Faulkner, Welty, Wright
Faulkner and Yoknapatawpha
2021

Faulkner, Welty, Wright
A Mississippi Confluence

EDITED BY
ANNETTE TREFZER,
JAY WATSON,
AND JAMES G. THOMAS, JR.

UNIVERSITY PRESS OF MISSISSIPPI
JACKSON

The University Press of Mississippi is the scholarly publishing agency of the Mississippi Institutions of Higher Learning: Alcorn State University, Delta State University, Jackson State University, Mississippi State University, Mississippi University for Women, Mississippi Valley State University, University of Mississippi, and University of Southern Mississippi.

www.upress.state.ms.us

The University Press of Mississippi is a member of the Association of University Presses.

Any discriminatory or derogatory language or hate speech regarding race, ethnicity, religion, sex, gender, class, national origin, age, or disability that has been retained or appears in elided form is in no way an endorsement of the use of such language outside a scholarly context.

Copyright © 2024 by University Press of Mississippi
All rights reserved

Library of Congress Cataloging-in-Publication Data

Names: Trefzer, Annette, 1960- editor. | Watson, Jay, editor. | Thomas, James G., Jr., editor.
Title: Faulkner, Welty, Wright : a Mississippi confluence / Annette Trefzer, Jay Watson, James G. Thomas, Jr..
Description: Jackson : University Press of Mississippi, 2024. | Series: Faulkner and Yoknapatawpha series | Includes bibliographical references and index.
Identifiers: LCCN 2024009253 (print) | LCCN 2024009254 (ebook) | ISBN 9781496851086 (hardback) | ISBN 9781496851093 (trade paperback) | ISBN 9781496851109 (epub) | ISBN 9781496851116 (epub) | ISBN 9781496851123 (pdf) | ISBN 9781496851130 (pdf)
Subjects: LCSH: Faulkner, William, 1897-1962—Criticism and interpretation. | Welty, Eudora, 1909-2001—Criticism and interpretation. | Wright, Richard, 1908-1960—Criticism and interpretation. | Authors, American—Mississippi—20th century. | American literature—Mississippi—History and criticism. | American literature—20th century—History and criticism.
Classification: LCC PS266.M7 F38 2024 (print) | LCC PS266.M7 (ebook) | DDC 810.9/9762—dc23/eng/20240318
LC record available at https://lccn.loc.gov/2024009253
LC ebook record available at https://lccn.loc.gov/2024009254

British Library Cataloging-in-Publication Data available

This volume of the Faulkner and Yoknapatawpha Series is dedicated to John Lowe

*In memoriam
John Wharton Lowe III*

August 10, 1945–August 5, 2023

Contents

Note on the Conference ix

Introduction 3
    ANNETTE TREFZER AND JAY WATSON

"What There Is to Say": Looking Back
at My Friendship with Eudora Welty 24
    SUZANNE MARRS

Visionary and Incomplete: Comparing Cultural Landscapes
of Faulkner, Wright, and Welty 42
    JULIA EICHELBERGER

Witnessing Jim Crow: Three Mississippi Writers
and the Politics of Critical Race Theory 63
    SUSAN V. DONALDSON

Kiese Laymon, Jesmyn Ward, and Natasha Trethewey:
Writers of Our Mississippi Moment Showing How to Read
Those We Had Read Before 86
    HARRIET POLLACK

Life in the Permanent War: Faulkner, Welty, and Wright
and the Nuclear Arms Race 112
    RYOICHI YAMANE

Welty and Wright and the Visual Idea of the American South 126
    W. RALPH EUBANKS

Literary Dispatches from the Postal South 144
    DONNIE MCMAHAND AND KEVIN MURPHY

"Burning in His Own Heart": Contrasting Visions
of Blindness and Invisibility as Social Death in
Wright's *Native Son* and Faulkner's *Light in August*   163
    BERNARD T. JOY

Criminality, Sexuality, and Violence in Faulkner and Wright:
Sanctuary and *The Long Dream*   183
    JOHN WHARTON LOWE

William Faulkner, Richard Wright, and the Writing
of African American Consciousness   202
    ANITA DEROUEN AND ANNE MACMASTER

The Transit of Memory: William Faulkner,
Jesmyn Ward, and Eudora Welty   217
    SARAH GILBREATH FORD

"We Listen for What the Waves Intone": Writing Black Women's
Liberatory Voices as Dialectical Ghosting in Eudora Welty's "The Burning,"
Margaret Walker's *Jubilee*, and Natasha Trethewey's *Native Guard*   239
    REBECCA MARK

About the Contributors   261

Index   265

Note on the Conference

The forty-seventh annual Faulkner and Yoknapatawpha Conference, "Faulkner, Welty, Wright: A Mississippi Confluence," was held remotely in the form of Zoom meetings and webinars between July 18 and July 21, 2021. Twelve presentations on the conference theme are collected as essays in this volume. A brief mention is made here of conference activities.

The program began on Sunday afternoon with keynote lectures by Jerry W. Ward Jr. and Susan V. Donaldson. That evening, Kathryn McKee presented the Eudora Welty Awards in Creative Writing, and the 2021 John W. Hunt Scholarships were announced. Presentation of the inaugural Ann J. Abadie Lecture in Southern Studies followed with a talk and poetry reading by Natasha Trethewey.

Monday's program began with a panel on "Racial Environmental Crossings in Faulkner and Wright," with Laura Wilson, William C. Palmer, Candace Waid, and Pei-Wen Kao presenting papers. A panel on "Remapping Southern Geographies" followed with papers by W. Ralph Eubanks, Gary Richards, and Hayley Wilson. The morning culminated with the panel "Mississippi Writers Then and Now: A Crowded Landscape of Mutual Hauntings." Julia Eichelberger, Rebecca Mark, Harriet Pollack, and Sarah Gilbreath Ford presented papers. Seth Berner gave a Zoom breakout-room lunch talk on "Collecting Faulkner," which was followed by a keynote presentation by Welty biographer Suzanne Marrs. Sharon L. Jones, John Wharton Lowe, and Anthony Dyer Hoefer gave the day's final paper presentations on the theme "Wright, Faulkner, Aesthetics, and Propaganda." The day ended with a virtual cocktail hour and a private viewing of the film *The Past Is Never Dead: The Story of William Faulkner* and discussion with the director, Michael Modak-Truran.

Tuesday's program began with a panel on "Archival Discoveries and Developments" with Benjamin B. Alexander, April Blevins and Forrest Galey, and Ryoichi Yamane presenting papers. A panel on "Racial Violence and Social Death in Faulkner and Wright" followed with presentations by Anne Bull, Ahmed Honeini, and Bernard T. Joy. The last panel of the morning, "Navigating Faulkner's World through Digital Yoknapatawpha: New and Featured Updates," included a discussion with Stephen Railton, John Padgett, Erin Penner, Johannes Burgers, and Theresa M. Towner. Ebony Lumumba and Rebecca Nisetich engaged in a conversation on "Reparative Teaching: Faulkner, Welty, and Wright in the Antiracist Classroom." A panel including Jacob Agner, Adrienne Akins Warfield, and Donnie McMahand and Kevin Murphy followed on the topic of "Crime Fiction, Prison Studies, and the P.O." The day ended with an online virtual cocktail hour.

Wednesday began with a "Teaching Faulkner, Welty, and Wright" session led by James Carothers, Jennie Joiner, Brian McDonald, and Theresa M. Towner, followed by a panel on "Regional Markings: Vision, Gender, and Style" that included papers by Carol Ann Johnston, Judy Butterfield, and Michal Choiński. A screening of *Almos' a Man*, the film adaptation of a short story by Richard Wright, followed with comments by Malcolm Wright, and Carl Rollyson then presented the annual Library Lecture on "*The Life of William Faulkner*: The Making of a Biography." Afternoon panels included "Going Digital, Going Modern, and Going to Jackson: Changing Media, Mode, and Mind in Faulkner, Welty, and Wright," with Michael Pickard and Rae Switzer, Michael Gleason, and Anita DeRouen and Anne MacMaster presenting, and "Radicality in Faulkner, Welty, and Wright," with Phillip Gordon, David McWhirter, and Christopher Curran. Another virtual cocktail hour concluded the conference.

The Faulkner and Yoknapatawpha Conference at the University of Mississippi is sponsored by the Department of English and the Center for the Study of Southern Culture and coordinated by the Division of Outreach and Continuing Studies. The conference planners are grateful to all the individuals and organizations that support the Faulkner and Yoknapatawpha Conference annually. In addition to those mentioned above, we wish to thank the College of Liberal Arts, the Center for the Study of Southern Culture, University of Mississippi Libraries, the City of Oxford, the Oxford Convention and Visitors Bureau, and the Mississippi Humanities Council.

Faulkner, Welty, Wright
Faulkner and Yoknapatawpha
2021

Introduction

ANNETTE TREFZER AND JAY WATSON

In downtown Jackson, Mississippi, there is a monument to the three writers who are the focus of this volume. In that monument—an oversized stone sculpture created by the Mississippi sculptor Rod Moorhead—each writer claims a space in the group of three, but the figures face away from each other. A viewer approaching the artistic group might only ever face one writer at a time. When looking directly at William Faulkner, the viewer sees Richard Wright and Eudora Welty from the back. Facing away from each other and looking in different directions, the figures offer an apt metaphor for a constellation of writers working closely in each other's orbit in Mississippi. Together they created a lasting portrait of southern culture, but each from a distinctly different vantage point, and each with an eye cast outward, on the world beyond. They responded in their own personal, political, and artistic ways to the histories and realities of their time and place. Born in 1897 in New Albany, Faulkner was a good decade older than Wright and Welty, who were born within a year of each other in 1908 and 1909, respectively. Despite each being raised less than a hundred miles away from each other, their differences in age, the middle-class upbringing Welty enjoyed in Jackson, and the poverty Wright experienced in his childhood home of Roxie placed these writers far apart.

Moorhead's public monument is a fitting entry into this volume's inquiry also because it places the writers together on shared ground in the same landscape. This spatial positioning largely supplants questions of Faulkner's primacy or his literary influence on the writers who came in his wake. Though literary genealogy is certainly a legitimate approach, neither Wright nor Welty have entertained the question of Faulkner's impact on their work. Welty's quip about Faulkner's literary influence exerted from Oxford, Mississippi, 150 miles north of her own hometown, is well known: "[I]t was like living near a big mountain, something majestic."[1] But, as Noel Polk reminds us, "what most often lives near a mountain is another mountain."[2] Over the span of half a century, Welty read Faulkner and occasionally commented on his work, beginning with her delightful 1930s caricature of Faulkner, a drawing she shared with her friend Frank Lyell, and ending with her 1987 speech at the University of Mississippi in celebration of the William Faulkner postage stamp. The irony of awarding a stamp to the postmaster who was fired from his job in 1924 permeates Welty's speech and celebrates the writers' joint appreciation of humor.

William Faulkner, in turn, read Eudora Welty. He was aware of the younger writer from Jackson. He sent a postcard from Hollywood in April 1943 after having read *The Robber Bridegroom* and having bought Welty's first short story collection, *A Curtain of Green and Other Stories* (1941). He offered praise and help: "You are doing very fine. Is there any way that I can help you? How old are you?"[3] Though there is no reply to Faulkner's postcard on record, the writers would meet six years later in Oxford for the world premiere of the Metro-Goldwyn-Mayer adaptation of Faulkner's *Intruder in the Dust*. On the occasion of the visit, Faulkner took Welty and her friend John Robinson for a sail on Sardis Lake in his boat, the *Ring Dove*.

In Welty's 1949 review of *Intruder in the Dust* for the *Hudson Review* she praised the novel as "marvelously funny" and "a double and delightful feat, because the mystery of the detective story plot is being raveled out while the mystery of Faulkner's prose is being spun and woven before our eyes."[4] Welty also defended Faulkner's novel against Edmund Wilson's unfavorable review of it in the *New Yorker*. Wilson charged Faulkner with writing about "an antiquated community" and compared his "provinciality, stubbornly cherished and turned into an asset," to the modernity of Gustav Flaubert, James Joyce, and Henry James.[5] Welty reacted strongly to the bias she perceived against writers from Mississippi in the *New Yorker* book review column, noting that "Mississippi was pushed under three times in two weeks."[6] The perceived lack of a southern writer's relevance to literary modernity struck close to home as Welty's own modernist masterpiece *The Golden Apples* was about to be published in the same year; it aligned Welty with Faulkner and lit her pen on fire: "[I]n criticizing a novel there should be more logic and purity of judgment than Mr. Wilson shows in pulling out a map."[7] Standing with writers from the South, she sharply adds, "[I]t's that combination of 'intelligent . . . despite' that we are given as a verdict each time. The 'intelligent' refers to the books or their characters and the 'despite' refers to the authors living in Mississippi."[8]

In essays on the craft of fiction, Welty repeatedly refers to Faulkner's work. In "Place in Fiction," she cites Faulkner as a "triumphant example in America today of the mastery of place in fiction," and she uses "Spotted Horses" as an example of the "fidelity of place" that lies at the heart of this tale's "comic glory."⁹ In "Looking at Short Stories," Welty includes Faulkner's "The Bear" alongside her analyses of well-crafted plots by Katherine Mansfield, Stephen Crane, James Joyce, Ernest Hemingway, D. H. Lawrence, and Anton Chekhov.¹⁰ In "Some Notes on Time in Fiction," Welty focuses on Faulkner's "distortion of time" in *The Sound and the Fury*, including the "dilations, the freezing of moments, the persistent recurrences and proliferations" at the heart of a novel whose chief subject, as Welty sees it, is the attempt to explode chronological time.¹¹

Whereas Faulkner becomes a handy reference point for Welty's discussions of craft or literary experimentation, Richard Wright finds no such mention. Welty refers neither to the writer nor his works. Although Welty and Wright both attended school in Jackson, they went to different high schools: "Richard Wright, who was seven months older than Eudora but whose formal schooling had been sporadic, entered the fifth grade at Jackson's all-black Jim Hill School as Eudora entered the eighth at Jackson High."¹² Welty biographer Suzanne Marrs reflects on the missed connections between the writers: "Wright knew a Jackson from which Eudora had largely been sheltered, one where because of race he was barred from libraries, denied opportunity for advancement, subjected to violence. An outstanding student nevertheless, he moved through his classes on an accelerated basis and graduated as valedictorian of Smith-Robertson School in 1925. He and Eudora never met, though both would eventually be numbered among America's finest writers."¹³ By the time Welty wrote most of the reviews and essays later collected in *The Eye of the Story*, Wright had long since left the South and the United States for Europe.

Like Faulkner, Wright was a voracious and largely self-educated reader who famously borrowed a library card from a coworker in Memphis to access books including H. L. Mencken's *Prejudices*, a collection of essays that awakened his consciousness to the possibility of writing as a vehicle of social and personal change. He read Henry James and Dostoevsky, Sherwood Anderson and William Faulkner, Theodore Dreiser and Ernest Hemingway, and other contemporaries. In a radio discussion of the Federal Writers Project on April 13, 1938, Wright said of Faulkner: "I know that Faulkner's books deal with a phase of the real South. He is the only white writer I know living in Mississippi who is trying to tell the truth in fiction."¹⁴ And comparing Faulkner to Andre Malraux, he said, "Faulkner shows how human beings are stunted in Mississippi, while Malraux shows how millions all over the world are trying to rise above a degraded status. I value Malraux higher than I do Faulkner because of the quality of heroic action Malraux depicts in his novels."¹⁵ When asked about his affinities for other American writers in an interview conducted in 1950, Wright again refers to Faulkner: "I admire Faulkner, but I do not know him personally. We have corresponded."[16] Indeed, in the fall of 1945, Faulkner wrote a letter to Wright sharing his reading experience and appreciation of *Black Boy*: "It needed to be said, and you said it well."[17] But ultimately Faulkner thought that *Native Son* was the superior literary achievement because "the good lasting stuff comes out of one individual's imagination and sensitivity to and comprehension of the suffering of Everyman, Anyman, not out of the memory of his own grief."[18] Faulkner's mid-century assessment of Wright's achievement reflects his own desire for artistic universality in fiction. It also highlights the fact that, unlike Wright and Welty, Faulkner did not attempt memoir or autobiography as a literary form. Astute contemporary reviewers like Alain Locke, however, drew attention to the shared modernity of their fiction. In his review of *Native Son* in the January 1941 issue of *Opportunity*, Locke places Faulkner and Wright into a tradition of realism that has "released us from the banal stereotypes—where all Southern ladies were irreproachable and all Southern colonels paragons of honor and chivalry." The result, Locke writes, is a type of fiction that cleared the way for new Black protagonists like Bigger Thomas.[19]

In interviews over the span of his career, Wright repeatedly refers to Faulkner, but he never once mentions Welty. This omission might reflect a contemporary gender bias (Wright overwhelmingly references male writers in interviews, as for that matter does Faulkner) or his increasingly European vantage point, shaped by his friendships with Gertrude Stein, Simone de Beauvoir, René Maran, and Jean-Paul Sartre. And Welty, as noted, never references Wright, although she must have been aware of *Native Son*'s spectacular success, which catapulted the author into the national spotlight in 1940 and caused the novel to be banned in Mississippi. However, Welty most certainly read her friend Hubert Creekmore's extensive review "Social Factors in *Native Son*" in the *University Review*, where he assesses the novel as both a "thriller" and a "proletarian romance" containing a great deal of "social editorializing."[20]

In this triangular comparison of the writers—Faulkner, Welty, Wright—the lacuna is the relationship between the Black male writer and the white female writer, a communication gap perhaps reflecting the deepest taboo of their segregated world. Wright wrote, "In Dixie there are two worlds, the white world and the black world, and they are physically separated. There are white schools and black schools, white churches and black churches, white businesses and black businesses, white graveyards and black graveyards, and, for all I know, a white God and a black God."[21] Seeking to escape from the social and intellectual disenfranchisement of segregated home space, Wright searched for a place in the world that would not delimit his talents and crush his desires for becoming a modern writer.²² He turned first to Chicago, then to New York—as indeed Faulkner and Welty had also done early in their careers, before returning to Mississippi—and then to Paris, where he found a community of expatriate intellectuals from the African diaspora. Perhaps the reception of Faulkner's work in France, where he was lionized long before American critics and readerships really warmed to him, helped signal to Wright that Paris could be that elusive place that would allow him to cultivate a life of the mind, a milieu where ideas and art were taken seriously no matter the color of one's skin. But in ultimately looking toward Europe and Africa, Wright literally turned his back on the two white Mississippi writers who created out of the raw materials of their state the apocryphal landscapes of Yoknapatawpha and Morgana. On some level, of course, Welty turned her back on him, given his conspicuous underrepresentation in her interviews and occasional writings. And both younger writers would have had to turn their backs on Faulkner to some extent simply to carve out their own niches and identities in southern letters, where the elder figure's monumental—or mountainous?—presence proved so vexing for his successors. (Flannery O'Connor's oft-quoted crack about the "Dixie Limited" barreling down on her little mule cart is symptomatic of the problem.) Again, Moorhead's installation seems to recognize these exigencies in the arrangement of its stone figures.

For at least the first decade of his career as a published author, Wright was recognized as a protest writer, to such an extent that James Baldwin was able to capitalize on the association in his 1955 essay "Everybody's Protest Novel," which voiced significant reservations about Wright's achievement in *Native Son*, in part by linking it, most unflatteringly, to Stowe's *Uncle Tom's Cabin*. (Recall here that Wright had titled his first book *Uncle Tom's Children*.) Though Baldwin faulted him for sentimentality (a charge Wright had already leveled at himself in "How Bigger Was Born"), most readers did not miss the blistering attack Wright's novel and early stories mounted against the white supremacist institutions, including but not limited to Jim Crow segregation, that bore down on Black life in the North and South.

If this might seem to distinguish Wright's work from that of his white Mississippi cohorts, however, a second look might be in order. Welty, for instance, was arguably writing her own version of protest fiction by uncovering the subtle everyday workings of white supremacy in the South. Her vision of Mississippi included the history, presence, suffering, and accomplishments of African Americans, and her writings directly address the Jim Crow color line and the landscape of segregation marked by unequal social power structures. Stories like "Keela, the Outcast Indian

Maiden," "Powerhouse," and "A Worn Path," all from her first story collection, *A Curtain of Green*, center on African American protagonists, and in subsequent stories and novels, Welty continues to address the South's racial inequalities, including the white majority's social hypocrisies and warped cruelties. Familiar with the rich traditions of African American folk art, Welty was interested in depicting Black resourcefulness and resistance in her writing and photography. In her fiction, racial injustices form a constant background noise as audible as the din of a cotton gin.

Turning to Faulkner, we find that by the 1940s—and due in part to the influence of *Native Son*—a proletarian strain in his work that had emerged in response to Depression-era economic and social injustice took a distinctively racial turn in a series of fictions, including "Pantaloon in Black," "Go Down, Moses," *Intruder in the Dust*, and even *Requiem for a Nun*, that featured Black protagonists and condemned both the extralegal violence of lynching and the institutionalized violence of the criminal justice and penal systems against African Americans. Though Faulkner attempted with less success to protest school segregation and continuing racial violence as a public figure in the 1950s—earning Baldwin's ire in 1956—his fictions speak louder and more incisively to the American dilemmas of racism and white privilege. Each of our featured authors, then, was protesting in her or his own way the inhumanity of a system of segregation born from plantation slavery and perpetuated well into the decades of their writing years.

In navigating between and among our three figures and their distinctive outlooks on modern regional and national life, we might take as our cue Wright's words about artistic perspective in his aesthetic manifesto, "Blueprint for Negro Writing" (1937). Perspective, he writes, is "that fixed point in intellectual space where a writer stands to view the struggles, hopes, and sufferings of his people. [. . .] At best, perspective is a pre-conscious assumption, something which a writer takes for granted, something which he wins through his living."[23] Wright, Faulkner, and Welty offer their narratives of Mississippi and its people from the different perspectives of their life's circumstances and individual observations. So, what can we gain by comparing these writers' lives and fiction? Beyond their sometimes vivid differences of biography, sensibility, and style, what comes into sharper focus when we read one writer in light of the other(s)? Some recent critics have expressed reservations about the comparative method as a window onto literary meaning. R. Radhakrishnan, for example, argues that "comparisons are never neutral" but in fact political through and through, that "they are inevitably tendentious, didactic, competitive and prescriptive. Behind the seeming generosity of comparison, there always lurks the aggression of a thesis."[24]

Other scholars, however, like Rita Felski and Susan Stanford Friedman, continue to extol the merits of comparative analysis, though on a qualified note that heads off naïve applications of the method. Friedman, for example, acknowledges that comparisons are "never disinterested" but for that very reason advocates a comparative practice based on "the dialogic pull of in/commensurability."[25] She proposes readings that are "juxtapositional, contrapuntal, and reciprocal, thus opening the possibility for a progressive politics of comparison" that can potentially avoid "the categorical violence of comparison within the framework of dominance." In a contrapuntal reading, "the distinctiveness of each" text "is maintained, while the dialogue of voices that ensues bring[s] commonalities into focus." Such readings might be all the more striking and insightful where there are the fewest overt links and greatest apparent gaps between the writers or artists in question. Indeed, historian Marcel Detienne favors the comparative method precisely for the unexpected but nevertheless constructive outcomes it is capable of yielding.[26] Comparative analysis challenges literary scholars to relational thinking; it offers new ways of understanding writers and forges new connections across texts, identities, and traditions.

To Friedman's account of the juxtapositional, the contrapuntal, and the reciprocal dimensions of comparative work, we propose to add a fourth term: the *confluent*. Confluence, of course, is a notion we borrow from Eudora Welty's Pulitzer Prize-winning novel *The Optimist's Daughter*, where the term literally refers to the merging of the Ohio and Mississippi Rivers, the coming together of great streams, and metaphorically to the conjoining of human lives. Welty's reflections on the nature of confluence also end her memoir *One Writer's Beginnings*, where she observes that "the greatest confluence of all is that which makes up the human memory."[27] A methodology based on confluences requires flexible, indeed fluid, modes of comparative judgment and seems especially fitting for the study of a trio of writers who hailed from a state whose geography, economy, and culture were profoundly shaped by the continent's mightiest river. Acknowledging that Mississippi ground was never level for any of the three, we have encouraged our contributors to turn from the familiar landscapes of single-author criticism toward a mode of analysis more receptive to the fluid mergings of creative currents. At the same time, we remain mindful of Felski and Friedman's guiding questions for a twenty-first-century comparative criticism alert to complexity and nuance: "How do ... new ... modes of analysis based on interrelations, conjunctures, networks, linkages, and modes of circulation draw on or enrich comparative thinking? What are the limitations of comparisons based on similarities and differences, and what other methods of comparative thinking might we envision?"[28]

The twelve essays gathered here respond to that call in spirited fashion. In the opening essay, "'What There Is to Say': Looking Back at My Friendship with Eudora Welty," biographer Suzanne Marrs offers a privileged glimpse into the personal and professional relationships she shared with the writer from Jackson. She recalls her own scholarly journey and the circumstances that led to her first meeting with Eudora Welty on a hot July day in 1983, a meeting that would prove providential and result in a friendship with the writer. Weaving together biography and autobiography, Marrs recounts the beginnings of her own career as it intersects with the life and work of the writer. As a scholar in residence at Mississippi Department of Archives and History in 1984, Marrs spent a year organizing the archival materials, including photographs, correspondence, and typescripts, of the Welty Collection. "During the archival portion of my grant," she writes, "my primary instructor was Eudora Welty herself." Marrs offers information on Welty's photographs and the origins of some of her short stories. Most of all, she gives us a good sense of Welty's personality, wit, and self-confidence. From the perspective of a close observer, Marrs reports on Welty's acquaintances and friends, and on her encounters with other writers, including William Faulkner. Shining a searchlight on the trio of writers in this volume, the biographer is certain, however, that Welty never met Richard Wright in person or on the page. She notes instead "a litany of missed opportunities" between the two writers, and she concludes that the silence about each other's work might convey "respect for the other's achievements" and a shared "rejection of racial injustice." Silences exist in literature and in the private life. Concluding her essay, Marrs reflects on matters Welty remained silent about, such as the nature of her relationship with Kenneth Millar (a mystery writer known by the pen name Ross Macdonald). Her essay invites readers to ask: What can ever be known of a person's life, and what remains a mystery—even for a trusted biographer and longtime friend?

Biography also plays a role in the approach Julia Eichelberger takes to the three writers in this volume. "Visionary and Incomplete: Comparing Cultural Landscapes of Faulkner, Wright, and Welty" examines the parallel lives of the writers who grew up and lived in Mississippi. Contrasting the privilege and relative ease of Faulkner and Welty's upbringing with the struggle of Wright's early years, Eichelberger argues that personal positionality and "contrasts in opportunity" crucially shaped the writers' different fictional treatments of the South. Though the writers enjoyed reading some of the same authors—H. L. Mencken, for instance—and worked with editors and friends in the publishing world who knew each other, their paths diverged in life and in their fiction as they "continued to draw upon sharply differentiated earlier experiences of the region." Eichelberger illustrates these different perspectives by examining two of each writer's short stories. She asks: What if this story had been told from the subject position of one of the other two writers? For instance, analyzing Faulkner's "A Rose for Emily," Eichelberger wonders about the Black character, Tobe: "Would Wright have thought it plausible that a Black man could have inherited, then kept Emily's house?" Drawing attention to the limits and blind spots in each writer's vision, she explores their approaches as shaped by different racial and gendered experiences in their native Mississippi. Each writer presents uniquely valuable but limited insights; together, Eichelberger argues, the writers offer a rich "composite vision" of southern place.

Amid current debates among US politicians, pundits, and educators over critical race theory (CRT), Susan V. Donaldson finds harbingers of its systemic approach to racism and white supremacy, its call "for a national reckoning with the country's long history of racial hierarchies and inequities," and its clear-eyed acknowledgment of "the daunting impediments to that reckoning" in the work of our trio of featured authors. "Witnessing Jim Crow: Three Mississippi Writers and the Politics of Critical Race Theory" draws on the work of Kimberlé Williams Crenshaw, Derrick Bell, Richard Delgado, Jean Stefancic, and others to introduce the reader to the history and theory behind this important and controversial intellectual movement. Donaldson then turns to Wright's 1942 novel *The Man Who Lived Underground* (unpublished in Wright's lifetime), to Faulkner's *Go Down, Moses* (also 1942), and to Welty's *New Yorker* stories, "Where Is the Voice Coming From?" (1963) and "The Demonstrators" (1966), to show how these Mississippi authors, "all compelled throughout their careers to confront the politics of visibility and invisibility defining the color line," lay bare, "in ways that critical race theorists would have instantly recognized and confirmed, the entrenchment and yet slow dissolution of an antiquated racial hierarchy both bolstered and diminished by white blindness and denial." Fred Daniels, protagonist of *The Man Who Lived Underground*, discovers among the sewers and basements of the modern city "a wholly different way of being and a possible alternative narrative" that help him recognize, over what remains of his short life, the structural impediments to his and others' Black thriving and respond with newfound agency and authority. The stories of *Go Down, Moses* present Black and white Mississippians alike as "imprisoned," albeit in different ways, "in family histories and racial hierarchies," yet they also offer hints of "just how susceptible to disruption the very definitions of whiteness and Blackness can be in the pre–civil rights South." Welty's civil rights tales, meanwhile, exhibit an acutely sensitive ear for the politics of speech and discourse as they expose "fissuring whiteness under siege" in her home state "by competing voices and stories liberated" by the civil rights movement and its "forces of sweeping change." Though Donaldson finds the three writers to be "hesitant," even "despairing" at times in their engagements with the nation's structural racism, the hauntedness she ascribes to their writings ultimately "suggests both the tenacity of white recalcitrance and the ultimate futility of resisting the monumental changes defining the country's emergence into a new multicultural age."

Harriet Pollack aims less at refracting the works of our Mississippi modernists through one another than at reframing their writings as in turn refracted through a second trio, comprised of twenty-first-century successors in the state's literary culture. "Kiese Laymon, Jesmyn Ward, and Natasha Trethewey: Writers of Our Mississippi Moment Showing How to Read Those We Had Read Before" revisits the technique of literary allusion with an eye to its *bi*directional movement, the way it allows authors not only to "write forward to produce new texts" with the aid of their predecessors' words, but also to "work back to alter the ways that we read and reread the referent texts." Faulkner, Welty, and Wright look and feel different after their fellow Mississippians of the new millennium engage with their literary efforts, sometimes respectfully, sometimes irreverently, sometimes questioning, but always creatively and purposefully. Refracted through Ward's National Book Award–winning novel *Salvage the Bones*, for instance, Faulkner's *As I Lay Dying* looks less like the last word in technical perfection than like "an anxiety-producing" textual "other" that neglects Black voice and interiority and ends its characters' individual narratives too conclusively to strike a chord with an African American reader. Ward's response is thus to "retrofit a second story of race and . . . the prospect of Black survival" onto Faulkner's fable of family and environmental crisis and, truer to Black lives in contemporary America, to end her novel with far more questions than answers about her characters' future. Refracted through Trethewey's insightful introductions to Welty's memoir *One Writer's Beginnings* and her volume of photographic works, Welty's "construction of her beginnings as artist" in a sheltered white household can nonetheless extend an invitation to "southern literary family belonging" across the generations—and the color line—to a young African American poet staking out her own place in the region's literature, in part by tapping deeply into the power of photography to channel, document, *and* challenge memories of place, race, and kinship of various sorts—a lesson learned in part from Welty. Refracted through Laymon's *Heavy*, "an American memoir" very much in the tradition of Wright's *American*

Hunger (his working title for *Black Boy*), Wright's autobiography leaves a bitter aftertaste in its "clear-cut celebration of Richard's escape from family and region." Laymon instead chooses to build *his* American story squarely around people who opt not to escape, who stay with the trouble of family, region, and nation in Mississippi—a roster that ultimately includes himself as returning son, grandson, and writer. The refractions mount: Laymon and Trethewey on Faulkner, Ward and Laymon on Welty. The result, in Pollack's words, is "a crowded landscape of mutual hauntings," one that not incidentally makes a powerful case for the latest wave of distinguished writing to emerge from the state as its own "Mississippi Renaissance" to complement and "counterpoint" the twentieth-century one.

Where Donaldson and Pollack situate Welty, Wright, and Faulkner within national conversations about race, Ryoichi Yamane widens the focus to address the writers in the mid-twentieth-century global context. And that means the Cold War. "Life in the Permanent War: Faulkner, Welty, and Wright and the Nuclear Arms Race" takes issue with US and southern literary studies for "underestimating the cultural impact of nuclear weaponry" and "the reality of nuclear militarism" in their assessments of Cold War–era literary production in the region and nation. The emphasis of this scholarship primarily on the projection of *soft* power via print culture, education, and other outlets neglects the issue of "what kind of power was needed to maintain the influence of the nation's liberal democratic, antitotalitarian culture" on world affairs: namely, the Bomb. Yamane calls our attention, for instance, to the appearance of both Faulkner and Welty in the March 5, 1956, issue of *Life* magazine, where, he argues, the two Mississippi artists performed important ideological work for the publication, at the time, according to one historian, "the most important print medium through which Americans formed their initial impression of the atomic bomb." The issue, which, according to Yamane, appeared as the magazine was shifting its editorial "focus from [a] humanism that included fear of nuclear warfare to the demonization of the foreign enemy newly equipped with nuclear weapons," strategically placed its Faulkner and Welty articles to contextualize them, implicitly, as regional and provincial: first a long article intended to stir up "anticommunist sentiments" by suggesting that the USSR was ahead of the US in the nuclear arms race, then a resumé of recent "civil rights actions against segregation" were followed, first, by Faulkner's infamous "Letter to the North," in which he urged desegregation activists to "go slow now" and advocated, in Yamane's words, "regional autonomy as a response to integration," and later by a review of the stage adaptation of Welty's *Ponder Heart*, in which the South was depicted as backward and comic. The sequencing of these articles carried the implicit message that "the social progress of the US South was problematically slow, while that of the USSR was distressingly fast"—and that a dose of militarized US nationalism was the answer to both crises. On another front—and continent—Richard Wright employs the atom as a key conceptual tool for protagonist Cross Damon in *The Outsider* (1953). Not only does light-skinned Damon deflect inquiries into his racial views—and by extension into his racial identity—by redirecting political conversations toward "the atom bomb" and its global threat to humanity, he also, with the narrator's collusion at times, turns to the atom as an analogy for his own selfhood: monadic, isolated, complete. In both ways, Damon seeks to frame his identity as "nothing in particular," free both of ideological partisanship and of the entangling bonds of intimacy and love. For Wright, however, Damon's nuclear anxieties allegorize the "terror in freedom" experienced by recently decolonized peoples "concern[ed] that their white former colonizers, equipped with nuclear weapons, would recolonize their newly liberated nations." But Cross's "permanent war" to safeguard his own freedom proves precisely too atomistic to be a viable response to mid-century realities. If Damon leans in, conceptually, to the atom as a metaphor for selfhood, Wright ultimately pulls back, "relativiz[ing]" the Western fetishes of radical freedom and individualism by dramatizing the collateral damage they lead to in other lives and the fetishist's own. These examples suggest that scholars of southern literature at the mid-twentieth century need to take more conscientious account of "the region's social reality" as "inseparable from the Atomic Age."

In "Welty and Wright and the Visual Idea of the American South," W. Ralph Eubanks compares the writers' photographic practices. Wright turned to photography twice in his writing life: in 1938, when he wrote *12 Million Black Voices*, a book with photographs by Farm Security Administration documentarians, and again in 1953, when he photographed extensively on a research trip to Ghana hoping to include his images in his book *Black Power*. Welty photographed Black Americans in the South during the Great Depression at the same time Wright wrote the text for *12 Million Black Voices*. Eubanks compares their photographic subject positions: Welty as a white woman photographing African Americans in the South; Wright as a Black American photographing the local population on what was called the Gold Coast. What is conveyed by their images? What role do they play as "forces of social change"? Eubanks argues that in the 1938 photobook, Wright is more overtly concerned "with the politics of Black representation, in spite of [the photographs] having been taken by white photographers." In his later *Black Power*, however, Wright uses the camera as an instrument of documentation;

"here Wright is the ethnographer." Comparing the photographic work of Wright and Welty, Eubanks concludes that "Welty simply wanted her photographs to portray life as she saw it," in contrast to Wright, who picked up the camera as a tool "to spotlight the real social inequities that Black southerners lived with." Yet both writers were "documentarians" of sorts who "shared love of the peculiar alchemy that takes place with the visual and the verbal."

Turning from photographs to fictional treatments of the southern past, the next essay, by Donnie McMahand and Kevin Murphy, examines thematic connections. In "Literary Dispatches from the Postal South," the authors highlight the historical role of the US Post Office as a workplace. As a federal institution, the post office employed African Americans and women in the post-Reconstruction period, a practice that led to backlash during the Jim Crow era. Beginning with an analysis of *Visible Spirits*, a historical novel by Mississippi author Steve Yarbrough, who fictionalizes the case of Indianola, Mississippi, postmaster Minnie Cox, the authors anchor their essay in racial history. They survey writing by Richard Wright, William Faulkner, Eudora Welty, Alice Walker, and Lewis Nordan to argue that these writers center the postal service in their fiction to "expose deep racial and economic rifts within southern populations, to exploit cases of rural isolation, and, conversely, to offer some relief to unwanted insularity." Welty in *Losing Battles* and Walker in *The Color Purple* focus on women's access to postal services to combat rural isolation and domestic oppression. Although they write about white and Black women, respectively, the authors create female protagonists who seek intimacy in letters and who find therapeutic potential in the rural delivery service. In the final part of their essay, McMahand and Murphy note that several writers had personal experiences working at the post office: Wright referred to his post office position as his "university," and Faulkner was famously fired from his job at the University of Mississippi post office. Examining the role of the post office in autobiographical narratives—Wright's *Black Boy* and Nordan's *Boy with Loaded Gun*—and in fiction such as Wright's early novel *Lawd Today!* and Nordan's short story "The Sears and Roebuck Catalog Game," the authors posit the post office—as institution and metaphor—as a crucial nexus among southern writers.

In taking stock of the relationship between Faulkner's work and Wright's, Bernard T. Joy turns to *Light in August* and *Native Son* as case studies in what we might call the visualization of Blackness, the making-visible of "the practical lives" of African Americans in a segregated society. "'Burning in His Own Heart': Contrasting Visions of Blindness and Invisibility as Social Death in Wright's *Native Son* and Faulkner's *Light in August*" draws on a range of phenomenological and antiracist thinkers from Maurice Merleau-Ponty and Frantz Fanon to Orlando Patterson, Paul Gilroy, and Abdul JanMohamed to explore "both the limitations on and the possibilities for redemption inherent in how Black bodies see and are seen" in two of the most important literary anatomists of Jim Crow: a world in which "Blackness is marginalized to the point of invisibility" yet simultaneously "set in stark contrast to the point of hypervisibility . . . within a ubiquitously supremacist taxonomy in which every symbol of authority is coded as white." Under such conditions, visibly Black Bigger Thomas has no recourse to what Fanon called the "real dialectic . . . between body and world" unencumbered by the epidermalization that constitutes the bedrock fact of his life, one against which, in Fanon's words, "no ontological resistance" can be mounted. What remains for Bigger, then, is to appropriate his own "inescapable visibility as Black . . . as a resource of emancipatory resistance against his dehumanization," a resistance he is gratified to see taking visual form in the newspaper coverage of his crime and fugitive flight from the law. Though Christmas also inhabits a world ruled by white "seeing," his light skin affords him the sometime luxury of "evad[ing] the essentializing, dehumanizing effects of racist blindness" and experiencing a "feeling of being . . . a universal, deracinated human being untouched by social arrangements." Each protagonist in his own way ultimately makes of his death a culminating act in the pursuit, by their different means, of a more authentic way of being. Faulkner's and Wright's antiracist fictions thus employ different but related strategies "for understanding the place of the body in the world from a greatly neglected historico-racial perspective."

John Wharton Lowe makes a different pair of novels the focus of his comparative treatment of Wright and Faulkner. "Criminality, Sexuality, and Violence in Faulkner and Wright: *Sanctuary* and *The Long Dream*" develops an extensive, fascinating list of parallels between Faulkner's 1931 novel and Wright's 1958 novel, the last one published in his lifetime. Both books mine the genre conventions of crime fiction, detective literature, and classical tragedy to portray the "sordid underbelly" of Mississippi life in sensationalistic terms. In both works, "prostitution runs like a tawdry red thread" through the narrative at the heart of an "unholy bond between the police and . . . brothel-capitalists." Both novels provide a "seamy but productive milieu for an exploration of the interbraiding of commerce, perverse sexuality, and violence." Both take up issues of incarceration and surveillance. Both detail the "moral disintegration" of key characters, including their protagonists, alongside "the venality of the state." Both link death and eroticism and mine the sensational potential of "the violated corpse." Suggestively, both narratives close by relocating an important character to Paris, far from the endemic corruption of Mississippi and Memphis. As such, both novels serve as "fiery jeremiads" that "systematically reveal the malignant side of every section of society." As we might expect, however, Wright's crime novel proves significantly more sensitive to racial issues than Faulkner's: *The Long Dream* takes up interracial sexuality, "colorism within the race," the moral failure of Black elites, and, especially, the "tangled relationship" between Black men and the police, in ways *Sanctuary* does not approach. That latter emphasis on police violence, Lowe argues, gives Wright's novel "more relevance today," in the era of Black Lives Matter, "than ever before."

Anita DeRouen and Anne MacMaster observe that in surveying the Faulkner-Wright literary relationship, "we might expect the main flow of influence to be from Faulkner to Wright," but in "William Faulkner, Richard Wright, and the Writing of African American Consciousness," they make a case for turning that hypothesis on its head. Following the intertextual back-and-forth between the authors from *Light in August* (1932) to *Native Son* (1940) to *Go Down, Moses* (1942) and *Intruder in the Dust* (1948), DeRouen and MacMaster focus on the depiction of Black characters, and in particular on "the rendering of Black consciousness into fiction," across that sixteen-year arc. *Light in August* takes formative steps toward engaging Black interiority by using free indirect discourse to take us into the mind of Joe Christmas, a racially ambiguous figure who nonetheless lives aspects of the African American experience, including the experience of racial injustice, at various intervals in his life. Yet as DeRouen and MacMaster show, the reader's access to Joe's inner world is abruptly shut down at the moment, following chapter 13, when he is arrested and publicly designated Black. Wright, by contrast, maintains the strategy of free indirect discourse for the entirety of *Native Son*, where both Bigger's "interior complexity and depth" and the reader's access to it actually deepen after the youth's arrest and racial vilification, when "the movement of [Bigger's] thoughts" in fact "becomes the main action of the novel." In the wake of *Native Son*, Faulkner tellingly revised his treatment of Lucas Beauchamp from a pair of magazine stories to *Go Down, Moses* precisely by developing new material that sounded the depths of Lucas's consciousness in circumstances of racial injustice. He also, in the figure of Rider from "Pantaloon in Black," produced "his finest achievement in writing from a Black point of view," granting his reader "a level of intimacy with the character equivalent to" his achievements in "the interior monologues of Benjy and Quentin Compson." Even *Intruder in the Dust*, which some critics consider a step back from *Go Down, Moses* in its treatment of African American characters, might be considered a further, modest "advance" in its engagement with racial issues. In dramatizing the limitations of Chick Mallison's racial imagination yet also depicting them as reparable, Faulkner may have been using his young white character to acknowledge his own authorial limitations and his difficult progress, with Wright's assistance, toward a more mature perspective on Black life and the Black mind.

With Sarah Gilbreath Ford's essay, the volume pivots from Faulkner and Wright to Faulkner and Welty, with a contemporary Mississippi author thrown in for good measure. In "The Transit of Memory: William Faulkner, Jesmyn Ward, and Eudora Welty," Ford follows Ward's epigraph in *Sing, Unburied, Sing* from Welty's memoir *One Writer's Beginnings*, in which she writes: "[T]he memory is a living thing—it too is in transit." Ford explores this idea, shared by her three writers, that time and memory are always "in transit" and that, as Faulkner famously said, "The past is never dead. It's not even past." Considering Ward's acknowledgments of literary influence, Ford proposes that questions of intertextuality are complex and often work like a "haunting." She argues, "[B]y allowing her novel to be haunted by Faulkner and Welty, Ward puts her work in conversation with the past. By haunting that tradition in turn, Ward claims ownership of a narrative of racial injustice." Haunting is an integral part of the southern literary tradition. Narratives abound in which linear chronology is abandoned to convey instead what Ford calls "a gothic sense of the fluidity of time." Ward specifically references Faulkner's *As I Lay Dying* as a novel on her mind when she was writing *Sing, Unburied, Sing*. In her essay, Ford puts Ward's novel into conversation with Faulkner's: in both, the dead are literally present and able to speak. They rupture the present moment to claim their identities by crafting their own narratives and selves. As Ford notes, Faulkner, Ward, and Welty all "allow the dead to wrest ownership of their [characters'] identity from the living." Welty's confrontations with specters occur not only in her memoir but in her Pulitzer Prize–winning novel, *The Optimist's Daughter*. In the latter work, a daughter hears her dead mother's accusing voice as she wrestles with her own memories and with the grief of loss. Spending a night in the family home that is no longer hers, Laurel Hand has "no need for mere material reminders" of her parents' lives; instead, she prefers the stories and memories from the past. Like Faulkner and Ward, Welty values "an atemporal coming together" of memories and stories in the "confluence" that is the individual human memory.

Our volume concludes with what Rebecca Mark calls "an interconnected-Mississippi web of what we could now call feminist and racial-justice storytelling." In her essay, "'We Listen for What the Waves Intone': Writing Black Women's Liberatory Voices as Dialectical Ghosting in Eudora Welty's 'The Burning,' Margaret Walker's *Jubilee*, and Natasha

Trethewey's *Native Guard*," Mark examines how Eudora Welty, Margaret Walker, and Natasha Trethewey return to the Civil War to destroy the Lost Cause myth and propose instead "a form of literary reparation." Positioning these writers vis-a-vis William Faulkner, whose narratives still attempt to grapple with the humanity of slaves, Mark illustrates that in *The Unvanquished* and *Absalom, Absalom!*, "[T]he embers of the Lost Cause myth are still burning." In her reading of Welty's "The Burning," a short story she calls "wildly problematic," Mark shows that Welty, "like Faulkner, tears down, burns, and sacrifices the white ladies of the Lost Cause myth, but unlike Faulkner she provides a sustaining narrative of regeneration." Welty images the rebirth of the enslaved woman Delilah from bondage into freedom and ends her narrative neither in nostalgia nor in despair. Margaret Walker also traces the transformations of her Black female characters in her 1966 novel *Jubilee*, allowing her characters "to transform, to thrive, to rebel, [and] to savor a moment of justice and retribution." More recently, poet Natasha Trethewey reflects on Mississippi's past—specifically, the history of the Native Guard, enslaved Black men who were stationed on Ship Island to guard Confederate prisoners of war—in order to braid those forgotten lives with her own experiences growing up on the Gulf Coast. Trethewey alternates personal poems about her abused and murdered mother with poems about Civil War history. Mark calls this juxtaposition "an undeniable statement" about neglected and abused bodies, the unburied ghosts of the South. She ends her essay—and our collection—in a powerful appeal to readers: "[I]t is our responsibility to highlight the voices of those who do not look longingly back to a plantation past for inspiration but instead insist on a solid, hard, personal narrative that cannot be ignored, walked past, or through and that must be grappled with."

Before concluding, it might be illuminating to follow our confluence of Mississippi modernists "downstream" a bit, toward successors whose work has been shaped and nourished by its currents. Their ranks would include the white sculptor Moorhead, of course, but also other African American writers who have reached instinctively toward the trio as a literary lodestone. For Margaret Walker Alexander, for instance, a younger contemporary of Wright and Welty who went on to considerable fame as a poet, novelist, and educator, the three authors laid much of the conceptual groundwork for twentieth-century southern writing. As Walker Alexander told an interviewer in 1974, Wright, Welty, and Faulkner "have dealt with three or four themes that seem to run through Southern literature," including race, violence, and decadence; moreover, "like all great writers in the world, they move from the local to the universal," finding in Mississippi a window onto the world and the human condition.[29] For two-time National Book Award–winner Jesmyn Ward, the trio served as a beacon for her youthful literary aspirations. As a Delisle, Mississippi, teenager, Ward remembers, she would look at a state literary map for Mississippi in her high school classroom, "and here's Faulkner and here's Welty and here's Richard Wright, and I think a part of me always dreamed or asked, 'What if? What would it be like to be on that map one day?'"[30] Thanks to her immense talent, Ward has learned the answer to those questions.

We could also turn to Kiese Laymon's extraordinary 2018 memoir *Heavy* for evidence of the ongoing literary legacy of our Mississippi troika. Unlike Walker Alexander and Ward, however, Laymon resolves the literary confluence into its component currents, which had varying degrees of impact on his authorial efforts and ambitions. Of Faulkner's *Absalom, Absalom!*, which young Laymon was assigned to read by his mother, a college professor, when he was twelve years old, he writes, "The first sentence in the book was a million words long, which was cool, and it used strange words like 'wisteria' and 'lattices.'"[31] Reading Faulkner made the boy "feel drunker than a white man," intoxicated with language, but the apprentice writer ultimately concludes, "I didn't know how to write like Faulkner and say anything honest about us," about the Black community in Mississippi.

Welty, whose fiction Laymon encountered in eighth grade, elicits a more layered response. When his teacher fell back on "historical context" to contrast "the 'quirky racism' of Welty's characters" with "the 'bad real racism' of most of the white characters in *Roots*," Laymon recalls, "I didn't like what 'historical context' and 'quirky racism' in our English class granted white folk. If we could understand historical context, we would understand how Eudora Welty could create fully developed, unreliable white protagonists who treated partially developed black objects like 'n[-----]s'" (Laymon, *Heavy*, 71). Even so, he admits,

> I felt a tug toward the interior of Welty's stories. . . . Welty didn't know a lick about Mississippi black folk, but she knew enough about herself to mock white folk in the most ruthlessly petty ways I'd ever read. . . . Welty reminded me of what my eyes and ears taught me: white folk were scared and scary as all hell, so scared, so scary the words "scared" and "scary" weren't scared or scary enough to describe them.

From the opening sentence of "Why I Live at the P.O.," Laymon writes, "I didn't just feel an intimate relationship to Welty's text; I felt every bit of Jackson," his hometown, "and really every bit of Mississippi" he had come to know and "fear" in his young life. At Millsaps College, only blocks from the Welty residence in Jackson's Belhaven neighborhood, Laymon would turn again to Welty's work to help articulate his even more powerful response to the short fiction of Toni Cade Bambara (130).

It was also at Millsaps that Laymon rediscovered Richard Wright. Rereading *Black Boy* among the largely white, largely affluent student body there, he reports, "felt like a call to arms" against, among other things, structural racism in his native land (137). "Richard Wright wrote about disasters and he let the reader know there wasn't one disaster in America that started the day everything fell apart." Rather, Wright's America *was* a disaster, an ongoing, intrinsic catastrophe, and the jolt of recognition this prompted in Laymon also kindled a desire to take up the pen and mount his own campaign against injustice. "I wanted to write like Wright far more than I wanted to write like Faulkner," he clarifies, but then again, "I didn't really want to write like Wright at all. I wanted to fight like Wright. I wanted to craft sentences that styled on white folk, and dared them to do anything about the styling they'd just witnessed" (137-38). The passage so closely tracks Wright's account of reading H. L. Mencken as a young man as to rule out any doubt about *Black Boy*'s importance as a literary model for *Heavy*:

> I was jarred and shocked by the style, the clear, clean, sweeping sentences. Why did he write like that? And how did one write like that? . . . [T]his man was fighting, fighting with words. He was using words as a weapon, using them as one would use a club. Could words be weapons? Well, yes, for here they were. Then maybe, perhaps, I could use them as a weapon?[32]

Indeed, the full title of Laymon's book, *Heavy: An American Memoir*, stages an intertextual dialogue with Wright's original title for his memoir: *American Hunger*. Both works enlist forms of malnutrition—undernourishment in Wright's case, obesity and anorexia in Laymon's—as overarching metaphors for the ontologically diminished condition of being Black in America.

Yet here, too, as with Faulkner and Welty, Laymon acknowledges limits to the impact of his Mississippi precursor on his aspirations for the writing life. Maligned and misunderstood at Millsaps, the young man could understand "why Wright left Jackson, left Mississippi, left the Deep South, and ultimately left the nation" (Laymon, *Heavy*, 138). But Wright's way was not to prove Laymon's. Even at this early stage in his development as a reader and author, Laymon's identification with Wright's quest for a world elsewhere is tempered by an interior tug toward family and home:

> I kept thinking about how Grandmama didn't leave [Mississippi] when she could. I thought about how [his mother] left and chose to come back. I thought

about how I chose to stay. I wondered if the world would have ever read Wright had he not left Mississippi. I wondered if black children born in Mississippi after Wright would have laughed, or smiled more at his sentences if he imagined Mississippi as home. I wondered if he thought he'd come back home soon the day he left for Chicago.

Though his career takes him to Ohio, Indiana, and New York, Laymon ultimately returns to Mississippi at the memoir's end, to write, teach, and rejoin his mother and grandmother. He thus extends the Mississippi confluence while also redirecting it in his own way, to suit his own vision.

Which is as it should be. The experience of this confluence will vary according to the tributary from which one enters it, the degree of one's immersion in its flow, and the downriver destination(s) one has in mind. We aim for this volume to achieve a similar confluence among its contributors with equally diverse and rewarding results for its readers.

NOTES

1. Linda Kuehl, "The Art of Fiction XLVII: Eudora Welty," in *Conversations with Eudora Welty*, ed. Peggy Whitman Prenshaw (Jackson: University Press of Mississippi, 1984), 80.
2. Noel Polk, *Faulkner and Welty and the Southern Literary Tradition* (Jackson: University Press of Mississippi, 2008), 6.
3. Eudora Welty, "Postcard from Hollywood" (1943), *On William Faulkner* (Jackson: University Press of Mississippi, 2003), 20.
4. Eudora Welty, "Review of *Intruder in the Dust*" (1949), *On William Faulkner* (Jackson: University Press of Mississippi, 2003) 25, 26, 27.
5. Edmund Wilson quoted in Eudora Welty, "Letter in Defense of Faulkner" (1949), *On William Faulkner*, 29.
6. Welty, "Letter in Defense of Faulkner," 28.
7. Welty, "Letter in Defense of Faulkner," 30.
8. Welty, "Letter in Defense of Faulkner," 28.
9. Eudora Welty, "Place in Fiction," *The Eye of the Story: Selected Essays and Reviews* (New York: Vintage, 1990), 126.
10. Welty, "Place in Fiction," 85.
11. Welty, "Place in Fiction," 171.
12. Suzanne Marrs, *Eudora Welty: A Biography* (New York: Harcourt, 2005), 11.
13. Marrs, *Eudora Welty*, 11.
14. Keneth Kinnamon and Michel Fabre, eds., *Conversations with Richard Wright* (Jackson: University Press of Mississippi, 1993), 10.
15. Harry L. Shaw Jr., Donald Thompson, James McGaw et al., "An Editorial Conference" in Kinnamon and Fabre, eds., *Conversations with Richard Wright*, 10.
16. Revista Branca, "Interview with Richard Wright," in Kinnamon and Fabre, eds., *Conversations with Richard Wright*, 141.
17. William Faulkner quoted in Hazel Rowley, *Richard Wright: The Life and Times* (New York: Henry Holt and Company, 2001), 325.
18. Faulkner quoted in Rowley, *Richard Wright: The Life and Times*, 325.

19. Alain Locke, "there is no title: *Opportunity*" in *Richard Wright: Critical Perspectives Past and Present*, ed. Henry Louis Gates Jr. and K. A. Appiah (New York: Amistad, 1993), 19.

20. Hubert Creekmore, "Social Factors in *Native Son*," *University Review* 8, no. 2 (Winter 1941), 139.

21. Richard Wright, "How Bigger Was Born," *Early Works*, ed. Arnold Rampersad (New York: Library of America, 1991), 857.

22. Thadious M. Davis, *Southscapes: Geographies of Race, Region, and Literature* (Chapel Hill: University of North Carolina Press, 2011), 137.

23. Richard Wright, "Blueprint for Negro Writing" (1937), *Richard Wright Reader*, ed. Ellen Wright and Michel Fabre (New York: Harper and Row, 1978), 45.

24. R. Radhakrishnan, "Why Compare?" in *Comparison: Theories, Approaches, Uses*, ed. Rita Felski and Susan Stanford Friedman (Baltimore: Johns Hopkins University Press, 2013), 16.

25. Susan Stanford Friedman, "Why Not Compare?" in *Comparison: Theories, Approaches, Uses*, ed. Rita Felski and Susan Stanford Friedman (Baltimore: Johns Hopkins University Press, 2013), 40.

26. Rita Felski and Susan Stanford Friedman, "Introduction," *Comparison: Theories, Approaches, Uses*, ed. Felski and Friedman (Baltimore: Johns Hopkins University Press, 2013), 3.

27. Eudora Welty, *One Writer's Beginnings* in *Eudora Welty: Stories, Essays, Memoir*, ed. Richard Ford and Michael Kreyling (New York: Library of America, 1998), 948.

28. Felski and Friedman, "Introduction," 1.

29. Margaret Walker Alexander quoted in Bill Sierichs, "Baptist TV Wins Welty Americana Award," *Jackson Clarion-Ledger*, November 10, 1974, 3.

30. Jesmyn Ward, interview with Melissa Block, *All Things Considered*, National Public Radio, August 31, 2017, https://www.npr.org/2017/08/31/547271081/writing-mississippi-jesmyn-ward-salvages-stories-of-the-silenced. Accessed July 9, 2023.

31. Kiese Laymon, *Heavy: An American Memoir* (New York: Scribner, 2018), 14. Hereafter cited parenthetically.

32. Richard Wright, *Black Boy (American Hunger): A Record of Childhood and Youth* (New York: HarperPerennial, 1993), 293.

"What There Is to Say"

Looking Back at My Friendship with Eudora Welty

SUZANNE MARRS

Fifty-one years after their first letters to each other, William Maxwell wrote to assure Eudora Welty that she need not worry about their waning correspondence. "What there is to say," he told her, "we have said."[1] That line has come to apply to almost anything I, at age seventy-six, might say in a formal paper about Welty and her fiction. What remains unsaid or uncompiled by me in my career as a Welty scholar is more autobiographical than critical. So, in this keynote address, I will attempt to fill that gap and outline the professional and personal relationships I had with Welty over the course of eighteen years. I'll report on the way I met her work and then met her, describe some of what she told me about her photographs, the origins of her stories, her sojourns away from Mississippi, her reading interests, and her fellow writers, and reflect on new discoveries I made after Welty had died.[2] Here is that story, loose though its plot may be.

In the late 1960s and early 1970s, I was trained as a generalist. My comprehensive exams spanned four periods of English literature and two of American—I was able to drop one British period because I was an Americanist. I had no training in literary theory, and to this day I recoil at having to read it. I also had no classes that featured works by Eudora Welty—I would meet her work in what may be the best way—reading it on my own and trying to comprehend the complex forces at work in it. And I would meet her work in the spirit in which it had been written. "I never doubted [. . .]," she once observed, "that imagining yourself into other people's lives is exactly what fiction writing is."[3] She might have added that imagining yourself into characters' lives, not applying a template to a text, is exactly what reading fiction is. This was a concept we shared, though it is regarded as old-fashioned by many in today's academic environment. Strangely enough, based on this background and reading strategy, I have become a specialist, though not with a theoretical bent.

I began to read Welty at the suggestion of my mother's college roommate, Elva Lewis, who knew I had been asked to teach a course about twentieth-century American women writers. (I was the third woman hired in the English Department at SUNY-Oswego, and a former chair of our department was fabled to have retired when forced to add women to the faculty—"Let someone else hire the bitches," he told his dean. So, I was the "bitch" assigned to teach women writers, and thank goodness I was.) Elva recommended that I teach *Losing Battles* by Eudora Welty. It was my first encounter with Welty's fiction, and it was a life-changing one.

When my 1980 sabbatical leave came around, I opted to study Welty. I went to the University of North Carolina and sat in on Louis Rubin's southern literature and Peter Walker's nineteenth-century southern history classes. I also spent time in the library, trying to track down sources for two Welty stories: "First Love" and "A Still Moment." That led to small publications and to new academic friendships. Mary Hughes Brookhart, a UNC PhD candidate, and I at first vied for books, but ultimately, we gladly exchanged and talked about them. A few years later, we decided to cowrite an essay, to journey to Jackson, Mississippi, immerse ourselves in the Welty archive at the Mississippi Department of Archives and History (MDAH), see the Natchez Trace landscape that inspired "At the Landing," and try to meet "Miss Welty."

I arrived first and sought to secure an appointment for an interview. I had written to Welty but had not had a response. At the Archives, I inquired about the possibilities and was told I should ask Miss Capers. Charlotte Capers, Eudora's lifelong friend, had retired from her position as director of MDAH, but she continued to field such requests as mine. She met me at the Department, checked me out, and said, "I think Eudora ought to see you." What was behind her decision? I'm guessing it was a personal affinity—she and I were destined to become good friends. I certainly would not have qualified based on my resume.

Anyway, an appointment with Miss Welty was scheduled, and Mary Hughes arrived from North Carolina to join me in the interview. Welty greeted us at her front door on a hot July 1983 morning, and she clearly remembered my unanswered letter to her. "I hope you're not trying to turn me into an Agrarian," she said firmly but kindly. Mary Hughes's interest in Proustian connections was more pleasing to Welty than my own interest in her southern context. We did talk about literary matters, but also enjoyed personal conversations. As was her propensity, she drew us out. I ended up telling her that the characters' names in *Losing Battles* reminded me of the names in my mother's family—my mother was burdened with the name Evounda Wandalene, suggested to her mother by a neighbor. "Write that name on my soda box," my grandmother requested of her neighbor, "so I can learn to spell it correctly." As an adult and a married woman, my mother ensured that her legal name would simply be Wanda Marrs. Welty loved that tale—our shared love of family and family stories would enhance our friendship. When this conversation eventually paused, we left Welty's house for lunch at a local restaurant and for a visit to Lemuria Bookstore. "Hi, boys," Eudora called out to John Evans and Tom Gerald when we entered the store, and I saw that her literary community was a close, but not primarily academic, one.

A year later, I returned for another summer research stint, then in 1985-86 spent a year in Jackson as the Welty Scholar in Residence at MDAH on a grant from the Mississippi Committee for the Humanities. My charge was double-pronged: 1) organize the Welty Collection and write a finding aid to it, and 2) talk about Welty in schools and libraries across the state. Both tasks were wonderful learning experiences for me. During the archival portion of the grant, my primary instructor was Eudora Welty herself. I met with Eudora to identify each of her photographs by date and by location, to discuss her correspondence held there, and to reorganize the typescripts and galleys of her stories, essays, and reviews.

What did she tell me? Well, I learned that she had taken photographs with three separate cameras, which each created different-sized negatives. The photographs could be roughly dated by the camera she had been using: a Kodak with a bellows from 1929 to 1935; a Kodak Recomar in 1935-36; and a Rolleiflex from late 1936 to 1950. She corrected the commonly held assumption that these photographs had been taken for the WPA during her few months working for that agency; not so. She had taken them for herself, before, during, and after her time on the Works Progress staff. As we jointly examined more than one thousand contact prints and Eudora commented on them, I saw that she had photographed many white and more Black Mississippians of all ages, at home and at work, at state fairs and parades and in church, in Jackson and Grenada, Pontotoc and Crystal Springs, Raymond and Utica, and beyond. She had recorded the resilience and the dignity, the joy and the pain, of individuals facing poverty and racial oppression, living lives as nurses and fortune tellers, bootleggers and store owners, washwomen, farmers and religious leaders. In her introduction to the new edition of Eudora Welty's *Photographs*, Natasha Trethewey expresses her admiration and gratitude for the diversity and authenticity of these images: Trethewey had not realized, she writes, "[A]midst the constant barrage of cultural images diminishing or rendering monolithic a people—*my* people, southern, black, of a particular time and place—that there was evidence of another way of seeing: a vision rooted in an unvarnished attempt to show reality. Eudora Welty's photographs provided that other way of seeing, the visual, historical evidence: 'a record,' she has said. 'The life in those times.'" Trethewey then adds, "That record was the lens I needed." It was the lens she needed to write poems about her grandmother, "to anchor visually" the cadence of her grandmother's voice as translated to the page.[4]

Tretheway's experience with the Welty photographs in many ways recapitulated Eudora's own. "I had to go on to fiction from photographing," Eudora told Hermione Lee. "That's the only way you can really part the veil between people, not in images but in what comes from inside, in both subject and writer."[5] A career as a writer, not a photographer, was her goal, but one art form could and did complement the other, just as it would for Trethewey. Though, as Eudora told me, she had not consulted her photographs when writing, the images she had seen through the camera's viewfinder were also recorded in her memory, ready to serve as visual anchors for her fiction. Let me mention just a few: the images of New York City that call to mind "Flowers for Marjorie"; "A Woman of the Thirties," which W. Ralph Eubanks believes conveys the spirit of Phoenix Jackson in "A Worn Path"; the bottle trees that in "Livvie" represent the quest of an elderly Black man to find a safe haven in a dangerous world; the photograph of a fisherman and his sons throwing knives that has its fictional counterpart in "At the Landing"; the portrait of a man with roses round his hat brim who appears as Plez Morgan in "A Shower of Gold"; the stile in Raymond, which is so like the one in "The Wanderers," where the story's white protagonist and an aged African American woman respond as one to the "magical percussion" of rain; and the New Orleans Mardi Gras revelers costumed as Death and the Medusa, who move from a snapshot into *The Optimist's Daughter*. In their fictional incarnations, some aspects of each photograph are faithfully portrayed; others are changed as they are transformed to words—these are keys to understanding the writer's imaginative process and a story's import. A good bit of work has now been done on this topic.[6] More remains to be explored.

In working with the Welty correspondence, fiction, and nonfiction, I sought her help in providing information about those with whom she corresponded, and I relied upon my own reading of stories and novels to identify textual variants in drafts and published texts. The information gleaned from these conversations and from my research informed the finding aid I was compiling for MDAH. I also began a long-term project for myself.[7] Even as I fulfilled my grant obligations and traveled the state talking about her fiction, I sought to discuss the origins of her stories with Eudora. She told me that "A Piece of News," set in rural Mississippi and first published in summer 1937, had been extrapolated from an experience that had taken place years earlier in Lewistown, Montana. Her memory of the locale and time of year was vivid, of the actual year a bit hazy. We can now be certain that late in 1929, Eudora traveled to this county seat of slightly more than five thousand citizens. There, she visited a friend and worked briefly at a newspaper edited and published by her friend's father.[8] During that stay, Eudora recalled, a woman snowshoed into town to demand that the newspaper print a retraction: her husband had not shot her as had been reported. In Welty's story, the woman is transformed into Mississippian Ruby Fisher, who imagines (based on a Tennessee newspaper story about a woman of the same name) that her husband Clyde has taken a gun to her, leaving her "beautiful, desirable, and dead."[9]

The origins of "The Whistle" lay closer to home. This story was inspired by a visit to nearby Utica, Mississippi, where Eudora's friend Dorothy Simmons lived. During an overnight stay, Eudora was awakened by the piercing sound of a whistle. She rushed from her room and roused Dorothy, who had a matter-of-fact explanation: there was going to be a freeze that night, and the surrounding tenant farmers needed to cover and protect their tomato crop. That urgent need is the subject of "The Whistle," but the story's key scene when farmers Jason and Sara Morton burn their last log and then their furniture in a futile effort to stay warm, that key scene was totally, Eudora told me, of her own making.

The origins of "A Curtain of Green" proved to be even more personal. In this story, Mrs. Larkin has witnessed the death of her husband, who has driven his car home from work only to have a chinaberry tree fall "exactly so as to crush him to death."[10] Grief-stricken, the young widow ventures daily into her garden, creating not a showpiece, but a jungle, in an effort to comprehend the forces of nature that have destroyed her husband and her happiness. "Were you thinking of your mother's response to your father's death?" I asked Eudora. "I hope my mother never realized that," she replied.

Eudora and I talked about the origins of many another story: the youthful experiences of summer camp that inform "Moon Lake," the journey by boat-train from London to Cork that is transformed into "The Bride of the Innisfallen," and her own transatlantic crossing that provides so much detail for "Going to Naples." But in looking at the origins of stories, I did not want to make the source of the story an end in itself, to "pick the story up by its heels (as if it had swallowed a button)," to use Welty's apt metaphor.[11] Instead each of our discussions was focused on the act of transformation, the making of something new and different and suggestive from something discrete and particular. She was telling me what I later discovered she had written to her friend John Robinson. Writing, she told Robinson, "purifies experience, in a way, and what hurts most about experience may not be its pain, which is pertinent but (I think this) its dross, its alloy, residue. You make something. Its truth is somehow related to your honesty and torment. It's a little like loving someone in that you can't let anything false go from you, it has to be true from a certain moment. Then you know the lovely ease this makes happen."[12]

Professional conversations aside, during my year as MDAH's Welty Scholar, I had many other opportunities to spend time with Eudora. We often met for drinks at her house or for dinner elsewhere. She came to the small apartment I had rented, or we ventured to Bill's or Nick's or the Elite or the Mayflower restaurants—she was no longer cooking. She took me as her guest to plays at New Stage Theatre; her tickets were always for opening night. And best of all, she introduced me to her family and included me in the groups of friends with whom she regularly gathered. Those friends included Charlotte Capers, Ann Morrison (educational programs coordinator at the Old Capitol Museum), Patti Carr Black (director of the Old Capitol Museum), and Jane Petty (director of New Stage Theatre). Conversations about travel, politics, literature, and the theater were always sparkling. When the BBC came to film an hour-long program about Eudora, I was charmed to be included in many conversations that Patchy Wheatley and her crew had with Eudora, conversations with well-turned phrases from both sides of the Atlantic. I was fortunate to join Eudora when she entertained local writers like Ellen Douglas and Willie Morris. And when more far-flung writers visited Jackson, I was lucky to meet them. Elizabeth Spencer was one, Reynolds Price another. The opportunity to listen to these talented individuals talk to each other was an invaluable experience for me as a person and a young scholar. Eudora and her friends, old and new, were teaching me what she asserts in her introduction to the *Norton Book of Friendship*: Friendship arises "along with—or through—the inspiration of language," and "friendship might have been the first, as well as the best, teacher of communication."[13]

After the year I spent at the Department of Archives and History, I began to apply for academic positions in Mississippi, and happily the one I found was at Millsaps College in Jackson. In 1988, back here in residence, I began to see Eudora on a more regular but less formal basis. I was no longer interviewing her about the Welty Collection, but primarily seeing her as a friend. Whenever we were meeting just as friends (which must have been at least 90 percent of the time), I took no notes during or after our meetings. That said, I was blessed with a good memory, and Eudora's conversations were worth remembering. When she later gave me permission to write her biography, I was able to draw upon those memories. Here are a few.

I loved hearing Eudora describe her days as a student at Wisconsin and Columbia. At Wisconsin, to the consternation of Professor Ricardo Quintana, she failed to qualify for Phi Beta Kappa because she was unaware she could drop a Latin class too advanced for someone with her high school training. She did not fail, however, to pick up a Wisconsin expression that described this misadventure and that she would regularly use for the rest of her life. I had often asked Eudora about the phrase "there you are—jackknifed." "This is not the time to talk about that," she would reply. But one evening over drinks at Charlotte Capers's house, I prevailed. It seems that when an itinerant carpenter built privies in the woods near Madison, he at times made the seat hole too large, and then there the unfortunate user was—through the hole with head to toe and bottom below—jackknifed.

In a literal sense, there were no such problems at Columbia. During the 1930–31 academic year, Eudora along with friends from Jackson lived in Johnson Hall, a graduate women's dormitory with indoor plumbing, a building that Columbia president Nicholas Murray Butler had, according to student gossip, commissioned so that he could move his sister, Eliza Rhees Butler, out of his home and into the dormitory as its resident director. Miss Butler was a tyrant, and Eudora and her Jackson cohorts both resented her and found her amusing. Stories about Miss Butler that I heard in Eudora's living room explain their plight and their response.

Miss Butler, Eudora recalled, conducted bed checks. She offered melodramatic, delusional advice to the young women: "Never accept an aspirin from a stranger," Miss Butler warned, "or the next thing you know you'll wake up in Buenos Aires, in a house of prostitution, with a friend of your father's looking down on you." She refused to give the Mississippi girls free tickets to the opera—coming from such a benighted state, they could never appreciate high art, she reasoned. The Mississippians managed to buy their own tickets and were delighted one night to hear the voice of their tormentor ring out over the opera hall: "I am Eliza Rhees Butler, and I have been seated behind a post."

Miss Butler notwithstanding, Eudora took full advantage of New York's cultural riches, and she often managed to stay out late and miss the Butler bed checks, most notably, perhaps, when her Jackson boyfriend George Greenway came to visit as a respite from his own graduate studies in North Carolina. Greenway was a musician who had taken Eudora on drives into the countryside around Jackson so that he could serenade her with his trumpet. In New York, the two Jacksonians relished hearing more accomplished musicians perform in the nightclubs of Harlem. Ten years later, Eudora saw Fats Waller play in Jackson, but the audience for this concert was not integrated as the ones in New York had been. Inspired by Waller's music and appalled at the situation, she wrote the story "Powerhouse." As that story draws to a close and as the title character (like Waller, a Black jazz pianist) looks out over an all-white audience that is both fascinated and frightened by him, his face is transfigured by "a vast, impersonal and yet furious grimace."[14] The fury and chagrin Powerhouse feels in the story Eudora would forcefully express in a 1945 letter to her local newspaper, a letter calling for the political defeat of two virulent racists, Senator Theodore Bilbo and Representative John Rankin. Almost twenty years later, she would express even deeper fury and anguish in her *New Yorker* story "Where Is the Voice Coming From?"—a story that translates into fiction the horror of Medgar Evers's assassination. Eudora's empathic concern for racial justice was expressed in many other stories and novels, in her 1950s participation in events at the historically Black Tougaloo College, including its Social Sciences Forum, and in her 1963 insistence that a contingent from Tougaloo be allowed to attend her reading at Millsaps as part of the Southern Literary Festival. For that occasion, she read "Powerhouse."

As a student in Wisconsin and New York and throughout her life, Eudora was a great "in-taker," to borrow a term she coined to describe Elizabeth Bowen. As a photographer, as a writer, and as a person, Eudora wanted to "see and hear and learn and feel and remember" everything she could about the world in which she lived.[15] She wanted to face its terrors and relish its pleasures, and travel was one of its great pleasures. "Tell me your trip" was her first request any time I returned to Jackson from vacations. But her trips and her accounts of them were far more interesting. She told me, for instance, about being in Paris in 1949. The British aristocrat Stephen Tennant managed to contact her there and took her out at least twice. The first was to a show at the Folies Bergère: when the scantily clad dancing girls emerged on stage, he whispered to Eudora, "Darling, I'd forgotten how ravishing blue ostrich can be." The next outing was to lunch at the Tour d'Argent. Eudora was on a budget and was thrilled at the opportunity to go at no charge to this renowned and famously expensive restaurant. She and Tennant had a delicious meal, but when the check arrived, he turned to her and said, "Darling, shall we share?"

I was not lucky enough to spend time with Eudora in New York or Paris. We did travel to a few somewhat distant locations, to Knoxville for the Fellowship of Southern Writers meeting in 1991, to my native Oklahoma when Eudora received the Helmerich Award in Tulsa later that year, and to Washington, DC, where the American Association of

State Colleges and Universities honored her in 1992. And we traveled all around Mississippi—to Columbus and Natchez and the Gulf Coast, to the Faulkner conference in Oxford in the summer of 1987 and to a three-day Welty symposium in Starkville that fall. At the end of the Starkville event, I joined Eudora, age seventy-eight, and her friend Jane Pepperdene of Agnes Scott College, age sixty-eight, for late evening drinks in Eudora's spacious hotel room. We each had one bourbon, then poured another. "You can't," as I often heard Eudora say, "fly on just one wing." But at least this once, the second drink proved too stiff for me. I was seated on the floor, and my two brilliant, articulate, and energetic compatriots saw me, their junior by decades, fall asleep at their feet. Eventually they woke me and said it was time to call it a day. Neither Jane nor Eudora was the slightest bit inebriated. Sobriety was a key reason, Eudora once told me, colleges and universities so often invited her to speak; they knew she would not get drunk as so many visiting writers did.

Needless to say, wherever we went together, I basked in Eudora's reflected glory, whether joining her for breakfast with Shelby Foote, Alfred Uhry, and Peter Taylor in Knoxville, or inviting my Oklahoma family and friends to meet Eudora in Tulsa or simply walking with her across a university campus. And in Jackson, Eudora's love of dining out with friends like me created unexpected special events for patrons in local restaurants. Once when my husband and I took my parents and Eudora to Crechale's restaurant, the woman in charge of the cash register came to our table and whispered in my ear, "Is that Eudora Welty? If not, she's a dead ringer for her." And at a more upscale establishment, my father was amazed when our fellow diners stood and bowed as Eudora passed their tables on her way out. Following right behind her, Dad was proud to acknowledge the bows for himself.

This is not to suggest that Eudora and I failed to discuss my work as a scholar. There was hardly a time when I was not writing an essay or a book chapter about her fiction, and every now and then I scheduled sessions to talk shop. At those meetings, I asked permission to take notes, and on two occasions I even asked Eudora to read drafts of the papers that emerged from our discussions. She had told me a good deal, for instance, about the derelict house Waverley near Columbus, Mississippi, that she visited as a college student and then used as the model for Marmion in *Delta Wedding*. I asked her to look over my account of biographical detail and artistic transformation in that novel. She did, objecting to neither, but finding fault with my portrait of the Fairchild family. I had quoted Michael Kreyling in making my argument, and in the margin of my essay Eudora wrote: "You and Michael Kreyling are wrong. These people are not bleak." When I told Michael of Eudora's response, he said,

"She's right." And she was. A different issue arose when Eudora agreed to respond to a lecture I was writing for a local library. I had taken the Jackson context of several stories as my topic, and she offered additional information to me. Still, she was a bit uneasy about my discussing these issues, especially biographical information, on the home front. Uneasy though she may have been, she did not attempt to change my lecture because of its venue.

Of course, Eudora and I also talked about other writers (from Chaucer to Chekhov to Virginia Woolf) and about writing itself. We both were ardent readers of murder mysteries, and she introduced me to novels by many a mystery writer: Elizabeth Daly, Tony Hillerman, Margaret Truman, Elliott Roosevelt, and the iconic Ross Macdonald among them. And we had many conversations, anecdotal rather than analytical, about writers of literary fiction she had known. One was E. M. Forster. She showed me a 1947 letter from him that she had framed and hung in her sitting room. It began, "Finding myself in your country, I feel I should like to give myself the pleasure of writing you a line and telling you how much I enjoy your work."[16] Amused by the phrase "finding myself in your country," she was delighted to be admired by a writer she revered. She met him seven years later, and during one of our conversations, Eudora told me of that occasion. She was in Cambridge to speak at an American studies conference, and Forster invited her to lunch in his rooms at King's College. Forster's manservant, who waited on them, was drunk, to the amusement of both writers. After a boozily served meal, Forster led Eudora across the King's College lawn, a perk reserved for fellows there, and into the famous chapel, where someone was playing Handel on the organ. As I recall Eudora telling me this story, I feel sure she said that she had gone to see Forster just after having been infuriated by a conference session during which Arthur Mizener had dismissed *A Passage to India* as a failed novel of manners. So upset was she that she accidentally kicked herself in the ankle and arrived at Forster's rooms with a wounded ankle and blood in her shoe. When I came to write a biography of Welty, I learned that in one small detail either Eudora's memory had been faulty, or as is more likely, mine had. In a 1954 letter to her friend Frank Lyell, she reported that the benighted remarks from Mizener and her self-inflicted wound had come in the evening after her lunchtime meeting with Forster. Such are the perils of writing biography based on remembered conversations not recorded contemporaneously.

I could now report on Eudora's conversational observations about Katherine Anne Porter or Walker Percy, Elizabeth Bowen or V. S. Pritchett, but let me focus on the writers who share the conference title with Welty. First, Faulkner. Eudora told me of meeting him in Oxford in May

1948 when John Robinson took her there. The two Jacksonians were invited to a small dinner party hosted by Robinson's friends, and the guests included William and Estelle Faulkner. The next day, Eudora and John visited the Faulkners at Rowan Oak and received a tour of the house. In August of 1949, she and John returned to Oxford and once more enjoyed a tour led by Faulkner—this time he took them sailing on Sardis Lake. At no point during these visits was there talk of books, alas. I don't think she saw Faulkner again until 1962, when she presented him with the Gold Medal for Fiction from the National Institute of Arts and Letters. Eudora told me that she was worried about dropping the heavy medal during the ceremony and asked Faulkner if she could give him the medal in advance and present him with an empty box. "If you so prefer," was his courtly reply.

Eudora never met Richard Wright, so there were no stories of personal encounters for her to tell. There were no fortuitous invitations like the ones that had allowed her to meet Faulkner on a few occasions; instead, there was a litany of missed opportunities. Both Welty and Wright were star Jackson students, but a segregated society precluded their meeting. In the mid-1940s, Eudora did meet Wright's friend and fellow author Ralph Ellison; her editor John Woodburn took her to dinner at Ellison's apartment, and a fast friendship was formed. This friendship brought Ellison to Jackson and Millsaps College in 1970, but a shared friendship with Ellison did not bring Welty and Wright together.[17] Neither did the fact that Wright's editor Edward Aswell was married to *Harper's Bazaar* fiction editor Mary Lou Aswell, who, in 1941, began to accept a number of Welty stories for publication. By the early 1940s, the Aswells' marriage was on the rocks, and it seems unlikely that the couple would have been entertaining their authors together.[18] Eudora's late 1949 time in Paris, where Wright had emigrated, might have led to an introduction if Wright hadn't been spending a full year away from France, primarily in Argentina for the filming of *Native Son*.[19] The possibility of the two ever meeting seems to have been star-crossed. Bad luck for them and for us.

Still, there can be meetings on the page as well as in person. Faulkner took note of Welty's work, writing her an encouraging letter in 1943, even though he confused her with Zora Neale Hurston. And Welty commented on Faulkner's fiction in essays and lectures, reviewed his novel *Intruder in the Dust*, and defended him in a letter to the editors of the *New Yorker* when the magazine published Edmund Wilson's grudging review of the same novel. In contrast, Welty and Wright seem almost to have been off each other's writing radar. He seems never to have mentioned her or her fiction in publications or interviews or correspondence, though a story like "Powerhouse," one that writers Al Young and Randall Kenan found so authentic, might potentially have won Wright's regard as well and led him to read more. In 1955, Wright may have read Welty's story "Keela, the Outcast Indian Maiden," when Whit Burnett suggested that it (along with stories by Faulkner, Ellison, and Ann Petry) be added to an anthology manuscript for which Wright had already written an introduction. There seems to be no record of Wright's endorsement of this suggestion or reworking of his introduction, but Welty's story did become part of the manuscript that circulated unsuccessfully among publishers.[20] Just as Wright failed to mention Welty's work, Welty made, as best as I can ascertain, no mention of his in interviews or correspondence, nor did she write about his work in essays or reviews.[21] In spring 1945, she was invited by the *Journal of Mississippi History* to review *Black Boy*, but declined, perhaps because she was absorbed in writing her novel *Delta Wedding* and was pressed by an ongoing commitment to the *New York Times Book Review*. Given her disgust with white racism in Mississippi and the admiration a good friend, Duke historian William Hamilton, had expressed for *Black Boy*, it seems likely that she would have been receptive to Wright's work. But, for whatever reason, the fact remains that neither Wright nor Welty appears to have mentioned the other's fiction or nonfiction either positively or negatively. We seem destined never to solve this mystery definitively, though perhaps their joint silence may indicate both a respect for the other's achievements and a preference for different narrative strategies, whether in fiction or autobiography. Welty was a writer who by indirections found directions out, Wright a writer who learned from Mencken to use words as weapons. Narrative strategies notwithstanding, there are affinities in the work of Wright and Welty—certainly there is a shared rejection of racial injustice, and Harriet Pollack has written that Welty's late unpublished story "The Shadow Club" offers an homage to Richard Wright—but such affinities must be analyzed by critics without help from the authors themselves.[22] In my classes and in community lectures, I at times placed books by Wright and Faulkner in conversation with ones by Welty. In retrospect, I wish I had addressed these pairings with Eudora, but I did not.

Neither did I inquire about details of her personal life. I once asked, "Eudora, have you ever been in love?" "Yes," was her reply, but she offered no additional information, and I did not ask for it. I knew Eudora did not want a biography, and I was not preparing to write one. But someone else was.

In 1993, Ann Waldron, an experienced biographer, determined that Eudora would be her next subject. Waldron was a thorough researcher and unearthed a good bit of previously unknown information. For instance, she discovered, hidden away in the New York Public Library's

New Yorker Collection, Eudora's 1933 application for a post at the magazine: "How I would like to work for you!" she wrote. "A little paragraph each morning—a little paragraph each night." And then Eudora concluded that if she couldn't work at the *New Yorker*, she could dance in Vachel Lindsay's *Congo*: "I congo on," she punned. "I rest my case."[23] But despite such felicitous discoveries, Waldron found much information denied her. Eudora had expressed opposition to the biography, declined to be interviewed, and asked her friends who had reported inquiries from Waldron to decline as well. I was one of those Welty friends Waldron contacted. "I'd be glad to help you use the Welty Collection at MDAH," I told her, "but Eudora has requested that I not talk with you about our friendship." Waldron did not want or need my archival assistance; she wanted the life stories Eudora had told me and that I had not yet put on paper. Moreover, what Waldron didn't realize, and what I did not at that point fully appreciate, was the wealth of correspondence and unpublished fiction that Eudora had not yet donated to MDAH. That trove was left to the Archives in her will and would come to the Collection only after her death. None of it was then available. When Waldron's biography finally went to press in 1998, it was doomed to be underinformed. She had not seen the most important source material, and she failed, to my way of thinking at least, to grasp the essence of Eudora's character. My husband had long urged me to undertake a biography. I began to think he was right and that I should.

Shortly afterward, Reynolds Price visited Jackson. Over lunch, my husband broached the subject of a biography by me, and Reynolds added his encouragement. I then asked Patti Black if she thought I should try to provide a more informed biographical record than now existed. "Yes, but don't tell Eudora you want to write a biography for her sake," Patti cautioned me. "Tell her this is a project that would mean a lot to you." And so it would, and so I asked. Eudora's response was instantaneous and generous. "Yes," she said, but added, "you may be getting into deeper water than you imagine."

Those deep waters were indeed ahead of me, but they involved not lurid details, but a more complex and demanding writing experience than I had ever attempted. Eudora more fully understood what the project would entail than I did. My knowledge of her life and work was extensive, but not as extensive as it would have to become. I would need to learn more about the times in which she had lived, about her family, about the friends who sustained her, about the conflicts she would face, about the political and social and cultural events to which she had responded. I would need to read thousands of letters that she had written or received, track down correspondence in archives across the country, interview those who knew her best, and check my memory of events against other sources. Doing so would occupy my life for the next seven years.

Hard work, yes, and in the best sense. It began in Eudora's house soon after she had granted permission. Her niece Mary Alice White and I went upstairs—Eudora could no longer manage the stairs—and Mary Alice showed me box after box in which Eudora had carefully organized and stored letters to and from her closest friends. At a desk that had once been Eudora's, in a room that had been her mother's, and in a house where Eudora would reside for three more years, I was privileged to read these letters and record their revelations. In the wake of her 2001 death, my ongoing biographical research became a way of maintaining rather than supplementing daily contact with Eudora, of continuing to hear her voice and her stories. Eventually, with the blessing of Mary Alice and her sister Liz Thompson, I sent a book proposal to Eudora's agent Tim Seldes, who had agreed to represent me, and he engaged Harcourt to be my publisher. As I drew closer and closer to a complete manuscript, I was loath to turn the results loose. I didn't want, metaphorically speaking, my one-on-one meetings with Eudora to end, and I was then, as I remain, a compulsive reviser. Finally, I asked Reynolds Price to look over the text I had produced. "Send it off," he said. "Are you sure?" I asked. "I wouldn't send you out to play in traffic," he replied. So, I mailed it to Harcourt in late June or early July 2004, and the top-notch editor Tim Bent and I went through the manuscript in detail, chapter by chapter. *Eudora Welty: A Biography* was published in 2005.

Was the person I met in doing research for my biography the same person I had known as a friend for fifteen years before I began writing it? For the most part, yes. I did, nevertheless, make two rather startling discoveries: 1) Eudora was a far more audacious young woman than I had anticipated. And 2) her reticence about personal matters was far deeper than I had realized.

Audacious? Yes. The letter of application Eudora had sent to the *New Yorker* might well have tipped me off. That was a daring attempt to show by example, not precept, that her contributions could complement S. J. Perelman's. But a letter that Beth Rigel Daugherty located at the University of Sussex displayed Welty's audaciousness at its peak. In this missive to Virginia Woolf, one filled with effusive praise, twenty-two-year-old Eudora Welty, five years before she had published anything for a non-student audience, offered some rather pointed criticism of the established writer: "'The Waves,'" she told Woolf, "is beautiful; there are places in it where, one feels, only you would not fear to tread; but the sections of the book about Bernard close over the divine footprints and almost make one doubt what is now obscured and roughened away by lesser surges of inspiration. The flaw, one feels, is [. . .] in your use of such an unworthy medium as Bernard's personality for your writing. It seems wrong for you to shine there within Bernard; the spirit has descended to inhabit at those times an object we cannot worship. And Mrs. Woolf, to end the book from his lips is cruel."[24] If Eudora were here today, she might be cringing, but I think she'd be smiling at the presumptuousness of youth.

Reticent? Of course Welty was reticent about personal matters. She had long resisted attempts by critics to delve into her personal life; she had long opposed a biography. Though she and I were good friends, I understood and accepted her reticence with me when it came to discussing the loves of her life. I was much younger than she, rather new on the scene, and I was in the business of writing about her work. But I was surprised at how reticent Eudora had been with old friends like Frank Lyell, Charlotte Capers, and Patti Black, perhaps even with Bill and Emmy Maxwell, though I can't be sure. To none of these friends had she confided the love that she and Ken Millar (whose mystery-writing pseudonym was Ross Macdonald) shared. As best I can ascertain, she confided only in Mary Lou Aswell, William Jay Smith, and Reynolds Price. With no one did she discuss whether or not the relationship had become a love affair. Tom Nolan, Millar's biographer, and I agree that it probably did not. It most certainly was, we also agree, an intensely loving friendship.

The two writers met in the lobby of the Algonquin Hotel in New York City in 1971. In 1973, Ken journeyed from his Santa Barbara, California, home, to Jackson for a state celebration called Eudora Welty Day, and in 1975, 1976, and 1977, Eudora attended the Santa Barbara Writers Conference at Ken's request. She would return to Santa Barbara in 1982 for a last opportunity to see him even though his memory had been decimated by Alzheimer's disease. Six meetings only, but they had begun to exchange letters even before they met and continued doing so, Ken until he was no longer able, Eudora even when he could no longer reply; today 345 extant letters comprise their correspondence. They each carefully saved letters from the other; Ken had hidden his from his wife Margaret Millar. Fortunately, Ken's friend Ralph Sipper discovered those and personally delivered them to Eudora. Eudora at one point contemplated destroying both sides of the correspondence, but was dissuaded by Reynolds, who ultimately told me about them.

The letters, which Nolan and I would eventually edit and would publish in 2015, proved to be long and engaging and crucial to my 2005 biography of Eudora. The correspondence began with an exchange of fan letters, written from writerly perspectives, praising the language and the structure of the other's work. Then, even before their Algonquin Hotel meeting, their letters became more intimate—Ken reporting the death of his thirty-one-year-old daughter and Eudora offering empathy.

This professional and personal affinity grew deeper and deeper over the ensuing years. Each dedicated a book to the other; Eudora credited Ken with inspiring her to write a key scene in *The Optimist's Daughter*, and he enlisted her recommendations for a mystery anthology he was editing. They discussed the writing process and rued their separate experiences of writer's block. They discussed politicians and public issues—disapproval of President Nixon, fear of environmental disasters, horror at the Christmas 1972 bombing of Hanoi. They reported on their reading, their friendships, and their travels. And, as Tom Nolan and I jointly observed, "[T]hey worried over, celebrated, and consoled one another—dreamt about each other, dreamt of dreaming about each other, sent one another messages in their dreams."²⁵ Put more succinctly, they loved each other.

In September 1978, with the shadow of Alzheimer's disease darkening his life, Ken wrote to Eudora: "I hope I was able to lean on your strength without abating it, and on your knowledge of trouble and its meanings without deepening your own troubles. The best thing that can happen to a man is to be known, and by a woman of your great kindness and light and depth." Eudora replied, "We do want to be known truly, and I want to know truly. I'm glad that you feel you can lean on me. . . . Depressed or happy and serene, our spirits have traveled very near to each other and I believe sustained each other—This will go on, dear Ken—Our friendship blesses my life and I wish life could be longer for it."²⁶ This exchange exemplifies the devotion each brought to the other, a devotion perhaps intensified by the atmosphere of privacy in which it flourished.

In allowing me to make public this most profound relationship, one whose existence she had carefully guarded, Eudora knew that I would be entering deep water. I am forever grateful that she trusted me to negotiate its depths, to know her more fully and more truly than I had in our previous fifteen years of friendship. Perhaps in so generously giving me her blessing, she had Ken Millar's concept of a biographer in mind. As he told Eudora when they were excoriating Arthur Mizener's biography of Ford Madox Ford: "Biographers should write about figures they love, or at least warmly hate."²⁷ I can safely say I satisfy the first half of that stipulation.

NOTES

1. Maxwell to Welty, December 19, 1993, *What There Is to Say We Have Said: The Correspondence of Eudora Welty and William Maxwell*, ed. Suzanne Marrs (Boston: Houghton Mifflin Harcourt, 2011), 440.

2. Some information recounted in the following pages has appeared in different contexts in books I have published: *The Welty Collection* (Jackson: University Press of Mississippi,

1988); *One Writer's Imagination: The Fiction of Eudora Welty* (Baton Rouge: LSU Press, 2002); *Eudora Welty: A Biography* (Orlando: Harcourt, 2005); *What There Is to Say We Have Said*; and *Meanwhile There Are Letters: The Correspondence of Eudora Welty and Ross Macdonald*, eds. Suzanne Marrs and Tom Nolan (New York: Arcade, 2015).

3. Eudora Welty, "Looking Back at the First Story," *Georgia Review* 33 (1979), 755 (101 in online edition).

4. Natasha Trethewey, "That's Just the Way It Was," introduction to Eudora Welty, *Photographs* (Jackson: University Press of Mississippi, 2019), x, xi.

5. Eudora Welty, interview with Hermione Lee, in *More Conversations with Eudora Welty*, ed. Peggy W. Prenshaw (Jackson: University Press of Mississippi, 1996), 151.

6. For illuminating discussions of Welty's photographs, see Geraldine Chouard, *Eudora Welty et la photographie: Naissance d'une vision* (Paris: Editions Michel Houdiard, 2012); Pearl McHaney, *A Tyrannous Eye: Eudora Welty's Nonfiction and Photographs* (Jackson: University Press of Mississippi, 2014); Harriet Pollack, *Eudora Welty's Fiction and Photography: The Body of the Other Woman* (Athens: University of Georgia Press, 2016); and Annette Trefzer, *Exposing Mississippi: Eudora Welty's Photographic Reflections* (Jackson: University Press of Mississippi, 2022). The 1977 catalog for an exhibition at the Old Capitol Museum in Jackson, Mississippi, paired Welty's photographs with excerpts from her stories: see *Welty*, ed. Patti Carr Black (Jackson: Mississippi Department of Archives and History, 1977). See also Harriet Pollack and Suzanne Marrs, "Seeing Welty's Political Vision in Her Photographs," in *Welty and Politics: Did the Writer Crusade?*, ed. Pollack and Marrs (Baton Rouge: LSU Press, 2001), 223–51.

7. The finding aid I compiled was published as *The Welty Collection*, and my study of the origins of Welty's stories informed my book *One Writer's Imagination: The Fiction of Eudora Welty*.

8. On Sunday, November 17, 1929, the *Clarion-Ledger* (Jackson, Mississippi) reported that "Miss Eudora Welty, gifted and popular young daughter of Mr. and Mrs. C. W. Welty, Pinehurst Place, left Friday for a visit to be enjoyed until Christmas with a stopover in Chicago and in Madison, Wisconsin, where she attended the University, after which she will proceed to Lewiston [*sic*], Montana, as the guest of Miss Maxie Stout, a former schoolmate" (p. 18). On November 30, 1929, the *Great Falls Tribune* (Great Falls, Montana) reported that "Miss Maxine Stout of Lewistown and Miss Eudora Welty of Jackson, Miss., who had been here for Thanksgiving Day, left Friday for Lewistown, where Miss Welty will visit for some time" (p. 7). Speaking to me in 1985, Welty thought that her visit had occurred during the Christmas break (1927–28) of her junior year in college; correspondence suggests such a trip to have been more likely during her senior year. But today, thanks to the miracle of Newspapers.com, which Welty would have loved, we can be certain that she, the holder of a five-month-old BA, was in Montana in 1929. The newspaper editor and publisher for whom Welty briefly worked was surely Tom Stout of the *Lewistown Democrat-News* and the *Judith Basin Farmer* (neither has been digitized). To me Eudora reported that her friend in Lewistown had been a classmate at the University of Wisconsin in Madison. I have not been able to document that fact.

9. Eudora Welty, "A Piece of News," in *Eudora Welty: Stories, Essays, & Memoir* (New York: Library of America, 1998), 19.

10. Welty, "A Curtain of Green," in *Eudora Welty: Stories, Essays, & Memoir*, 133.

11. Welty, "Writing and Analyzing a Story," in *Eudora Welty: Stories, Essays, & Memoir*, 774.

12. Eudora Welty to John Robinson, August 17 [1946], quoted in Suzanne Marrs, *Eudora Welty: A Biography*, 146.

13. Eudora Welty, introduction to the *Norton Book of Friendship*, eds. Eudora Welty and Ronald A. Sharp (New York: W. W. Norton and Co., 1991), 40.

14. Welty, "Powerhouse," in *Eudora Welty: Stories, Essays, & Memoir*, 170.

15. Welty, *One Writer's Beginnings*, in *Eudora Welty: Stories, Essays, & Memoir*, 918.

16. E. M. Forster to Eudora Welty, April 28, 1947, as quoted in Marrs, *Eudora Welty: A Biography*, 156.

17. Ellison spoke at Millsaps College on April 9, 1970, and then attended a reception hosted by Lee and Gerry Reiff at their home. Lee Reiff was a professor of religious studies and his wife Gerry a librarian at Millsaps. Thanks to Joseph Reiff, professor emeritus at Emory and Henry College, who, in a July 26, 2020, email, told me about these events and provided me with copies of pages from a signed guestbook his parents had kept. Ellison fondly recalled the lecture in a June 16, 1993, letter to Willie Morris: "I remember the gig at Milsaps [sic] College with pleasure, and all the more because I associate it with Eudora Welty and the coincidence that my mother was a Milsap from a rural area near Savannah, Georgia." See *Selected Letters of Ralph Ellison*, eds. John F. Callahan and Marc C. Conner (New York: Random House, 2019), 982.

18. Mary Lou Aswell's daughter has written that "by the time I *was* born, in 1940, my parents' marriage was crumbling" (Mary Aswell Doll, "Beyond Myth and Memory: Ghostwriting Wolfe," *Thomas Wolfe Review* 33, nos. 1–2 [2009], 86-87). The Aswells divorced in 1946 (Doll, "'Lost and found, lost and found': Remembering Thomas Wolfe and My Father," *Thomas Wolfe Review* 39, nos. 1–2 [2015], 87). Doll refers to troubles during the interim in her book *To the Lighthouse and Back: Writings on Teaching and Living* (New York: Peter Lang, 1995), 66-67. Eudora reported seeing both Mary Lou and Edward Aswell at a party given by Henry Volkening in November 1941, but when shortly afterward Mary Lou invited Eudora to lunch, it was for the two women only. See Marrs, *Eudora Welty: A Biography*, 82.

19. Eudora was in Paris from mid-November 1949 to early January 1950, stopping by briefly in spring 1950 on a return from London. Her travels in Europe had begun in October 1949 and extended to June 1950. Wright was traveling out of France, primarily to Argentina, from August 1949 to August 1950. Welty would not return to the Continent until 1974. See Marrs, *Eudora Welty: A Biography*, 174-209, 400-401; Hazel Rowley, *Richard Wright: The Life and Times* (2001; repr., Chicago: University of Chicago Press, 2008), 382-88.

20. A copy of Wright's introduction to *The Violent Conflict* is held by the Beinecke Library at Yale University, JWJ MSS 3, box 8, folder 191. Correspondence from editor Whit Burnett to Wright is held by Yale, JWJ MSS 3, box 106, folder 1625, and by the Firestone Library at Princeton University, CO 104, box 37, folder 45. A list of the manuscript anthology's contents is held at Princeton, CO 104, box 38, folder 11. In his correspondence with Wright, Burnett recommended adding stories by Welty, William Faulkner, Ann Petry, and Ralph Ellison. Works by each became part of the manuscript, seemingly without comment by Wright, and Wright's introduction to the volume remained as written before these additions. Only one book by Welty was part of Wright's personal library, an English edition of *Delta Wedding*—see Michel Fabre, *Richard Wright: Books and Writers* (Jackson: University Press of Mississippi, 1990), 170.

21. In an interview with Miriam Horn ("Imagining Others' Lives," *US News and World Report*, February 15, 1993, 78), Welty rued the segregated social structure of the southern past and the fact that it had kept her from meeting Wright when they were both children in Jackson. I have not located any other comment on meeting or failing to meet Wright. Welty makes no mention of his work that I can find, and there are no Wright titles in Welty's personal library (Eudora Welty House catalog).

22. Harriet Pollack, "Evolving Secrets: Welty and the Mystery Genre," *Detecting the South in Fiction, Film, and Television*, eds. Deborah E. Barker and Theresa Starkey (Baton Rouge: LSU Press, 2019), 149-52.

23. Eudora Welty to the *New Yorker*, March 15, 1933, in *What There Is to Say We Have Said*, 20.

24. Eudora Welty to Virginia Woolf, November 23, 1931, Monks House Papers, University of Sussex Library Special Collections, Brighton, England, quoted in Marrs, *Eudora Welty: A Biography*, 38-39.

25. Marrs and Tom Nolan, introduction to *Meanwhile There Are Letters*, xv-xvi.

26. Millar to Welty, September 18, 1978; Welty to Millar, 23 September 1978, in *Meanwhile There Are Letters*, 405, 408.

27. Millar to Welty, April 6, 1971, in *Meanwhile There Are Letters*, 12.

Visionary and Incomplete

Comparing Cultural Landscapes of Faulkner, Wright, and Welty

JULIA EICHELBERGER

What I have sought to do was to be faithful to the time and place as it presented itself to those involved. This has meant trying not to make people aware of what with hindsight they should have been aware of but weren't. Some of what I failed to see when it lay all around me is difficult to credit. I am thinking in particular to matters of civil rights and economics.
—LOUIS D. RUBIN[1]

This essay compares six potentially troubling texts: "A Rose for Emily" and "That Evening Sun" by William Faulkner; "The Ethics of Living Jim Crow" and "Long Black Song" by Richard Wright; and "Livvie" and "Moon Lake" by Eudora Welty.[2] Set in Mississippi in the Jim Crow era, they are filled with slurs, casual racism, and racialized and misogynist violence. Discussing these topics can result in discomfort and pain. Since 2020, when the notorious killings of unarmed Black citizens Ahmaud Arbery, Breonna Taylor, and George Floyd led to widespread protests and what some called a "summer of racial reckoning,"[3] such texts may strike us as even more difficult to read and discuss in our classrooms.[4] Do these texts adequately critique the harms they portray, or do they ultimately expose the classism, racism, and/or sexism of their creators?

I propose a comparative reading of these texts alongside each writer's personal history and subject position to illuminate more clearly what each writer did and did not perceive. Despite their many intersections of geography and era, and despite their tremendous powers of creative imagination, each writer perceived their shared cultural surround quite differently, meaning that for each writer, significant cultural realities went unperceived. Faulkner, in the words of Noel Polk, "saw what he saw, as Shakespeare did, and we are immeasurably the richer for it. But he didn't see it all, nobody can."[5] Likewise, Welty and Wright saw what they saw, creating texts that are both visionary and incomplete. Collectively, however, the gaps and insights of all three writers' works can reveal a more complete cultural landscape. By "landscape" I mean the physical and cultural environment portrayed in a text—the environment that characters perceive and the further possibilities it holds, whether or not the characters perceive them. Each writer vividly renders the characters' subjective accounts of their landscape— physical perceptions, memories, and expectations for how to interact with what they encounter. These perceptions constitute the characters' sense of possibility—their sense of who they are and what they are able and unable to do in a given moment. Ecological psychologist James Gibson coined the term "affordances" to denote features of one's environment that an organism knows it can interact with. Recently, scholars have used the term *landscape of affordances* to mean "the total ensemble of available affordances for a population in a given environment," as distinct from *field of affordances*, which includes only the things that "are salient at a given time" to an individual.[6] In literary texts, this dynamic creates dramatic irony when a character overlooks possibilities that others know to be present. Writers may signal to readers that additional possibilities exist, as when the pharmacist in "A Rose for Emily" chooses not to require Emily to tell him what the poison will be used for. In this essay, I am suggesting that readers can see more possibilities, or affordances, in the Mississippi landscape than each text has accounted for. These possibilities become visible through a comparative reading of these texts informed by a comparison of the writers' subject positions.

One way to visualize the authors' separate perspectives on their home state appears in a book on quantum physics that Welty was reading in 1934. Physicist Arthur Stanley Eddington, who'd published research verifying Einstein's theory of relativity, explained "new physics" to nonscientists in *The Nature of the Physical World*. Welty was fascinated, writing to her friend Frank Lyell, "Apply the Einstein relativity formula + Eddington's time frame and space-frame conceptions to the problem of communication between [two] people."[7] Eddington's book included diagrams portraying two individuals' experiences of the present moment, represented as two different lines. The drawings were titled "Present moment of 'myself'" and "Present moments of 'myself' and 'yourself'" (see figure 2.1 and 2.2).

"Certainly it looks from the picture as though my instants were more natural than yours, but that is because *I* drew the picture," Eddington

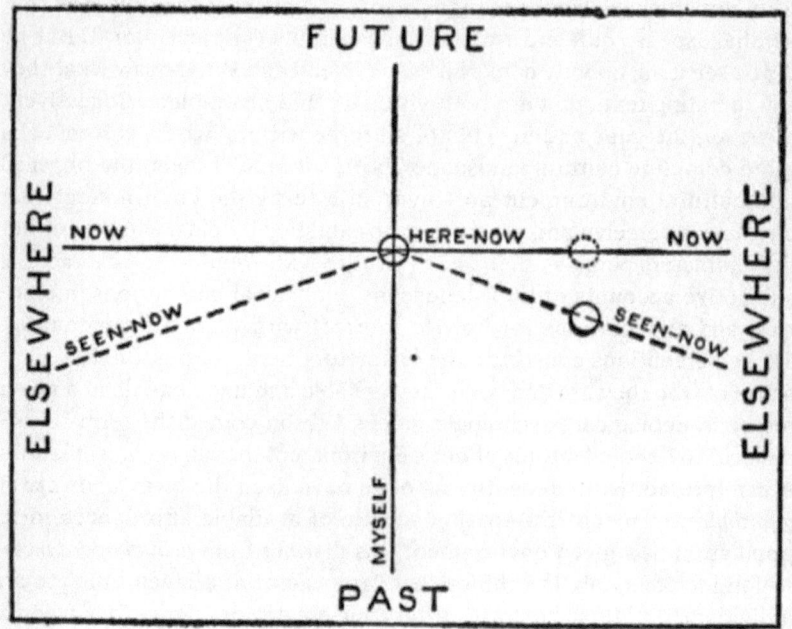

Figure 2.1

wrote. "You would redraw it with your Now lines at right angles to yourself" (46), adding later, "Nature provides no indication that one of these [space-time] frames is to be preferred to the others" (61). There are multiple realities, Eddington explained: "The external world of physics is thus a symposium of the worlds presented to different view-points" (284).[8] In this essay, I attempt to incorporate the multiple realities experienced by all three writers into my readings of each story.

"Let us begin with the claim that knowledge is always socially situated," as standpoint theorist Sandra Harding has proposed,[9] a claim I make for these writers' knowledge of life in twentieth-century Mississippi. The social position of these writers has been much discussed but infrequently compared. Faulkner's position in a patriarchal, white supremacist society is widely acknowledged. Many Welty readers examine, sometimes with mistrust, her identity as a white, middle-class, polite southern woman ("a perfect lady," as one *New Yorker* essayist called her, not meaning it as a compliment).[10] And readers frequently cite Wright's experiences, particularly traumas undergone as a Black southerner, when interpreting his writing. But scholars have not examined these lives together often enough; the three almost never make it into the same work of criticism or biography for more than a sentence or two.[11] A side-by-side comparison

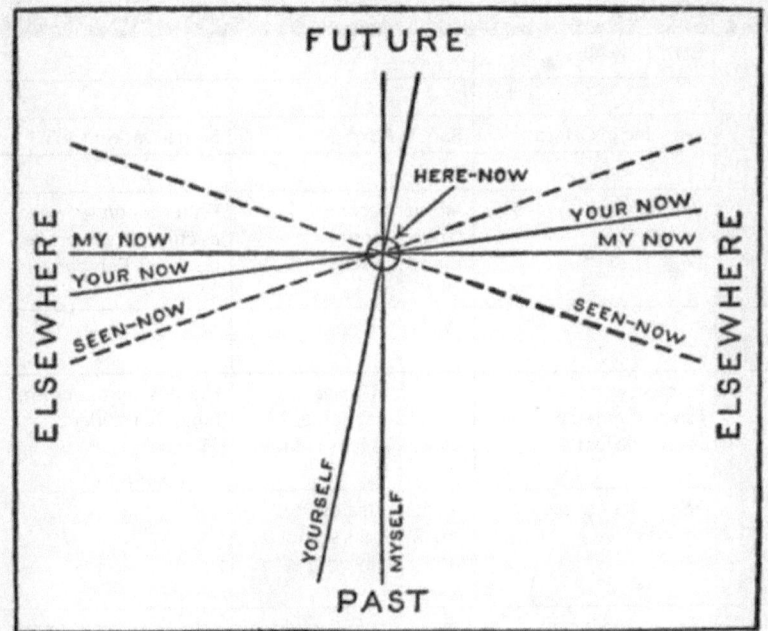

Figure 2.2

of the writers' lives draws each writer's relative position into sharp relief.[12] In the following table (see table 1), the young Faulkner's racial privilege and material comfort contrast with Wright's family's vulnerability to poverty and racism, a very different Jackson experience from a childhood Welty described as "sheltered," provided by her hardworking but securely middle-class parents.[13]

One item in the table—a 1908 lynching occurring blocks from eleven-year-old Faulkner's home—is particularly revealing of the white supremacist landscape these writers inhabited. Scholars have discussed this event's relevance to Faulkner, but it was also proximate to Richard Wright's life, occurring four days after he was born. A lynching took place in 1908 when Lawson "Nelse" Patton, charged with killing a white woman, was in the Oxford jail. A mob broke in, shot him dead, threw his body from the jail, mutilated it, dragged it through the streets, and hanged it outside the courthouse. Teenage boys, including the son of former Senator W. V. Sullivan, had entered the jail first, acting as shields for their fathers, knowing guards would not shoot them. Sullivan told reporters he was proud to have directed the lynching. The following day, the *Los Angeles Evening Express* reported an inquest's conclusion: "the death was at the hand of unknown parties."[14] In this era, white Mississippians viewed such executions as a

	WF	RW	EW
1897	Born, New Albany, MS		
1905			
1908	Lynching in Oxford	Born in Roxie, MS	Born in Jackson, MS
1909			
1916	Works in bank owned by grandfather	Mother becomes ill; family lives in Jackson, then Arkansas	Father continues work as officer in Lamar Life Insurance Company
1917		Uncle murdered in Arkansas	
1918	Former sweetheart Estelle marries; WF trains in Canada for RAF	When family needs coal to heat home, RW scavenges it by railroad tracks	Finishes fourth grade as honor roll student
1919	Enrolls in university courses	Mother's health worsens, RW quits school to work; family returns to Jackson	
1921	Begins working at university post office	Begins grade 5; works selling Black newspapers	Attends summer camp; begins grade 8 in fall

Table 1

proper response to Black identity straying from its subaltern position. Nine years later, Richard Wright's uncle, whose "crime" was apparently owning a successful business, was killed by whites in Arkansas.

The table also includes a few examples of the privilege Faulkner, grandson of an influential businessman, enjoyed, even as he chafed at the expectations of his family and town. These experiences informed his expectations for how one might escape from such confinements. When he tired of high school, he received a job in his grandfather's bank.[15] Back from Canada after the Great War, he enrolled in university courses, skipping quizzes and exams and earning passing grades; professors knew his grandfather and father were a trustee and officer. After a sojourn working in a New York bookstore, Faulkner returned to Oxford where another job awaited him: university postmaster of a tiny mailroom that housed a barber's chair and a soda fountain. Reportedly ignoring customers, reading and playing cards with two assistants he had been allowed to hire, he held onto this job until 1924, and later would famously recall it as a period of semi-imprisonment.[16]

The year Faulkner began this post office job, Richard Wright, two years behind his age group after missing so much school, began fifth grade in Jackson. Wright's eventual escape from his confining Mississippi life began through reading, when reading material was available, about the world outside Mississippi. While Faulkner read magazines in the university post office, Wright read the *Chicago Defender* and *Crisis* in the office of the *Southern Register*, whose newspapers he sold to Black Jacksonians. That same year, Welty began eighth grade at age twelve. A precocious child nurtured by well-educated parents who surrounded her with books, she had skipped first grade. Her academic successes, like those of other white Jackson children, were praised in local newspapers, as were her awards for art and poetry.

Contrasts in opportunity are further evidenced in 1925's relocations: Faulkner to Europe for travel, Wright to Memphis to find work, Welty to Columbus, Mississippi, to college. Welty couldn't go as far away as she wished; her parents wanted their sixteen-year-old close to home. Wright left Jackson, alone, at seventeen, after working numerous jobs, finishing ninth grade and briefly attending high school. In Memphis, he found work and more to read, including H. L. Mencken, whom Welty playfully invoked in *Oh, Lady*, a college humor magazine she cofounded. In 1927, it published Welty's drawing of a mock abstract painting titled "H. L. Mencken Singing the 'Star-Spangled Banner' in His Morning Tub."[17] Doubtless Welty, a lover of irreverence, appreciated Mencken's withering mockery of American culture. Wright had a somewhat different response to Mencken, whom he encountered in books he borrowed from the public library by pretending they were for a white coworker. Wright felt exhilarated to see a writer using words "as a weapon," castigating received ideas and cultural practices that Wright knew could have lethal consequences.[18] He would soon move to Chicago, gain enough weight to qualify for the postal exam and a post office job, and meet Black writers.

For Faulkner, more than a decade older than Wright and Welty, these were years of intense productivity and personal upheavals, occurring within a context of privilege and protection. He'd begun writing about the Compson family and drafted his fourth novel when he married the newly divorced Estelle Franklin. After a summer-long, somewhat unhappy honeymoon in Pascagoula,[19] he returned to Oxford, soon taking another job available to a man with university connections: "supervisor" of the coal-powered boiler that generated electricity for the campus.[20] Astonishing publications followed: *The Sound and the Fury* (1929), *As I Lay Dying* (1930), and *Sanctuary* (1931). In Chicago, Wright, lacking white privilege, connections, or financial sponsorship, was laid off from the post office in 1930 when demand for mail fell during the Depression. Welty's situation was far more secure: her parents could afford to support her 1930–31 year at

	WF	RW	EW
1924	Loses post office job due to negligence.		
1925	Travels in Europe. Publisher accepts *Soldiers' Pay* and offers option on next 2 novels.	Completes 9th grade, valedictorian. Works numerous jobs, starts high school, then leaves Jackson alone, age seventeen.	Finishes high school, begins college, age sixteen.
1927	*Mosquitoes* published, drawing on WF's experiences in New Orleans.	Joined in Memphis by mother, brother. Borrows library card, reads H. L. Mencken. Moves to Chicago.	Publishes mock abstract art named for Mencken in MSCW humor magazine; transfers to University of Wisconsin.
1928	Begins writing about the Compson family in several works including "That Evening Sun."	Family joins him in Chicago. Underweight, he fails postal service exam, resumes dish-washing job.	
1929	Publishes *Sartoris*. Marries, honeymoons in Pascagoula, works at university power plant, publishes *The Sound and the Fury*.	Gains weight, qualifies to work at post office. Joins Black literary group.	Creative writing thesis earns grade of B. Graduates from Wisconsin, returns to Jackson.
1930	Buys house with no down payment. "A Rose for Emily," *As I Lay Dying*. Mencken cuts items from "That Evening Sun" that might shock readers.	Loses job after postal usage declines in Depression. Begins writing novel about Chicago.	Takes graduate courses in advertising at Columbia University.
1931	"That Evening Sun" in *American Mercury*, then in *These 13* with "A Rose for Emily." *Sanctuary*.		Finishes first year of Columbia program; does not return after father's death.

Table 2

Columbia University, where she and several Jackson friends took graduate courses and enjoyed life in the city. Welty's father, having worked his way up to president of his insurance firm, believed his daughter should learn marketable skills, so she studied advertising and business. Faulkner's novels were not earning enough for the lifestyle his new family expected in Oxford. (Still, he and Estelle could buy a large, if decaying, antebellum house and four acres with no down payment.) Seeking higher, quicker royalties, he submitted short stories to national magazines, publishing both "A Rose for Emily" and "That Evening Sun" in 1930 and 1931 respectively in the *American Mercury*. Its sometime-iconoclast editor, Mencken, asked Faulkner to cut a few details from "That Evening Sun" (a character named Jesus, an out-of-wedlock pregnancy) that he thought readers might find shocking. Faulkner made the cuts, then restored most of them when the story was published in *These 13* later that year.

In 1932, Faulkner left Oxford to begin his first stint at the screenwriting work he did periodically for the next fourteen years, earning a Hollywood salary while escaping some pressures of home and small-town life. Even before that income boost, Faulkner's financial circumstances would have been exceedingly welcome to Wright, who went on relief that year. Faulkner took up flying in 1933; Wright joined the John Reed Club. By 1934, he joined the Communist Party and read numerous modern authors, including Faulkner. Welty, positioned somewhere in between these men, worked part-time jobs in semiurban Jackson and periodically sought a more interesting life in New York City. Less free than Faulkner or Wright to travel or live alone, Welty lived with her mother, often hosting Jackson pals in her brothers' old playhouse, where high-spirited intellectuals drank bootleg whiskey and discussed high and low culture. Not wealthy but never in want, these fledgling scholars, writers, and artists entertained themselves by staging campy photographs and dancing to jazz records.[21] They named themselves the "Night-Blooming Cereus Club," with the motto, "Don't take it cereus. Life's too mysterious."[22]

In 1935, Richard Wright, still hustling in Chicago, worked for the Federal Writers' Project and published "Between the World and Me," a poem about lynching, during the same year Welty was writing society columns for the *Memphis Commercial Appeal*. She was also reading modernist fiction and a book on quantum physics and teaching herself to be a photographer. In 1936, a year of important publications by Faulkner and Wright, she worked a few months for the Mississippi WPA, took more photographs, and published her first story in a national magazine. In 1938, Wright spoke on a New York radio program, mentioning Faulkner admiringly. Welty published more short stories and joined the Jackson Junior League. Together, these details highlight the contrasting

	WF	RW	EW
1932	Writing for MGM. *Light In August*.	Selling insurance, then on relief in Cook County.	Writes for WJDX, a Jackson station sponsored by father's insurance company.
1933	Takes up flying, writes for MGM.	Joins John Reed Club.	Unsuccessfully seeks work in NYC.
1934	Writing at Universal Studios.	Joins Communist Party. Reading including Stein, Joyce, Faulkner.	Reading includes Stein, Woolf, *Nature of the Physical World* (Eddington).
1935	Writing at Twentieth Century-Fox.	"Between the World and Me." Hired by Federal Writers' Project.	Writes society columns for *Memphis Commercial Appeal*, tries to sell art photographs.
1936	*Absalom, Absalom!* published with genealogy and map.	"Big Boy Leaves Home"	Works for Mississippi WPA. "Death of a Traveling Salesman" published. NYC gallery exhibits photographs.
1937		Breaks with Communist Party; moves to Harlem. "Ethics of Living Jim Crow" published in Federal Writers' Project anthology.	Publishes four short stories.
1938	*The Unvanquished*	"Long Black Song" in 1st edition of *Uncle Tom's Children*. On Federal Writers' Project radio program, praises Faulkner's depiction of the South, but prefers novels by Malraux.	Joins Jackson Junior Auxiliary (Junior League); publishes short stories, photographs.
1939	*The Wild Palms*. On the cover of *Time*.	Finishes writing *Native Son*.	Publishes more stories.

Table 3

circumstances that shaped each writer and formed the standpoints from which, as Polk would put it, they saw what they saw.

The writers' separate lives became slightly more aligned in the 1940s, when all enjoyed increased royalties and recognition. Welty wrote "Livvie" in 1942, shortly after her first book of short stories appeared and the US entered the war. *Black Boy*'s royalties would enable Wright to leave the United States. Faulkner wrote Wright that the book "said what needed to be said," but that *Native Son* was better.[23] Each writer was increasingly successful; Welty was about to publish her fifth book by the time "Moon Lake" was published in 1949.[24] Faulkner earned a large sum for the movie rights to *Intruder in the Dust*. Wright, living comfortably abroad, returned for the filming of *Native Son* in 1949, and Welty made her first overseas trip. The writers now even had a few friends in common: Ben Wasson, Faulkner's friend and sometime agent, published Welty's "Music from Spain" in 1948. Wright's editor, Ed Aswell, was the first husband of Mary Lou Aswell, who became Welty's close friend and her editor at *Harper's Bazaar*. After Ed Aswell's death in 1958, Tim Seldes became Wright's editor at Doubleday, and in 1973, Seldes became Welty's agent at Russell & Volkening. The three writers' texts, however, continued to draw upon sharply differentiated earlier experiences of the region.

I will now analyze these writers' texts. As a thought experiment, I will try to identify what each text contains that another writer, viewing the topic from another standpoint, might have presented differently.

"A Rose for Emily," the first text to be published, is an impressive journey beyond Faulkner's subject position, considering his personal immersion in a white supremacist society that seemed to him both artificial and permanent. However, while Faulkner does imagine a Black character, Tobe, with more agency than many whites in the story seem to believe he has, other questions about Tobe's life remain, gaps that seem more like misunderstandings than mysteries. Since Emily's "house was all that was left to her" (123), she cannot pay Tobe for his services, which included fetching food from somewhere, "going in and out with a market basket" (122). Perhaps grocers in Jefferson wrote off Emily's bills, just as city officials remitted her taxes (128), because everyone had considered her "a tradition, a duty, and a care; a sort of hereditary obligation upon the town" (119). But why would Tobe work without payment? Faulkner's own experience provides one possible explanation; in 1930, Faulkner sometimes could not pay his Black employees wages, but only board and clothing.[25] Would this have sufficed for Tobe? The published story suggests strongly he knew of Emily's crime and might have hoped to be rewarded for years of loyal secret-keeping. In the manuscript version of "Emily," Faulkner further imagined why Tobe worked so long wage-free before his abrupt, darkly comic exit.

	WF	RW	EW
1940		*Native Son* and *Uncle Tom's Children* second edition, including "Ethics of Living Jim Crow," published.	Hires literary agent to help place stories in national magazines and with publishers.
1941		*12 Million Black Voices* photo essay, with RW's text.	*A Curtain of Green*
1942	*Go Down, Moses*		"Livvie Is Back," *The Robber Bridegroom*
1943	Writes postcard offering help to Welty.		*The Wide Net*
1944		"The Man Who Lived Underground"	Writes for *New York Times Book Review*, sometimes under male pseudonym.
1945	Writes RW about *Black Boy*.	*Black Boy* denounced by Mississippi Senator Bilbo.	*Delta Wedding*, begun as short story, grows into novel.
1946	*The Portable Faulkner* reprints out-of-print works and new map.	In Paris; helps found *Presence Africaine* magazine.	*Delta Wedding* published; writes short fiction, reviews, literary criticism.
1947	In interview, praises EW's *The Robber Bridegroom*.	Returns to US, then leaves again. In London, buys copy of *Delta Wedding*.	Spends months in San Francisco. Lectures on short story. Writes "Moon Lake."
1948	*Intruder in the Dust*	Begins writing *The Outsider*.	Meets Faulkner.
1949	Film version of *Intruder in the Dust*.	Film version of *Native Son*.	*New Yorker* publishes her defense of Faulkner. "Moon Lake," *Golden Apples* published. First trip abroad.

Table 4

In a scene cut from the published story, Emily promised Tobe, who knows what's upstairs in the locked bedroom, that he would inherit the house when she dies. As they discuss the matter, Tobe, described as "a secret and unfathomable soul behind the death-mask of an ape and haloed like an angel," says he does not want to inherit and sell the house or leave town.[26]

What if this story had been told from Richard Wright's subject position? Would Wright have thought it plausible that a Black man could have inherited, then kept, Emily's house? In the manuscript's unpublished section, Emily assures Tobe that Colonel Sartoris will "see they don't rob you," forgetting Sartoris is long dead. If Tobe inherited property whose taxes had been remitted or uncollected for decades, would Emily's special privilege have transferred with the title, and no back taxes assessed? Tobe was no more likely to receive that consideration than to get away with murder, as Emily did, by purchasing poison and defiantly refusing to disclose its purpose. Wright would also have seen how precarious Tobe's position could become once a white woman was found dead where he worked. Bigger Thomas's frantic missteps notwithstanding, would Wright portray a Black man lingering on the premises as long as Tobe did in Faulkner's story? Maybe Faulkner fully understood Tobe's vulnerable position, but in the story he wrote, when Tobe's services as house- and secret-keeper are no longer required, he disappears, no longer significant to the narrative. Imagining Tobe's story from Wright's subject position, we may conclude that, just as the townspeople knew less about Emily than they believed, their creator, too, may not have understood all that was possible and impossible for Jefferson's Black residents.

The Black characters in "A Rose for Emily" are servants: Tobe and the unnamed women who cannot "appear on the streets without an apron" (119–20), wearing the costume of a domestic. "That Evening Sun" opens with Quentin's memory of Nancy and other Black women carrying laundry, but in this story, Black characters also sometimes act independently, not obeying whites' directions. This doesn't work out well for Nancy; even Quentin, a child not fully accustomed to the contradictions and cruelties of white supremacy, knows that white men in Jefferson assault her. While being arrested, Nancy is brutally beaten by Mr. Stovall, who faces no consequences. When she attempts to end her life, she is prevented, then beaten again. Her subaltern status is perceived by whites as normal, even if not entirely permanent, in the sense that, as the jailer said, "a n----r full of cocaine wasn't a n----r any longer" (291). Faulkner's Black characters articulate their positions with striking clarity. Jesus describes his inferior status in a white-dominated world: "I can't hang around white man's kitchen. . . . But white man can hang around mine. . . . When white man want to come in my house, I aint got no house" (292). Nancy both accepts and protests her position, saying, "I aint nothing but a n----r.... It aint none of my fault" (293).

Faulkner rightly indicts the Compson family; years later, he stated that he intended the story to show that Nancy, after having "given devotion to the white family, knew that when the crisis of her need came, the white family wouldn't be there."[27] Yet his story's emphasis, shifting quickly from Nancy's imprisonment to her pregnancy and Jesus's anger, suggests that Nancy's "crisis" is caused by her vengeful husband. "[J]ust let white men alone," Mr. Compson advises (295), oblivious to the possibility that Nancy's sexual activity may not have been consensual, or that other men besides Jesus could hurt her.

Wright, of course, knew this was possible. By the time "That Evening Sun" was published, Wright's own "Jim Crow education" had included witnessing a Black woman being beaten in a Jackson store while police stood nearby. Later, he wrote that after this woman "came stumbling out, bleeding, crying, and holding her stomach," police arrested her for drunkenness (230). "I was learning fast, but not quite fast enough" (231). Wright's perspective, therefore, could have given Nancy's predicament a different emphasis. She could have been coerced into sex; the Compsons may have paid her very little, and she could have chosen to seek other sources of money; Mr. Stovall, for one, had paid Nancy at least once (291). If Wright had told Nancy's story, he might have linked Jesus's words more explicitly to what Wright learned as a teenager: white men were free to do whatever they wished, at any time, to a Black body. The character who states this truth in Faulkner's story is a lawless, dangerous figure scarred by previous fights, who may be lurking somewhere "with that razor in his mouth" (295). Wright's version of this story might have devised a more credible speaker of the truths of Jim Crow, suggesting more strongly that Nancy had men other than Jesus to fear.

Additional insight on how Wright might have told Nancy's story appears in "The Ethics of Living Jim Crow." Its incidents lay bare Wright's subject position within the chronic vulnerability of Black bodies in the Mississippi of his boyhood, with no time for Faulkner's long-form ruminations, melancholia, or musings about what other people in the past might have done. Wright navigates scenes and spaces in Jackson that Welty never saw—sites of danger, brutality, and relentless thwarting of intellectual opportunity—unlike the sinecures available to Faulkner or the education and nurturing provided to Welty in the same city Wright felt compelled to leave.

"The Ethics of Living Jim Crow" analyzes the catch-22 of Jim Crow in a way that sometimes resembles the contradictory conclusion reached by Faulkner's jailer in "That Evening Sun" when he stated that with cocaine, "a n----r ... wasn't a n----r any longer." In "Ethics," inescapable illogic hemmed Wright in as he faced whites' active hostility or casual disdain. He had to respond to their disapproval in real time rather than in the slow-motion gloom of Emily's house, its dust "spinning with slow motes" in the parlor (120) or "patient and biding" in the upstairs bedroom (130). In Wright's telling, Blacks do not accept their abjection because of alcohol, prostitution, or a belief that, as Nancy said, "I hellborn" (298). Instead, Wright states at the end of "Ethics" that Blacks submit to their Jim Crow status because they know what "them polices 'n' them ol' lynch mobs" (237) will do to those who violate the rules of white supremacy.

As Wright's works were being published, Welty's subject position was widening beyond the "sheltered life" she recalled in her 1984 memoir. She lacked Wright's experiences that would have shown her the immense power of white supremacist terror. She had something else in the 1930s, though: an inkling of Black Mississippians' independent subjectivities, glimpsed through her camera lens and later as she printed her photographs.[28] This activity afforded Welty what one theorist calls a "third eye" for seeing beyond the given realities of her society, past her own privilege and into lives she had not lived.[29] Having created, in her first published story, a salesman who realizes he's misunderstood the people who are providing him shelter, Welty continued writing stories from the viewpoint of characters who, unlike herself, were fully dispossessed by poverty and racism in 1930s Mississippi. Her story "The Whistle," about white tomato packers nearly freezing to death, was published the same year Wright published *Uncle Tom's Children*, in which some Black farmers join unions ("Fire and Cloud") and fight back against whites.

Wright's "Long Black Song," also appearing in *Uncle Tom's Children*, widens our view of Faulkner's stories. In Silas's drive to acquire more land and his precarious dominion over it, we can reimagine Faulkner's Tobe refusing to work without wages or being eager to inherit property rather than expressing his plans, in Faulkner's unpublished version of "Emily," to stay in the poorhouse and watch trains. "That Evening Sun" and Wright's biography enable us to interrogate his presentation of a Black woman in "Long Black Song." Sarah is subject, like Nancy, to advances or assault by white men who can, just as Jesus observed, come into her house whenever they want to. Sarah's response to the salesman's behavior, interpreted by Silas as a betrayal, has been read as consent by many, as may have been Wright's view. Margaret Walker's biography reads this apparent victim-blaming as a reflection of Wright's subject position, his personal history of resenting and blaming Black women in his life, and limiting the agency he ascribed to them in his writing.[30] Walker's convincing analysis helps us account for misogyny in the story's presentation of sexual activity, making Sarah, rather than the salesman, responsible for the events that lead to Silas's act of revenge and his death.

Even so, Wright accords Sarah a wider subjectivity than Nancy seems to have in "That Evening Sun," where escape seems only possible via cocaine or death. Sarah sees more in the landscape than the squabbling white children or vengeful husband commanding Nancy's attention. Wright shows Sarah, who married a man with property, recalling a former love, now far away: "Against the plush sky she saw a white bright day and a green cornfield and she saw Tom walking in his overalls" (331). She is profoundly touched by the graphophone's music, "feeling the rise and fall of days and nights, of summer and winter; surging, ebbing, leaping about her, beyond her, far out over the fields to where earth and sky lay folded in darkness" (335). Wright's character, limited though her imagination may be, lifts her gaze beyond the everyday.

Meditations in which characters imagine other locations and times appear in all these texts, but contemplation by Faulkner's characters often leads nowhere. The narrator of "Rose for Emily" recalls the "tableau" townspeople imagined when thinking of Emily's father, "a spraddled silhouette in the foreground, his back to her and clutching a horsewhip" (123). In the unpublished section, Tobe describes a future where he'll "set on that hill in the sun all day and watch them trains pass. See them at night too, with the engine puffing and lights in all the windows"—trains he will not take. In "That Evening Sun," the landscape menaces Nancy as she imagines Jesus hiding in a ditch; Nancy's story emerges from a memory of a landscape in the adult Quentin's mind, triggered by looking at Jefferson and seeing an absence—women no longer carrying laundry on their heads as Nancy once did (289). By contrast, in Welty's "Livvie" and "Moon Lake," scenes of contemplation function as pivotal components of the story, rather than introductions or interludes.

"Livvie" and "Moon Lake" reflect Welty's writerly goal of "try[ing] to enter the mind, heart, and skin of a human being who is not myself. [. . .] It is the act of a writer's imagination that I set most high" (829). Reading these stories alongside Faulkner and Wright, we can discern more clearly what Welty sees and does not see in each Mississippi landscape. What she does see, in "Livvie," is a Black woman whose husband has owned property for decades, taking satisfaction in keeping her own house, rather than somebody else's. Livvie's house, like those owned by Faulkner's and Wright's characters, sets its owners apart from unpropertied Mississippians, like Cash. Solomon's property could have motivated the teenage Livvie to marry him, as it may have motivated Sarah in "Long Black Song" to marry Silas instead of Tom. Even as Solomon nears death, this house is lively compared to Wright's or Faulkner's houses, with Livvie's dust-free marble-top table, decorative feathers, and silverware in glass jars (276–77). She is timid, but Livvie's imagination ranges more freely than Faulkner's Black female characters. While watching her sleeping husband, she thinks,

> there he lay having a dream. Now what did he dream about? For she saw him sigh gently as if not to disturb some whole thing he held round in his mind, like a fresh egg. So even an old man dreamed about something pretty. [...] He might be dreaming of what time it was, for even through his sleep he kept track of it like a clock, and knew how much of it went by. (281)

Welty shows readers freedom and power in Livvie's subjectivity, imagining the subjectivity of Solomon.

In Welty's Natchez Trace landscape, she has also imagined a young Black man, Cash, who seems completely unconcerned with white Mississippians. When Cash appears at Livvie's door in a zoot suit, he's admiring himself, "lifting his peg-top pants the higher to see fully his bright socks. His coat long and wide and leaf-green he opened like doors to see his high-up tawny pants.... [H]e reached gently above his wide platter-shaped round hat, the color of a plum, and one finger touched at the feather, emerald green" (285). Cash got his outfit in Natchez; he exults: "*I ready for Easter!*" (285). Welty had seen suits like these in Jackson. She wrote Diarmuid Russell about them in April 1942, enclosing a sketch of a man in a zoot suit and feathered hat. She'd seen this "in the colored section where all the clothes are the most imaginative and really the most effective on shining dark skin, when you get right down to Easter egg colors." These men had "a style all their own—not copied from white people, and it is a delight."[31] Like them, Cash does not follow white imperatives or fashion trends.

In Welty's story, as in Wright's, a white sales agent tries to cajole a lonely woman into buying an item that meets no practical need. Livvie is stirred by the product Miss Baby Marie offers, as Sarah was stirred by the graphophone in "Long Black Song." But unlike Sarah, Livvie does not swoon into a state of acquiescence, rendered abject by what she can't have, when she smells a scent like chinaberries in the lipstick.

> In an instant she was carried away in the air through the spring, and looking down with a half-drowsy smile from a purple cloud she saw from above a chinaberry tree ... and there was her home that she had left ... her mama holding up her heavy apron, ... her papa holding a fish-pole over the pond, and she could see it transparently, the little clear fishes swimming up to the brim. (283)

In Welty's cultural landscape, vibrant subjectivities have agency, even while facing limitations—Livvie lacks money to buy lipstick, but she can imagine herself outside the house where Solomon wants her to stay. Welty's characterization suggests that Livvie could be resilient enough to find new forms of joy with Cash. Possibilities appear to expand in the final scene: "The redbirds were all flying and criss-crossing, the sun was in all the bottles on the prisoned trees" (290).

When reading Welty's celebration of poor, rural Mississippians' vitality, however, we should be mindful of Faulkner's Mississippi landscape, in which a swaggering Black man like Cash is not safe. If Faulkner had told Livvie's story, his own subject position, as a man psychologically surrounded by family unwilling to disrupt Oxford's social status quo, could have interpreted her situation differently, concluding that interpellations of family and history would inevitably block Livvie from the freer life she only imagines is possible. Readers can also notice realities Wright would have perceived that Welty, in 1942, did not.[32] Miss Baby Marie, despite her comic presence, is also a possible menace as a white "lady," a perpetual pretext for accusing Blacks of threatening southern womanhood. Wright would be more conscious than Welty could have been of the precarious future of unpropertied Cash, seemingly not versed in the lessons Jim Crow taught Wright.[33] Welty, who wrote Russell of driving into "the colored section" of Jackson to see Easter fashions, was probably unaware that young men like Wright were sometimes assaulted just for entering neighborhoods like hers.

Welty's "Moon Lake" provides a counterpoint to Nancy's abjection, Emily's self-imprisonment, Tobe's silent disappearance, and Sarah's helpless sorrow. Welty's story, written in 1947 after *Native Son*, *Go Down, Moses*, "The Man Who Lived Underground," and *Delta Wedding*, resonates powerfully with each writer's personal and fictional landscapes. Set in a summer camp in the woods like the one Welty had attended in childhood, its protagonist, Nina, realizes—if only temporarily—what she doesn't know. In one scene, after walking off the trails and into the forest, Nina senses something else in the Mississippi landscape, different from what Wright or Faulkner showed readers. She hears "the swamp sounds—closer to the ear and nearer to the dreaming mind." She sees that "[v]ines, a magnificent and steamy green, covered more and more of the trees, played over them like fountains" (424–25). Welty's woods contain energies and transgressive powers that do not play assigned roles in a white supremacist drama.

To be sure, that drama *is* at work at camp, where the town girls witness, in Easter and other orphans, the vulnerability of female bodies. Yet when Nina stares into the night, she questions social roles that others accept. Other possibilities, already present but unrecognized, now enter her field of inner vision.

> The orphan! she thought exultantly. The other way to live. There were secret ways. She thought, Time's really short, I've only been thinking like the others. ... To slip into them all—to change. To change for a moment into Gertrude, into Mrs. Gruenwald, into Twosie—into a boy. (435)

The day Easter almost drowns, these options linger in the steamy air, even as Black characters perform the roles whites assign to them: Marvin carries watermelons; Twosie cooks; Exxum is designated a predator. Wright's works can help readers recognize the limits of Nina's view of Exxum and perhaps Welty's limits as well: onlookers hold him responsible for Easter's fall into the lake. "He gave Easter's heel the tenderest, obscurest little brush, with something of n----r persuasion about it" (437). Whether startled into falling or not, Easter is rescued, then forced back into life by Loch, a well-trained Boy Scout employing a strangely violent lifesaving procedure. As the girls look on, "[t]he Boy Scout crushed in her body and blood came out of her mouth. For them all, it was like being spoken to" (445). This recalls how Faulkner's Nancy was prevented from completing her suicide and then beaten. Welty's Easter is pulled from the water only to be immersed in a different loch/lake, the masculine regulation of her body. "Can't any of us help it," one of the counselors says, weeping. "Can't any of us. It's what he came for" (442).

Yet Easter survives the rescue; she "kick[s] the Boy Scout," then sits up, eventually commanding the middle-class girls, "Carry me" (447-48). That evening, the lake that did not drown her glimmers with mysterious powers, "rimmed around with its wall-within-walls of woods.... The lake grew darker, then gleamed, like the water of a rimmed well" (449). Welty's landscape contains possibilities that are dangerous and beautiful, lethal and life-giving; few people perceive them all. When Nina resumes her life back home, these possibilities will be largely forgotten, judging from Nina's appearance thirty years later, holding a gold-rimmed teacup in "The Wanderers," the story that ends Welty's *Golden Apples*. But "Moon Lake" shows readers a landscape that white supremacy cannot completely define, during a summer when "the other way to live" was briefly visible.

Faulkner, Welty, and Wright's texts provide visionary insights into what ecological psychologists might call "the field of affordances" visible to characters in the Mississippi landscape. Each text provides evocative glimpses of additional possibilities—the "landscape of affordances" that also exist if someone is brave or crazy enough to make use of them. But the full picture of these writers' home state—"the very crossgrain and bottom truth about Mississippi," as Welty put it—is not available to any individual character or artist.[34] To see this landscape, we should strive to assemble, in Arthur Eddington's words, "a symposium of the worlds presented to different viewpoints."

Jesmyn Ward suggests this sort of multivalent landscape in her *Sing, Unburied, Sing* (2017), turning up the volume on Faulkner's ever-present past. Ward's Mississippi contains all the cruelty, suffering, and self-destruction Faulkner or Wright found, and then some. In a post-Katrina world that seems far beyond repair, it takes a ghost, Richie, to reveal unseen realities to Jojo, whose family was traumatized by Parchman Penitentiary. Richie tells Jojo that Parchman "was past, present, and future all at once"[35] (186). He's only one of many who have suffered and whose stories must be told. "There's so many . . . . So many of us," Richie says (282). Jojo hears their stories in a landscape that narrates itself: "The song. In snatches. The stars. A record. The sky. A great record. The lives. Of the living. Of those beyond. See it in flashes. The sound. Beyond the waters" (281).

Mississippi's landscapes, past and present, are as crowded as Ward's, humming with more than meets the eye. If we, as citizen-scholars, hope to repair the broken places in landscapes we now inhabit, we need a composite vision of the past and its continuing presence. Placing these writers and their works side by side, we can expect to find not just an author's visionary genius, but also what these writers could not see. This comparative standpoint approach will yield greater truth-telling about the South: what was possible or impossible, what was suffocating or beautiful, what stories people told to make sense of it all, and which of these stories were lies.

NOTES

1. Louis D. Rubin, *Uptown, Downtown in Old Charleston: Sketches and Stories* (Columbia: University of South Carolina Press, 2010), ix.

2. I wish to thank Annette Trefzer and Jay Watson for their encouragement and helpful comments as I was revising this essay for this volume. Parenthetical references to the six works I analyze come from Faulkner's *Collected Stories* (New York: Vintage International, 1995), Wright's *Early Works* (New York: Library of America, 1991), and Welty's *Stories, Essays, and Memoir* (New York: Library of America, 1998).

3. Ailsa Chang, Rachel Martin, Eric Marrapodi, "Summer of Racial Reckoning," National Public Radio, August 16, 2020.

4. At the 2021 Faulkner conference's session "Reparative Teaching: Faulkner, Welty, and Wright in the Antiracist Classroom," Ebony Lumumba and Rebecca Nisetich noted that in facilitating class discussions and community agreements, they found standpoint theory to be helpful for reminding participants to speak from their own subject position and not to claim to speak for others. To foster equitable discussion, as in a restorative practice circle, all participants are asked to "step up and step back" or to "take up space and leave space"—to listen as well as to speak. For an introduction to these concepts, see "Standpoint

Theory" in *Dictionary of Human Geography* (Oxford University Press, 2013); Anna Jane High, "Using Restorative Practice to Teach and Uphold Dignity in an American School District," *McGill Journal of Education* 52, no. 2 (Spring 2015), 525-33.

5. Noel Polk, "Welty and Faulkner and the Southern Literary Tradition," in Eudora Welty, *On William Faulkner* (Jackson: University Press of Mississippi, 2003), 95.

6. Maxwell J. D. Ramstead, Samuel P. L. Veissière, and Laurence J. Kirmayer, "Cultural Affordances: Scaffolding Local Worlds through Shared Intentionality and Regimes of Attention," *Frontiers in Psychology* 7 (2016): 1-21. For further discussion of landscapes, see Manuel Heras-Escribano and Manuel De Pinedo-García, "Affordances and Landscapes: Overcoming the Nature-Culture Dichotomy through Niche Construction Theory," *Frontiers in Psychology* 8 (2017): 1-15. For an introduction to affordances, see Manuel Heras-Escribano, *The Philosophy of Affordances* (Cham, Switzerland: Palgrave Macmillan, 2019).

7. Welty to Lyell, May 11, 1934, box 126, folder L25, Eudora Welty Collection, Mississippi Department of Archives and History.

8. Diagrams from Arthur Eddington, *The Nature of the Physical World* (New York: Macmillan, 1929), 43, 45. Quotations from 46, 61.

9. *The Feminist Standpoint Theory Reader*, ed. Sandra Harding (Milton Park, UK: Routledge, 2004), 7.

10. Claudia Roth Pierpont, "A Perfect Lady," *New Yorker* (October 5, 1998), 94-104.

11. Thadious Davis concludes that "in their choices of how to portray the southern land and its inhabitants, Wright and Faulkner were faithful to their separate racial memories, perspectives, and observations of the South" (477). See "Wright, Faulkner, and Mississippi as Racial Memory," *Callaloo* no. 28 (Summer 1986), 469-78.

12. Most biographical information appears in numerous sources. I have relied particularly on Joseph Blotner's one-volume *Faulkner: A Biography* (New York: Random House, 1984), Margaret Walker's *Richard Wright: Daemonic Genius* (New York: Warner Books, 1988), Arnold Rampersad's chronology in the Library of America volumes of Wright's works, and Suzanne Marrs's *Eudora Welty: A Biography* (New York: Harcourt, 2005). Page references refer to these biographies.

13. Welty uses the term in *One Writer's Beginnings*, which concludes, "As you have seen, I am a writer who came of a sheltered life. A sheltered life can be a daring life as well. For all serious daring starts from within." *Stories, Essays, and Memoir*, 948.

14. Christian Middleton, "'Epilogue and Epitaph': Oxford Attempts to Reconcile Legacy of Racism and Lynchings," *Mississippi Free Press*, January 11, 2021; Thadious Davis, *Faulkner's "Negro": Art and the Southern Context* (Baton Rouge: LSU Press, 1983), 162-64; "Former Senator Admits He Led Lynching Mob," *Los Angeles Evening Express*, September 10, 1908, 15; Don H. Doyle, "Faulkner's Civil War in Fiction, History, and Memory" in *Faulkner and War*, ed. Noel Polk and Ann Abadie, (Jackson: University Press of Mississippi, 2001), 3-19.

15. In 1931, Faulkner recalled that while working in the bank, he "learned the medicinal value of [grandfather's] liquor. Grandfather thought it was the janitor. Hard on the janitor" (Blotner, *Faulkner*, 53).

16. Often quoted is the remark he claims to have made when leaving: "Thank God I won't ever again have to be at the beck and call of every son of a bitch who's got two cents for a stamp" (Blotner, *Faulkner*, 110-11).

17. Eudora Welty, *Early Escapades*, ed. Patti Carr Black (Jackson: University Press of Mississippi, 2005), 27.

18. Richard Wright, *Black Boy*, in *Later Works* (New York: Library of America, 1991), 237.

19. Blotner, *Faulkner*, 242. Blotner notes that Estelle's mother sent her family's maid along for the summer.

20. Blotner explains, "The job was supervisory, with two Negroes to provide the labor. Estelle recalled that he would go to work after dinner, immaculate, and return before breakfast, still immaculate" (Blotner, *Faulkner*, 248).

21. Jackson friend and composer Lehman Engel, a member of this group, later stated that Welty "really invented 'camp.'" *This Bright Day: An Autobiography* (New York: Macmillan, 1974), 41.

22. Marrs, *Eudora Welty*, 45.

23. Faulkner wrote, "It needed to be said, and you said it well. Though I am afraid [. . .] it will accomplish little of what it should accomplish, since only they will be moved and grieved by it who already know and grieve over this situation. [. . .] Because I think you said it much better in *Native Son*, I hope you will keep on saying it, but I hope you will say it as an artist, as in *Native Son*." Qtd. in Hazel Rowley, *Richard Wright: The Life and Times* (New York: Henry Holt, 2001), 324–25.

24. "Moon Lake" was rejected by six periodicals before being accepted by a small quarterly, *Sewanee Review*. For sending schedule, see Noel Polk's *Eudora Welty: A Bibliography of Her Work* (Jackson: University Press of Mississippi, 1994), 455–56.

25. Blotner says this arrangement "was exactly what Mammy Callie and Uncle Ned expected" (*Faulkner*, 262).

26. Stephen Railton, "Manuscripts Etc.: 'A Rose for Emily,'" *Digital Yoknapatawpha*, University of Virginia, http://faulkner.drupal.shanti.virginia.edu/node/7862?canvas. (Date added to project: 2015). The three-page excised section is viewable there.

27. *Faulkner at the University*, ed. Frederick L. Gwynn and Joseph L. Blotner (Charlottesville: University Press of Virginia, 1959), 21.

28. Welty later wrote that her 1930s photographs revealed their significance gradually: "It was after I got home, had made my prints in the kitchen and dried them overnight and looked at them in the morning by myself, that I began to see objectively what I had there," in *One Time, One Place: Mississippi in the Depression* (New York: Random House, 1971), 7.

29. Susan Donaldson argues that Welty's 1930s works used what Fatimah Toby Rony called the "third eye," which, in Donaldson's words, finds "a way of looking back and resisting the eye of power." Of Wright and Welty, Donaldson writes, "In their art and perhaps in their lives as well, these two Mississippi writers discovered just how empowering the third eye could be in its capacity to subvert, expose, and block the objectification and dehumanization intended by the white gaze of Jim Crow." See Donaldson, "Parting the Veil: Eudora Welty, Richard Wright, and the Crying Wounds of Jim Crow," in *Eudora Welty, Whiteness, and Race*, ed. Harriet Pollack (Athens: University of Georgia Press, 2013), 50, 68.

30. Walker, *Richard Wright*, 107–8, 117–18.

31. Welty to Russell, April 5, 1942, *Tell about Night Flowers: Eudora Welty's Gardening Letters, 1940–1949*, ed. Julia Eichelberger (Jackson: University Press of Mississippi, 2013), 56.

32. In a 1978 interview, Welty recalled that in childhood, she "never saw black people except in a white household as a servant or something, and . . . I never heard black people talking among themselves." Jeanne Rolf Nostrandt, "Fiction as Event: An Interview with Eudora Welty," in *More Conversations with Eudora Welty*, ed. Peggy Whitman Prenshaw (Jackson: University Press of Mississippi, 1996), 14.

33. A real-life Cash might have had greater earning power in 1942, compared to most Black Mississippians in the 1920s and '30s. Tom Sancton (a friend of Welty's) wrote that many Blacks were "quitting their menial jobs for white employers to take better-paying jobs in defense industries." See Sancton, "Race Fear Sweeps the South," *New Republic*, January 18, 1943, 83.

34. Welty to John Robinson, May 21, 1946, *Tell about Night Flowers: Eudora Welty's Gardening Letters*, ed. Julia Eichelberger (Jackson: University Press of Mississippi, 2013), 188.

35. Jesmyn Ward, *Sing, Unburied, Sing* (New York: Scribner, 2017), 186. Hereafter cited internally.

Witnessing Jim Crow

Three Mississippi Writers and the Politics of Critical Race Theory

SUSAN V. DONALDSON

Once confined to advanced law school courses, the phrase "critical race theory" has since the spring of 2020 dominated local and state legislative brawls over education, antiracist programs in corporations and government agencies, and even the assignment of American history texts and novels in high school classrooms. But far from being a radically new issue in political discourse, critical race theory itself began shaping public discussions about race in American life as far back as the 1970s, when historians and legal scholars sought explanations in the law, history, and "systemic" racism for economic, social, and political inequities blocking African American advancement decades after the successful passage of 1960s civil rights legislation.[1] Even earlier, Mississippi's three greatest writers, Richard Wright, William Faulkner, and Eudora Welty, made use of their fiction to probe the underpinnings of Jim Crow and white racism in American culture. Drawing much of their attention in the turbulent decades of the 1940s, 1950s, and 1960s, as it did with critical race theorists, for that matter, was the growing imperative for a national reckoning with the country's long history of racial hierarchies and inequities—and the daunting impediments to that reckoning.

In May 2020, though, critical race theory took on an unexpected new urgency when it was repeatedly invoked by both left and right commentators—on cable television, social media, newspapers, and radio—to defend Black Lives Matter demonstrations protesting the televised murder of a Black man named George Floyd in police custody and to condemn the explicitly antiracist demonstrations just as passionately. If anything, former president Donald Trump intensified ongoing debates in September 2020 by publicly denouncing "this divisive, false, and demeaning propaganda of the critical race theory movement" and by banning federal antiracist-training programs supposedly inspired by critical race theory.[2] From the perspective of conservative activist Christopher Rufo, whose language shaped Trump's executive-ordered ban and his denunciation of critical race theory, such programs constituted "humiliation."[3] By then the very phrase *critical race theory* had been conflated in the minds of a good many white Americans with rapid demographic change and the growing visibility of minority voices in American public life. Those changes were evoked most powerfully by the 2019 publication of the *New York Times Magazine 1619 Project*, which reenvisioned American history through the lens of slavery and its lasting legacy for African Americans and racial relations in American culture.[4]

The language often wielded by opponents of critical race theory—"divisive," "demeaning," and "humiliating"—reveals responses ranging from open fear of racial violence to a strong discomfort on the part of many white Americans with the relatively new emphasis upon racial consciousness in public discourse, in part because of long-term goals of transcending race, implicit then and now in key terms like "colorblindness" and "post racialism," driving the civil rights revolution of the 1960s.[5] Two leading conservatives have publicly referred to critical race theory as "a kind of revenge." Televangelist Pat Robertson argued on his show *The 700 Club* that this particular approach to analyzing systemic racism encouraged people of color—in Robertson's words—"to rise up and overthrow their oppressors." For good measure, he added ominously, "And then, having gotten the whip handle—if I can use the term—then to instruct their white neighbors to behave." Fox News television host Tucker Carlson openly speculated that critical race theory may even result in "genocide" and asked, "How do we save this country before we become Rwanda?"[6] Right-wing worries of this sort, strikingly enough, echo much earlier white fears of Black revenge and violence dating back to Reconstruction, the Civil War, and slavery.[7]

Critical race theory had, in fact, become a catch-all phrase—"a new bogeyman of the political right," as the *New Yorker* termed it—for a good many white Republicans worried in general about demographic changes over the next few decades, the impact of those changes at the ballot box in future elections, and the consequences for public education, in particular, the teaching of race and racism in K-12 public education.[8] By the fall of 2021—over four short months—Fox News had mentioned the phrase 1,300 times, and one Republican candidate—Glenn Youngkin—had won the governorship of Virginia by attacking antiracism programs in public schools, a campaign he continued to pursue by creating a tip line for Virginians to complain about "divisive topics" taught in public classrooms. That same year, nine Republican-controlled legislatures passed laws restricting discussion of race, racism, gender, and inequalities in public classrooms, and four other states set up restrictions on classroom discussions of those politically charged topics through executive branch actions. In 2022, 112 bills calling for similar restrictions were introduced in thirty-four state legislatures.[9] By the spring of 2023, anti-critical race theory measures had been introduced in forty-nine states, and 241 had been adopted. The language of these new laws and/or bills is especially worth pondering. Texas's new law going into effect in the fall of 2021 restricted teaching "of currently controversial issues" that could make students feel "blame," "guilt," or "psychological distress" on account of their race.[10]

Such language, in turn, linked with the mere mention of the phrase *critical race theory*, bears faint but unmistakable echoes of earlier formal and informal prohibitions imposed on critical discussions of race and racism, like Mississippi's 1920 state law banning the advocacy of social equality and intermarriage.[11] Perhaps even more pointedly, restrictions in recent and proposed state laws banning discussion of critical race theory in public schools also echo the complicated taboos that African Americans like Richard Wright had to navigate around in everyday life before segregation began to be dismantled in the 1950s and 1960s. Toward the end of his 1945 autobiography *Black Boy*, Wright captures the dangers awaiting young Black men in casual conversations:

> Among the topics that southern white men did not like to discuss with Negroes were the following: American white women; the Ku Klux Klan; France, and how Negro soldiers fared while there; Frenchwomen; Jack Johnson; the entire northern part of the United States; the Civil War; Abraham Lincoln; U. S. Grant; General Sherman; Catholics; the Pope; Jews; the Republican party; slavery; social equality; Communism; Socialism; the 13th, 14th, and 15th Amendments to the Constitution; or any topic calling for positive knowledge or manly self-assertion on the part of the Negro.[12]

It is precisely this kind of enforced silence on issues of race and racism, along with the agitated opposition to the very term *critical race theory*, that has motivated legal scholars like Kimberlé Williams Crenshaw and Derrick Bell since the 1990s to resort to the lens of critical race theory—by exposing the "systemic nature" of white supremacy, its invention and reinvention in American history, law, and institutions, and by indicting the denial and blindness required to maintain racial inequalities.[13]

Unsettling and new as this critique of white supremacy and of its tenacious hold on American history appears to a good many white Americans in the twenty-first century, similar charges of white blindness, denial, and disavowal have punctuated some of the most daring fiction by Wright, Faulkner, and Welty, whose lives and careers were shaped by the rise and fall of Jim Crow segregation. All three were born at the turn into the twentieth century—in what one eminent historian has labeled the "most race-haunted of all American states"—just as disfranchisement and legalized segregation were taking hold in the US South.[14] All three were accordingly compelled throughout their careers to confront the politics of visibility and invisibility defining the color line during its last decades in mid-twentieth-century Mississippi, but nowhere more so than in three texts written during the racial upheavals of the early 1940s and the 1960s: Wright's 1942 novel manuscript "The Man Who Lived Underground," Faulkner's 1942 short story cycle *Go Down, Moses*, and Welty's two civil rights stories, "Where Is the Voice Coming From?" and "The Demonstrators." What could be seen in that world and what required erasure to maintain a racial hierarchy dating back to slavery? What stories could be told and what could not? And how could those untold stories be retrieved by writers attuned both to the changing politics of race during and after World War II and to the multiplicity of language and narrative defining literary modernism? Many of the answers to those questions arrived at by Wright, Faulkner, and Welty were hesitant at best and markedly different in degree of intensity, but ultimately these texts exposed, in ways that critical race theorists would have instantly recognized and confirmed, the entrenchment and yet slow dissolution of an antiquated racial hierarchy both bolstered and diminished by white blindness and denial.

To be sure, answers suggested by these texts and others fell far short of the radical polemics of critical race theorists in general or their widespread disillusionment with the stalled civil rights movement and the political backlash of the 1970s and 1980s, all of which gave rise to ongoing discussions in the academy about fighting new forms of racism. Indebted to perspectives developed earlier by critical legal studies in law schools and radical feminist scholarship, critical race theorists interrogated triumphalist accounts of landmark cases like *Brown v. Board of Education* for failing to take into account administrative and legal setbacks; developed the notion of "legal indeterminacy" posing multiple alternatives for court decisions in lieu of a "correct" one for each case; explored the nexus between power and the social construction of race, gender, and class; and drew attention to real-world consequences of legal, historical, and social theories. With these central aims in mind, critical race theorists, as summarized by Richard Delgado and Jean Stefancic in their 2001 introductory volume *Critical Race Theory*, came to agree to five basic "tenets":

1) the "ordinary" nature of racism in general, rather than defining racism in general as "exceptional"; 2) "interest convergence"—or the recognition that large sections of the country, including political and economic elites, have a vested interest in maintaining the hierarchical racial status quo; 3) the social construction of race and races, invented and reinvented according to social and political dictates; 4) "differential racialization," which is to say, stereotypes and racial categories that change according to societal needs and pressures, along with the complexity of individual identity drawing from multiple sources—or "intersectionality, and anti-essentialism"; and 5) the special authority and competence awarded to minority voices to address issues of race and racism and to tell their own stories of racism and the law.[15]

A more direct and compact definition of this form of racial critique is offered by Kimberlé Williams Crenshaw, who is usually cited as coining the phrase *critical race theory* back in the 1990s.[16] For her, critical race theory "is a way of seeing, attending to, accounting for, tracing and analyzing the ways race is produced, the ways that racial inequality is facilitated, and the ways that our history has created these inequalities that now can be almost effortlessly reproduced unless we attend to the existence of these inequalities."[17] But that historical and political lens, Crenshaw argues, also "documented the ways in which the reproduction of racial power and domination requires particular forms of disavowal and denial"—a failure on the part of whites in general to imagine the world differently.[18] The key term in this summary is "seeing," or rather, not seeing—taking for granted racial hierarchy, denying its long-term history, and turning a blind eye to alternative racial and social possibilities. Critical race theory, in short, challenges the national faith in progress and triumph over history by offering a counternarrative of white denials and entrapment in a history long defined by the legacy of slavery, segregation, violence, and racial injustice.[19] As Crenshaw herself argues, such a counternarrative is partly a response to the overly optimistic claims of colorblindness and post-racialism characterizing a good deal of conservative political rhetoric in the 1970s and 1980s—and the sense of widespread disappointment with the possibilities of ending American obsessions with race and racism after the 2008 election of Barak Obama.[20]

Unsettling as this basic approach to racism as both ordinary and persistent has been to a good many white Americans in the twenty-first century, charges of white blindness, denial, and disavowal of racial injustice punctuating critical race theory scholarship are even more disturbing to those who consider the very notion of white supremacy—and its relevance to their own daily lives—a relic of now-distant history. To Wright, Faulkner, and Welty, though, grappling with Mississippi's history of racial violence and the state's pioneering role in legislating de jure segregation and disfranchisement, white supremacy was a present reality reinforced by law, white blindness, history, and violence, literal and figurative. If anything, even Crenshaw's direct and focused definition of critical race theory would have proven far too tentative and abstract for Wright to describe the violence and trauma he experienced throughout his life navigating "The Ethics of Living Jim Crow" in the autobiographical sketch included in his short story collection *Uncle Tom's Children*. Each section of the sketch begins with a lesson to be learned in encountering whiteness and ends with a reaffirmation of Wright's heightened sense of vulnerability under the unblinking gaze of whites. For what each encounter with whiteness confirms in the sketch, as well as in the whole of *Black Boy*, is that whiteness in a segregated world is premised on Black subjugation and submission, to be performed over and over again to confirm and reconfirm a racial hierarchy dating back to slavery and redefined through decades of de jure segregation.

This is the lesson that Wright as a child learns in the first section of the sketch, when he's punished so severely by his mother for fighting white boys that he suffers nightmares of looming white danger: "All that night I was delirious and could not sleep. Each time I closed my eyes I saw monstrous white faces suspended from the ceiling, leering at me."[21] In the sketches that follow, Wright learns that even the slightest appearance of less-than-full submissiveness will lose him promising jobs, attract physical blows, and threaten his very existence, and in this respect, his writing sadly anticipates and confirms one of the central tenets of critical race theory: the tenacious persistence of racial hierarchy among the elite members of society who have a vested interest in maintaining the status quo.

The only recourse in the end is flight, and hence, Wright, as a teenager, joined the Great Migration north, first to Memphis and then to Chicago, a trajectory that he retraces in *12 Million Black Voices*, his 1941 folk history of the Great Migration in photographs and poetic, heartbreaking prose. By his lights, *12 Million Black Voices* served as a chronicle of the racial injuries suffered by those trapped behind the color line, whether defined by Jim Crow in the South or casual racism in the North, and he took as his primary responsibility "to place within full and constant view the collective humanity whose triumphs and defeats are shared by the majority."[22]

Even in the North, though, Wright's efforts to display the humanity of his fellow migrants and his own were blocked by yet another white gaze—this time from white northerners—relegating the migrants to the poverty of menial jobs, substandard neighborhoods, and blighted prospects. His collective first-person narrator declares: "We remain to live in the clinging soot just beyond the factory areas, behind the railroad tracks, near the river banks, under the viaducts, by the steel and iron mills, on the edges of the coal and lumber yards. We live in crowded, barn-like rooms, in old rotting buildings where once dwelt rich native whites of a century ago."[23] There, they remain trapped in the white gaze, rendered mute and powerless, and their plight is evoked nowhere as vividly as in Wright's unpublished 1942 novel *The Man Who Lived Underground*, first published in abridged short story form in the 1961 collection *Eight Men* and issued at full length in 2021, along with his highly revealing essay, "Memories of My Grandmother," which recounts the origins of the story, the racial injuries it evoked, and above all, the violence required in maintaining white supremacy.

The Man Who Lived Underground originated in a crime story Wright read in a "very cheap magazine"—a 1941 issue of *True Detective*, according to the afterword in the Library of America edition.[24] The article recounted the story of a man living underground and tunneling into nearby businesses to rob in Hollywood, California, during the 1930s, a plot that Wright borrowed for his novel. His own underground story, he maintained, also originated in his dead grandmother's "ardent and volatile religious disposition," her firm belief in a God invisible to her, and Wright's own obsession with "the idea of invisibility" taken from a current Hollywood series of movies about an invisible man.[25]

The result was a liberating writing experience for Wright, one that opened him to new ways of seeing and writing as well as representing the reality of police violence in northern cities. "I have never written anything in my life," Wright wrote in "Memories of My Grandmother," "that stemmed more from sheer inspiration, or executed any piece of writing in a deeper feeling of imaginative freedom, or expressed myself in a way that flowed more naturally from my own personal background, reading, experiences, and feelings than *The Man Who Lived Underground*."[26] The freedom that he felt had a good deal to do with finding a voice in the improvisation of jazz and surrealism, enabling him to weave together the dreamlike adventures led by his protagonist Fred Daniels, who finds refuge underground from the violent police interrogation he suffers as well as a measure of invisibility awarding him his own gaze and briefly entrapping his persecutors.[27]

The refuge that Daniels finds is all the more striking because from the beginning of the narrative, opening with his arrest for burglary and murder, he is trapped in the glare of a white gaze that defines his race, his supposed criminality, and ultimately his lack of humanity. In the first few sentences, he learns that he has no way of asserting his own sense of self—as gainfully employed, a prospective father, and a respected church member—because the arresting police officers see not him but a criminal guilty because of his race and because of his being in the wrong place at the wrong time, a well-to-do white neighborhood requiring vigilant white protection. "He grew hysterical," the third-person narrator tells us, "as he felt that he did not exist for them."[28] Brutalized by the interrogation he undergoes, Daniels loses all sense of autonomy and self, and signs the confession forced upon him. His sense of entrapment is captured in the single sentence: "Invisible hands seemed to be pressing some alien destiny upon him."[29]

It's not until Daniels finds a moment apart from the unrelenting scrutiny of the three white policemen who extort a confession out of him that he is able to elude not just the glare of their defining gaze but the narrative that is about to incarcerate him literally and figuratively. He slips out a window, into the street, and through a manhole into the underground of sewers and basements underlying the city, and therein lies "an illusion of another world with other values and other laws," an invisible, oddly ghostly narrative other than the one aboveground that has defined him as a guilty criminal.[30] Looking upon scenes featuring both whites and Blacks who are blind to his presence, Daniels seems to discover an alternative gaze and an alternative narrative far beyond the ken of the white world aboveground. He wanders through basements and rooms revealing a Black church service, a movie theater, an undertaker's establishment with corpses awaiting treatment, workrooms with toolboxes that may prove useful, even hallucinatory visions that may or may not be real—a brown baby in the sewer water, and a nude woman with a nude baby, both of whom sink into the depths of the sewer. Peering through cracks and stepping through holes in walls, he even witnesses the theft of money from an insurance office, a police interrogation of two accused thieves, and the suicide of a possible accomplice. Seeing what whites cannot above ground, he is seemingly free from scrutiny to steal what he wants, money in the insurance office and diamonds in a jewelry store, along with tools and even a radio. He makes use of these items any dreamlike way he wants, from grinding diamonds into the floor of a cave he finds to papering its walls with stolen dollar bills. Underground, away from the white gaze that confines and defines him, he constructs a surrealistic counternarrative out of these fragments testifying to his new sense of freedom. "He was filled with reflection," the narrator suggests, "experiencing again that high pitch of consciousness, gazing like an invisible man hovering in space upon the life that lived aboveground in the darkness of the sun."[31]

Below ground, out of sight, Daniels conjures up any number of possible narratives invisible to anyone aboveground. But once he climbs out of the manhole—and out of the darkness that has protected him—he seems to lose both the sense of invisibility empowering him belowground and its accompanying empowerment. He actually retreats to the police station where he is originally interrogated and tries his best—without success—to explain to the same white policeman who arrested him and beat a confession out of him that he has discovered underground a wholly different way of being and a possible alternative narrative, one that he ultimately cannot articulate or even connect in a recognizable narrative. As the narrator remarks, "He was full of what he wanted to say, but he could not say it. He groped for words, but none came."[32] He even goes to the trouble of telling the policemen what he has seen from his hiding place underground and to direct them to the manhole where he found escape in invisibility and alternative possibilities, only to discover that they cannot see or hear what he has to say. They simply cannot imagine the alternative scenario he has to offer. What they do see, though, is the threat that his short sojourn underground, away from their defining gaze, poses to their authority as police officers, to their whiteness, and to the racial status quo aboveground.

That Daniels dies in the end, murdered by those police officers and interred in the sewer where he took shelter and from which he emerged to take some control of his life, does not minimize the sense of agency he has seemingly acquired—with a new sense of sight excavating the visible from the invisible and his new ability to formulate the beginnings of narrative, that of his own innocence and his own authority. Falsely accused of murder, he is nonetheless able to bear "testimony," in Wright's words, to "look at life from a position of enforced severance."[33] Beginning with his brutal beating by the police in a scene that evokes for contemporary readers the murder of George Floyd, Fred Daniels finally, as Wright notes at the end of his extraordinary essay, "emerges from the underground to communicate what he has seen, and to give testimony to what one feels is a right worth dying for."[34]

No such freedom, however, seems to await Wright's fellow Mississippi author William Faulkner or his Black and white characters, especially not in Faulkner's own 1942 text *Go Down, Moses*, the "negro stories," as he called them in his correspondence, arguably the culmination of an extraordinary series of novels and short stories exploring the color line at a time when segregation and racial categorization seemed to be firmly in place in American culture.[35] It was also a time, though, when the state of Mississippi was on the verge of monumental change because of the advent of World War II and the increasing restlessness of Black Mississippians joining the Great Migration north in growing numbers. As historian Neil R. McMillen reports, in the decade of the 1940s, 314,000

African Americans left the state, the largest number since 1870.[36] That demographic movement in turn is detectable in the occasional departures and disappearances of African American characters northward from the stories in *Go Down, Moses* that trace the intertwined legacy of slavery, rape, incest, peonage, and racial hierarchy of two closely related families in north Mississippi—the Black Beauchamps and the white McCaslins and Edmondses. But despite those periodic departures, the world of *Go Down, Moses* and its Black and white characters appears to be as much imprisoned in family histories and racial hierarchies as any of Richard Wright's tormented race rebels.

That sense of imprisonment is most pronounced in the opening stories "Was" and "The Fire and the Hearth," which feature African American characters who boldly test the boundaries of racial categories imposed upon them by white relatives, first under slavery and then under tenant farming. "Was" portrays a runaway slave determined to court his sweetheart on a neighboring plantation and, in doing so, manages to set the pace and the terms of the slave hunt that ensues. As half-brother to the white men who have inherited him and a host of other slaves, Tomey's Turl is able to take only partial authorship of the comedy of courtship that follows for whites and slaves alike, and in the end, manages to win his bride and only a small measure of autonomy. Despite the comedy and the protoabolitionist tendencies of his owners, Tomey's Turl remains a slave from start to finish, confined in his subjugated status by his white slaveholding father and white half-brothers. In the following story, "The Fire and the Hearth," it is left to one of his children, Lucas Beauchamp, a tenant farmer employed by his white cousin Carothers Edmonds, to test the boundaries of racial subjugation and its accompanying etiquette. Driven by the sense of dispossession he suffers as one of his white grandfather's Black descendants, Lucas pursues moonshine rivalries, an obsessive search for buried treasure, wheeling-dealing with white antagonists, and most energetically, his ongoing feud with generations of white employers who are also his white cousins. For Lucas, a descendant of Black slaves and white slaveholders, inheriting a racially charged history requires both acknowledgment and resistance by playing the role of the subservient Black underling on the one hand and, on the other, taking every opportunity to disrupt the power dynamics of racial construction and subjugation. He does so by repeatedly outwitting his white employer in one money-making scheme after another and by challenging his employer's father decades earlier to protect his marriage and his sense of manhood. Even his partial success in defying the racial status quo against all possible odds reveals just how susceptible to disruption the very definitions of whiteness and Blackness can be in the pre–civil rights South. Lucas's white employer and cousin, Carothers ("Roth") Edmonds, admits as much after turning a blind eye to a good many of Lucas's rebellious antics and challenges to the very notion of white supremacy. Pondering how permeable the color line is between Lucas and his white grandfather, Roth salutes Lucas with equal measure of anger and admiration: *"He's more like old Carothers than all the rest of us put together, including old Carothers. He is both heir and prototype simultaneously of all the geography and climate and biology which sired old Carothers and all the rest of us and our kind, myriad, countless, faceless, even nameless now except himself who fathered himself, intact and complete, contemptuous, as old Carothers must have been, of all blood black white yellow or red, including his own."*[37]

Lucas Beauchamp is, in fact, a good deal more successful in disrupting the racial status quo that has been imposed upon him by the legacy of slavery than his white cousins Roth Edmonds and Ike McCaslin are in seeing alternatives to the white domination that they themselves have inherited. Roth, for one, learns what it means to accept the designation of whiteness when he suddenly assumes white superiority over his childhood Black playmate and thereby betrays their longstanding emotional intimacy and his own sense of family crossing racial lines. In doing so, he is able to assert his own sense of white prerogative and privilege. As the third-person omniscient narrator tells us, it was then that "the old curse of his fathers, the old haughty ancestral pride based not on any value but on an accident of geography, stemmed not from courage and honor but from wrong and shame, descended to him."[38] Even as a child, Roth is able to define himself as white at the cost of humiliating his friend whose subordination is based only on color. Of Roth's discovery of his own whiteness, the third-person narrator remarks: "So he entered his heritage. He ate its bitter fruit."[39]

Ultimately, Roth Edmonds is imprisoned in his whiteness, symbolized by the power he holds over his Black employees and relatives and the plantation he has inherited from his white forebears who themselves defined their own sense of white privilege, power, and property by means of the slaves and later-hired laborers who made the plantation profitable. He may turn the occasional blind eye to the money-making schemes of his cousin and employee Lucas, but he is ultimately impervious to the possibility of considering alternatives to the racial status quo long enjoyed by his slaveholding forebears. If anything, Roth ends up repeating the sins of those forebears every time he asserts his sense of white superiority—including the on-and-off affair with a Black cousin he initiates and eventually repudiates.

In contrast, Ike McCaslin does attempt to consider alternatives to the racial status quo established by his McCaslin and Edmonds relatives—what Ike refers to as "the communal anonymity of brotherhood" he has glimpsed on his youthful hunting trips in the Mississippi wilderness under the mentorship of the master woodsman Sam Fathers, a former slave still bound to the McCaslins and Edmondses.[40] In the wilderness and in the simple purity of the bear hunt marking his coming of age, Ike sees something like a refuge from the burdens of family history and hierarchies of race and class defining life in late nineteenth-century Mississippi. Armed with those brief glimpses, Ike manages to decipher his family's history of slavery, property, and exploitation recorded in the plantation ledgers. Anticipating the analytical skills of critical race theorists to come, he pores over accounts of slave purchases, births, deaths, and manumissions and learns that he owes his identity and his privileges as a white man in a race-obsessed society to the brutal legacy of enslavement, exploitation, incest, and Black subjugation bequeathed to him by his grandfather, Lucius Quintus Carothers McCaslin. This discovery, in turn, awakens him to his own complicity in the elaborate plantation economy that links Black labor with white profits and Black subordination with his own sense of whiteness: "that whole edifice intricate and complex and founded upon injustice and erected by ruthless rapacity and carried on even yet with at times downright savagery not only to the human beings but the valuable animals too, yet solvent and efficient and, more than that: not only still intact but enlarged, increased."[41]

Ike McCaslin's discovery in turn leads him to identify his family legacy with that of the South itself, "that chronicle which was a whole land in miniature, which multiplied and compounded was the entire South, twenty-three years after surrender and twenty-four from emancipation."[42] It is a chronicle, though, with which he refuses to accept his own complicity and which he ultimately repudiates, a response that he half-heartedly tries to explain to his cousin McCaslin Edmonds upon his twenty-first birthday when he renounces the plantation that is his by right of birth and race. "Sam Fathers set me free" is the final explanation Ike offers for his repudiation after recounting a faltering, revised history of slavery, the Civil War, Reconstruction, and the segregated South that denies his own complicity.[43] Ultimately, he defends his decision to repudiate his inheritance—and to insist upon his own innocence—as part of a divine plan to rectify the wrongs of slavery and his family's legacy.

But is he really free—to reject the wrongs of the past and the identity of whiteness bequeathed to him by slavery? Or does his family inheritance, so closely intertwined with southern history—with the legacy of slavery as an institution and with racial injustice—overshadow any individual effort at rectification, as the whole of Faulkner's own fiction and contemporary critical race theorists seem to suggest about the "systemic" nature of racism? The remaining narratives in *Go Down, Moses*—the last two sections of "The Bear," "Delta Autumn," and "Go Down, Moses"—repeatedly question the value of his freedom or the viability of his repudiation. Indeed, as the narratives progress, the ghostly presence of Ike's grandfather—"that evil and unregenerate old man" seemingly rejected by Ike as the source of the family's original sin of slavery and brutality—makes itself even more pronounced and sinister with each passing year.[44] The more Ike tries to distance himself from that legacy, the more his grandfather's actions impinge upon his own until even half-hearted gestures of rectification to Black relatives blur into empty assertions of white innocence marred by acts of denial repeating past callousness and brutality.

By the penultimate story, "Delta Autumn," Ike is left stranded in his own diminished whiteness, still weighed down by the family legacy he has repudiated and still unable to rectify the wrongs of the past, whether his family's or his own. Even in the remaining Delta wilderness, which at the start of World War II is rapidly disappearing, Ike is unable to see past the afterlife of slavery and the racial status quo in the present. Confronted with a newly discovered kinswoman who is also racially mixed, McCaslin can see, ultimately, only a threat to his own whiteness as he urges her to leave for parts North rather than seek recognition from him and his white family. But his is a world, he realizes when she leaves, in which the strict boundaries of whiteness and Blackness have already dissolved, in part with the departure of African Americans in the migration North:

> This Delta. *This land which man has deswamped and denuded and derivered in two generations so that white men can own plantations and commute every night to Memphis and black men own plantations and ride in jim crow cars to Chicago to live in millionaires' mansions on Lakeshore Drive . . . and usury and mortgage and bankruptcy and measureless wealth, Chinese and African and Aryan and Jew, all breed and spawn together until no man has time to say which one is which nor cares.*[45]

In the end, he is left only with the remnants of his own empty whiteness, no longer bolstered by the presence and subordination of Blackness, no longer anchored by Black objects in the white gaze. It is a singular loneliness anticipating, oddly enough, Kenneth B. Clark's shrewd assessment of the utter dependence of a certain historically situated whiteness upon Black subordination. "It would probably be a calamity," Clark once observed, "for the average American white for the Negro either to disappear or for him to succeed in translating the words and promises of democracy into day to day reality. It would then be necessary for the

American whites to find other scapegoats, or to face again the intolerable state of their own emptiness."[46]

A similar sense of white abandonment—of a once familiar world emptying out altogether—can be discerned in the concluding story of "Go Down, Moses," which begins, notably enough, with a scenario of a census taker earnestly seeking to interview one of those Black Beauchamps who joined the Great Migration northward: Samuel Worsham Beauchamp, or Butch, imprisoned in a prison cell and awaiting execution. Frustrated by the prisoner's lack of responsiveness to questions, the census taker finally asks, "If they don't know who you are, how will they know—how do you expect to get home?" To which Beauchamp rightly replies, "What will that matter to me?"[47] After execution, his remains are sent back by train to Jefferson, Mississippi, and taken to the cemetery by a hearse paid for by the whites who gather to watch the procession pass—marked by a curious kind of nostalgia. The crowd of whites and Blacks who gather briefly to watch the hearse carrying Beauchamp's body go by commemorates the return not so much of a prodigal son lost to the Great Migration as of a Black man whose presence, even in death, helps configure the whiteness of the spectators. It's a scene that suggests that the unity of the whites gathered around the town square to watch Beauchamp finally come home is brief, the result of efforts by the garrulous lawyer Gavin Stevens to collect money by hook or crook. "It's for Miss Worsham," Stevens tells those he duns, referring not to Butch Beauchamp's grieving grandmother Mollie Beauchamp, who blames Roth Edmonds for selling her Benjamin into Egypt, but to the white woman who serves as patron of sorts to Mollie and her family.[48] Stevens's gesture, ultimately, suggests not recognition or culpability but an attempt at self-absolution and concealment of the "complicity with often brutal domination" that Renato Rosaldo finds at work in "imperialist nostalgia," which involves mourning the loss of what one has destroyed in the name of "progress," power, and authority.[49]

Ruth Frankenberg suggests that in times when constructions of whiteness are undergoing transformation and reconfiguration in response to changing historical conditions, whiteness becomes "highly visible, named and asserted, rather than invisible or simply 'normative.'"[50] It is that visibility—and its emptiness, I think—that Faulkner came to contemplate in the slow dismantling of what Robyn Wiegman calls the "tenuous geometry of public gazes" marking segregation and its own peculiar definitions of whiteness and Blackness.[51] What is left, Faulkner seems to suggest in the last two stories of *Go Down, Moses*, is a mere husk of whiteness, but even those fragments continue to assert a power of sorts—and to suggest the limitations and confinements of whiteness that Faulkner's characters and Faulkner himself faced.

Two decades after the publication of *Go Down, Moses*, and immediately after the murder of civil rights activist Medgar Evers, during the height of racial violence and unrest in 1960s Mississippi, Eudora Welty herself was besieged by late-night telephone callers who demanded to know just what she was "going to do about it."[52] Welty responded to those late-night callers first with a story whose title pondered an even more unsettling question, "Where Is the Voice Coming From?"—published in the *New Yorker* just after Evers's murder—and then a few years later with "The Demonstrators." Following that first title is a nonstop, first-person monologue by a hate-spewing racist whose sense of his own whiteness seems to depend upon killing a Black civil rights leader and thereby asserting his control over what can and cannot be seen. "Never seen him before," the first-person narrator tells us, "never seen him since, never seen anything of his black face but his picture, never seen his face alive, any time at all, or anywheres, and didn't want to, need to, never hope to see that face and never will. As long as there was no question in my mind."[53] But the question of where the voice is coming from and to whom it is directed remains, along with the question of just how much control the speaker has indeed achieved over who and what he is. In the end, after exulting in the brief sense of victory that murder bestows upon him, the killer retreats to a corner, strums his guitar, and sings a fragmentary refrain—"Sing a-down, down, down, down"—like a diminished, whimpering ghost with no one left to hurt or haunt.[54]

Welty's angry exposé of hate bonded with white grievance and racial violence is in fact something of a ghost story detected in the narrator's keening monologue and his haunting sense that his story and sense of self are increasingly overshadowed by events and figures out of reach and out of sight. In this respect, "Where Is the Voice Coming From?" meets the criteria of ghost stories and hauntings established by Avery Gordon in her 1997 volume *Ghostly Matters: Haunting and the Sociological Imagination*. Gordon's definition of ghostliness emphasizes a suspicion of authorized stories and histories that are linear, separating the past from the present, and that require certain kinds of "exclusions and invisibilities," knowledge visual and verbal that is subjugated, as it were, in the interest of unity and coherence.[55] Among other things, turning our attention to such "exclusions and invisibilities" provides tools for recovering hidden layers of history beneath the easily readable surface, and by doing so, exposes a palimpsest of competing stories through a process that Toni Morrison, no stranger herself to hauntings and ghost stories, would see as "rememorying" and recovering "discredited knowledge."[56]

The curious thing about this story and about Welty's subsequent story "The Demonstrators," published in 1966 as yet another response to those late-night callers, is the portrait that emerges of fissuring whiteness under siege by competing voices and stories liberated by the civil rights movement and the forces of sweeping change. In both stories, white resistance to those forces and voices is captured in language that can only be described as hate speech or words designed to exert mastery and inflict injury in the sense meant by Jeremy Waldron in his 2012 book *The Harm in Hate Speech* and by Judith Butler in *Excitable Speech*. Waldron sees hate speech as "the use of words which are deliberately abusive and/or insulting and/or threatening and/or demeaning directed at members of vulnerable minorities, calculated to stir up hatred against them."[57] Stirring up hatred by Waldron's lights also means awakening past nightmares in order to attack "the public good of inclusiveness."[58] Above all, though, hate speech represents an effort to control visibility and invisibility, precisely because, Waldron maintains, hate speech "can become a world-defining activity, and those who promulgate it know very well—this is part of their intention—that the visible world they create is a much harder world for the targets of their hatred to live in."[59] We know from Toni Morrison's 1993 Nobel Prize address that hate speech "does more than represent violence." In Morrison's words, "it is violence."[60] Judith Butler quotes those words in *Excitable Speech*, but she notes that the violence of abusive language also exposes "a prior vulnerability to language, one that we have by virtue of being interpellated kinds of beings, dependent on the address of the Other in order to be."[61] Calling out hurtful names by Butler's sights inflicts injury, but it also constitutes a form of address and recognition, a call for response that in itself inadvertently acknowledges agency, and strangely enough, Butler says, "our dependency on the ways we are addressed in order to exercise any agency at all."[62]

It is this sense of dependency—and even a sudden onslaught of ghostliness—that the nameless speaker in "Where Is the Voice Coming From?" inadvertently reveals as he first exults in his act of murder and then discovers that his victim remains highly visible in death even as the speaker himself seems to fade from the very story he is narrating. Just so does Dr. Richard Strickland, the apparent protagonist of "The Demonstrators," exhibit his increasing marginality and irrelevance, even his own invisibility, on a night visit to the African American community, where he seemingly fails to see and recognize lifelong neighbors and subordinates and displays a callous indifference that amounts to a genteel form of hate speech. Both Strickland and the narrator of "Where Is the Voice Coming From?" assume centrality and autonomy in their stories only to reveal their own fissuring whiteness and impotence amid the clamor of competing voices and stories emerging in the turmoil of the 1960s.

No narrator could be more certain of his sense of control and mastery than the speaker of "Where Is the Voice Coming From?" He declares from the outset that murdering the civil rights leader is his idea and no one else's, not even Governor Ross Barnett's. He insists as well that from start to finish his execution plan underscores his own sense of mastery and centrality—in a word, his whiteness. Waiting outside the civil rights leader's house, the speaker exults in his sense of control: "That was him. I knowed it when he cut off the car lights and put his foot out and I knowed him standing dark against the light. I knowed him then like I know me now. I knowed him even by his still listening back."[63] And once he fires his gun, he feels compelled to spell out just how his sense of self—and whiteness—has been fortified through murder:

> I stepped to the edge of his light there, where he's laying flat. I says "Roland? There was one way left, for me to be ahead of you and stay ahead of you, by Dad, and I just taken it. Now I'm alive and you ain't. We ain't never now, never going to be equals and you know why? One of us is dead. What about that, Roland?" I said. "Well, you seen to it, didn't you?"[64]

In the aftermath of the murder, though, the speaker discovers that the story he tells of the civil rights leader's death is not so much his story as that of the man he has killed, who remains in the news while the speaker slowly fades into the shadows, relegated to the margins of the event he has engineered: "They know who Roland Summers was without knowing who I am. His face was in front of the public before I got rid of him, and after I got rid of him there it is again—the same picture. And none of me."[65] Hearing theories about the murder on the news and in the street, the speaker senses that he has failed to exert control over what can be seen and heard. What remains is the misgiving of defeat rather than any hope of victory. "You can't win," he observes tersely, and as he anticipates a manhunt or even an onslaught of racial violence, he fades farther and farther into the background of the story itself, a voice muttering in the shadows like a newly made ghost.[66] In the concluding paragraph, the speaker strums his guitar and sings to himself—apparently with no audience, no company, and no recognition of who and what he is, certainly no acknowledgment of his whiteness and his brief murderous act of self-assertion. The speaker is left alone with his unheard songs, a ghost haunting his own story drowned out by the force of events.

If anything, words seem equally injurious and life-denying in "The Demonstrators," published like "Where Is the Voice Coming From?" in the *New Yorker*. In this story, words and white public discourse in particular seem to serve as barricades between white and Black. The opening scenario suggests as much in its description of a visit paid by the demoralized, numb white protagonist Dr. Strickland to one of his shut-in patients, Miss Marcia Poe, who recites "great wads of Shakespeare and '*Arma virumque cano*.'"[67] The narrator declares that the "more forcefully Miss Marcia Pope declaimed, the more innocent grew her old face—the lines went right out."[68] Like his patient, Dr. Strickland is surrounded by declaiming words presuming and assuming innocence—those of newspaper stories, photographs, and captions and of charges and countercharges hurled by combatants over civil rights. So too is the young Black woman he visits to treat an ice pick wound closed in by public words—in a house filled with stacks of newspapers and divided by "newspapered walls."[69] The woman he treats is singularly quiet, so much so that Strickland feels compelled to pepper the crowd of people in the house with questions about who she is and what has happened—to which the crowd responds, tellingly, "'Don't you know her?' . . . as if he never was going to hit on the right question."[70] He finally does recognize the young woman in a manner of speaking when he realizes that she is Ruby Gaddy, the maid who cleans his office building, but that recognition is contingent of course on placing her in the age-old white script of the Black servant. Only with great difficulty does he come to understand the circumstances of her wounding—by Dove Collins, a Black man whose own wounds Strickland has repeatedly treated in the past.

Strickland reassures the crowd that he knows Ruby Gaddy, Dove Collins, and all the rest of them, for that matter, but if he does, it is only because he has "inherited" them in a sense—from his own childhood and from his father, whose medical practice he has taken over. Still, he leaves the house acknowledging, if only to himself, that he doesn't know the name of one woman there who has always been a part of his life. What he does know and recognize—and this one easy recognition is highly revealing—are the dresses hanging across the front of the house, the laundry farmed out by his mother, sister, and wife, and a porcelain cup in which he is offered a drink of water. The accoutrements of whiteness and privilege, parts of his own identity, are far more accessible to him than anything else in the house. It is telling that he leaves the house encased in his own sense of callous indifference and supposed autonomy. As the narrator tells us, "Then he stepped across the gaze of the girl on the bed as he would have had to step over a crack yawning in the floor."[71]

In the end, Strickland leaves behind a narrative of events that has apparently escaped him, a story that briefly remains untold beneath the clamor of words strangely illegible and inaccessible to the figure who is ostensibly the protagonist and central point of view. Or is he? The third-person narrator tells us that Strickland drives back to the unlighted town as he hears "the throbbing mill, working on its own generator," suggesting nothing so much as a cacophony of stories beyond his ability to read or see—or even to avoid eventually.[72] Stopping at the railroad crossing bordered by the throbbing mill, Strickland ponders the tumbled cotton bales on the mill's loading platform revealed by the headlight of a passing freight train, and as he does, he remembers his lost daughter and his estranged wife and even a civil rights worker who defended the misrepresentations of a false news story as justified political weapons. Having long felt embittered and numbed by his losses, Strickland suddenly feels at the railroad crossing a sudden inexplicable surge of well-being: "Was it the sensation, now returning, that there was still allowed to everybody on earth a *self*—savage, death-defying, private? The pounding of his heart was like the assault of hope, throwing itself against him without a stop, merciless."[73] But that feeling of well-being—one might say of whiteness reassured—is momentary. Almost immediately thereafter, Strickland discovers a wounded man lying in the moonlight, who turns out to be Dove Collins and who begs the doctor to hide him and then hemorrhages—almost as though to underscore that the doctor's brief sense of well-being and whiteness reassured is made possible, if only briefly, by the kind of violence suffered only by African Americans in the small town of Holden.

If there is any sense to be made of either Strickland's brief sense of whiteness reassured or the sequence of events leading to the wounds suffered by Ruby and Dove, it seems on the face of things to be the town's newspaper story issued the next day, which declares "No Racial Content Espied" in the deaths of Ruby and Dove and the violence leading to their deaths.[74] Citing white authorities like Holden marshal Curtis "Cowboy" Stubblefield, the Rev. Alonzo Duckett, pastor of the Holden First Baptist Church, and country sheriff Vince Lasseter, the story concludes that no "outside agitators" were involved and that "[n]o cause was cited for the fracas."[75] It is, ultimately, the "official" story told by white authorities—to a white newspaper speaking to white readers—but strangely enough, the official story is presented as an afterthought, and not a very persuasive one at that. This is a narrative that interrogates the cacophony of words imprisoning white and Black alike and suggests that in the end, Strickland himself, the town doctor, is relegated to the margins of the town and its narratives, a ghostly remnant of whiteness under siege by a growing clamor of words and voices testifying to the sweeping presence of change. That brief sense of well-being he experiences at the railroad crossing is as ephemeral as the white newspaper account of the night's events, its own words as dehumanizing and as injurious as hate speech, designed to control and manipulate what in the end can be seen and heard. And so are those protestations of white innocence underscoring the news story. "That's one they can't pin the blame on us for," County Sheriff Vince Lasseter declares. "That's how they treat their own kind. Please take note our conscience is clear."[76] It is a protestation that is finally empty, a ghostly excuse overshadowed by the events preceding it, and in that contrast, we can detect Welty's own condemnation of the injurious language and the violence required to maintain even the semblance of whiteness in an era when it is increasingly revealed to be nothing more than ghostliness.

There is, finally, a muted, even despairing tone to these late stories by Eudora Welty, as there is in William Faulkner's self-consciously described "negro stories" and far more emphatically in Richard Wright's unpublished novel of the 1940s. They are narratives reflecting upon the increasing untenability of the color line in Jim Crow America and the fierce resistance to change posed by the intensified racism of white blindness. The ghostliness that haunts all of these texts suggests both the tenacity of white recalcitrance and the ultimate futility of resisting the monumental changes defining the country's emergence into a new multicultural age. Above all, these are texts that serve as devastating critiques of the country's reluctance to relinquish a familiar racial hierarchy—and the white blindness and violence accompanying that reluctance. Literary pieces they may all be, but they nonetheless serve notice of the country's failings and the imperative for African Americans in particular, in the words of critical race theorist and activist Derrick Bell, to "confront and conquer the otherwise deadening reality of our permanent subordinate status."[77] But for both critical race theorists and for Mississippi's greatest writers, the obstacles to genuine change and transformation—the lingering legacy of slavery, the long-term embedding of racial hierarchy in law and institutions, and even the looming presence of the past—remain stubborn and seemingly immovable features of the present.

NOTES

1. Richard Delgado and Jean Stefancic, introduction to *Critical Race Theory: An Introduction*, ed. Delgado and Stefancic (New York: New York University Press, 2001), 3–5; Jacey Fortin, "Critical Race Theory: A Brief History," *New York Times*, November 8, 2021, https://www.nytimes.com/article/what-is-critical-race-theory.html; Kimberlé Crenshaw, "Twenty Years of Critical Race Theory: Looking Back to Move Forward," *Connecticut Law Review* 43, no. 5 (July 2011): 1253–352.

2. Benjamin Wallace-Wells, "How a Conservative Activist Invented the Conflict over Critical Race Theory," *New Yorker*, June 18, 2021, https://www.newyorker.com/news/annals-of-inquiry/how-a-conservative-activist-invented-the-conflict-over-critical-race-theory?utm_source=onsite-share&utm_medium=email&utm_campaign=onsite-share&utm_brand=the-new-yorker.

3. Benjamin Wallace-Wells, "How a Conservative Activist Invented the Conflict over Critical Race Theory."

4. Jack Silverstein, "Why We Published *The 1619 Project*," *New York Times Magazine*, December 20, 2019, https://www.nytimes.com/interactive/2019/12/20/magazine/1619-intro.html.

5. Gery Peller, "Race Consciousness," *Duke Law Journal* 4 (September 1990): 759–60.

6. Qtd. in Zak Cheney-Rice, "The Right's New Reason to Panic about 'Critical Race Theory' Is Centuries Old," *New York Intelligencer*, June 30, 2021, https://nymag.com/intelligencer/2021/06/the-white-panic-behind-critical-race-theory.html.

7. See in particular Matthew J. Clavin, *Toussaint Louverture and the American Civil War: The Promise and Peril of a Second Haitian Revolution* (Philadelphia: University of Pennsylvania Press, 2010), 144–61; and Henry Louis Gates Jr., *Stony the Road: Reconstruction, White Supremacy, and the Rise of Jim Crow* (New York: Penguin Press, 2019).

8. Lauren Michele Jackson, "The Void that Critical Race Theory Was Created to Fill," *New Yorker*, July 27, 2021, https://www.newyorker.com/culture/cultural-comment/the-void-that-critical-race-theory-was-created-to-fill.

9. Ronald Brownstein, "Red States Are Reworking the Civil Liberties Landscape," CNN Wire, February 22, 2022, https://www.cnn.com/2022/02/22/politics/republicans-civil-liberties-abortion-voting-race/index.html.

10. States News Service, "Lawmakers Introduced 563 Measures against Critical Race Theory in 2021 and 2022," States News Service, April 6, 2023, https://advance-lexis-com.proxy.wm.edu/api/document?collection=news&id=urn:contentItem:67Y9-9411-JCBG-S234B-00000-00&context=1516831; Jackson, "The Void That Critical Race Theory Was Created to Fill": and Kmele Foster et al., "We Disagree on a Lot of Things, Except the Danger of Anti-Critical Race Theory Laws," *New York Times*, July 5, 2021, https://www.nytimes.com/2021/07/05/opinion/we-disagree-on-a-lot-of-things-except-the-danger-of-anti-critical-race-theory-laws.html.

11. Neil R. McMillen, *Dark Journey: Black Mississippians in the Age of Jim Crow* (Urbana: University of Illinois Press, 1989), 8.

12. Richard Wright, *Black Boy (American Hunger): A Record of Childhood and Youth*, rev. ed. (1945; repr., New York: Harper Perennial, 1993), 252–53.

13. Kimberlé Williams Crenshaw et al., introduction to *Seeing Race Again: Countering Colorblindness across the Disciplines*, ed. Crenshaw et al. (Berkeley: University of California Press, 2019), 14; Kimberlé Williams Crenshaw, "Race, Reform, and Retrenchment: Transformation and Legitimation in Anti-Discrimination Law," *Harvard Law Review* 101, no. 7 (1988); Kimberlé Williams Crenshaw et al., eds., *Critical Race Theory: The Key Writings That Formed the Movement* (New York: New Press, 1995), 116.

14. McMillen, *Dark Journey*, xiii.

15. See Delgado and Stefancic, *Critical Race Theory: An Introduction*, 2–9 and 14–17, with special attention to 7, 8, and 9.

16. For a quick review of the origins of critical race theory, see Fortin, "Critical Race Theory: A Brief History."

17. Qtd. in Fortin, "Critical Race Theory: A Brief History."

18. Crenshaw et.al., introduction, 14; Crenshaw, "Race, Reform, and Retrenchment," 116.

19. Kimberlé Williams Crenshaw et al., "Praying to the Disciplinary Gods with One Eye Open," in *Seeing Race Again: Countering Colorblindness across the Disciplines*, ed. Crenshaw et al., 14; see also Crenshaw, "Race, Reform, and Retrenchment," 116; and George Lipsitz, "The Sounds of Silence: How Race Neutrality Preserves White Supremacy," in *Seeing Race Again: Countering Colorblindness across the Disciplines*, ed. Crenshaw et al., 23–25.

20. Kimberlé Williams Crenshaw, "How Colorblindness Flourished in the Age of Obama," in *Seeing Race Again: Countering Colorblindness Across the Disciplines*, ed. Crenshaw et al., 128–52.

21. Richard Wright, "The Ethics of Living Jim Crow," in *Uncle Tom's Children* (New York: Harper & Row, 1940), 5.

22. Richard Wright, *12 Million Black Voices* (New York: Thunder's Mouth Press, 1941), xix-xx.

23. Wright, *12 Million Black Voices*, 103.

24. Richard Wright, "Memories of My Grandmother," in *The Man Who Lived Underground* (New York: Library of America, 2021), 197; and Malcolm Wright, afterword to Richard Wright, *The Man Who Lived Underground*, 222.

25. Wright, *The Man Who Lived Underground*, 164, 176-78.

26. Wright, *The Man Who Lived Underground*, 163.

27. Wright, "Memories of My Grandmother," 185-88.

28. Wright, *The Man Who Lived Underground*, 23.

29. Wright, *The Man Who Lived Underground*, 43.

30. Wright, *The Man Who Lived Underground*, 53.

31. Wright, *The Man Who Lived Underground*, 103.

32. Wright, *The Man Who Lived Underground*, 136.

33. Wright, "Memories of My Grandmother," 188-89.

34. Wright, "Memories of My Grandmother," 200.

35. Qtd. in Joseph Blotner, *Faulkner: A Biography*, rev. ed. (1974; repr., New York: Random House, 1984), 420.

36. McMillen, *Dark Journey*, 259.

37. William Faulkner, *Go Down, Moses*, rev. ed. (1942; repr., New York: Vintage International, 1990), 114.

38. Faulkner, *Go Down, Moses*, 107.

39. Faulkner, *Go Down, Moses*, 110.

40. Faulkner, *Go Down, Moses*, 244.

41. Faulkner, *Go Down, Moses*, 283-84.

42. Faulkner, *Go Down, Moses*, 279.

43. Faulkner, *Go Down, Moses*, 285.

44. Faulkner, *Go Down, Moses*, 280.

45. Faulkner, *Go Down, Moses*, 346.

46. Qtd. in David R. Roediger, ed., *Black on White: Black Writers on What It Means to Be White* (New York: Schocken, 1998), 380.

47. Faulkner, *Go Down, Moses*, 352.

48. Faulkner, *Go Down, Moses*, 360.

49. Renato Rosaldo, "Imperialist Nostalgia," *Representations* 26 (Spring 1989): 108.

50. Ruth Frankenberg, "Introduction: Local Whitenesses, Localizing Whiteness," in *Displacing Whiteness: Essays in Social and Cultural Criticism*, ed. Frankenberg (Durham, NC: Duke University Press, 1997), 5.

51. Robyn Wiegman, *American Anatomies: Theorizing Race and Gender* (Durham, NC: Duke University Press, 1995), 41.

52. Eudora Welty, "Must the Novelist Crusade?," in *The Eye of the Story: Selected Essays and Reviews* (New York: Vintage, 1978), 147.

53. Eudora Welty, "Where Is the Voice Coming From?," in *The Collected Stories of Eudora Welty* (New York: Harvest-Harcourt Brace Jovanovich, 1980), 604.

54. Welty, "Where Is the Voice Coming From?," 607.

55. Avery Gordon, *Ghostly Matters: Haunting and the Sociological Imagination* (Minneapolis: University of Minnesota Press, 2008), 17.

56. Toni Morrison, *Beloved* (New York: Plume/New American Library, 1987), 215; Christina Davis, "An Interview with Toni Morrison / 1986," in *Conversations with Toni Morrison*, ed. Danille Taylor-Guthrie (Jackson: University Press of Mississippi, 1994), 226.

57. Jeremy Waldron, *The Harm in Hate Speech* (Cambridge, MA.: Harvard University Press, 2014). 9

58. Waldron, *The Harm in Hate Speech*, 5–6.
59. Waldron, *The Harm in Hate Speech*, 74.
60. Toni Morrison, "The Nobel Prize in Literature," in *What Moves at the Margin*, ed. Carolyn C. Denard (Jackson: University Press of Mississippi, 2008), 201.
61. Qtd. in Judith Butler, *Excitable Speech: A Politics of the Performative* (New York: Routledge, 1997), 9, 26.
62. Butler, *Excitable Speech*, 27.
63. Welty, "Where Is the Voice Coming From?," 604.
64. Welty, "Where Is the Voice Coming From?," 604.
65. Welty, "Where Is the Voice Coming From?," 606.
66. Welty, "Where Is the Voice Coming From?," 606.
67. Eudora Welty, "The Demonstrators," in *The Collected Stories of Eudora Welty* (New York: Harvest-Harcourt Brace Jovanovich, 1980), 608
68. Welty, "The Demonstrators," 608.
69. Welty, "The Demonstrators," 610.
70. Welty, "The Demonstrators," 610.
71. Welty, "The Demonstrators," 614.
72. Welty, "The Demonstrators," 615.
73. Welty, "The Demonstrators," 618.
74. Welty, "The Demonstrators," 619.
75. Welty, "The Demonstrators," 620, 621.
76. Welty, "The Demonstrators," 621.
77. Derrick Bell, *Faces at the Bottom of the Well: The Permanence of Racism* (New York: Basic Books, 1992), 1.

Kiese Laymon, Jesmyn Ward, and Natasha Trethewey

Writers of Our Mississippi Moment Showing How to Read Those We Had Read Before

HARRIET POLLACK

Contributing to a collection dedicated to three twentieth-century Mississippi writers brings certain questions to mind. Why do we place writers together in comparative study? Is it because juxtapositions grow our picture of an era, its history, its aesthetics, its concerns and preoccupations? When teaching courses on or writing about periods, we routinely place novels and poems in conversation with one another, conversations that create and define a sense of a literary and cultural era. And as a critic often studying this volume's three Southern Renaissance writers in particular—Faulkner, Welty, and Wright—I routinely ask how the cluster of works composed by these creators of different backgrounds, of diverse personal identities, and of varied experiences collaboratively reveals both their region's history and what is omitted from its official histories.

Today, as in the twentieth century, contemporary Mississippi writers dominate the literary field. Together, writers of then and now interact in a crowded landscape of mutual hauntings as the presence of older texts hovers in the new. Kiese Laymon, Jesmyn Ward, and Natasha Trethewey represent a current Mississippi Renaissance in counterpoint with this volume's primary trio. As I focus on the interactions of these six writers, I acknowledge that Ralph Eubanks's recent book *A Place Like Mississippi: A Journey through a Real and Imagined Literary Landscape* makes clear the subjectivity of selectively privileging three or even six writers from all of Mississippi's astonishing abundance, which Eubanks, by mapping writers to their distinct in-state regions, shows representing different places, different Mississippi stories. Yet the dialogue between these six writers adds to, comments on, and revises comprehension of our nation's cultural landscape—for much like Leigh Ann Duck, Imani Perry, and others, I read the texts of the South as key to understanding the nation.[1]

Most crucially for this essay and as a critic who has in detail explored Eudora Welty's uses of allusion to rewrite and revise texts of the past, I find myself now considering a different aspect of allusion than I have treated before. Previously, I've written about Welty's modernist play with literary memory. Her tendency is to evoke a familiar literary pattern, genre, or text and then veer from the expectations created by it. Her inclination is to call on but sport with readers' literary competencies rather than to fulfill the anticipations these produce. Her female swerve and artistic innovation have built on manipulations of and references to older texts and familiar genres.[2]

But now with focus on references *to* Welty, Wright, and Faulkner, I note that allusions also work *in reverse*, to complicate the texts alluded to, to show us new ways to read that which we thought we had fully read before. Consequently, I mean to explore how allusions to earlier writers' products not only write forward to produce new texts but also work backward to alter the ways that we read and reread the referent texts. And in the work of Laymon, Ward, and Trethewey, we are particularly concerned to write/unwrite the fraught narrative of race in the United States—and to attend to the story of the child. Arguably, all six of the writers meeting in this discussion are especially adept at portraying childhood socializations to race or whiteness in America. That is unsurprising given that, as Neely Tucker recently commented in a review of a John Grisham novel, "to ignore race in Mississippi is to write about Arizona and ignore the desert."[3]

Kiese Laymon and Eudora Welty

In *How to Slowly Kill Yourself and Others in America* (2020), Kiese Laymon explicates his burdened personal history of meeting Eudora Welty and William Faulkner in the Mississippi educational system. "For a long time," he writes,

> I hated on Eudora Welty's narrative abilities because ... teachers made us read her every year from seventh to twelfth grade, and I knew that that Ms. [Margaret] Alexander's *Jubilee* and "For My People" were way better or at least as good as anything Ms. Welty did. Ms. Welty was dope. She was. [...] But Mississippi is the home of the best sentence creators in the world. How come Ms. Welty was the one who got all the shine when I was in school?[4]

With that reframing, Laymon conveys the resentment of racial exclusion, an exclusion he also connects to the absence of Richard Wright in his school curriculum, a felt erasure.

But it's in *Heavy: An American Memoir* that Laymon moves his focus from Welty's Mississippi reception to her writing. *Heavy* is his account of systemic racism and its impact on Black love, measured in family, friend, and educational relationships. There, Laymon, with blatant honesty, recalls his discomfort in an otherwise white eighth-grade classroom.

> Somewhere around our third quarter, Ms. Stockard made us read . . . Faulkner and . . . Welty stories and watch *Roots* for black history month. . . . Ms. Stockard talked a lot about the work of Eudora Welty all year. She talked . . . about "historical context" when speaking about the "quirky racism" of Welty's characters . . . compared . . . to the "bad real racism" of . . . the white characters in *Roots*. I didn't like what "historical context" and "quirky racism" . . . granted white folk.[5]

Laymon felt heavy racial weight in that classroom. But he confesses to also feeling something he "was embarrassed to admit," that is, "a tug toward the interior of Welty's stories" (*H*, 71). And, unlikely as it first seems, the story he's tugged toward is "Why I Live at the P.O."

> Even though there were bold boundaries between my imagination and Welty's, when she started . . . with the sentence "I was getting along fine with Mama, Papa-Daddy, and Uncle Rondo until my sister Stella-Rondo . . . came back home again," I didn't just feel an intimate relationship to Welty's text; I felt every bit of Jackson, and really every bit of the Mississippi [my mother] had taught me to fear.
> Welty didn't know a lick about Mississippi black folk, but she knew enough about herself to mock white folk in the most ruthlessly petty ways I'd ever read. [. . .] White folk were capable of anything and not to be provoked, but Welty reminded me of what my eyes and ears taught me: white folk were scared and scary as all hell, so scared, so scary the words "scared" and "scary" weren't scared or scary enough to describe them. (*H*, 71)

Laymon's presentation of "Why I Live at the P.O." as a depiction of scared white folk is an altering reframing. It recharacterizes Welty's wack white characters, self-absorbed with First World problems, scared and therefore scary in their narcissism. Before Laymon's comment, had I fully seen the conflict between privilege and anxiety in the "main people in China Grove"?[6] Now I reconsider the fullest class implications of Stella Rondo, who "always had anything in the world she wanted and then she'd throw it away" (*CS*, 46), coming home with what Mama pointedly and meaningfully calls a "marvelous blonde child" that she insists is adopted because she is evidently much too afraid to confess having been pregnant before married (*CS*, 46). I also have another look at Mama begrudgingly turning "both the Negroes loose" (*CS*, 50) for a holiday only because "no earthly power could hold one anyway on the Fourth of July." And I revisit Papa Daddy who articulates his regret at having finagled, on the merits of his connections, Sister's position as postmistress—for which he now avows, rather than admits, she's not particularly qualified ("he said if Uncle Rondo could only fathom the lengths he had gone to get [her] that job!" [*CS*, 48]). Although Papa Daddy "would of gone on till nightfall" (*CS*, 47) speaking of hussies, and despite dictatorially insisting they "all sit ... and remember [his] words" (*CS*, 48) while he goes to "lie in the hammock," this comic southern patriarch flashes terror at his older daughter's challenges to his authority—fretfully broadcasting his farcical dread that she wants to cut off his beard. All told, Laymon has directed me to see "the main people in China Grove" as potentially dangerous white people, scary because scared as they anxiously tend their place in a power structure. The postmistress, their daughter, is not persuasive as she insists she has "got everything cater-cornered, the way [she] like[s] it" (*CS*, 56), and Laymon shows me that white folks like these—who don't have everything just as they like it—are ones who may act purely cornered.

And so, while I knew how in so many of Welty's signature stories ("The Winds," "A Memory," "June Recital," "Moon Lake," to name a few) girls are a revealing filter for the limiting culture of whiteness regulating them, Laymon has made visible how Welty's comedy also gleans and mocks the backdrop of white insecurity. That technique unexpectedly links Welty and Laymon's comic voices; his satire of that same target in *Long Division* has a family resemblance to hers in "Why I Live at the P.O."

Laymon, William Faulkner, and Richard Wright

About William Faulkner, Laymon repeatedly and across his works sounds the refrain of being instructed to imitate Faulkner's white excellence, creativity, and command of language, of being told to learn to write as the "master" wrote. In his essay "What I Pledge Allegiance To" in *How to Slowly Kill Yourself and Others in America: Essays* (2020), Laymon sums up the story:

> As a Black child from Central Mississippi, I was encouraged by my mother and teachers to imitate the work of William Faulkner. Mama thought imitating Faulkner could protect me, ironically, from white men, white men's power, and all men's bullets. By the time I was fifteen, I'd read everything Faulkner had written. I knew *my* Faulkner like I knew *my* Ice Cube, *my* Voltron, *my* En Vogue, *my* Good Times, *my* banana-flavored Now and Laters. [...] Somewhere around eleventh grade, though, my body tired of imitating white writers who simply could not see, hear, love, or imagine Black folk as part of, or central to, their audience. (*HSKY*, 23)

Here Laymon is abridging the story told in *Heavy*, where the character of young Kiese reports on the predictable home assignment he has received from his mother—a college professor resolved to mentor and enrich her son's education.

> I was ... supposed to read the first chapter of William Faulkner's *Absalom, Absalom!* and imitate Faulkner's style when writing a short story placed in Jackson. The first sentence in the book was a million words long, which was cool, and it used strange words like "wisteria" and "lattices," but I didn't know how to write like Faulkner and say anything honest about us. . . . So I decided I'd take the whupping from you or write lines when I got home. (*H*, 14)

Working on self-education, finding a voice, and choosing literary guides, mentors, and influences, young Kiese contemplates lines written by Margaret Walker Alexander, Mississippi's still-underappreciated Black woman writer who, like his mother, worked at Jackson State University:

> "They will distract you. They will try to kill you. Do not be distracted. Be directed. Write to and for our people."
>
> I loved those sentences, but I didn't understand the difference between "writing to" and "writing for" anyone. No one ever taught me to write to and for my people. They taught me how to imitate Faulkner and how to write to and for my teachers. And all of my teachers were white. When writing to you, I wrote in the hopes that what I wrote was good enough for me to not get beaten. (*H*, 106)

In this story of mother, son, educational aspirations, literary training, and love expressed in family violence, I hear Laymon choosing another mentor for himself: not Faulkner, but Richard Wright in his own memoir *Black Boy* and its portrayal of how white racism leads to self-destructive Black behaviors—among them, the harsh parenting provided ostensibly to protect a boy from the dangers met while living Black. Throughout *Black Boy*, "hit" and "beat" are words that repeat (altogether, there are seventy-five uses) as the child is "educated." Unruly young Richard knows he will be walloped when he burns his house curtains and indeed is "lashed so hard and long" that he loses consciousness.[7] Next, the child "hits," learning to fight back at the felt offense of his father's resented verbal blows. "Kill that damn thing!" his father declares, referring to the mewing kitten that is a double to Richard's own disruptive noisiness, and the boy—intentionally misconstruing the rough statement by taking it literally—hangs the pet in an act of rebuke and violence against paternal instruction (*BB*, 15-16). Then the child "hit[s] again and again" the bully street boys that his mother forces him to fight rather than avoid (*BB*, 21), intending to teach him to withstand assault. Next, when youthful Richard hears that a Black boy has been severely beaten by a white man, he "assume[s] that the 'white' man must have been the 'black' boy's father," a response that tells us first how little the child knew about race but that also obliquely associates parental harshness and racial danger (*BB*, 26–27). Later, adolescent Richard hears of bullets that hit Black men and of the deadly consequences of being a Black man who hit a white woman (*BB*, 59, 70). Arguably the pattern of violent education reaches an apex in Richard's conflict with his harsh Aunt Addie; after she—who is also his schoolteacher—takes a switch to his hand and legs in the classroom, he flips her script during yet another corrective assault at home. Then he warns, "If you hit me I'll fight you!" which he does (111).

The Addie passage explicitly echoes in *Heavy* when the character Kiese snatches the belt that his mother brandishes after opening her son's college report card. It is a scene unobtrusively prefaced by explicit references to rereading *Black Boy* in college.

> Reading the book at Millsaps felt like a call to arms. Reading the book in my bed, a few feet from your room, in our house, felt like a warm whisper. [. . .] I wanted to write like Wright far more than I wanted to write like Faulkner, but I didn't really want to write like Wright at all. I wanted to fight like Wright. I wanted to craft sentences that styled on white folk, and dared them to do anything about the styling they'd just witnessed. (*H*, 137–38)

Here Laymon is defining a relationship between literacy, creativity, fight, and possibility. The outburst that next materializes, set against the bookcase that presumably contains these writers' works, figuratively and literally closets its echoes of that moment in *Black Boy* when Richard grabs for a knife in self-defense against his Aunt Addie's assault—when she intends to "educate" him not to lie, although he had not lied. The allusive resonances are palpable:

> I had not been a perfect student.
> I stood in front of the bookcase waiting for you. You marched into your room, went in the closet, and came out with a belt. You brought one lash down across my shoulder. You brought another lash down across the front of my stomach. I didn't move. You went on and on about ruining the only chance I had to get free.
> I grabbed the belt, snatched it from your hand, and threw it against the bookcase. You looked at me for the first time in my life the same way you looked at [your physically abusive lover] when he was angry. I knew your body

was afraid of mine. You knew, for the first time in our lives, my body was not afraid of yours. (*H*, 138–39)

Here Laymon, fighting now in words, reminds us too of the moment in Wright's *Black Boy* when Richard discovers H. L. Mencken as a "man . . . fighting with words. He was using words as a weapon, using them as one would use a club" (*BB*, 251). That finding, and the transition from one kind of battling to another, is as important to Laymon as it is to Wright.

In 2020, Laymon brought out a new version of *How to Slowly Kill Yourself and Others in America*, originally published in 2013 but bought back, along with his 2013 novel *Long Division*, from its first publisher at three times what Laymon had been paid for it, so the author might revise both books as the author, not his editor and press, desired, exiting a constraining relationship that Laymon writes he had wishfully first imagined as a nurturing friendship. In his 2020 reintroduction to *How to Slowly Kill Yourself*, Laymon alternatively writes of the "radical friendship" he found reading Black writers with whom he connected. "Toni Cade Bambara and Richard Wright were my super oldhead friends. [. . .] We spent tens of thousands of hours in each other's homes, wandering around each other's guts" (*HSKY*, xii). In his choice of his friends and influencers, his camaraderie with oldhead Wright shows. Like *Black Boy*, *Heavy* is not simply or primarily about Black family dysfunction but about first understanding the cultural backdrop of racism that produces damage and then learning to fight both cause and effect. Like Wright's memoir, Laymon's books are full of educational spaces that provide the wrong lessons for young Black men—as in the "Can You Use That Word in a Sentence" contest that opens Laymon's novel *Long Division* and goes wrong when the quiz words to be employed are first "chitterlings" and then "niggardly."[8] These classrooms teach the performance of race rather than achievement, the lessons of history, or self-respect.

Heavy reveals a cycle in which American racism produces colluding self-destructive behaviors spread from parent to child, in which living with racism leads individuals to become agents of their own self-harm. We may feel Wright's original title for *Black Boy*—*American Hunger*—in the story of Kiese's self-destructive overeating, initially portrayed as a direct response to what he diagnoses as his mother's pattern of enduring abusive relationships:

Malachi Hunter said he was sorry for punching you in your face, sorry for making you bleed, sorry for fighting your son, sorry for punishing you for wanting to know the truth. You told Malachi Hunter you wanted a daughter and you were sorry for running away.

> I went back to my room and heard your bedroom door unlock and lock again. [. . .] I walked in the kitchen, got the biggest spoon I could find, and dipped it halfway in the peanut butter. . . . I dipped the same spoon a quarter deep into Grandmama's pear preserves and put the whole spoon in my mouth. I did it again and again until the jar of peanut butter was gone. (*H*, 47)

Heavy is brutal in its outing connections between racism and in-league, symbiotic, self-damaging behaviors resulting in wild fluctuations between success, failure, success, failure, success.

Returning through Laymon's allusions to Wright's *Black Boy* to reread what we had read before, I revisit and begin to interrogate Wright's clearcut celebration of Richard's escape from his family and region. Reentering the classic, a reader may ask about Richard's degree of self-analysis—does his telling stop just short of the self-reflection that *Heavy* pitilessly risks? In *Heavy*, Laymon explicitly questions Wright's pattern of flight: "I understood why Wright left Jackson, left Mississippi, left the Deep South, and ultimately left the nation. [. . .] I wondered if the world would have ever read Wright had he not left Mississippi. [But also] I wondered if black children born in Mississippi after Wright would have laughed, or smiled more at his sentences if he imagined Mississippi as home" (*H*, 138). Here Laymon is asking about remaining in the southern family in order to possibly break its patterns, to attempt change, truth-telling, and healing, and so to improve Black love, self-love, all (American) love. And Laymon's allusions to Faulkner, Welty, and Wright (Mississippi literary relatives) are part and parcel of the family work he is undertaking in that location.

For Wright and Laymon each, a personal solution is found in the power of memoir. Like *Black Boy*, *Heavy* is a culturally significant account on two levels. It is a generalizable national story—as all great American autobiographies carry the quality of being the bildungsroman of both self and others. And like *Black Boy*, it is also the history of an eminent American writer (albeit creatively managed and productively fictionalized as great autobiographies are). Laymon's book is, to apply the title of Eudora Welty's memoir, the story of one writer's beginnings, in this case seemingly composed with confident (and correct) knowledge that, like *Black Boy*, the frank, free-spoken Mississippi chronicle of race and damage in the US will take the author's art and his reputation to international importance.

Jesmyn Ward and William Faulkner

Similarly, Jesmyn Ward—who won the 2011 National Book Award in Fiction for her second novel, *Salvage the Bones*, and then the 2017 Award for her third, *Sing, Unburied, Sing*—is a contemporary Mississippi writer of recognized international importance whose work is also in conversation with the writers of the twentieth-century Southern Renaissance. Her intriguing repurposing of William Faulkner's *As I Lay Dying*[9] in both of those acclaimed books has been thoroughly analyzed, notably in articles by Sinead Moynihan (on *Salvage*), John T. Matthews (on *Salvage*), and Greg Chase (on *Sing*).[10] By comparison, the use of Ward's reference to Eudora Welty in *Sing, Unburied, Sing* has received less attention previous to this volume.

Ward herself has commented on her relationship to Faulkner's *As I Lay Dying*, repeatedly describing the envy and admiration that book triggered: "I thought, oh God, I should just quit. There's something he's captured about the [S]outh that I can't even articulate. I recognised it in my bones"; "I was so awed I wanted to give up. I thought, 'He's done it, perfectly. Why the hell am *I* trying?'"[11] Although demonstrably an ardent fan, Ward continues with tempering reflections on Faulkner's handling of race: "But the failures of some of his black characters—the lack of imaginative vision regarding them, the way they don't display the full range of human emotion, how they fail to live fully on the page—work against that awe and goad me to write."[12] Nuancing her criticism in yet another interview, Ward protests Faulkner's mixed-race characters in *Absalom, Absalom!* (1936): "They aren't coming alive like the [white] characters; these characters feel flat to me."[13] These remarks set the backdrop for Ward's extensive uses of and allusions to Faulkner's texts (and also for her choices of what *not* to reuse).

In *Salvage*, for example, it is not only Ward who has read Faulkner but also Esch, Ward's fifteen-year-old Black narrator and central character, an adroit reader who "made an A" on an English assignment when she "answered the hardest question right: *Why does the young boy think his mother is a fish?*"[14] We can only guess at the right answer, but the reference to Vardaman Bundren first signals Ward's extended reworking of the earlier text. Matthews, summarizing discussions of Ward's interaction with Faulkner's novel, notes how "the characters of the Bundrens and Batistes line up suggestively: a recently lost mother mourned by a feckless father, children who include a practical-minded older brother, another who is a protector of a ferocious prized animal, a third an uncomprehending seven-year-old, and a pregnant teenage daughter" ("Heirs-at-Large," 39). And yet these correspondences are not neat—rather, the novel broadly sustains the profuse fusion of innumerable echoing elements. For instance, as Moynihan also points out, Skeetah, obsessed with his dog, resembles Jewel with his horse, and at the very same time is more like Darl, "the odd one" (*STB*, 33), "the one that folks say is queer" (*AILD*, 24). Likewise, drink-addicted Daddy Claude

Batiste parallels inept Anse Bundren, but when Daddy rallies to earnestly attempt to protect his family from Hurricane Katrina (the coming flood that echoes the high water in *As I Lay Dying*), his carpentry—accompanied by the refrain of "*Thwack, thwack, thwack*" (*STB*, 109)—instead recalls Cash Bundren and the chorus of "Chuck. Chuck. Chuck" that is the sound of his work on his mother's coffin (*AILD*, 5).

Moynihan explains—and this is a point critical to my extended argument about how these contemporary writers of our Mississippi moment are using allusion—that these echoes do not function, say, as in feminist fiction, where they might be written in opposition, to deconstruct a referent text, but rather that they constitute repurposing through acts of recycling and salvage linked here to the plot, themes, and title of Ward's novel.[15] The Batistes, surviving southern poverty, live in The Pit—a space filled with rusting appliances and vehicles from which they "salvage and reuse as much as possible, thus calling into question the status of that which Esch herself calls 'detritus.'" With this strategy, they persist in a culture that has thrown away Black bodies as easily as used-up equipment, a scenario witnessed nationally after Hurricane Katrina (565). Ward and the outlasting Batistes both have the habit of salvage. Moynihan maps the family work of scavenge and reclamation, especially at Mother Lizbeth's house (566). From it, the Batistes remove and repurpose "couch by chair by picture by dish until there was nothing left" (*STB*, 58). And then they repurpose the remaining shell itself—their salvation when forced to flee their own house as floodwaters rise.

Ward's allusive form fits her content. She is herself engaging in subversive salvage, and not only from Faulkner. Her narrating character Esch has read *As I Lay Dying*, but now the pregnant teen is reading Edith Hamilton's *Mythology* and, in particular, its chapter "The Quest of the Golden Fleece." Trying to understand her own relationship with her unreliable lover Manny, Esch is drawn to the counterpart story of Medea's ardent love of Jason, for whom Medea uses her powers—even killing her brother—before witnessing Jason's callous betrayal in choosing another to be his wife. Medea, we know, takes revenge, slaying her rival and then brutally murdering her own children to protect them from retribution. In her 2011 *Paris Review* interview, Ward glosses her recycling of this mythology. "Medea is in China," she observes, referring to Skeet's pit bull, a fierce warrior who kills one of her own puppies. Likewise, "Medea is in Hurricane Katrina because her power to unmake worlds, to manipulate the elements, closely aligns with the storm. And she's in Esch, too, because Esch understands ... Medea's tender heart, and responds to it."[16]

Moreover, *Salvage the Bones*' story of a Black child's pregnancy and uneasy preparation for motherhood doubles with the stories of Addie and Dewey Dell Bundren in *As I Lay Dying*, narratives of what Matthews intriguingly calls woman's "forced labor" (pun appreciated).[17] Ward's Esch in 2005, like Faulkner's women of the 1920s, lacks resources for the control of her body—even though it is still seventeen years before the US Supreme Court backpedaled to further limit women's right to abortion. Esch considers eating a pack of birth control pills that she couldn't afford in the first place or drinking bleach to induce a miscarriage. But her conclusion that "these are my options, and they narrow down to none" (*STB*, 103) helps us to revisit both Addie's anger when Anse rejects her gesture toward choice ("Nonsense . . . you and me aint nigh done chapping yet, with just two" [*AILD*, 173]) and Dewey Dell's resignation when pharmacists Moseley and MacGowan thwart her efforts to buy an abortifacient—with a lecture on morality from the former and her rape by the latter.

With these allusions as backdrop, further consider how Ward creates doubles by manipulating these salvaged and repurposed texts. Having myself written a book largely about Eudora Welty's uses of the double of the "other woman," I salvage some bones of my former analysis to highlight the method's characteristics.[18] Doubling is a technique often useful in signifying internal conflict and self-division. Doubles both appall and attract as they embody a central character's internal conflicts. The double typically expresses both apprehension about the meaning of the other and a desire for transformation of and difference in the self. The double becomes a lightning rod, drawing flashes of indirect and unforeseen self-revelation. The double can be both a model and a grotesque—that doubleness precisely expressing anxiety about choices. And "the power of the double lies in its ambiguity."[19]

What we see in *Salvage* is doubled doubling, simpler in the case of Esch's twinning with China and Medea than in the case of Ward's own doubling with Faulkner. In the explicit textual associations between China, who kills her puppy, and Medea, the double clearly embodies pregnant Esch's fear of what she might be / become / be thought to be, a doubling expressing areas of anxiety in the teen's readying for early motherhood, as she pictures ways of enacting the role. But more complicated and more interesting still is Ward's doubling of *Salvage the Bones* with *As I Lay Dying*. That doubling is an expression not of personal but of cultural anxieties that Ward is attending through her Yoknapatawpha-like creation of Bois Sauvage. If "Yoknapatawpha," derived from the Chickasaw words *yakni* and *patafa*, means "split land," Bois Sauvage—derived from the French—translates as "savage/wild wood."[20] Consider the implications of Ward's choice of this name for the fictional twin of her hometown—DeLisle, Mississippi—in the context of her project to counter

American misunderstandings of Blackness. Like Richard Wright, who so often plunged directly into American problematics, Ward dives into risk. Tellingly, when asked not about the name Bois Sauvage but about her book title, Ward obliquely turned her response, saying "*salvage* is phonetically close to *savage*. At home, among the young, there is honor in that term. [. . .] You survive. You are a savage."[21] Ward ends the Batistes' told story on the cusp of Katrina's aftermath—a future painfully and unforgettably known now in our national past. The entire family story thus becomes a reframing of Black and savage, in which savage is a valorized term, an asset for survival, indicating a determination to salvage.

In this twinning of books, consider *As I Lay Dying* as the double Ward will not write, the anxiety-producing other. Through doubling, Ward makes use even of what she chooses not to recycle. Recall Faulkner's *comic* wind-ups for the Bundrens' survival—narrative conclusions that drive Darl Bundren to uncontrollable laughter even as he is being institutionalized. *As I Lay Dying* differs from *Salvage the Bones* in closing each Bundren quest unambiguously. Recalling that "the power of the double lies in its ambiguity," consider that Ward's novel leaves the reader not with Faulkner's finalizing comic closures but with open uncertainties, themselves by and large shaped by the Faulkner doubling. Will Daddy Batiste, like Cash, be crippled by his wound of severed fingers (lost limbs that Skeeter laughingly but direly suggests might be salvaged as "free protein" for China [*STB*, 187])? Has the floodwater infected Claude's wound, and might he die as medical support fully deteriorates after the storm? Or will Mr. Claude be healed by Big Henry's mama, Ms. Bernadine, and, Anse-like, make her the new Mrs. Batiste? Will Skeetah (his real name Jason, as in the story of Medea) be unable to relinquish his obsession with the now-missing China, the dog who was a diversion from grief over the family's lost mother, but who evolved into a compulsion, imaginably a fixated proxy for the mother—a haunted doubling of Jewel's similar relationship with his horse? During the storm, Skeetah has only—but meaningfully—surrendered the animal from his impassioned grip in order to prioritize reaching for his sister as waters rise, as Jewel was forced to surrender his horse for Addie. But after the emergency, will Skeetah abandon all reason and proportion in his obsessive hunt for his lost dog and, like Darl, be considered insane? Or might he before long find that China has survived Katrina's floodwaters to mother another litter of puppies? Will Esch die in childbirth as her mother has? Or will she recognize Big Henry as the respectful, true, supportive, and satisfying lover that Manny could never be? Will her delivered child be lost as China's puppies are to sickness, to flood, to their mother's unpreparedness to nurture? Or will her offspring thrive as a result of their mother's teaching herself to be a savage warrior for survival? Will the family break apart under the strain of illness, poverty, and dependence on others, or will they unite and transcend Faulknerian Black endurance in a community bonding to savagely salvage lives?

The power of this contrast between doubles has turned us to retrieve and reconsider *As I Lay Dying*, a text that we thought we had fully read before. Ward's recycling from Faulkner's novel choosily salvages many useful struts of wood from that reclaimed henhouse, bringing them to Ward's newer place down the road to retrofit a second story of race and to renovate for the prospect of Black survival.

Ward and Eudora Welty

If the relationship between Ward and Faulkner has received excellent critical attention, the connections between Ward and Welty are still largely open for development. Yet one of the three epigraphs that open Jesmyn Ward's *Sing, Unburied, Sing* is an excerpt from Welty's memoir *One Writer's Beginnings* (1984): "The memory is a living thing—it too is in transit. But during its moment, all that is remembered joins, and lives—the old and the young, the past and the present, the living and the dead."[22] That passage and its notions, moreover, had previously lived and breathed in both Welty's *Losing Battles* (1970) and *The Optimist's Daughter* (1972), where the "alive and . . . dead" are "all part of it together."[23] These are familiar words that Welty and Ward *both* are salvaging and recycling, as their meanings accrue.

Ward uses the allusion to prepare us to meet her ghosts: her 2017 novel's young "living dead" victims of racism haunting the present from their undead past. Thus, she puts the zombification of young people who died violently in conversation with Welty's recurrent notion of confluence in memory. In situ, Welty's meaning can seem quite different than Ward's—her uses of memory, even when filled with hurt as in *The Optimist's Daughter*, strive to join the living and the dead against loss. In Ward, traumatized memory reveals inexorable haunting loss, loss walking with the living. Ward uses Welty's passage alongside two other epigraphs, one a West African chant about the disappearance of Equiano, an African boy:

> Who are we looking for . . . ?
>> It's Equiano we're looking for.
>> Has he gone to the stream? Let him come back.
>> Has he gone to the farm? Let him return.
>> It's Equiano we're looking for. (*SUS*, n.p.)

The mourning chant's theme of the boy lost to the farm, whom we want to return, attaches to the novel's ghost, Richie. And the farm that twelve-year-old Richie has gone to and been lost at is Parchman Farm, the brutal plantation-style penitentiary, filled with young Black men arrested for minor offenses, sentenced to serve hard time providing "free" labor at the twenty-eight-square-mile Delta work camp that echoes slavery. David M. Oshinsky's 1996 study of the prison complex—a book Ward acknowledges that she drew on[24]—is in truth titled *Worse than Slavery: Parchman Farm and the Ordeal of Jim Crow Justice*. There, convicts picked cotton under the watch of the prison's most violent offenders, now gun-armed "trusty-shooters," whose convictions for brutal offenses served as recommending qualifications for their role in institutional oversight.[25]

The novel's characters Pap, Stag, Richie, Bishop, and Michael have at points all been incarcerated at the prison farm. White Michael, in for drug use, says, "This ain't no place for no man. Black or White. Don't make no difference. This a place for the dead" (*SUS*, 96). Understood, but the reasons for Black imprisonment are different than for white. Twelve-year-old Richie is sentenced to three years for stealing food. And fifteen-year-old River (now Pap) is imprisoned for having been in the same room when his brother is arrested.

And verdicts are so different. White Michael's angry racist cousin, who deliberately shoots and kills Pap's seventeen-year-old son Given, another of the novel's ghosts, on a hunting trip and calls it an accident, is sentenced to a mere five years, and worse, serves only three. To be clear, Black Richie, stealing food, is sentenced to serve the same time that Michael's white cousin serves for his murder of a Black boy. Michael himself is discharged after two years and three months (incidentally the exact term served by the white man who, driving under the influence, killed Ward's brother, a story told in *Men We Reaped*). Also, by contrast, the likelihood of going home relatively intact is scant for what Patricia Yaeger might recognize as "throwaway" Black inmates.[26] Black lives, treated as disposable, are routinely used up by Parchman. Richie dies in the penal complex. But undead, his ghost echoes Welty's words, not her meaning, when he thinks that "Parchman was past, present, and future all at once," a confluence showing "time [to be] a vast ocean" where he "was trapped" (*SUS*, 186).

Richie's transformation of Welty's words again returned me to reconsider what I've read before: Welty's own use in *Losing Battles* not only of memory joining the living and the dead but of Parchman Farm itself—in a comic performance where timbre is as murky as in Coen brothers films, tonally ambiguous noir comedies that typically show some affection for the best values of a region but also let loose, confess, and inspect appallingly vicious acts and the cultural presumptions behind them—including, as here, presumptions about race.

In *Losing Battles*, Jack returns from Parchman to his family in the Mississippi hill country to describe the ploughing he did at the penitentiary, in a nod to the place's brutality. Just as Pap does for Jojo, Jack describes the prison as a landscape without end. But Welty allows Jack successfully and comically to escape Parchman—by riding a trusty's horse off the farm. When Aunt Birdie speculates, "Did you scoot right quick through the fence?" Jack replies:

> "Parchman is too big to fence. There's just no end to it, that's all. [. . .] I come out on Dexter. [. . .] There's a overseer that rides him every day but Sunday. The kind of horse Dexter is, he's almost an overseer himself. He took me overseeing all over those acres, and finally he conducted me out onto a little road that meant business." (*LB*, 196)

When juxtaposed to the failed and lethal escape of the brutally beaten child Richie, Welty's comic uses of Parchman compare to Faulkner's portraits of that same prison in *The Wild Palms* and *The Mansion*, portraits that satirize the law. Similarly, in *Losing Battles*, the law as represented by local marshal Curly Stovall and by justice of the peace Homer Champion is shady. We even wonder about decent Judge Moody. At great length, Moody precisely weighs the legal nuances of whether Jack should be prosecuted for possibly marrying his cousin. But disturbingly, the judge says absolutely nothing about Nathan Beecham's unexpected but explicit confession to letting a Black mill worker hang for his, Nathan's own, felony murder of Herman Dearman, the ruthless entrepreneur who rose to power—like a Sutpen or a Snopes—by violating land and persons.

Satire is of course a powerful weapon against injustice, but re-entering *Losing Battles* directly from *Sing, Unburied, Sing* helps me see Welty's novel as considerably more about whiteness than generally recognized.[27] White Jack can escape Parchman, echoing Oshinsky's story of white Russell Montgomery, "the rodeo cowboy who escaped Parchman on a prison horse" quite like Jack.[28] But Black Richie cannot escape. Oshinsky describes Montgomery as among those white convicts—like "Hogjaw" Grammar and Kinnie Wagner, who both become characters in Ward's novel—legendary for their resistance of the "prison environment geared to the discipline and punishment of Negroes."[29] The implication of these legends is that white resisters became fabled heroes while Black resisters were considered doomed threats to society.

It is Jack's Uncle Nathan Beecham, of course, who has centrally benefited from community assumptions that culprits are Black and that Black lives do not matter. Rereading what we've read before, I also now see that the conviction of a Black surrogate, possibly by law but unmistakably by lynching, is carefully prepared for by Welty throughout her novel—in the family's uses of the N-word and more.[30] One instance of this foreshadowing specifically concerns the prison farm. In their ignorance, the family astoundingly describes Parchman as a paradise. Speaking of Jack's internment there, they say,

> "Jack's in the Delta. . . . Clear out of the hills and into the good land."
> They smiled. "That Jack!"
> "Where it's running with riches and swarming with n[-----]s everywhere you look." (*LB*, 70)

In these lines, Welty's white Mississippi hill farmers grieve their own land that "wouldn't hardly give a weed comfort and sustenance" but picture Parchman's free Black labor as profitably "swarming"—both to produce wealth and, in their white racist view, like vermin. White acceptance of racism is detectible even in the novel's most open-minded characters. Sensitive and intelligent young Vaughn, often celebrated as the promise of change in the family's future, thinks of Nathan as "one who had killed a man" (*LB*, 365). It is unfortunately utterly predictable that a child in this family, even an aware and growing one, acknowledges only that his uncle has killed one man, and not two.

Overall, Ward uses her Welty epigraph to highlight the false boundary between the past and present in the American story of race. And Welty's own repetition in *One Writer's Beginnings* of memory as "living" and "joining" used in *Losing Battles* combines with Ward's corrective rewriting of the Welty novel's story of Parchman Farm to show meanings accruing between writers. The conversation uncovers Welty's discernable attempts to address the story of the Mississippi color line in her own tale of whiteness and race, *Losing Battles*. Permit me now to turn one more page to discuss the work of Natasha Trethewey, who, like Laymon and Ward, is remarkable for narrating untold histories of race in America.

Natasha Trethewey and William Faulkner

In interviews, Natasha Trethewey frequently explicates her work by referring to one very familiar Faulkner quotation. Speaking to David Haney in 2003, for example, she comments:

> Isn't it William Faulkner who says, the past isn't dead, it's not even in the past, it's not even past? And that's what I think, that it constantly lives all around us.

> My project has been and continues to be to try to find a way to restore lost narratives to our collective and public memory. . . . I'm bringing that past to bear on this moment.³¹

Speaking to Christian Teresi in 2009, in a remark that also reverberates with Ward's *Sing*, she observes: "As Faulkner says, 'The past isn't dead, it isn't even past.' It's always here. The dead are always here with us" (*CNT*, 116).

The past that Faulkner and all the other writers in this conversation refer to is also a place: Mississippi. And Trethewey traces the history of that locale in her own present—she tells the story of the trauma that is Mississippi as felt in her relationship to her own mixed-race body. In her poetry's chronicle of Mississippi—its erasures, its violations, its atrocities—the political is personal as she writes about this state "that made a crime / of me," having made her interracial existence an illegality.³² In her essay "Why I Write" (a title transforming Welty's "How I Write"), she states:

> I have inherited from this geography both great cultural richness and great suffering. [. . .] I am tethered to a place whose Jim Crow laws rendered my family, my people, second-class citizens, whose laws against miscegenation rendered my parents' marriage illegal, my birth illegitimate not only in the customs but also in the constitution of the state. Thus, I write to claim my native land even as it has forsaken me, rendered me an outsider. I write so as not to be a foreigner in my homeland. I write from a place of psychological exile. I take up the burden of history. I am guided by King's words: "No lie can live forever."³³

In this context, Trethewey's connections and allusions to the work of Faulkner and Welty—whom she assertively claims as literary ancestors—are different. In her references to Faulkner, as she puts it in an interview with the late Jake Adam York, Trethewey is sometimes "stamping her foot," though the total relationship (as she says of the Fugitive poets) "is not antithetical at all" (*CNT*, 19–20).³⁴ Meanwhile, her references to Welty are, by comparison, more collaborative. As in the case of Jesmyn Ward, there is currently a substantial commentary on Trethewey's direct uses of Faulkner in her poems "Pastoral" and "Miscegenation," but less on her uses of Welty's work.³⁵

Her Faulkner poems appear in *Native Guard* (2006), a volume in which she builds two monuments. One is for the supervising squadron of Black Civil War soldiers—former slaves—who guarded captive Confederate soldiers on Ship Island, off the Mississippi coast, but were unmentioned and erased in the tourist park's commemorations. And the second is for

Gwendolyn Ann Turnbough, Trethewey's murdered mother, a memorial the poet continues to construct in her 2018 volume, *Monument: Poems New and Selected*, and in her 2020 memoir, *Memorial Drive*, both of which make visible the effects of racism on and in her mother's two marriages and the narrative surrounding the tragedy of her death.[36] The two poems in *Native Guard* alluding to Faulkner, "Pastoral" and "Miscegenation," belong to the collection's third (and final) section, which Trethewey has also referred to as "testament" (while describing the volume's first section as "document" and its second section as "monument").[37] Here she is speaking back to Mississippi history as she proclaims her place in its artistic canon.

In "Pastoral," the poet, in a wry dream, poses for a picture with a group of twentieth-century southern poets: the white male Fugitive/Agrarian group. Appropriate to their aversion to the modern, they stand in front of a photographer's scrim that obscures the actual landscape behind them—Atlanta's skyline and unseen bulldozers that nevertheless can be heard—with the bucolic illusion of "soft-eyed cows / lowing" in a pasture.[38] The poet-persona is there, asserting her presence, but the episode is not about her belonging. The group's photographer croons: "*Say 'race.*'" The poet finds herself "in / blackface" when the flash freezes them. In comic self-defense, she blurts out that her father is "*white ... and rural,*" as if to offer appropriate membership criteria. The poem finishes by re-engineering the line with which William Faulkner's Quentin Compson closes *Absalom, Absalom!*, his ambiguous assertion now turned into an uncertain question: "*You don't hate the South? they ask. You don't hate it?*"

In *The Sound and the Fury*, Quentin Compson commits suicide due to the weight of his southern burden—he is young enough and late enough in history that he might be expected to reject his problematic inheritance, but he finds instead that he is fully shaped by faulty southern precepts and caught in their contradictions between the ideal and the real, purity and pollution, honor and accommodation. In *Absalom, Absalom!*, his situation is restated: "Quentin Compson who was still too young to deserve yet to be a ghost but nevertheless having to be one for all that, since he was born and bred in the deep South."[39] His concluding proclamation—that he does not hate the South—is suspect. In "Pastoral," however, his unconvincing assertion becomes an ambivalent question for the mixed-race poet's persona, a woman who lives a different southern point of view. The reinscription conveys the uncomfortable but accepted challenge of interjecting oneself as a woman poet of color into the canon comfortably represented by Robert Penn Warren, Allen Tate, and William Faulkner, writers specifically called up by the poem.

In her 2007 interview with Pearl McHaney, Trethewey explicates the poem, saying, "I am very much asking, after Eric Foner's *Who Owns*

History?, 'Who owns southern history or southern poetry?'" (*CNT*, 60). Asked by Daniel Cross Turner in 2010 about "the nature of 'Southernness'" in her poetry, Trethewey is—as in "Pastoral"—perhaps smiling as she stamps her foot to say:

> I am the quintessential Southern writer! Quintessentially American too! Geography is fate. Of all the kinds of fate swirling around my very being, this place in which I was born and this particular historical moment matter deeply. The story of America has always been a story of miscegenation, of border crossings, of integration of cultures, and again, I embody this in my person. To me, I fit in as the quintessential Southerner. Perhaps even now my role is to establish what has always been Southern, though at other points in history it has been excluded from "Southernness." (*CNT*, 165-66)

Trethewey directly follows "Pastoral" with "Miscegenation," also haunted by Faulkner. It begins with a fact: "In 1965 my parents broke two laws of Mississippi."[40] That is, Trethewey's parents left the state where—one Black, one white—they could not wed, then returned to Mississippi married, first transgressing the state's Jim Crow miscegenation law and then, near Easter in 1966, infringing it again with the birth of their mixed-race daughter. The poem turns on a contrast between the poet's persona and Faulkner's Joe Christmas in *Light in August* (1932). The contrast develops around the topic of naming but obliquely around the behavior of name-calling. Trethewey writes, "Faulkner's Joe Christmas was born in winter, like Jesus, given his name / for the day he was left at the orphanage, his race unknown in Mississippi." And before the poem is over, the poet-persona, comparing and contrasting her mixed-race self to Joe, speaks her own name and identity: "I know more than Joe Christmas did. Natasha is a Russian name— / though I'm not; it means *Christmas child*, even in Mississippi."

In *Light in August*, Joe Christmas is the orphan of unknown origins who, with skin the color of parchment, is fit to be written on; as readers, we arguably will never know if he is racially mixed. And it does not matter. The novel shows us that race is socially constructed, not related to levels of melanin in the skin. Philip M. Weinstein writes of Joe Christmas, names, and name-calling in this way:

> [Y]ou are who you are by virtue of how you have been called. [...] We are called long before we ever answer—called as infants before we can even talk—and our answer to these calls is our reflexive way of knowing who we are. [...] Joe Christmas becomes (and it takes all of *Light in August* to tell this story) a "little n----r bastard." It is stared and punished into him. [...] [Faulkner] shows us ... how many damage-dealing others it takes ... [to] turn Joe Christmas into [that].[41]

It is the understanding of identity, naming, and name-calling that is the something "more" the poet-persona knows that distinguishes her from Christmas. She not only knows who her parents are and that she is mixed race, but also what she tells just a few pages further on, in "Southern Gothic." There, she considers "words that take shape / outside us" and comprehends the effects of schoolyard words of violation: "*peckerwood* and *n----r* / *lover, half-breed* and *zebra*," the kinds of racial slurs that have damaged and determined the child Joe Christmas.[42] Trethewey conveys the destructive power of how we are called, when calling is both an act of violence and our means of knowing who we are. Natasha "know[s] more than Joe Christmas did"—she knows she is not "the same," though similarity is evoked in the poem—because, understanding naming, she is prepared to transform damage-dealing histories and words by reinscribing them.

Trethewey assertively claims herself "the quintessential Southern writer" exactly because and not in spite of her mixed-race body having broken the culture's marginalizing Jim Crow rules, and just because she as person and writer bridges the culture's policed divisions and exclusions. In this way, she refuses the "damage-dealing" alienation name-called into her as a child and insists on her family tie to the canon of white southern literary tradition. Hence, she finds words central to the work of William Faulkner pivotal in her own, again causing us to reread, reframe, and recycle what we thought we had fully read before.

Natasha Trethewey and Eudora Welty

Natasha Trethewey in 2019 and 2020 produced forewords for two reissued Welty works. Reintroducing Eudora Welty's *One Writer's Beginnings*, Trethewey describes the worn, heavily annotated copy on her desk. While she swaps out other books as she moves from project to project, Welty's memoir remains, and it is "heavily annotated: passages underlined, once, twice, in different colored ink—one for each successive reading—or highlighted in yellow, dotted with stars or exclamation points in the margins that bear, on many pages, a record of my thoughts on a given day, my responses to Welty's words."[43] Trethewey's commentary, like mine in this essay, is about reading and rereading, meeting your own "former self—the reader you were at another time," and about intimacy with another—across difference and through reading. Welty, Trethewey writes, "shares her experience while reminding us of how similar we are despite how vastly different the particularities of our experience may be" (*I*, x). Their intimacy is "a convergence of two women, two Mississippians—one white, one black—born more than half a century apart.

It is that convergence, what Welty would call confluence, that each of us enacts when reading this slender and lovely narrative. Our separate journeys converging" (*I*, xi).

Confluence noted, and with the work of a poet whose project crucially doubles poetry and memoir. Like Wright and Laymon, Trethewey repeatedly realizes the power of memoir to report the ordeal of being a child within the American story of race. That she uses Welty's construction of her beginnings as an artist as inspiration seems a radical act as well, in keeping with her "stamping [her] foot" to assert southern literary family belonging.

This radical confluence is also felt in Trethewey's introductory reframing of the University Press of Mississippi's 2019 update of Welty's 1989 volume *Photographs*. The new preface even more profoundly informs the connections between the two artists, as Trethewey establishes Welty's photography's influence on her life as an *ekphrastic* poet. There, Trethewey tells us that during her first year of graduate school, she received a gift copy of *Photographs* that was, for her, "transformative."[44] The student had been planning poems about her maternal grandmother—"a black woman born in Gulfport, Mississippi, in 1916." She doesn't say, but we know, that the project would lead to *Domestic Work*, the collection that in 1999 won the Black poetry foundation Cave Canem's prize for a first book. Trethewey tells us that, having been born in 1966 "on the heels of . . . the Civil Rights and Voting Rights Acts," she was exerting herself to imagine her grandmother's Jim Crow world. She writes, "[T]he Mississippi I was trying to document," the Mississippi that "my grandmother had grown up in, the world Welty had photographed," had been "straining the limits of my vision." Welty's photos let Trethewey see "the street scenes, the candid expressions and subtle interactions, the intimacies and ordinariness, the details on a dress or apron . . . sewn from cotton cornmeal sacks" (*TJWW*, x). She recounts having found in the snapshots "the truth" of Welty's imagination, "but also . . . a record of what [Welty] had *seen*" (*TJWW*, ix). The photos captured, as Welty herself said, "the life in those times" and became the lens Trethewey had needed. This "documentary evidence" (*TJWW*, ix) allowed her to know an earlier time and place: "I began writing poems with those images in mind, each one a starting place to anchor visually what I'd heard in the cadences of my grandmother's voice" (*TJWW*, xi).

This vicarious *photographic* experience of a past not her own most importantly began Trethewey's habit of writing *ekphrasis*, the technical term for poetic responses to productions in other, often visual, artistic media. Learning from her early encounter with Welty's photographs, images she entered and imaginatively narrated, Trethewey has gone on repeatedly to write poems, in *Domestic Work, Bellocq's Ophelia, Thrall*, and *Monument*—really, in all her work— that over and again read graphic images to connect the past and the present. It is a signature ekphrastic approach that informs the body of her work. Recently, I was able to ask Trethewey if this early encounter with Welty's photography was indeed the trigger for all that would follow, and she answered:

> It absolutely was. [. . .] When my stepmother gave me that copy of Welty's *Photographs* and said, "why don't you write about some things here" . . . I think she knew that I would find something of my own vanished past in those photographs, that I would find a visual articulation of my grandmother's stories about her life growing up in Jim Crow Mississippi.
>
> And so, beginning [then] to write about Eudora Welty's *Photographs*, one of the first . . . I wrote about, and there's no existing poem now about this . . . there's a [Welty photo of a] woman with a folded newspaper over her head because of the rain, she's . . . keeping her hair from the rain. [. . .] I allowed the photograph to be a window to a memory I had about getting my hair hot-combed as a child, a ritual my cousins would do. [. . .] I didn't [need a hot-comb] but I wanted to be part of the community, so I would get my hair hot-combed too. Welty's photographs . . . showed me . . . how my thinking always worked very visually the way that you know some people remember or . . . are moved more by smell or sound. [. . .] So, when I started writing poems, if I could make a photograph . . . in my head, in my mind's eye, then I knew I could write the poem. [. . .] I started reading Welty's photographs, and then paintings in the same way, for not only the literal things that are going on, but also for the figurative possibilities in the gestures of the people and the objects that you see in juxtaposition.[45]

In her earliest volume, *Domestic Work*, I recognize the presence of Welty's 1930s photos, showing Black women in both disheartening labor and vibrant lives. In the poems of that collection, we don't see one-to-one matching of particular Welty photos to poems so much as a correspondence to the collection of images Welty first published in *One Time, One Place* and organized there by the divisions (sections) *Workday, Saturday,* and *Sunday*. That conceptual structure becomes the narrative itself in Trethewey's title poem, "Domestic Work, 1937." Its speaker tells us of a woman who has all week cleaned others' houses:

> But Sunday mornings are hers—
> church clothes starched
> and hanging, a record spinning
> on the console, the whole house
> dancing.[46]

In Trethewey's new preface to *Photographs*, she interprets one Welty image in particular, causing us to reread what we thought we had read before. It is the book's new cover image: a street scene, picturing "a young woman ... poised on a curb, as if about to step off and cross the street" (*TJWW*, x). Trethewey reads her as "on the verge of something ... a woman with places to go." She notes, "[h]er hair is perfectly waved beneath her proper hat, and she stands ... to display a smart day coat ... a clutch bag under her arm," her hands clad in black leather gloves. Trethewey first calls this Black woman "a picture of elegant nonchalance." But then she writes that the look on the woman's face is something else: "What? Wariness? Awareness ... ?" The image, she says, catches "the ambiguity, the woman's inner complexity." And yet, in it, Trethewey sees her young grandmother, "in charge" and equal to her reality.

Her older grandmother, the one she grew up with, self-employed and "making draperies in the front workroom of her house," Trethewey suggests was a strong independent heroine very much like the woman posing in Welty's photographs of Ida M'Toy, midwife and businesswoman, "standing on her porch" and displaying "quiet pride," with the hint of an "enigmatic smile teasing the corners of her mouth" and "wisdom ... etched lightly on her smooth face" (*TJWW*, x). Trethewey's reframing of Welty's photography highlights its record of Black experience. And as I have written elsewhere, Welty's photos of Black women captured stages of social mobility, bringing attention to social change even in the midst of segregation and economic depression.[47] These are portraits that stand in contrast to other images of Welty's time that spoke the more standard grammar of racial representation, associating Black subjects with rough shacks and dire poverty rather than beauty, pride, and self-creation, as Welty's photos do.

• • •

Returning to the question of why we place writers together in comparative study, the now apparent further answer is that writers often open these conversations themselves through allusion. We have seen that Kiese Laymon, Jesmyn Ward, and Natasha Trethewey are defining a new period in southern literary history by entering, altering, and bringing readers into a conversation begun by William Faulkner, Eudora Welty, and Richard Wright, one that attends the narrative of growing up in the US, land of the color line. Laymon in *Heavy* appreciates Welty's comic mockery of the obsessions and insecurities of whiteness before he chooses Wright as his "oldhead" ancestor over Faulkner. His allusions to the twentieth-century Mississippi literary trio are part and parcel of the family work that his chronicle undertakes to break entrenched racial patterns and create change without abandoning home. In *Salvage the Bones*, Ward's allusions cause readers to retrieve and reconsider *As I Lay Dying* as she salvages and recycles what she loves in Faulkner's work while retrofitting the southern house of fiction for a better understanding of Black character, experience, and survival. In *Sing, Unburied, Sing*, Ward uses Welty's echoing words on memory as a "living thing" joining "the living and the dead" to highlight the false boundary between the past and present in the American narrative of race and also to frame her extension of *Losing Battles*' story of Parchman Farm, now elucidated and exposed by a Black perspective. In interviews and poetry, Trethewey emphatically proclaims herself "the quintessential Southern writer," refusing the "damage-dealing" alienation that earlier constructions of (white) southern literary tradition implied. Hence, she finds words central to the work of Faulkner pivotal in her own, again causing us to reread, reframe, and recycle what we thought we had fully read before. While "stamping her foot" at the Agrarians and Faulkner, she describes collaborating with Welty to locate and develop her signature ekphrastic poetic technique. And the interactions among these six Mississippi writers clearly define as well as revise comprehension of the child who must decipher our nation's cultural landscape.

NOTES

1. See Leigh Ann Duck, *The Nation's Region: Southern Modernism, Segregation, and U.S. Nationalism* (Athens: University of Georgia Press, 2006) and Imani Perry, *South to America: A Journey below the Mason-Dixon to Understand the Soul of a Nation* (New York: Ecco, 2022).

2. Harriet Pollack, "On Welty's Use of Allusion: Expectations and Their Revision in 'The Wide Net,' *The Robber Bridegroom*, and 'At the Landing,'" *Southern Quarterly* 29, no. 1 (Fall 1990): 5–33. Reprinted in *Eudora Welty*, ed. Harold Bloom (New York: Chelsea House, 2004), 113–40.

3. Neely Tucker, "John Grisham's New Novel Wades into Mississippi's Racist Past," *Chicago Tribune*, October 19, 2018, https://www.chicagotribune.com/entertainment/books/ct-booksthe-reckoning-john-grisham-review-20181018-story.html.

4. Kiese Laymon, *How to Slowly Kill Yourself and Others in America: Essays* (New York: Scribner, 2020), 59. Hereafter cited parenthetically as *HSKY*.

5. Kiese Laymon, *Heavy: An American Memoir* (New York: Scribner, 2020), 70–71. Hereafter cited parenthetically as *H*.

6. Eudora Welty, *The Collected Stories* (New York: Houghton Mifflin, 1980), 56. Hereafter cited parenthetically as *CS*.

7. Richard Wright, *Black Boy: A Record of Childhood and Youth* (New York: Harper, 1945), 9. Hereafter cited parenthetically as *BB*.

8. Kiese Laymon, *Long Division* (New York: Scribner, 2021), 26, 34.

9. William Faulkner, *As I Lay Dying* (New York: Vintage International, 2011). Hereafter cited parenthetically as *AILD*.

10. Sinead Moynihan, "From Disposability to Recycling: William Faulkner and the New Politics of Rewriting in Jesmyn Ward's *Salvage the Bones*," *Studies in the Novel* 47, no. 4 (Winter 2015): 550–67; John T. Mathews, "Heirs-at-Large: Precarity and Salvage in the Post-Plantation Souths of Faulkner and Jesmyn Ward," *Faulkner Journal* 32, no. 1 (Spring 2018): 33–50; Greg Chase, "Of Trips Taken and Time Served: How Ward's *Sing, Unburied, Sing* Grapples with Faulkner's Ghosts," *African American Review* 53, no. 3 (Fall 2020): 201–16. All cited parenthetically hereafter.

11. Emma Brockes, "Jesmyn Ward: 'I Wanted to Write about the People of the South,'" *Guardian*, December 1, 2011, https://www.theguardian.com/books/2011/dec/01/jesmyn-ward-national-book-award; Elizabeth Hoover, "Jesmyn Ward on *Salvage the Bones*," *Paris Review*, August 30, 2011, https://www.theparisreview.org/blog/2011/08/30/jesmyn-ward-on-salvage-the-bones/.

12. Hoover, "Jesmyn Ward on *Salvage the Bones*."

13. Brockes, "Jesmyn Ward: 'I Wanted to Write about the People of the South.'"

14. Jesmyn Ward, *Salvage the Bones* (New York: Bloomsbury, 2011), 7.

15. Moynihan, "From Disposability to Recycling," 552.

16. Hoover, "Jesmyn Ward on *Salvage the Bones*."

17. John T. Matthews, "*As I Lay Dying* in the Machine Age," *boundary 2* 19, no. 1 (1992): 80.

18. See Harriet Pollack, *Eudora Welty's Fiction and Photography: The Body of the Other Woman* (Athens: University of Georgia Press, 2016), 8.

19. Milica Živković, "The Double as the 'Unseen' of Culture: Toward a Definition of Doppelganger," *Facta Universitatis: Linguistics and Literature* 2, no. 7 (2000): 121.

20. See "A Chickasaw Dictionary," Chickasaw Nation (2020), https://www.achickasawdictionary.com/. Many sources incorrectly render the terms as *yocona* and *petopha*, perhaps because their spelling more closely suggests Faulkner's own: see for instance "Yoknapatawpha County," Wikipedia, https://en.wikipedia.org/wiki/Yoknapatawpha_County.

21. Hoover, "Jesmyn Ward on *Salvage the Bones*."

22. Jesmyn Ward, *Sing, Unburied, Sing* (New York: Scribner, 2017), n.p. Hereafter cited parenthetically as *SUS*.

23. Eudora Welty, *Losing Battles* (1970; repr., Vintage International, 1990), 345. Hereafter cited parenthetically as *LB*.

24. In her interview on NPR's *All Things Considered*, Ward states, "I was doing research about Parchman prison in order to write about it. [. . .] And I was reading a book called *Worse than Slavery*" by David Oshinsky" (https://www.npr.org/2017/11/28/566933935/for-jesmyn-ward-writing-means-telling-the-truth-about-the-place-that-i-live-in).

25. David M. Oshinsky, *Worse than Slavery: Parchman Farm and the Ordeal of Jim Crow Justice* (New York: Free Press, 1996), 125, 131.

26. On the concept of the throwaway body, see Patricia Yaeger, *Dirt and Desire: Reconstructing Southern Women's Writing, 1930–1990* (Chicago: University of Chicago Press, 2000), 61–87.

27. For the earliest and still groundbreaking discussion of race in the novel, see Rebecca Mark, "A 'Cross-mark Ploughed into the Center,'" in *Eudora Welty and Politics: Did the Writer Crusade?*, ed. Harriet Pollack and Suzanne Marrs (Baton Rouge: Louisiana State University Press, 2001), 123–54.

28. Oshinsky, *Worse than Slavery*, 146. Welty must have known the story too.

29. Oshinsky, *Worse than Slavery*, 146.

30. Here I am making the point that I have developed at greater length in "When a Mystery Leads to Murder: Genre Bending, 'Homme Fatals,' Thickening Mystery, and the Covert Investigation of Whiteness in Eudora Welty's *Losing Battles*," in *Eudora Welty and Mystery: Hidden in Plain Sight*, ed. Jacob Agner and Harriet Pollack (Jackson: University Press of Mississippi, 2022), 146–77.

31. Joan Wylie Hall, ed., *Conversations with Natasha Trethewey* (Jackson: University Press of Mississippi, 2013), 20. Hereafter cited parenthetically as *CNT*.

32. Natasha Trethewey, "South," *Native Guard* (New York: Houghton Mifflin, 2006), 46.

33. Natasha Trethewey, "Why I Write," *South Central Review* 31, no. 1 (Spring 2014): 6.

34. Trethewey continues, "I don't see my work as antithetical to a tradition of Southern poetry, but very much a synthesis because those spaces are there. It's not like I'm creating them, I'm fitting something in. The spaces are there for what we will re-remember" (*CNT*, 29–30).

35. See in particular Georgia De Cenzo, "The Native Guard of Southern History," *South Atlantic Review* 73, no. 1 (Winter 2008): 20–49; and Malin Pereira, "Re-reading Trethewey through Mixed Race Studies," *Southern Quarterly* 50, no. 4 (Summer 2013): 123–52.

36. In *Monument*, Trethewey collected her poetry to date. In shaping the compilation, however, the poet revised the narrative arc of her previous volumes, forwarding her memorial to her mother, Gwendolyn Ann Turnbough. To *Native Guard*, however, she made no change, no restructuring, and no abridgement in the later volume, perhaps suggesting that book's centrality to her understanding of her work. About the project of memorializing her mother, she has said that when she wrote the early poem "Graveyard Blues" and described the "hard, or cold comfort" of laying her head down on her mother's tombstone, she felt she needed to write more "to undo the lie that I told. . . . My mother does not have a stone or any marker at all. [. . .] So I started writing the poem 'Monument.' [. . .] It was the realization that I needed to fix the lie that made me realize exactly why those elegies to my mother should be in the same book with the Native Guards" (*CNT*, 48).

37. Charles Henry Rowell, "Inscriptive Restorations: An Interview with Natasha Trethewey," *Callaloo* 27, no. 4 (Autumn 2004): 1030.

38. Natasha Trethewey, "Pastoral," *Native Guard* (New York: Houghton Mifflin, 2006), 35.

39. William Faulkner, *Absalom, Absalom!*, rev. ed. (1936; repr., New York: Vintage International, 1990), 4.

40. Natasha Trethewey, "Miscegenation," *Native Guard* (New York: Houghton Mifflin, 2006), 36.

41. Philip M. Weinstein, *What Else but Love: The Ordeal of Race in Faulkner and Morrison* (New York: Columbia University Press, 1996), 170.

42. Natasha Trethewey, "Southern Gothic," *Native Guard* (New York: Houghton Mifflin, 2006), 40.

43. Natasha Trethewey, introduction to *One Writer's Beginnings*, by Eudora Welty (New York: Scribner, 2021), ix. Henceforth cited parenthetically as *I*.

44. Natasha Trethewey, "That's Just the Way It Was," in *Photographs*, by Eudora Welty, rev. ed. (1989; repr., Jackson: University Press of Mississippi, 2019), ix. Henceforth cited parenthetically as *TJWW*.

45. Trethewey answered my question during a "Welty-At-Home" Book Club meeting on August 26, 2021. The Zoom session is now on YouTube at https://www.youtube.com/watch?v=atF8MN1Ah2I.

46. Natasha Trethewey, "Domestic Work," *Domestic Work* (Saint Paul, MN: Graywolf, 2000), 13.

47. Pollack, *Eudora Welty's Fiction and Photography*, 95.

Life in the Permanent War

Faulkner, Welty, and Wright and the Nuclear Arms Race

RYOICHI YAMANE

The Nagano Seminar in August 1955 included an enigmatic historical testimony to US-Japan cultural diplomacy in the early Cold War era. Masayoshi Higashiyama was a faculty member at Kwansei Gakuin University in Hyogo, Japan, and one of the Japanese scholars who attended William Faulkner's lecture during the seminar. After the event, some of the Japanese participants left farewell notes for the novelist on a *kakejiku*, a hanging scroll typically used for the exhibition of Japanese calligraphy and paintings. What Higashiyama wrote there is unusual: while most left casual, heartfelt messages expressing their gratitude to the novelist who played a role as a cultural ambassador, he merely wrote, "$E = mc^2$."[1] Higashiyama thus referenced the formula by Albert Einstein, who had issued the Russell-Einstein manifesto, a call for global nuclear disarmament, with philosopher Bertrand Russell in July of the same year.

For reasons known only to him, Higashiyama wrote the formula with no further comment. If it were not a mere imitation of the kitschy, popularized image of the formula occasionally accompanied by that of a mushroom cloud found in the artistic and political realms of US Atomic Age culture,[2] he might have been attempting to express his own opinion about the postwar US-Japan political relationship. In any case, Higashiyama stopped short of referring to the traumatic issues surrounding the Japanese participants in the seminar: atomic bombs had been dropped on Hiroshima and Nagasaki a decade previously, and the incident of *Lucky Dragon No. 5*, a Japanese tuna fishing boat exposed to the deadly radiation caused by the US thermonuclear weapon test at Bikini Atoll, had occurred in March 1954. While the "Atoms for Peace" speech by Dwight D. Eisenhower at the United Nations General Assembly in 1953 put emphasis on the peaceful use of nuclear energy, the years from 1945 to 1955 in Japan witnessed a nationwide movement for nuclear disarmament that collected signatures from approximately one-third of the nation's population; the movement led to the First World Conference against Atomic and Hydrogen Bombs in Hiroshima during the same month as the Nagano Seminar.[3]

The collocation of Faulkner's name and Einstein's formula on the hanging scroll opens a path to examine the pitfalls of underestimating the cultural impact of nuclear weaponry. Although a growing body of scholarship has clarified how US cultural diplomacy in the early Cold War period informed Faulkner's art, discussion of this topic tends to omit the reality of nuclear militarism in the same period. More specifically, those interested in the link between the Cold War and the southern US novelist are deeply inspired by Lawrence H. Schwartz's classic work, *Creating Faulkner's Reputation* (1988), while being indifferent to an equally classic work on the culture of the Atomic Age by Paul Boyer, *By the Bomb's Early Light* (1985), despite the contemporaneity of the two books' subjects. This academic separation is exemplified by efficient works such as Greg Barnhisel's *Cold War Modernists* (2015) and Jordan J. Dominy's *Southern Literature, Cold War Culture, and the Making of Modern America* (2020), both of which refer to Schwartz in examining the complicity of US containment culture and the institutionalization of literary modernism represented by Faulkner[4]; however, both arguments omit any inquiry into what kind of power was needed to maintain the influence of the nation's liberal democratic, antitotalitarian culture on the Cold War world—i.e., any investigation into the link between US Cold War culture and the nation's nuclear arsenal.

My aim is to make southern US Cold War cultural studies engage in a dialogue with nuclear discourse by focusing on three significant Mississippi-born writers: William Faulkner, Eudora Welty, and Richard Wright. Furthermore, I suggest that the three novelists' perceptions of race and racism in the 1950s can be interpreted through the lens of global military history framed by the proliferation of nuclear weapons. This perspective, compounding the two meanings of the word "race," identity and competition, is not necessarily new. Stating that "the atomic bomb acted as a bifocal lens,"[5] Abby J. Kinchy's 2009 monograph revisits African American newspapers and magazines published in the period from the end of World War II to the civil rights movement, unraveling how racism and the nuclear arms race were interconnected issues for African American leaders such as Langston Hughes, Paul Robeson, W. E. B. Du Bois, and Martin Luther King Jr. Vincent J. Intondi extends this inquiry, adding to the aforementioned figures Barack Obama as "not only the first African American president, but also the most antinuclear president in US history."[6] This color-based approach to the history of nuclear disarmament movements has foregrounded the long conflict of nuclear powers and antiracist, anticolonialist movements.

However, these scholars' perspectives on racism and the nuclear arms race cannot cover the potential significance of Higashiyama's enigmatic nuclear imagining that accompanied Faulkner's footprint in Japan. Of importance here is not the exploration of a Japanese perspective, which would lead to a political discussion on Afro-Asian coalitions against white nuclear imperialism such as the Bandung Conference in April 1955 (it is noteworthy at this point that the Nagano Seminar coincided with Wright's reportage on this meeting in Indonesia, "Indonesian Notebook," in the August 1955 issue of *Encounter*, the CIA-funded publication produced by the Congress for Cultural Freedom).[7] More important for my argument is that Higashiyama's message at the Nagano Seminar suggests that the imagery of nuclear energy or weaponry inherent in the formula was so prevalent as to intrude upon the aesthetic individualism that Faulkner would have represented.[8] Welty and Wright were not immune to nuclear-related issues during the Cold War, either. Their writings on race and racism in the 1950s became correlative with the nuclear arms race due to the breaking out of not just the Cold War, but also what is now called a state of permanent war. As Joseph Darda concisely states of the logic underlying this war, "Race excused war, and war made race."[9] In other words, in the name of national defense and the protection of Western (white) civilization and norms within and beyond the nation, the United States has racialized foreign others—e.g., communists, drug dealers, and terrorists—in justifying endless militarization since the mid-twentieth century, the period marked by the combination of the US military-industrial complex, global interventionism, and liberal democratic consensus.[10] Thus a reciprocal interdependence between racism and war was forged by virtue of the principle of defense. Projecting the logic of permanent war onto the three Mississippi-born novelists' works related to racial and nuclear issues would eventually reveal nuclear blindness in the southern US literary arena.

Faulkner, Welty, and *Life*

According to Boyer, *Life* magazine was arguably "the most important print medium through which the American people formed their initial impressions of the atomic bomb."[11] Along with a cover photograph of General Carl "Tooey" Spaatz, a director of the atomic bombings of Hiroshima and Nagasaki, smoking a cigarette, the August 20, 1945, issue of *Life* displayed photos of mushroom clouds and the shockingly different appearances of Hiroshima before and after the atomic attack.[12] What follows these images is "The Atomic Age," an editorial that discusses the impact of the new weapon and offers a warning about the next chapter of human history: "The thing for us to fear today is not the atom but the nature of man, lest he lose either his conscience or his humility before the inherent mystery of things."[13] However, by the time the US monopoly on atomic weapons was over and the Cold War world entered the phase of the nuclear arms race (primarily between the US and the USSR), this magazine ceased to moralistically discuss how humanity should deal with nuclear power. Faulkner and Welty were in the midst of the shift of *Life*'s focus from the humanism that included the fear of nuclear warfare to the demonization of the foreign enemy newly equipped with nuclear weapons in endorsing the reinforcement of US military power.

The March 5, 1956, issue of *Life* was a point of convergence for the topics of racism and the nuclear arms race, including such articles as "The Golden Youth of Communism," "A Bold Boycott Goes On," Faulkner's "A Letter to the North," and "The Trials of Uncle Daniel." The last item is a review of *The Ponder Heart*, a theatrical adaptation of the 1954 novella by Welty. There were cases where the magazine flexibly changed its plans for which content was to be printed in an issue to offer new, updated information;[14] however, this particular issue has intertextuality among these four articles, a solid context in which each of them is to be read. To begin with, "The Golden Youth," the longest article of the four, informs readers of the rise of aspiring young engineers and students in the USSR. The article stimulated the anticommunist sentiments of its US readers when it reported, "Russia, in desperate need of trained metallurgists for its jet engine, atomic and guided missile research programs, has raised the stipends of metallurgy students higher than the rest."[15] The accompanying huge photograph of Russian and Chinese students studying in the same lecture hall, which is extended to two pages (36–37), expresses the potential for integrated multiethnicity in the USSR. The article describes "Russian lecture halls with seas of solemn, attentive faces attracted from every corner of the Communist empire" (36). At the end of the main text is a quote from atomic submarine developer Rear Admiral Hyman Rickover: "In rate of progress they are, in fact, already ahead of us" (36). With its visual impact and sense of crisis, the article establishes the overall mood of the magazine, placing the following articles in the racial-military context of the nuclear arms race.

The racial mixture of young students in the USSR provides a stark contrast with what is presented in "A Bold Boycott." This report on the civil rights actions against segregation since the Montgomery Bus Boycott, which began the previous December, includes a photograph of African American leaders standing at the State Capitol of Alabama. There is a caption under the photo: "Where Alabama voted 95 years ago to secede and Jefferson Davis was inaugurated president of Confederacy, 83 indicted boycott leaders gather."[16] The magazine thus connects the memory of the Civil War to the contemporary movement for integration, anticipating the defeat of the Jim Crow South. From a different angle, this image of integration printed in the magazine also invokes a sense of urgency not to be outstripped by the integrated USSR's academic institutions; juxtaposing this article with "The Golden Youth," *Life* captures the nation's burden to deal with the two meanings of "race" at the same time.

After these articles comes Faulkner's controversial essay. In "A Letter to the North," he writes to the leaders of the NAACP and northerners who demand integration in the novelist's region from outside: "Go slow now. Stop now for a time, a moment. You have the power now; you can afford to withhold for a moment the use of it as a force."[17] Considering the militaristic, competitive tone of this particular issue of *Life*, the phrase "go slow" appears as a fetter for the nation competing against the USSR and its multiethnic group of communist youth who would contribute to the stockpile of their nuclear weapons. To be fair, there was no reason for the novelist to revisit his statement in his Nobel Prize Banquet Speech in 1950, especially when bent on restoring peace in the destabilized racial and social structure of his hometown; in Stockholm, Faulkner had expressed his fear of nuclear warfare briefly with "[t]here is only the question: When will I be blown up?";[18] the expression of his anti-apocalyptic belief in humanity that followed in the speech advertised a humanistic aspect of US culture to the contemporary global literary market. Nevertheless, Faulkner, in 1956, had to handle a clearer and more immediate danger to himself than the speculative vision of nuclear warfare. James W. Silver recollects how Faulkner sought to mitigate the racial tension in his local community that escalated following the Supreme Court decision in *Brown v. Board of Education* in May 1954 and the death of Emmett Till in August 1955: "He never was one for extended conversation, but he said over and over, as if to himself, 'We are sitting on top of a powder keg.'"[19] *Life* was not so kind as to deliver his moderate views on his communal race issues by themselves, but displayed them in a negative manner as an example of dilatory southern US exceptionalism in contrast to the rapidly militarizing, integrating communist enemy.[20]

But this perception is not the case with one of Faulkner's fellow southern novelists. Aware that the review of the theatrical version of her novella would be in the same issue of *Life* as Faulkner's contribution, Welty read his essay and wrote a letter to her literary agent Diarmuid Russell saying that "Faulkner has a good letter to the North in the same issue."²¹ How seriously she took the other article on the US-USSR conflict in the same issue is unknown, but her attitude at least insinuates little interest in the nuclear arms race when reading Faulkner's claim for regional autonomy as a response to integration. As for Welty's regionalism, its backwardness is overemphasized by the magazine and the play *The Ponder Heart* itself: although Granville Hicks praises the original by writing, in analogy with Faulkner, that Welty also exceeds "the limitations of regionalism,"²² and though the author herself was satisfied with the play to a certain degree,²³ the review in *Life* introduces the play version as a mere comical portrait of the region, where "the dignity of the law suffers almost beyond repair."²⁴ The photos accompanying the review capture, for example, Uncle Daniel's young bride Bonnie Dee using an electric toaster as her mirror (111), a salesman selling women's underwear in court (114), and Uncle Daniel raging on the witness stand (116). Overall, the tenor of this 1956 issue showed that, simply put, the social progress of the US South was problematically slow, while that of the USSR was distressingly fast.

In this issue, *Life* moreover casts a skeptical light on pacifism when the editorial "The New Communist Line" claims that the regime of Nikita Khrushchev was pursuing world revolution even after Stalinism, this time with a new tactic of ostensible pacifism: "To continue overtaking the capitalist world in industrial and atomic strength they clearly need an interval of peace, and they are buying it for its going rate in Western markets, i.e., nothing."²⁵ This editorial page appears immediately after the boycott article and before Faulkner's essay, separated only by advertisements. When reading those articles in the page order and in relation to the sense of crisis expressed in "The Golden Youth," some readers would have perceived the domestic, regional issues of racism within the wider network of Cold War nuclear militarism. Certainly, others would have been able to separate these issues, but such a compartmentalizing mode of reading would have been viewed as synonymous with condoning regression in the nuclear arms race. This approach is clearly not what the *Life* editorial was attempting to cultivate. This issue of the magazine placed Faulkner and Welty in such a way that racism in their region, regardless of their intentions, became materially contiguous to the nuclear arms race.

The Atoms in *The Outsider*

Richard Wright's 1953 novel, *The Outsider*, includes various atomic references around his African American protagonist Cross Damon. One example is found in the character's first encounter with District Attorney Ely Houston on the train from Chicago to New York. In the conversation with Houston, who is "profoundly interested in the psychological condition of the Negro in this country,"[26] Cross feels uncomfortable with his racial interest and, in an apparent attempt to avoid it, discusses the deepest fear of human civilization in the Atomic Age: "We talk about what to do with the atom bomb . . . But man's heart, his spirit is the deadliest thing in creation" (506, ellipsis in original). Following this dreadful view of humanity, Damon boldly comments on ontological anxiety: "Maybe man is nothing in particular" (507). Later, he is confronted by a Communist Party member named Blimin. Asking him, "Can atom bombs correct a man's sense of life?" (764), Cross declares that desires for "the total and absolute in modern life" (763)—for instance, a desire for modernity materialized by electronic media and atomic energy[27]—reside in both capitalist and totalitarian nations. From this viewpoint, he shows himself as existing between the two positions, and therefore not a menace to the party. His atomic bomb imaginings first and foremost reflect his own personal desire to be "nothing in particular," an exceptional existence not to be framed by any racial or political identification.

Investigating physical and psychological conflicts in the Black experience and movement beyond national boundaries, Paul Gilroy argues that Wright's 1950s works, including *The Outsider*, present "the tension between the claims of racial particularity on one side and the appeal of those modern universals that appear to transcend race on the other."[28] I add a wrinkle to this tension, rephrasing it as a tension between self-defense and perpetual war. *The Outsider* is a narrative of the self-defense of the angst-ridden African American protagonist by means of atomic imagery and violence, a grim example of a life entangled in an endless fight for individual freedom. When Darda theorizes the interdependence of racism and permanent war in the US, he also writes on how the nation's ideal can work to make this racist-military nexus formidable: "Liberalism defines the human by universalizing the characteristics of white Western man and valuing all others based on their adoption of, or failure to adopt, his characteristics" (12). A consequence of this white liberalist US universalization or domestication of racial others can be found in the life of Cross; in the aforementioned train scene, the African American character needs to disguise himself with the Atomic Age expedient to convince Houston of his grandiose ideas about humanity because, before their conversation, Cross has killed a former colleague in Chicago to begin his new life with a clean slate. However, after reaching New York, Cross commits the further murders of those who have oppressed him; before his own death, he kills a fascist landowner and two communists, then loses his beloved Eva Blount, who commits suicide after finding out about his horrible deeds.

The continuity of self-defense and offense against his surroundings in Cross's violent life has affinity with the complex postcolonial condition the author experienced and witnessed. Vaughn Rasberry examines the protagonist in *The Outsider* in relation to what Wright calls "terror in freedom"[29] in *White Man, Listen!* (1957). This terror occupies the post-World War II, Third World mentality of African and Asian elites; it is the urgent concern that their white former colonizers, equipped with nuclear weapons, would recolonize their newly liberated nations. Rasberry applies the psychology the novelist observed at the Bandung Conference to his reading of *The Outsider*, defining it as "a fictional response to what Wright perceived as the condition of 'terror in freedom' afflicting the postcolony."[30] Whereas this terror construes a cause for Third World nations' or for Cross's fight for freedom in Rasberry's argument, it is also possible to perceive another aspect of the emotional and mental constitution of the formerly colonized by visiting another phrase in *White Man, Listen!*: "the Nuclear Revolutionary Motive" (688), the sense of a void within Asian and African people as a result of their Westernization, an emptiness in life to be filled by an ideology that would accommodate their feelings and offer them a reason to live. Wright does not fully explain why he uses the term "nuclear" here, but it evokes the image of the nucleus of an atom, the power expressed in its division from and joining to another nucleus, which can metaphorically indicate the core, movement, and energy of the Asian and African mindset at the 1955 conference in Indonesia. For Wright, these psychological traits of Asians and Africans were familiar; two years before the Bandung Conference, he had already created a character who conceptualized the human being as "nothing in particular" and who had a fatal involvement with Communist Party members. Moreover, as Rasberry again indicates, the 1953 novel itself is in congruence with "Wright's reimagining of Jim Crow as a totalitarian regime" (91), which had begun much earlier in his literary career.

What distinguishes *The Outsider* from Wright's fiction published before the atomic bombings in 1945 is its use of the word "atom" in association with the apocalyptic imagery attached to atomic weaponry, as shown in the conversation between Cross and Houston. Additionally, the terrified, emptied nonwhite psychology illustrated in *White Man, Listen!* resonates with some of the novelist's atomic expressions in *The Outsider*. Aside from the atomic bomb images, the novel uses the word "atom" to emphasize Cross's anxious, alienated status. After murdering Gil Blount, an official of the Communist Party, he faces the suspicious gaze of Jack Hilton, Gil's subordinate. Cross's nerves are stretched to their utmost limit because he cannot determine at this point whether the communist considers him a suspect: "Cross held himself alert, every atom of him striving supremely to be aware of what was taking place" (628). Eva, who is a white painter and Gil's widow, emotionally depends on Cross when she attempts to cut her ties with the Communist Party, but she cannot reach his inner world: "She would never be able to comprehend that he was a lost soul, spinning like a stray atom far beyond the ken of her mind to conceive" (717). These atomic references function not only as a shelter for the protagonist against Communist involvement in his life, but also as a double-edged means of self-defense that eschews love as well as politics.

The use of "atom" in the novel explains more than the Third World mentality, predicting a foreseeable future for the author's home country as a nation armed with nuclear weapons. Through its protagonist's expansive conceptualizing of modern civilization in the Atomic Age and his atomic-inspired self-consciousness, *The Outsider* presents the process in which the pursuit of individual freedom leads to relentless assaults against racial and ideological others, a process analogous to the decade of US international politics following the atomic attacks in Japan. As mentioned earlier, the universal humanism of the postwar Atomic Age had transformed into the logic of perpetual war by the time of the nuclear arms race—that is, the logic of the reciprocal interdependence of the US national defense of individual freedom and the nation's racialization of communist enemies in the Cold War. This shift has a concrete example in the difference between the claim on conscience in the 1945 issue of *Life* and the endorsement of the nuclear arms race in its 1956 issue. Published during the period between these two issues, *The Outsider* provides an objective view on the stances of both *Life* issues with a global viewpoint that Faulkner and Welty, two white Mississippi natives, did not have: the African American novelist, who left the Jim Crow South for Chicago, New York, and Paris, finished writing his novel in London, where he became an occasional guest at Trinidadian writer George Padmore's apartment to discuss Kwame Nkrumah's recent efforts toward African independence in the Gold Coast.[31]

Toward the end of *White Man, Listen!* Wright refers to the motivations of Nkrumah and his people in seeking liberation from the West: "One set of men, black in color, had to organize and pledge their lives and make grievous sacrifices in order to prove to another set of men, white in color, that they were human beings! What a perversion of the energies of human life!" (807). This humanist observation inherently differs from the Atomic Age conscience expressed in the postwar *Life*; while the latter eventually paved the way for advocating the nuclear arms race, Wright's approach to African psychology is fundamentally pacifist. He asks his white readers, "Is the West free enough of its own fears to let these people know that they will not be resubjugated? That is the question" (810).

Rereading *The Outsider* in conjunction with this demand for a humanist understanding of racial others offers an insight into the bewildered rendering of Cross Damon; Wright endows this African American character with a white, Westernized concept of individual freedom and, at the end of his life, makes him understand what the author attempts to make his white readers understand in *White Man, Listen!*: that humans are *not* just "nothing in particular," nor is the character himself just a mere synthesis of atoms, a frightened and barren existence that the word "atom" and the concepts of "terror in freedom" and "the Nuclear Revolutionary Motive" indicate. Houston asks Cross in his dying moment what lessons he has learned from his bloody life, and Cross responds: "Men hate themselves and it makes them hate others ... We must find some way of being good to ourselves ... Man is all we've got" (840, ellipses in original). Thus, Wright relativizes the Western belief in individual freedom by portraying the destructive life it leads to in his African American character, who finally understands that his freedom is not worth death, including his own.

Toward the Concept of Nuclear Southern Studies

Faulkner's and Welty's unintentional involvement in the discourse of the nuclear arms race in *Life* and Wright's atomic imagery in *The Outsider* may offer a new horizon in current academic trends in southern US literary studies. In the introduction to *A History of the Literature of the U.S. South* (2021), Harilaos Stecopoulos provides the following overview of the new southern studies (NSS): "For NSS critics, the literature of the South is comprehensively a literature of race and racism that demands new ways of thinking about subjectivity, property, and power."[32] Frustrated with the fixed regionalist image chiefly cemented by the alumni of Vanderbilt University and the literature of the Southern Renaissance, NSS intellectuals have been interested in widening their scope to look beyond the Mason-Dixon line, as well as to look more extensively and deeply into the region's racial and social structure; in so doing, however, they have been inclined to omit examination of the region's social reality (and the rise of southern studies itself as a field) as inseparable from the Atomic Age, as exemplified by the absence of this topic in the anthology edited by Stecopoulos. The fact that Welty's words "one place comprehended can help us understand other places better"[33] are quoted in Lindsey A. Freeman's *Longing for the Bomb* (2015) suggests that examining the US South in relation to the nation's nuclear issues may yoke together the global and the local as effectively as NSS seeks to. Freeman's book argues that for the local community around the Oak Ridge National Atomic Laboratory in Tennessee, the fear of extinction and hope for economic growth coexist—that is, there is an ambivalence inherent within any modern civilization dependent on nuclear energy.

At the same time, Freeman, quoting the novelist, fails to address an issue of aesthetic distance between US southern literature of the Cold War era and the region's nuclear culture. Welty's interview in the 1977 *New York Times*, "Eudora Welty in Type and Person," demonstrates how she avoids nuclear anxiety. The interviewer is her dear friend and writer Reynolds Price, who observes of her essay collection, *The Eye of the Story*,

> as your uses of *radiance* began to mount, I came to feel that the essays combined to advance a concept of the great writer as a kind of nuclear power plant, a large center of energy, radiating for us; and that the nuclear fuel is love, a deep tender fascination with human life.
>
> E.W. That *is* what it is. It goes to the center of my being, my feeling for what I've read. It's a *vital* force.[34]

One who remembers Schwartz's argument in the 1980s might be tempted to mix and recompose the two phrases "the center of my being" and "a *vital* force" to evoke Arthur M. Schlesinger Jr.'s title phrase in *The Vital Center* (1949), an Atomic Age publication that presents patriotic belief in freedom of expression and individualism as what Dominy calls "key tenets of American democracy" (77). However, what is more obvious in this interview is that both interviewer and interviewee view nuclear power plants only positively, as energy sources. Both seem oblivious to the dangers of radiation.[35] This conversation took place one year before Allen Ginsberg participated in the antinuclear protest against radioactive contamination from the Rocky Flats nuclear weapons plant near Golden, Colorado. His "Plutonian Ode" (1978) exposes what Kristin George Bagdanov calls "America's nuclear unconscious," a collective mentality that disassociates military and peaceful uses of nuclear energy in order to forget the danger both pose for, in Joseph Masco's terminology, "America's radioactive nation-building project."[36] This project for military buildup and economic prosperity by means of nuclear energy had apparently succeeded in inscribing the nuclear unconscious in the minds of Welty and Price. Their aestheticization of nuclear energy speaks volumes about how readily they could disconnect nuclear weapons from nuclear power plants in their aesthetic imaginations by that time. If this is typical of "vital center" novelists, then US (southern) Cold War literature brought with it a repression of the nuclear threat.

A new, synthetic image of southern US literature should not depend on the extent to which its regional representations can be distanced from nuclear weapons and industry. A closer look at nuclear culture in and around the region would contribute to excavating insights for perpetual peace rather than causes for permanent war from its cultural soil. We should cast a critical eye on nuclear culture in the region and beyond, not just because Faulkner, Welty, and Wright were part of it, but because their nuclearized imaginations, intentionally or unintentionally, can otherwise offer a reason to normalize life in a state of permanent war.

NOTES

1. *Messages on a Hanging Scroll to William Faulkner*, the Faulkner Corner, Nagano City Library, Nagano City, Nagano, Japan. This scroll, at the request of the Faulkner family, was returned to Nagano by James B. Meriwether on November 14, 1987, and has been preserved at the library since then. At the center of it is a calligraphy inscription, which is a Japanese translation of Falconer, *takajou* (鷹匠), a phonetic equivalent to Faulkner. See Ohashi Kenzaburo, "Takajou toha [What Falconer Means]," *Faulkner* フォークナー, no. 4 (April 2002): 174–75; Alexander Zabusky, "TRAVEL ADVISORY; For a Change of Pace, Faulkner in Nagano," *New York Times*, January 18, 1998, https://www.nytimes.com/1998/01/18/travel/travel-advisory-for-a-change-of-pace-faulkner-in-nagano.html (accessed February 27, 2022). I have discussed Higashiyama's writing on this *kakejiku* in more detail elsewhere; see for example Ryoichi Yamane, "Sono koudai na shimen nite: William Faulkner to bunka reisen no gengo ariina [On the Wide-open Space of the Paper: William Faulkner and the Language Arena of the Cultural Cold War]," in *William Faulkner no Nihon houmon: reisen to bungaku no politikusu [William Faulkner's Visit to Japan: Politics of Cold War and Literature]*, ed. Hiroaki Soda (Kyoto: Shoraisha 松籟社, 2022), 97–118.

2. A. Costandia Titus, "The Mushroom Clouds as Kitsch," in *Atomic Culture: How We Learned to Stop Worrying and Love the Bomb*, ed. Scott C. Zeman and Michael A. Amundson (Boulder: University Press of Colorado, 2004), 107, 119.

3. Lawrence S. Wittner, *Resisting the Bomb: A History of the World Nuclear Disarmament Movement, 1954–1970* (Redwood City, CA: Stanford University Press, 1997), 8–9.

4. Greg Barnhisel, *Cold War Modernists: Art, Literature, and American Cultural Diplomacy* (New York: Columbia University Press, 2015), 124; Jordan J. Dominy, *Southern Literature, Cold War Culture, and the Making of Modern America* (Jackson: University Press of Mississippi, 2020), 30–31. Hereafter cited parenthetically.

5. Abby J. Kinchy, "African Americans in the Atomic Age: Postwar Perspectives on Race and the Bomb, 1947–1967," *Technology and Culture* 50, no. 2 (2009): 291.

6. Vincent J. Intondi, *African Americans against the Bomb: Nuclear Weapons, Colonialism, and the Black Freedom Movement* (Redwood City, CA: Stanford University Press, 2015), 108.

7. Richard Wright, "Indonesian Notebook," *Encounter* 5, no. 2 (August 1955): 24–31.

8. Lawrence H. Schwartz, *Creating Faulkner's Reputation: The Politics of Modern Literary Criticism* (Knoxville: University of Tennessee Press, 1988), 202–3.

9. Joseph Darda, *Empire of Defense: Race and the Cultural Politics of Permanent War* (Chicago: University of Chicago Press, 2019), 4. Hereafter cited parenthetically.

10. The rising academic trend of studying perpetual or permanent war, which includes Darda's book, underscores the growth of the military-industrial complex since the early Cold War era. See Jonathan Vincent, "American Culture and the (Permanent, Global) Cold War (on Terror)," *American Literary History* 32, no. 2 (2020): 354.

11. Paul Boyer, *By the Bomb's Early Light: American Thought and Culture at the Dawn of the Atomic Age* (1985; repr., Chapel Hill: University of North Carolina Press, 1994), 8.

12. "War's Ending," *Life*, August 20, 1945, 25-31.
13. "The Atomic Age," *Life*, August 20, 1945, 32.
14. See Edward K. Thompson, *A Love Affair with Life and Smithsonian* (Columbia: University of Missouri Press, 1995), 192-205, specifically 192-93, where Thompson writes on how he, as the managing editor, dealt with three issues published in 1956, one of the most productive periods for the magazine.
15. "The Golden Youth of Communism," *Life*, March 5, 1956, 32. Hereafter cited parenthetically.
16. "A Bold Boycott Goes On," *Life*, March 5, 1956, 43.
17. William Faulkner, "A Letter to the North," *Life*, March 5, 1956, 52.
18. William Faulkner, "I Decline to Accept the End of Man," *Perspectives USA*, no. 1 (Fall 1952): 9. I use this version of Faulkner's Nobel Prize banquet speech in the first issue of *Perspectives USA* to indicate how this speech resonated within US Cold War culture. See Barnhisel, *Cold War Modernists*, 194.
19. James W. Silver, *Mississippi: The Closed Society* (1964; repr., Jackson: University Press of Mississippi, 2012), xiii.
20. The image of Mississippi that Silver provides is connected to totalitarianism abroad in the context of regional exceptionalism. See Joseph Crespino, "Mississippi as Metaphor: Civil Rights, the South, and the Nation in the Historical Imagination" in *The Myth of Southern Exceptionalism*, ed. Matthew D. Lassiter and Joseph Crespino (Oxford, UK: Oxford University Press, 2010), 101.
21. Welty to Russell, March 1, 1956, the Eudora Welty Collection, Mississippi Department of Archives and History, Jackson, Mississippi, quoted in Suzanne Marrs, *Eudora Welty: A Biography* (Orlando: Harvest Books, 2005), 257. Hereafter cited parenthetically.
22. Granville Hicks, "Two Novels about Youth and Age by Jessamyn West and Eudora Welty" (1954), *Eudora Welty: The Contemporary Reviews*, ed. Pearl Amelia McHaney (Cambridge, UK: Cambridge University Press, 2005), 105.
23. See Marrs, *Eudora Welty*, 256-57.
24. "The Trials of Uncle Daniel," *Life*, March 5, 1956, 111. Hereafter cited parenthetically.
25. "The New Communist Line," editorial, *Life*, March 5, 1956, 44.
26. Richard Wright, *The Outsider*, in *Later Works*, ed. Arnold Rampersad, rev. ed. (1953; repr., New York: Library of America, 1991), 499. Hereafter cited parenthetically.
27. Cross states, "Communication, inventions, radio, television, movies, atomic energy . . . create the conditions for the creation of organizations reflecting the total and absolute in modern life" (763).
28. Paul Gilroy, *The Black Atlantic: Modernity and Double Consciousness* (1993; repr., London: Verso, 1996), 147.
29. Richard Wright, *White Man, Listen!*, in *Black Power*, ed. Cornel West (1957; repr., New York: Harper, 2008), 683. Hereafter cited parenthetically.
30. Vaughn Rasberry, *Race and the Totalitarian Century: Geopolitics in the Black Literary Imagination* (Cambridge, MA: Harvard University Press, 2016), 345. Hereafter cited parenthetically.
31. This novel Wright finished writing in London in 1952 is considered a turning point for the author that cemented his interest in Africa and antitotalitarianism. See Hazel Rowley, *Richard Wright: The Life and Times* (Chicago: University of Chicago Press, 2001), 402-6.
32. Harilaos Stecopoulos, "Introduction: Reconstructing Literary History," *A History of the Literature of the U.S. South*, ed. Harilaos Stecopoulos (Cambridge, UK: Cambridge University Press, 2021), 4.
33. Lindsey A. Freeman, *Longing for the Bomb: Oak Ridge and Atomic Nostalgia* (Chapel Hill: University of North Carolina Press, 2015), xv.

34. Eudora Welty, interview by Reynolds Price, "Eudora Welty in Type and Person," in *Conversations with Eudora Welty*, ed. Peggy Whitman Prenshaw (Jackson: University Press of Mississippi, 1984), 232.

35. For Welty, from the outset of the Atomic Age, the weapons were dreadful but not completely evil; according to Suzanne Marrs, in a letter to John Robinson, Welty expressed her fear of atomic bombs in 1945 but ultimately accepted them as a "tragic necessity" (quoted in Marrs, *Eudora Welty*, 133) to end the war. I am indebted to Suzanne Marrs for bringing this episode to my attention.

36. Kristin George Bagdanov, "Addressing the Atomic Specter: Ginsberg's 'Plutonian Ode' and America's Nuclear Unconscious," *symplokē* 27, nos. 1-2 (2019): 188.

Welty and Wright and the Visual Idea of the American South

W. RALPH EUBANKS

The great twentieth-century photographer Dorothea Lange once claimed that the camera is an instrument that teaches people how to see without a camera. If photography is a way of seeing, the fictional worlds created by Eudora Welty and Richard Wright were influenced in some way by their individual visual practices as photographers. Welty documented Depression-era Mississippi with what she called her photographic "snapshots," which included many portraits documenting the lives of Black women. Welty never consulted her photographs when writing fiction because she believed the image she had seen through her camera's viewfinder was set in her memory. Yet the detail Welty uses in her fiction often has a documentary quality to it. It is difficult to read the description of Welty's character Phoenix Jackson in her story "A Worn Path" and not think of Welty's photographs of Black women. In that story, here is how Welty describes Phoenix Jackson: "She looked straight ahead. Her eyes were blue with age. Her skin had a pattern all its own of numberless branching wrinkles and as though a whole little tree stood in the middle of her forehead, but a golden color ran underneath."[1]

Richard Wright's visual practice involved the use of photography more directly as an *aide-mémoire*. On a research visit to Chicago in 1938 while completing *Native Son*, he took a newly acquired camera to make photographs of court facilities, holding cells, and even the electric chair in the Cook County jail in an effort to get a sense of the world Bigger Thomas would enter after his arrest for the murder of Mary Dalton.[2] Fifteen years later, during a ten-week-long trip in Africa, he took fifteen hundred photographs that he wanted to use as part of the book *Black Power: The Record of Reaction in a Land of Pathos*. So, photography was more directly a part of his creative process. However, in spite of being an aspiring photographer, he used the work of other photographers—primarily from the Farm Security Administration—for his book *12 Million*

Black Voices: A Folk History of the Negro in the United States. The book is a sweeping narrative of the Black American experience, one that seems to be written in response to Mary Dalton, who commented to a frightened Bigger Thomas that she wanted to "just *see* how your people live."[3] *12 Million Black Voices* shows readers what Wright thought Mary Dalton should see through documentary images.

The first edition of *12 Million Black Voices* only includes one of Wright's photographs—it was dropped from subsequent editions—yet the documentary images selected for the text reflect Wright's concerns with the politics of Black representation in spite of having been taken by white photographers. More than nine thousand images were considered for the text, and Wright met with University of Chicago professor Louis Wirth, who provided him with a reading program in sociology.[4] According to correspondence between Wright and Louise Rosskam, wife of Edwin Rosskam, the FSA office also provided research to Wright, including an assortment of government pamphlets, Thomas Jackson Woofter's *Black Yeomanry*, and Gunnar Myrdal's *An American Dilemma*. "I'm afraid we're going to make your desk look like a forest of reports and pamphlets before long," she wrote in January 1941.[5]

The influence of sociology comes through in the text. In the opening section of *12 Million Black Voices*, when Wright says, "[O]ur outward guise still carries the old familiar aspect which three hundred years of oppression in America have given us," he is proclaiming both a historical truth and a social truth.[6] He is also saying that the book derives its power from the image. While the images and their accompanying text acknowledge sociologist W. E. B. Du Bois's idea of Black dual consciousness, Wright makes it clear in the preface that these are not images of the "Talented Tenth," like those images of middle-class life that Du Bois compiled for the 1900 Paris Exposition on the American Negro, which were largely portraits of Black Americans in respectable and prim Victorian dress. Although Wright does not say it explicitly, his text and images deal with what Du Bois would have deemed the "submerged tenth," the most economically disadvantaged and least educated.

Wright is direct in the opening words of his book, claiming that the combination of images and text he will put to use will use the power of photography to be subversive. As Roland Barthes notes in *Camera Lucida*, photography is "subversive not when it frightens, repels, or even stigmatizes, but when it is pensive, when it thinks."[7] Knowing that his book would reach a largely white audience, Wright was hoping that his subversiveness would force his white audience to think. At the same time, Wright hoped the text would instill a sense of pride in its Black readers and that they would see it as an empowering narrative. That came through in a November

3, 1941, letter to Wright, in which Ralph Ellison declares, "[T]he book makes me feel a bitter pride; a pride which springs from the realization that after all the brutalization, starvation, and suffering, we have begun to embrace the experience and master it. And we shall make of it a weapon more subtle than a machine gun, more effective than a fighter plane!"[8]

In the work of Welty and Wright—Welty's photos of Depression-era Mississippi and the images Wright selected for *12 Million Black Voices*—we see how photography can be used to examine social hierarchies, just as they explored those same hierarchies in their fiction. In Wright's photographs taken for his book *Black Power*, we can see how his photography, like that of Welty's, used photographic formalism in composing portraits, though for Wright, it seems to be a more intentional decision than it was for Welty. Wright's portraits of the people he encountered during ten weeks in Africa in 1953 and Welty's in her journeys around Mississippi reveal both what separates and divides their artistic sensibilities as photographers. It is Wright's self-conscious invocation of modernist photography that separates it from what Welty described as her "snapshots."

Wright described Bigger Thomas in *Native Son* as a kind of recording instrument late in the novel, a machine whose hands are "electric wires" with the mission to find out if "other hands connected with other hearts."[9] This is a description of the work of a documentary photographer, whose work it is to elicit a shock of recognition by the viewer, and in Welty's fiction, the viewer discovers a sense of what she felt about the place and people she photographed. In her story "A Worn Path," Welty holds up a mirror to the power dynamic at work against her character Phoenix Jackson. Phoenix is viewed as a "charity case" by both the white medical service professionals with whom she interacts and the white hunter she encounters in the woods. Throughout this story, Welty finds ways to remind the reader of the history of structural injustice that has determined Phoenix's social and economic position, much like she did in her photographs of Black Mississippians. It is in these two writer's individual documentary sensibilities that we also see different views of the American South, particularly in the ways they portray ideas of race, place, and public memory. What the two writers had in common is that their documentary efforts reveal that both were aware of the social hierarchies that governed the American South and the impact that the social structure had on Black lives. In Wright's later images of Africa, as it moves from colonialism to independence, we see how his work in *12 Million Black Voices* affected him as he stood behind the camera in Africa, "faced with the absolute otherness and inaccessibility of this new world."[10]

• • •

Figure 6.1. "For Rent" placard, photo by Richard Wright, ca. 1941 (from *12 Million Black Voices*). Richard Wright Papers, Yale Collection of American Literature, Beinecke Rare Book and Manuscript Library, courtesy of Julia Wright.

In July 1940, only weeks after *Native Son* came into print, Richard Wright began a collaboration with FSA photographer and administrator Edwin Rosskam that resulted in *12 Million Black Voices*. The book has long been considered a text that is a footnote to Wright's career or merely an application of the FSA documentary project to the Black experience. Since all the photographs except one by Wright were taken by white photographers, it is also a book considered to be examining Blackness through a white gaze. Wright's sole photo in the book is a shot of a "for rent" placard advertising rooms "Just Open to Colored" (see figure 6.1). In *12 Million Black Voices*, Wright seemed to be conscious of the separation of words and images along racial lines. If photographs are a way of imprisoning reality, Wright used his text to correct the power imbalance inherent in the book's images. It is Wright's text that allows readers to see the images as he interpreted them rather than simply through the vision of the person behind the camera. As critic Geoff Dyer notes in his book *The Ongoing Moment*, there is a unique alchemy between the visual and the verbal.[11] Wright understood that alchemy, and he sharpened his text in a way that left room for his personal documentary vision in the images for the book. Wright's text served as a counterbalance to the images of Black life documented by white FSA photographers who often took their images with a sense of detachment.

In the two chapters of the text devoted to the American South, text and image are artfully orchestrated to convey to the reader an idea of what Black life was like at that time. While Wright may have only taken one image for this book, his documentary sensibilities are conveyed in both the text and the images. Wright describes in intimate detail for his readers images of Black farmworkers, laborers, cooks, elevator operators; all, as he said, were linked in "a knot of pain and hope whose snarled strands converge from many points of time and space."[12] The images may not be Wright's, but he is validating the authenticity of them through his text.

In the first two chapters of *12 Million Black Voices*, Wright is looking at the Black Americans of the South as the inheritors of a legacy of slavery in the not-so-distant past. Bear in mind that until World War II, three-quarters of Black Americans lived in the South, in many ways making it a nation within a nation. The photographs in part 2 of his book elicit this feeling of exile and separation. The opening image of the chapter titled "Inheritors of Slavery" is a portrait rather than an image of a laborer. The image was taken by Jack Delano of a preacher and his wife at their home in Heard County, Georgia, seated beneath photographic portraits of themselves taken twenty years previously. This image evades the FSA trope of the shack or cabin. The walls are tight and neatly trimmed. Yet their clothing is utilitarian, frayed and heavily patched. This was an image Wright most certainly had included to allow viewers to engage with the dignity of the subjects with a degree of intimacy (see figure 6.2).

The inclusion of an image by Ben Shahn of two cotton workers continues Wright's movement toward photographic intimacy.[13] Shahn's image of these cotton pickers in Pulaski County, Arkansas, feels profoundly personal, which might be attributed to his use of an angle finder that allowed him to shoot subjects frontally without direct contact.[14] The image is also cropped—excluding a woman standing on the right—which also heightens the power of the image. It also appears in a segment of the text that is one of the most quoted: "[W]hether it is spring or summer or autumn or winter, time slips past us remorselessly, and it is hard to tell of the iron that lies beneath the surface of our quiet, dull days" (see figure 6.3). Although Wright is not the photographer, he uses his text to set up an idea that permeates the text: that Black people are looking into the white man's mind to see what is there. It seems as if that is exactly what these two people in this photograph are doing.

In *On Photography*, Susan Sontag wrote, "Socially concerned writers have not taken to cameras, but they are often enlisted, or volunteer, to spell out the truth to which photographs testify."[15] Wright is doing what James Agee did in *Let Us Now Praise Famous Men*, a book published the same year as *12 Million Black Voices*: his text works as an extended

Figure 6.2. Jack Delano, *Sharecropper and Wife, Georgia, 1935* (from *12 Million Black Voices*). Library of Congress, Prints and Photographs Division, FSA/OWI Collection.

Figure 6.3. Cropped Ben Shahn photo from *12 Million Black Voices* (left), original uncropped image (right). Library of Congress, Prints and Photographs Division, FSA/OWI Collection.

caption on the moral meaning of the images. Wright is using his text to attest to the reality of life for the submerged tenth of Black Americans in the South, his own version of Agee's "cruel radiance of what is." Wright might not have been behind the camera, but the images have a complex, dialectal relationship with the narrative he creates.

Much has been made of Wright's repeated use of "we" in *12 Million Black Voices*.[16] Through this use of a collective "we"—meaning all Americans—Wright is seeking to advance the deep and problematic connection between American exceptionalism and racial subjugation. *12 Million Black Voices* is part of a group of well-known Depression-era books of documentary photography, including Erskine Caldwell and Margaret Bourke-White's *You Have Seen Their Faces* (1937), Dorothea Lange and Paul Taylor's *An American Exodus* (1939), and the previously mentioned *Let Us Now Praise Famous Men* (1941). These other texts tend to evoke the dignity of impoverished Americans rather than confront their connection to wider patterns of human displacement, alienation, and resilience. Wright, on the other hand, was much more concerned with the systemic problems of what he believed was a racist economy. By using "we," Wright wanted his readers to understand that all Americans are implicated in the circumstances of the people in the photographs, not just "the Lords of the Land" in the American South. Photographs are often a means for making things real for the privileged, but Wright's use of "we" connotes that the reader is connected to the circumstances depicted in the photograph. As Susan Sontag notes in *Regarding the Pain of Others*, "No 'we' should be taken for granted when looking at other people's pain."[17]

• • •

Although *12 Million Black Voices* includes only one photograph by Wright, he shot over 1,500 photographs with his own professional-grade camera during the ten weeks in 1953 that he spent living, traveling, and writing in Africa. As he traveled what was then Africa's Gold Coast—today known as the independent nation of Ghana—Wright went to great lengths to develop and print his negatives, yet only thirty-four of Wright's photographs of Africa were published in the UK edition of his book *Black Power: The Record of Reaction in a Land of Pathos* (1954). Further, contrary to Wright's wishes and intentions, the US edition included no photographs at all. With his images of Africa, Wright's body of photographic work can be compared more equally to that of Welty's, since it is largely perceived as being separate from a text Wright created. But it is by examining the text of *Black Power* that a viewer can understand fully the context of Wright's photographs. This is a collection of photographs that can be examined through the ways in which the photographs connect to Wright's previous photographic practice, particularly in *12 Million Black Voices*, as well as to how Wright's documentary and political sensibilities became wrapped together as he became what some have described as a "Western man of color."

As Wright photographed Africa as it moved toward independence from colonialism, he asks himself early in the text of *Black Power*, "How much am I a part of this? . . . Why could I not feel [racial belonging]?"[18] Judging from the text of *Black Power*, Wright seems to feel less of a connection to what he is seeing and photographing in Africa than he does with the FSA images created by other photographers in *12 Million Black Voices*. Perhaps that is because in his work for *12 Million Black Voices*, he could see the power imbalance captured in the images. In the photographs for *Black Power*, Wright is the one wielding power. Wright knew that photography, more than any other art form, is subject to intense moral scrutiny. In his text for *Black Power*, Wright is often mirroring the scrutiny that he knew would be given to his text and images.

New Deal-era photography served as a model for Wright's photographic work, which might be why when he writes about seeing the soil of the Gold Coast for the first time, he says, "I saw Africa for the first time with frontal vision: black life was everywhere."[19] The frontal gaze that is a large part of New Deal-era photography is also part of Wright's photography and is as much of a powerful ethnographic gaze as that of the photographers who photographed Black southerners in *12 Million Black Voices*. The only difference is that here, Wright is the ethnographer. He remains a stranger in Africa since he cannot see a connection between his identity and history and that of Africa. Wright's photographs for *Black Power*, which are dominated by frontal views of his photographic

Figure 6.4. Richard Wright, untitled, Gold Coast, 1953, from *Black Power*. Richard Wright Papers. Yale Collection of American Literature, Beinecke Rare Book and Manuscript Library, courtesy of Julia Wright.

subjects, have detachment as part of their composition and reflect his self-identification as a stranger in what to him feels like a strange land, albeit one to which he senses a connection.

The title of Wright's book, *Black Power*, has a special resonance for readers who are more familiar with the 1960s use of "Black Power" with respect to an American social movement. Wright's text predates the Black Power movement by a decade. Yet the power Wright is referencing here is the nationalist aspirations of African nations seeking to be independent of colonial powers. However, Wright's *Black Power* is often viewed as a travel narrative written in a colonial context, given his difficulty in getting "my eyes ... accustomed" to the landscape.[20]

In *12 Million Black Voices*, Wright could write passionately and knowledgeably about the American past, and the accompanying images mirror

Figure 6.5. Walker Evans, *Floyd Burroughs, Hale County Alabama, 1936*. Library of Congress, Prints and Photographs Division, FSA/OWI Collection.

the emotion of the text. But when confronted with the African past and present, Wright merely relied on a formulaic visual structure in his photographs. In a photograph of an Ashanti chief, Wright takes a tight shot at ground level and the image foregrounds the ruler's baton and captures his feet. But it is not a face-to-face exchange—we never see the chief's face—which leads the viewer to wonder whether Wright was uncertain of how to confront the chief's gaze (see figure 6.4).

When Wright does confront his subject's gaze, it is with a detachment reminiscent of Walker Evans's portraits of tenant farmers in Hale County Alabama (see figure 6.5). In one of his photographic encounters, Wright describes himself as "suddenly . . . self-conscious" about his own presumptions. While Wright thought of himself as a transnational Black intellectual, in both his text and his photographs, the reader sees how he is questioning himself about what he is seeing and is restraining himself

Figure 6.6. (Left) Richard Wright, untitled, Gold Coast, 1953, from *Black Power*. Richard Wright Papers. Yale Collection of American Literature, Beinecke Rare Book and Manuscript Library, courtesy of Julia Wright. (Right) Eudora Welty, *Woman of the Thirties*. Copyright © Eudora Welty LLC, used by permission of Russell & Volkening on behalf of Eudora Welty LLC, Mississippi Department of Archives and History.

from imposing standards of Western modernity on it, while at the same time using the power of the Western gaze in constructing his images of Africa. Wright is seeking to engage with the idea of "Black Power" as it relates to colonialism in Africa, while not being able to free himself from his Western sensibilities.

If Wright's portrait of a tribal elder is placed beside Welty's *Woman of the Thirties*, one can see a difference in the two writers' photographic sensibilities (see figure 6.6). Wright's photograph is a frontal portrait, one in which the elder's hut is only a backdrop, much like the worn wood of the tenant farmer's shack is only a backdrop in Walker Evans's portrait of Floyd Burroughs. Welty's *Woman of the Thirties* captures the house in the background, although her subject's body covers part of the building. Place and landscape are both part of the composition of Welty's image, and the image's title evokes a specific time as well. Perhaps because of Wright's uncertainty about his connection to Africa, he seems to rely on capturing his subject out of time and as a formal Western portrait, one that renders his subject as a radical other. Wright's sense of dislocation is

Welty and Wright and the Visual Idea of the American South   137

Figure 6.7. *Segregated Theater Entrance, Jackson, Mississippi, 1930s.* Copyright © Eudora Welty LLC, used by permission of Russell & Volkening on behalf of Eudora Welty LLC, Mississippi Department of Archives and History.

Figure 6.8. *Club Float, Black State Fair Parade, Jackson, Mississippi, 1930s.* Copyright © Eudora Welty LLC, used by permission of Russell & Volkening on behalf of Eudora Welty LLC, Mississippi Department of Archives and History.

part of the way his photographs of Africans are composed and is echoed in the text. However, when the photographs are thought of as belonging to Wright's text, they create a fuller portrait of the tensions that were a part of his African journey.

Toni Morrison once famously said that Eudora Welty wrote "about Black people in a way that few white men have ever been able to write. It's not patronizing, not romanticizing—it's the way they should be written about."[21] I would say the same thing about her photographs of Black people: she captured them the way they wanted to be captured. The African American women that Welty photographed often look directly into the camera, displaying trust rather than trepidation. While Wright sought to capture the memory of the pain of the southern past in the photographs in 12 Million Black Voices, Welty sought to capture a shared past, while still acknowledging the existence of segregation. That is exactly what she does in an image of an entrance to a segregated theater (see figure 6.7), as well as in an image of the Black state fair parade. Blacks could only attend the fair on what were designated as "Negro Days," and the photograph is one of only a few of Welty's images that include both Blacks and whites (see figure 6.8). Likewise, Welty captures the joy and camaraderie of three women embracing at the midway of the state fair, again, on what would have been a designated day for Black citizens to attend the fair (see figure 6.9).

Figure 6.9. *Midway, Mississippi State Fair, 1939.* Copyright © Eudora Welty LLC, used by permission of Russell & Volkening on behalf of Eudora Welty LLC, Mississippi Department of Archives and History.

These three images reveal the way Welty documented social hierarchies in the South, yet in a way that is quietly subversive. What separates Welty and Wright is that while Wright created commentary on those hierarchies through the work of those who documented the South, Welty chose to simply document the existence of the hierarchies. While some might argue that Welty's approach is problematic because she does not engage with Black suffering in her images, I would argue that, just as in her fiction, Welty resisted the impulse to crusade. She was far more interested in her snapshots, as she called them, capturing the dailiness of life rather than its trials. Welty said it best in the introduction to *One Time, One Place*: "My wish, indeed my continuing passion, would be not to point the finger in judgment but to part a curtain, that invisible shadow that falls between people, the veil of indifference to each other's presence, each other's wonder, each other's human plight."[22] But it is in that documenting of dailiness that viewers can engage with an expanded perspective on the South and the reality of social structures in existence during the Great Depression.

Welty believed in the intrinsic value of the photographic image to capture a past reality more than she believed in the power of the image

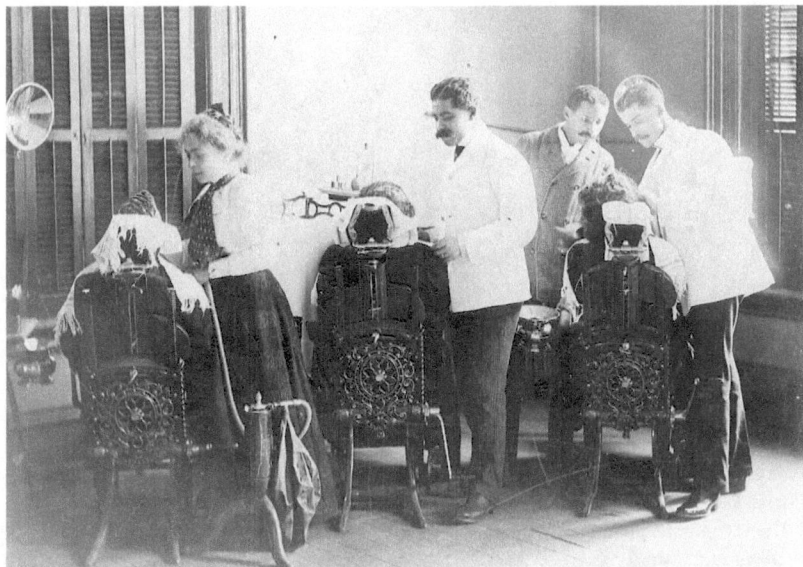

Figure 6.10. *Howard University Dental School. Photo from the American Negro Exhibit, 1900 Paris Exposition*. Library of Congress, Prints and Photographs Division, Daniel A. P. Murray Collection.

as a force of social change. In describing her snapshots, Welty notes, "They were taken spontaneously—to catch something as I came upon it, something that spoke of the life going on around me. A snapshot's now or never."[23] This capturing a past reality was not for the sake of the viewer to take action or journey down a nostalgic path of memory. Welty only wanted to represent the essence of the past in her images with some certainty. During a time when a white photographer might have engaged with Black female stereotypes—such as the mammy or temptress—Welty sought to capture her photographic subjects in the spirit of Du Bois's Paris exposition photographs. Du Bois sought to capture what he deemed "a small nation of people, picturing their life and development without apology or gloss."[24] As Welty herself noted, her photographs were "made in sympathy, not exploitation. If I had felt that way, I would not have taken the pictures."[25]

Although Welty herself would have not made the Du Boisian connection with her photography, her images reveal that she, like Wright, had little interest in the Talented Tenth. In her photographs, she chose to capture the submerged tenth. Rather than making images of primly dressed women in sewing classes or the dapperly dressed men at the Howard University Dental School taken by photographer Thomas Calloway and commissioned by W. E. B. Du Bois (see figure 6.10), Welty went down rural roads capturing

Figure 6.11. *Window-Shopping, Grenada, Mississippi, 1930s.* Copyright © Eudora Welty LLC, used by permission of Russell & Volkening on behalf of Eudora Welty LLC, Mississippi Department of Archives and History.

hog-killing time, cotton chopping, cotton and plum pickers, and washer women. She also, however, captured an image of a woman window-shopping in Grenada, Mississippi, standing looking dignified as she contemplates something that catches her eye. In this image, what happens outside the frame is as important as what happens inside it (see figure 6.11).

The contemplative pose could have been of any woman—Black or white—on a Saturday afternoon in small-town Mississippi. Well into the mid-twentieth century, Saturdays in small towns in Mississippi were one of the few times during the week when both races would have been on the street. As historian Grace Elizabeth Hale notes, "Saturday afternoon shopping belonged to all southerners as black and white, middle-class and poor, men and women crowded into towns," which was one of the great ironies of that time in the segregated American South.[26] In Welty's photograph, not only does the glass separate her photographic subject from the goods she is viewing through the window, but it also represents the system of segregation that would have determined what the window-shopper could do when she entered the store. The woman looking through the window would not have been able to try on a dress or a hat or any other object she desired. What Welty captures here is the muddle that segregation created in the South, particularly on a day when everyone in the town shared the same social space. The woman was a shopper just like anyone else, but her race set her apart in how she could act upon her window-shopping impulse.

Figure 6.12. Marion Post Wolcott, *Segregated entrance of movie house on Saturday afternoon, Belzoni, Mississippi, 1939*. Library of Congress [LC-DIG-ppmsca-12888], Prints and Photographs Division, FSA/OWI Collection.

Although Welty would never have claimed to have been making social commentary, examining these photos through the lens of history forces the viewer to ponder what exists beyond the frame. Welty does document white shoppers by photographing a gathering of whites on the Grenada town square that same day, and that image captures the circumstances of her time just as clearly as when she photographs a "colored entrance" to a theater, much like Marian Post Wolcott did in Belzoni, Mississippi, around the same time (see figure 6.12). "Photographs are a way of imprisoning reality," Susan Sontag writes in *On Photography*. "Or they enlarge a reality that is felt to be shrunk, hollowed out, perishable, remote."[27] Once the viewer places them in historical context, Welty's photographs both freeze images in time and enlarge the reality of that time.

Eudora Welty wanted her photographs to capture a particular time and place in the South. Richard Wright, on the other hand, wanted his commentary on FSA photographs for *12 Million Black Voices* to spotlight the real social inequities that Black southerners lived with (see figure 6.13). Yet what connects these two very different writers as documentarians is a shared love of the peculiar alchemy that takes place with the visual and the verbal. For both writers, language was a part of their visual practice, so they understood the power of the visual to enhance the details

Figure 6.13. (Left) Eudora Welty, *Day's End, Jackson, 1930s*. Eudora Welty/Eudora Welty LLC, Mississippi Department of Archives and History. (Right) Jack Delano, *The Black Sharecropper*, from *12 Million Black Voices*. Library of Congress, Prints and Photographs Division, FSA/OWI Collection.

of a story. Wright understood that one thing a photograph cannot do is speak, so he used his accompanying text to illuminate the work of other documentary photographers and to reveal a truth he wanted his readers to encounter. In his text and photographs for *Black Power*, Wright sought to capture the tensions of change and displacement that were part of his experience in Africa. Given the way Wright understood how the visual and verbal worked together, had photographs been more a part of the narrative of *Black Power*, it would have added to the reader's experience. Welty simply wanted her photographs to portray life as she saw it, and her camera captured her own unique visual poetry. Yet it is what Welty *doesn't* say about her photographs that reveals their connection to the truth of the southern past and their connection to Richard Wright.

NOTES

1. Eudora Welty, "A Worn Path," in *The Collected Stories of Eudora Welty* (New York: Harcourt Brace, 1980), 142.
2. Sara Blair, *Harlem Crossroads: Black Writers and the Photograph in the Twentieth Century* (Princeton, NJ: Princeton University Press, 2007), 69.
3. Richard Wright, *Native Son*, rev. ed. (1940, repr., New York: HarperPerennial Classics, 1993), 79.
4. Laurence Cossu-Beaumont, "Twelve Million Black Voices: Let Us Now Hear Black Voices," *Transatlantica*, no. 2 (2014), https://doi.org/10.4000/transatlantica.7232.
5. Richard Wright Papers, Yale Collection of American Literature, box 105, folder 1585.
6. Richard Wright, *12 Million Black Voices* (New York: Thunder Mouth Press, 1988), 11.
7. Roland Barthes, *Camera Lucida: Reflections on Photography* (New York: Hill and Wang, 2010), 38.
8. Ralph Ellison to Richard Wright, November 3, 1941. Richard Wright Papers, Yale Collection of American Literature, box 97, folder 1314.
9. Richard Wright, *Native Son*, rev. ed. (1940, repr., New York: HarperPerennial Classics, 1993), 419.
10. Richard Wright, *Black Power: A Record of Reactions in a Land of Pathos*, rev. ed. (1954, repr., New York: HarperCollins, 1995), 40.
11. Geoff Dyer, *The Ongoing Moment* (New York: Pantheon Books, 2005), 169.
12. Wright, *12 Million Black Voices*, 11.
13. Wright, *12 Million Black Voices*, 34.
14. Blair, *Harlem Crossroads*, 87.
15. Susan Sontag, *On Photography* (New York: Picador, 2001), 107–8.
16. The best discussion of this idea can be found in Jeff Allred, "From Eye to We: Richard Wright's *12 Million Black Voices*, Documentary, and Pedagogy," *American Literature* 3, no. 78 (September 2006): 549–83.
17. Susan Sontag, *Regarding the Pain of Others* (New York: Picador, 2003), 7.
18. Wright, *Black Power*, 63.
19. Wright, *Black Power*, 38.
20. Wright, *Black Power*, 43.
21. Toni Morrison, interview by Mel Watkins, "Talk with Toni Morrison," in *Conversations with Toni Morrison*, ed., Danille Taylor-Guthrie (Jackson: University Press of Mississippi, 1994), 43–47.
22. Eudora Welty, *One Time, One Place: Mississippi in the Depression: A Snapshot Album* (New York: Random House, 1971), 8.
23. Eudora Welty, *Photographs* (Jackson: University Press of Mississippi, 1989), xiii.
24. David Levering Lewis and Deborah Willis, *A Small Nation of People: W. E. B. Du Bois and African American Portraits of Progress* (New York: Amistad, 2003), 18.
25. Lewis and Willis, *A Small Nation of People*, xxvi.
26. Grace Elizabeth Hale, *Making Whiteness: The Culture of Segregation in the South, 1890–1940* (New York: Pantheon Books, 1998), 182.
27. Susan Sontag, *On Photography*, 163.

Literary Dispatches from the Postal South

DONNIE McMAHAND AND KEVIN MURPHY

Rarely has the notion of cultural flux more fittingly applied to the American South than during the century that followed Reconstruction (1863 to 1877), a century influenced by increased infrastructure and New South ideals of economic reform. The United States Postal Service, increasingly installing offices across the region, signified an unavoidable federal presence in cities and backwaters staunchly protective of their local customs and conventions. Depictions of the post office by southern writers offer readers a wide prism of responses to its presence, not merely as a federal institution but also as a system of internal operations. Every letter, postcard, and engraved announcement passing through a postal worker's hands extends a story, and the stories the South tells about the anticipations, delights, misfortunes, misdeeds, and daily minutia characterizing the postwar years are incalculable. All the ways in which these stories diverge and intersect vis-à-vis the postal service work to delimit a composite representation of the time. In selected works by Eudora Welty, Richard Wright, Alice Walker, Lewis Nordan, and Steve Yarbrough, mail delivery acts as an indiscriminate agent of paradigmatic change. Each text an open invitation to the past, its unfolding confers the intimacy of a letter or personally inscribed postcard. At the same time, collective narratives that centered on restricted political freedoms would only lengthen and calcify in the post-Reconstruction South, a reality integral to the stories these writers tell.

Bound by the period's intense racial divide, what W. E. B. Du Bois predicted in 1903 would be "the problem of the Twentieth Century," residents of the postwar South assessed the relevance of the postal service in their lives precisely from the side of the color line they occupied.[1] Recent histories by Devin Leonard and Winifred Gallagher have clarified the US Postal Service's impact on Black Americans' lives. In *Neither Snow nor Rain: A History of the United States Post Office,* Leonard describes Postmaster General Gideon Granger's urgent proposals during the early 1800s to discontinue allowing free and enslaved Blacks from carrying mail. Leonard reprints Granger's letter to the Senate, which in part reads, "By travelling from day to day, and hourly mixing with people ... [Blacks] will acquire information. ... One able man among them ... might lay a plan which would be communicated by your post-riders from town to town, and produce a general and united operation against you."[2] Congress took up Granger's warning and, seeking to prevent slave insurrections, restricted Blacks from carrying mail for the US Postal Service. The ban lasted from 1802 until after the Civil War. Like Leonard, Gallagher marks the war's end as the beginning of a profusion of Black labor into the civil service, with many Black Americans filling the ranks of mail carriers, clerks, and postmasters. Gallagher writes in *How the Post Office Created America*, "Most of the early black postmasters worked in small offices in rural districts."[3] Bolstered by an increasingly efficient rail system that cut through and slowly connected a disparate postbellum South, these postmasters would provide greater opportunities for correspondence and commercial distribution to the most isolated Americans, Black and white. Notably, the capacity for such support would wane under the impact of Jim Crow laws and fervent anti-Black sentiment pervading policies at the local level all over the South.

The rise to positions of public prominence for Black Americans placed them at greater peril in local communities, a reality perhaps best exemplified by the case of Minnie Cox. In 1891, Cox became the first African American woman appointed to a postmaster position. Having graduated from Fisk University in Nashville, Tennessee, with a teacher's certificate, she excelled at her post in Indianola, Mississippi, but her career ended abruptly in 1903, when she fled her job in fear for her life. Many of the white citizens of Indianola, envious of Cox's prominence, demanded her resignation and created such a hostile environment that Cox left her post over the objections of President Theodore Roosevelt, who initially rejected her resignation and temporarily rerouted Indianola's mail service to Greenville, Mississippi.[4] This resistance toward any push for political and social equality establishes a fundamental reality in the development of what we term the "Postal South." At the core of this formation exists a ferocious intersection between local authorities and federal interventions. The South's earliest responses to Reconstruction policies contradictorily placed segregation and female domesticity against corporate industry (however corrupt) and opportunities for education (however inconsistent). Based on these historical happenings, our notion of the Postal South refers to literary memory and production, a probative retelling or untelling of circumstances and events, actual and imagined.

Mixing the actual and the imagined, the writers included in this discussion explore mail delivery in the South with varying degrees of directness. The most direct, Steve Yarbrough's 2001 novel *Visible Spirits*, looks back the furthest in time, to 1903 and Cox's expulsion. Like Wright, Walker, and Nordan, Yarbrough represents the South (Indianola being his hometown) from his residence in another state. Both Wright and Nordan cast backward glances at their native Mississippi in autobiographies pointedly recalling the impact of the postal service on their individual creative imaginations. Wright's posthumously published first novel *Lawd Today!* (1963) and Nordan's Sugar Mecklin stories impart nuanced, conflicted assessments of the postal service, exposing its potential for facilitating fraudulent or manipulative commerce and communication.

In fictions focusing on women's differing attitudes about mail delivery, Welty and Walker demonstrate how the characters' social positions deeply impact their viewpoints. Not unlike Julia Mortimer in Welty's *Losing Battles* (1970), Celie Johnson, the heroine of Walker's epistolary novel *The Color Purple* (1982), regards mail delivery as a viable source of meaningful exchange. Lacking Julia's agency, though, Celie traverses a pathway clearly divergent from Welty's heroine, and yet as women inhabiting the modern South, they experience firsthand the radical power and futurity of the US Post Office. Every textual site of our mapping of the Postal South reveals representative facets of a changing cultural landscape and the struggles of isolated individuals seeking to correspond with their neighbors and the world. Like the residents of the postwar South, the people and places brought to life by Welty, Wright, Walker, Nordan, and Yarbrough fashion a robust literary correspondence, building and detailing a diagram of memory, history, and imagination. Evoking the disruptiveness imposed by modern mail delivery on southerners' lives and perspectives, Welty, Wright, Walker, Nordan, and Yarbrough specifically mark the ability of the Postal Service to expose deep racial and economic rifts within southern populations, to exploit cases of rural isolation, and, conversely, to offer some relief to unwanted insularity.

The South Unburied: Yarbrough's *Visible Spirits*

Memory, history, and imagination forcefully synthesize throughout *Visible Spirits*, with Yarbrough parsing through the official record, adding new characters, and, except for Roosevelt, renaming the historical ones (Cox appears as Loda Jackson in the novel). What animates these figures, besides the cinematic clarity of the novel's prose, is Yarbrough's willingness to pry into every character's innermost thoughts, including those of his Black characters. Sensitive to the issue of cultural appropriation, Yarbrough asserts, "If I happened to care about somebody who was in a lot of ways different than me, then I felt that I could tell that story."[5] To suggest that only a Black woman can convincingly write (or should write) Minnie Cox's story is to revert to essentialist logic. Ultimately, Yarbrough's Black characters, like their white counterparts, prove multidimensional, imbued by the immediacy and complexity of the historical moment.

Much of Loda's story occurs internally through a series of observations and memories, her rational thoughts all but replaced at novel's end by lingering visions of loved ones no longer living. Loda quietly bears her secrets (the biggest consisting of her filial link to her former owner Samuel Payne), confiding little to her husband, Seaborn Jackson, a man for whom she harbors more ambivalence than affection. Balancing her time between the post office and caring for Miss Bessie, an old survivor of the Payne plantation, Loda constantly assesses the dangers and threats her white neighbors pose, particularly the threat posed by her half-brother, Tandy Payne. His character is a fictionalized version of Mississippi's James K. Vardaman, who, first as governor and then as senator, sought to forge a political consensus among poor and wealthy white Mississippians and who openly advocated for legalized white supremacy. In the novel, Loda and Tandy, not having seen each other for several years, cross paths passing two mating dogs. Before handing her his petition to have her removed as postmistress, he impugns her husband's manhood, and, provocatively placing his hand on her shoulder, intimates his desire to give her a doggish "rut"; her reaction, a slap "so hard that his head snapped back and his hat flew off," shows her careful calculations giving way to indignation.[6] This showdown between Loda and Tandy tacitly invokes the sexual violence and institutionalized assault recurrent throughout the slave era. After walloping him, she half expects him to cry when, instead, he lets out a disingenuous laugh. In a scene wired for maximum tension, the region's history threads tightly along the characters' backstories: although Loda rejects Tandy's attempt to animalize her, to reenact a humiliation enslaved women routinely suffered, their altercation frames a future of continuing violence and racial enmity.

Tandy's first attempt at robbing Loda of her position makes a strategically indirect strike, drawing on the trope of Black male rapaciousness. Propping himself up as a defender of white woman virtue, Tandy sets down in an editorial what he hopes will rouse the townspeople's racial paranoia: "*Do we the citizens of Loring that pay our taxes to the United States Government really want to send our womenfolks into a place where a colored man hangs around for no good purpose?*" (43). The "colored man" referred to is Blueford, Loda's childhood friend, who, unlike Seaborn, refuses to grovel to whites. Blueford's presence at the post office during Tandy's visit gives Tandy the opening he has been looking for—if only his brother, Leighton, Loring's mayor and newspaper editor, would cooperate. When his plan with the editorial fails, Tandy spreads a petition, stoking the racist ire of his friends, who in the dead of night abduct and severely beat Blueford, strap him naked to a horse, paint a white line along the full length of his body, and pin to his flesh a note that reads: *"This white line is where we will divide his black carcase next time he forgets the Good Lord saw fit to put the mark of Cain upon him"* (104).

While Blueford's humiliation presages further incidents of violence, this attack specifically serves as a substitute for Tandy's thwarted designs on his half-sister. Implying Loda has more than a friendly regard for Blueford, Tandy alerts her to the terrible unknowns awaiting her loved ones: his petition, he tells her, "will be the least of your problems, bitch" (95). For Tandy, sexual violation of the Black body reassures his own manhood, at least temporarily. Years ago at the Deadening, his father's plantation, he forced Loda to watch him pleasuring himself, while "desperate sobs shot from his throat" (95). Describing the assault on Blueford, Yarbrough stresses its sexual subtext—hinting at something besides literal castration—in the victim's unspoken fears, *"No, Lord. No, Jesus,"* while one of his assailants "began to undo [Blueford's] pants" (102).

Radically shifting in significations, Loring's post office operates as a historical metonymy publicly projecting the characters' ambitions, anxieties, anger, and shame. Day laborers and sharecroppers are among the first to discover the spectacle of Blueford's savaged body tied to a joist in front of the post office, now a site of white terror. This gory site serves as a reminder to the laborers and sharecroppers, the so-called children of Cain, to abide in the shadows. Meanwhile, the ordeal occasions kindness from Leighton, who removes the pin and releases Blueford from his entanglement. Clearly, then, the post office denotes for Leighton and Tandy two enormously different breaks from the Deadening. The sons of a sadistic slaveowner and planter, Samuel Payne, they separately align with two categories of postbellum southerners put forward by W. E. B. Du Bois in his seminal sociological tract *The Souls of Black Folk* (1903). Exhorting Black Americans to be discerning in their appraisals of southern whites, Du Bois insists, "the ignorant Southerner hates the Negro, the workingmen fear his competition, the money-makers wish to use him as a laborer, some of the educated see a menace in his upward development, while others—usually the sons of the masters—wish to help him to rise" (42–43). If Leighton personifies those white southerners appealing for Black progress, Tandy, filled with bile and a feeling of displaced supremacy, figures as his brother's antithesis. To grapple with the forces and counterforces of history is to draw upon whatever reserves, admirable or not, are available to a person, or as Thomas E. Dasher puts it, "History is both the facts of what happened and the uncertainties of how that history plays out in [an] individual."⁷ What may prove true in principle for the Payne brothers holds up for Loda as well. For her, like other Black Americans, postal work signals a step out of the shadows, an escape from determinist labor like sharecropping; however, the post office also represents the mortal dangers that surround such acts of ambition.

Welty's and Walker's Womanly Interventions (1920s-1930s)

After the hardening of Jim Crow laws following Reconstruction, few, if any, Black women like Loda (Minnie Cox) rose to positions of prominence in the Postal South, leaving white women the most visible beneficiaries of a reinvigorated color line. As telling as Welty's treatments of marriage, rural isolation, and a modernized postal service prove—not least in her novel *Losing Battles* and the stories "Asphodel" and "Ladies in Spring"—her focus on white womanhood unavoidably produces only a partial view of the Postal South. In "Why I Live at the P.O.," "At the Landing," and "Ladies in Spring," the post office lends agency to Welty's white women characters, while in "Asphodel" and *Losing Battles*, white women either embrace modern mail delivery or oppose it. This opposition stems from their desire to cling to marriage, domesticity, and the insularity of tight-knit, rural communities that they perceive to be threatened by the communicative power of the postal service. The characters who oppose the post office find validation and status in their placement on the pedestal.

Despite the considerable interest Welty devotes to Black women's lives in her photography and fiction, she never explicitly portrays Black women sending or receiving letters or holding forth inside a post office. These women do not visibly populate Welty's Postal South. As David McWhirter observes, "Welty is always attuned to . . . [her characters'] desire not to be known or tell or be told."⁸ "Ladies in Spring," for instance, entices readers with a glimpse at Black life without extending the contact into a bona fide encounter. In this piece and others, Welty makes the racial divide eventful, and this conspicuous obscuring of Black bodies clearly intimates the incompleteness of the narrative's vantage point.

Walker's portrayals of disenfranchised, rural Black women and the potentialities of the US Postal Service not only align with Welty's formulations, but they also, where necessary, restructure them. While white southerners after Reconstruction forcibly removed African Americans from postmaster positions and sometimes segregated Black and white mail on rural routes,⁹ the Rural Free Delivery program provided mail delivery to residents, Black and white, living mostly on farms and rural residences like those depicted in Welty's and Walker's fiction.¹⁰ Both

Welty and Walker lift the veil long shrouding rural Black and white women's lives during segregation. After interviewing Welty at her family residence in Jackson, Mississippi, in 1973, Walker confirmed for herself the insuperable barrier dividing their lives, a break borne out of the differences in their race, age, and political forwardness, as well as by the imprint of history and habit on their imaginations. Whatever Welty and Walker might share as women, southerners, and writers, Walker insists, "[W]e are more strangers, because the past will always separate us."[11] And yet, both writers pilot separate but modally similar passages through the South's racial divide. Remarkably, Welty and Walker achieve this similarity not by inscribing (or prescribing) a synthesized perception of the Black-white boundary, but by implicitly setting one raced perspective opposite the other. As Welty's white characters regard the post office either in agreement or in competition with the pedestal, Walker's Black characters occupy its absence. Contrary to Welty's contradictory presentations of the post office and the pedestal, Walker's fiction imparts a singular view, reflective of her characters' intense subjugation and the post office as their only pathway to the wider world.

Published the same year as the interview, Walker's story "Strong Horse Tea" renders the danger of depending solely on the post office. In the story, Rannie Mae Toomer eschews the homeopathic knowledge of her uneducated Black neighbors in favor of an imaginary white physician to treat her dying son, Snooks. Holding vigil at his bedside, Rannie Mae watches her child wheeze with whooping cough and double pneumonia. Her distrust of home remedies causes her to waste vital time petitioning her friendly mailman to send back a doctor: "'White mailman, white doctor,' she chanted skeptically, under her breath, as if to banish spirits."[12] Only when old Aunt Sarah darkens her door to explain no doctor is coming, that the mailman has only bothered to relay the message to her, does Rannie Mae, albeit too late, follow Sarah's suggestion that the child ingest horse urine. The mailman's view of rural Blacks can hardly be clearer: "He wished she would stand back from his car so he could get going. But she clung to the side gabbing away about 'Snooks' and 'NEW-monia' and 'shots' and how she wanted a 'REAL doctor.' ... Black people as black as Rannie Mae always made him uneasy" (91). Pinning her hopes on the mailman, Rannie Mae, absurdly pathetic and isolated, mistakes his politeness for genuine concern; more importantly, she has internalized white supremacy, while fatally overlooking the durability of the Black-white boundary.

The indifference to Black suffering also informs the singular mention of a specific African American in Welty's *Losing Battles*, a nameless and innocent sawmill worker hanged for a crime Uncle Nathan commits, the murder of Herman Dearman.[13] Focusing not on the emotional fallout the Black man's death has upon his family, the novel instead probes, as Rebecca Mark notes, "the isolationist instincts of the people of Tishomingo County," an almost exclusively white section of northeast Mississippi, to reveal how such an absenting of Black life is possible.[14] In a novel built upon the sharing of stories, this instinct for the characters' silence in the face of racial injustice remains an important one, underscoring Welty's own characterization of this episode as "very telling and essential."[15]

Where Welty's novel fronts an exclusively white perspective, Walker's *The Color Purple* offers an almost entirely Black one with only fleeting references to white characters. Regardless of this stark difference, both novels reveal that even as postal routes shorten the distance between regions and individuals, history, law, and convention continue to reinforce the Black-white boundary. Although *Losing Battles* and *The Color Purple* similarly take place in backwater communities—in Mississippi and Georgia, respectively—and although both narratives occur in the 1930s, the women in these texts offer significantly different responses to disconnection and seclusion. Not to minimize the sacrifices the women make for marriage in *Losing Battles*, Welty at least spares them the patrilineal violence Celie suffers in *The Color Purple*. When Celie's stepson Harpo asks his father Albert why he beats his wife, he answers, "Cause she my wife. Plus, she stubborn," upon which Celie silently reflects: "Remind me of Pa."[16] That Celie mistakes her stepfather for her actual father does nothing to diminish this pattern of sexual tyranny.

Like Gloria and Beulah in *Losing Battles*, Celie conforms to the definitions of marriage and domesticity given to her, but without the pedestal Gloria and Beulah possess, tokenized as it may be, the impetus for Celie to secure a community outside that of her in-laws' and husband's friends becomes paramount for her. In the first half of the novel, Celie's "letters"—topped with the salutation "Dear God"—register as cosmic outcries against her loneliness and disempowerment. As Linda Selzer acknowledges, Celie's recovery of Nettie's letters "begins the transformation of Celie from writer to reader."[17] As a reader, the lonely seeker locates her tribe, her extended self. Whereas Gloria in *Losing Battles* nonchalantly dismisses letter writing, thereby sealing her commitment to her husband, Jack, Celie turns inwardly away from hers, her innermost thoughts fixed on unreceived letters from her beloved sister Nettie, whom Albert bans from his house for refusing his sexual propositions.

Both Welty and Walker present the suppression of women's access to postal services. Veritable agents of obstruction, Lexie in *Losing Battles* and Albert in *The Color Purple*, rationalize their actions by viewing their captives as undeserving of private correspondence: Lexie likely tosses Julia's letters in a pigsty, and Albert bars Celie from the mailbox, burying Nettie's letters in a covered trunk containing his own cherished objects. Driven by distorted masculine pride, Albert dominates his wife to suppress his own incipient sense of sexual inadequacy. From either side of the color line, Lexie and Albert initially appear to have little in common, but as obstructionists, they pursue similar objectives and comparable strategies of containment. Most importantly, Lexie and Albert work to oppress individuals already oppressed, furthering the familiar narrative that women, regardless of color, figure most fittingly as socially peripheral or ancillary.

As Lexie and Albert seek to contain, control, and suppress, they inevitably inflict great suffering on the women they cut off from private correspondence, leaving both Julia and Celie captive to their respective controllers. Never shrinking from a fight, however, Julia redoubles her defiance against her captor. At the family reunion, Lexie recalls chasing after a distraught Julia along "the empty road" in front of her house where Julia would "even crack open her mailbox, and look inside!" (716). After uncovering Nettie's letters, Celie finds her sadness narrowing into rage-filled fantasies in which Albert "fall[s] dead every which a way" (120). These scenes of anguish novelize the historical reality of extreme rural isolation. As Gallagher notes, the therapeutic potential of the Rural Free Delivery Program (RFD), launched nationwide in 1902, became apparent to Postmaster General George Meyer who, convinced by medical testimonials and tributes, declared in 1907 a considerable decrease in cases of mental illness throughout the nation's secluded areas and territories because of the program. Gallagher explains, "In addition to information from the outside world, the carriers brought friendly faces and news of recent events" so that now the most alienated populations "had, right at their doorsteps, a bridge that united them with a larger America."[18] All told, the literature, medical writing, and written history uniformly confirm the primal, existential need for finding connections beyond immediate personal contact.

The disparity between Celie's and Julia's outcomes rests on the guarding of white woman respectability, a crucial element in Julia's life but materially absent from Celie's. For these reasons, a woman as bold and brazen as Shug Avery could not exist in the Mississippi Welty imagines. In Walker's story, Shug personifies the mythic traits of the blues musician—women like Bessie Smith and Ma Rainey—fusing lust for life and wanderlust, a woman setting her own life's terms, and seeking pleasure anywhere she can. When Celie and Shug secretly become sexually involved, they explode the patriarchal bounds of their respective marriages to Albert and Grady. Shug's spiriting Nettie's latest letter from Albert to give to its rightful recipient breaks Albert's postal blockade, initiating not simply Celie's recovery of stolen letters but also her self-recovery as well as the reclamation of the novel's global community scattered across Africa and America. Unpersuaded by the narratological structure of Celie's transformation, author and social critic bell hooks maintains that Celie lacks "a true correspondence" with Nettie—that her letters only offer "the illusion of intimacy."[19] What hooks fails to articulate is that Nettie's writings, many of them focused on her missionary work in Africa, continually open Celie's consciousness, bending it, molding it, filling it with geographies, experiences, and realities unavailable to Celie otherwise. To dismiss Nettie's letters as inauthentically intimate diminishes their effect on their recipient and, more than that, overlooks the operative forces of the US Post Office and post offices around the world, which make Nettie's communication with Celie at all possible.

Despite the differences between Julia's and Celie's narratives, they similarly extol literacy and education as liberating powers. Although Celie's education takes a less conventional route than Julia's, it proves instrumental in reuniting her with Nettie. Meanwhile, Julia's passion for learning and teaching forges in the community a mostly veiled legacy, except in the life of Jack's younger brother, Vaughn, who drives the bus for Banner School. Vaughn so adores his job and the school that "he would have beaten sunup and driven there now, if the doors had had any way of opening for him" (806). Welty describes the school bus as Noah's Ark, which Rebecca Mark thoughtfully reads as a metaphor of "salvation from certain death by the flood of violence and ignorance"[20] in Mississippi in the 1960s. To preserve and further his imagination, Vaughn must look outward, figuratively departing the place of his family, friends, and neighbors.

If Lexie and Gloria act as agents of obstruction in *Losing Battles*, the bus and the school function as forces of cultural shift, challenging the community's proscriptive views and customs primarily through exposure to perspectives broader than those already uniformly accepted. Conversely, a school and a school bus could work to preserve the conformity, prejudice, and isolation ingrained in Banner's people, but with the mention of Vaughn's new, cherished geography book, Welty's "ark" more clearly points toward an anticipation of paradigmatic change. Looking forward to his next day at school, holding the geography book close to his face, "he could smell its print, sharper, blacker, dearer than the smell of new shoes" (806). Here the narration links Vaughn's and Julia's reverence for education, and by aligning Vaughn with the school, the novel stresses its anxious balance between clannishness and boundary breaking. Vaughn's geography book doubles as Julia's posted letters and seeds, and like the book, the bus serves to dislocate Vaughn—as the school and post office do for Julia—displacing him from his community as much as daily routines also center him there.

Clearly, Vaughn has opportunities unavailable to Julia or Celie.[21] Unrestricted by the pedestal or by race, Vaughn nevertheless hides his book (bartered from a family rival) and suppresses his excitement about learning, wary it will affront the machismo his family and neighbors admire and his brother wears like a shield. What Vaughn, Julia, and Celie all require is an ally, a friend, a figure of inspiration to light their path even partway. No one opens the door to the outside world for them or encourages their fascination with it. Instead, they meet with rejection and betrayal: Gloria disowns Julia's attempts to widen her worldview in favor of convention and domesticity formalized by her marriage to Jack. By contrast, Shug smashes the oppression Celie has known her whole life by connecting her to a world Nettie's letters construct for her—or begin to construct. Where Julia presses forward on her own, Celie relies on other women (Nettie and Shug) as she forges a self-determination explicitly free of male control. Of course, alliance does not necessitate perpetual harmony. As Suzanne Marrs notes, "To Welty, even letters filled with lacerating wit were a way of reaching for connection."[22] Nevertheless, without the allowance to reach out, to make contacts, Welty's and Walker's characters struggle with the thwarting of the possible self—what the self might become, pursue, produce, rebuff, and accept, what the self might imagine, calculate, and decide, if left uninhibited to converse with other people with opposing and sympathetic views across short and long distances.

Southern Exiles: Wright and Nordan
Writing the Postal South in the North (1940s–1950s)

Like Welty and Walker, Richard Wright and Lewis Nordan look to the post office as an attractive agency of viability, connection, and exchange. Narrating the impact of the post office on their self-formations, both Wright and Nordan trace how access to its services decidedly altered the trajectories of their lives. Although written while living outside the geographical boundaries of the Postal South, Wright's *Black Boy* (*American Hunger*) (1945) and Nordan's *Boy with Loaded Gun* (2000) detail the pivotal role the post office played in expanding their consciousness beyond the conditioning of their southern experiences. Both native sons of Mississippi who later resettled in the North, Wright and Nordan, though from opposite sides of the color line, recount the impact southern racial violence had on their decisions to migrate north. Born in Roxie, Mississippi, in 1908, and having also lived in Arkansas and Tennessee, Wright developed a chronic fear of white people, his psychic and physical survival dependent on his steering clear of the violent threats they posed. Throughout *Black Boy*, Wright chronicles the indelible imprint this fear has on his interactions with whites; he characterizes his years living in the South as "the terror from which I fled."[23]

Born in 1939 in Forest, Mississippi, more than three decades after Wright, and raised in Itta Bena, about a half hour from where Emmett Till was lynched, Nordan acknowledges in *Boy with Loaded Gun* that "the death of Emmett Till had been the final reason, if I had needed one final reason, that I left Itta Bena to try to find a life in the larger world."[24] Although Nordan eventually escaped the South to settle permanently in Pittsburgh, Pennsylvania, the epicenter of his fiction remained in Mississippi, his vision cast permanently behind him to the origin of his psychic wounds.

Wright's and Nordan's fictional depictions of the post office paint a decidedly unromantic portrait of the postal service and its possibilities; meanwhile, their autobiographical writings underscore its initially positive interventions in their lives. Wright's temporary stint working at the Chicago post office, which he depicts in *Black Boy*, provided him a financial security he had not previously known and created the opportunity for meaningful cross-racial friendships. Left malnourished from a poverty-induced lack of food in the South, Wright, who weighed under the minimum 125 pounds required for full-time employment at the post office, received a temporary clerk position, a job for which he "earned seventy cents an hour," allowing him to go "to bed each night now with a full stomach for the first time in my life" (264–65). That Wright eventually lost the postal job that allowed him to eat enough ironically highlights the ongoing somatic toll his southern upbringing inflicts upon him.

Wright initially claims he "had no friends . . . and felt the need for none," but the post office altered this situation, providing him contact with a like-minded, well-read group of friends (265). Far from the experience of the singular rural postmaster or postmistress depicted in Welty's fiction, the northern urban post office provided Wright a much larger community of workers that defied the anti-intellectualism of his previous employer and members of his own family. Wright befriended an "Irish chap" with whom he "had read a lot in common," and they happily shared a cynical worldview (271). Eventually, the friendship expanded to include "a 'gang' of Irish, Jewish, and Negro wits," their lives troubled by a "childhood disease of metaphysical fear" that led them to poke "fun at government, the masses, statesmen, and political parties" (271–72). So studious are the friends he meets there that, as Wright biographer Michel Fabre notes, "the post office was jokingly referred to as 'The University.'"[25]

Unlike the post office in Chicago that facilitates Wright's formation of ethnically diverse lifelong friendships, community arrives for Nordan by way of a mail order catalog. The catalog opened distant worlds to the young Nordan, who increasingly felt alienated by geography and the limitations of small-town life in Mississippi: "Montgomery Ward was an escape hatch, its opening as thin as a reed, but somehow I might squeeze through it and pop out the other end into rarer air" (52). Seeing in the catalog "real worlds toward which [he] might flee," Nordan initiates a mail order buying spree he likens to scientists sending "out signals to the stars in hopes of contacting extraterrestrial life" (52). Nordan's point of departure is his hometown post office, where he purchases a money order, his "first ticket out," to buy "coffee cups and saucers" for his parents (53).

While the possibilities of mail order clearly expand the scope of Nordan's imagination, the reality of his "cosmic" postal exploits initially proves more mundane. Taking advantage of the send-away opportunities in his comic books, Nordan joins boys' clubs, like the Junior G-Men, and fan clubs, like Dick Tracy and Little Lulu, all in the hopes of making contact and establishing himself as part of a larger, national community. Establishing community via mail order, however, depends on the intentions and ethics of the consumer, a point underscored by Nordan's postal purchase of a gun with which he tries to shoot his stepfather. Acknowledging his relief at the gun's misfire primarily because he did not kill his stepfather, Nordan explains how this event could have unraveled all he had hoped to achieve through the postal service: "I had cast my line through mail order catalogs and comic books and old barbershop magazines . . . in hopes of snagging a way out, a map with the route marked, a clear set of instructions. A bullet in my father's chest . . . would have kept me there in Itta Bena, in the cramped spaces of my limited imagination, forever" (71).

Except for the gun purchase, which nearly derailed his escape entirely, the success of Nordan's postal connections rests on a financial agency fundamentally denied to Wright. Such differences in their economic realities determine the writers' interactions with and perceptions of the post office that inevitably filter into their fictional representations. Despite these differences in economic circumstances, their visions of the postal service align in Wright's novel *Lawd Today!* and Nordan's story "The Sears and Roebuck Catalog Game" (1986). Containing autobiographical elements, these texts transform aspects of Wright's and Nordan's personal experiences with the post office into bleak tragedies, initiating a pessimistic turn away from the ambivalence their memoirs signal about the institution's benefits.[26] Depicting the illusory happiness promised by American consumerist culture, a myth disseminated in part by the United States Postal Service, both works feature unhappy marriages with alcohol-dependent husbands and lonely, desperate wives prone to suicidal ideation, who turn to religious magazines or catalogs to escape their dissatisfaction. Whether located in Depression-era Illinois as in Wright's novel or mid-twentieth-century Mississippi as in Nordan's story, the postal service appears fundamentally altered by the shift away from personal correspondence to advertising and mail order catalogs.

Following a day in the life of Chicago postal worker Jake Jackson, Wright's novel *Lawd Today!* depicts an urban landscape inundated with advertising so omnipresent that it intrudes upon Jake's sleep and reaches into his home via the mail. The radio program that opens the novel and bleeds into Jake's dream announces the time, eight o'clock, "COURTESY THE NEVERSTOP WATCH COMPANY,"[27] and when Jake checks his mailbox before leaving for the day, he finds only circulars, no letters from family or friends, no personal greetings, no meaningful news. The fliers, from companies like "THE MYSTERIOUS THREESTAR MEDIUM," "THE EASTERN CELESTIAL MAGIC COMPANY," "THE DEMOCRATIC PATENT MEDICINE STORE," "VIRGIN MARY'S NEVERFAIL HERB AND ROOT TONIC FOR NERVOUS AND RUNDOWN WOMEN, INC.," and "THE SUREFIRE TREATMENT COMPANY, INC.," advertise dubious spiritual mediums promising wealth and charlatans hawking cures for lethargy, impotence, and alcoholism (38, 39, 41, and 42). Ostensibly, the lack of first-class mail is due to a holiday, Lincoln's birthday, but Wright's implication is clear: in the facilitation of an exploitative American capitalist system, the postal service loses its interpersonal communicative power, rendering recipients as little more than gullible consumers without legitimate hope of relieving the ills that blight urban life. The last two companies hail from Jake's home state of Mississippi, but what passes for interregional postal connection amounts to an ineffectual substitute for a more sustaining Black religious experience. Possibly to underscore the irony of a Mississippi company in the 1930s promising to cure the troubles of Blacks living in the North, Wright depicts Jake immediately walking into the street after pocketing circulars he finds appealing and catching a glimpse in a newspaper of "a black and white picture of a nude, half-charred body of a Negro swinging from the end of a rope" (43). Set against such racial terror, these southern-born panaceas of the circulars belie the systemic racism that poses an existential threat to Black survival.

Portraying Jake's wife, Lil, as more likely to die by his hands than a lynch mob, Wright presents an uncomfortable truth that not only confounds critics' expectations of Black male heroism but also challenges any monolithic assessment of Wright's depiction of the postal service without respect to gender. Routinely beaten, verbally assaulted, and tricked by Jake into having an abortion that results in ongoing medical problems, Lil turns to the mail-distributed spiritual publication *"UNITY*

...*A MAGAZINE DEVOTED TO CHRISTIAN HEALING*" to sustain her in her otherwise insufferable marriage (7). *Unity*, the historical magazine published in Kansas City, Missouri, reached a national audience when postal reforms subsidized second-class mail delivery and allowed for the proliferation of advertising typified by the circulars Jake pulls from his mailbox. Characterizing this historical shift in mail delivery, Winifred Gallagher contends that this revolution "also had a dark side," including the increase in fraud that left postal inspectors regularly pursuing "vendors of quack remedies."[28] Whether Lil's embrace of this Christian magazine becomes yet another iteration of Wright's critique of a fraudulent consumerist culture remains open to critical debate. Finding sincerity in Lil's attachment to the magazine, Brannon Costello sympathetically argues that "it is perhaps [her] only access to religion or to any sort of broader community," and from it, "she draws some of the strength that allows her to survive."[29] While this is undoubtedly true, Wright also questions the efficacy of Lil expecting physical relief from a magazine that pictured "a haloed, bearded man dressed in white folds" resting his hand "upon the blond curls of a blue-eyed girl" (7).

With this image of a white-robed man protecting a white child who could not look more different than Lil, Wright underscores the futility of placing trust in white paternalism, which has already proven to be an abysmal failure, evidenced by her repeated attempts to talk to Jake's white boss at the post office to stop her ongoing domestic abuse. When Jake appears on the precipice of losing his job for his latest act of abuse, he foils her attempt by paying Doc Higgins, a prominent Black businessman, to bribe those with connections to the postmaster who ultimately orders for Jake not to be fired, once again making Lil's complaints of domestic abuse disappear. If white paternalism is Lil's only beacon of hope, either spiritually via *Unity* or institutionally via the post office, it remains a very dim one indeed and ultimately does nothing to address the physical abuse that causes her to utter by novel's end, "Lawd, I wish I was dead" (219).

Though separated by time, race, and geography, Lil and the unnamed wife in Nordan's story "The Sears and Roebuck Catalog" both turn to the postal service to provide an imagined community in otherwise isolated situations. Depressed and unhappy in her marriage with a man who "had no imagination,"[30] the wife creates fictional lives for the models she encounters in the Sears and Roebuck catalog. As Sugar, a thinly veiled fictionalized Nordan, says of his mother's game, "Sears and Roebuck was a real world to me, with lakes and cities and operas and noisy streets and farmlands and neighborhoods" (15). For his mother, the game becomes an imaginative act of inventing alternative worlds to escape the loneliness and boredom of small- town living and enduring a marriage with an alcoholic man she does not love. Suggesting a biographical influence in the origins of such a game, Nordan writes in his memoir that his "mother's use of the catalog was to inspire dreams of worlds she did not really believe existed and was resigned to know only in fantasy" (52). Like Lil's turn to *Unity*, the wife's game with the Sears and Roebuck catalog, "soon known as 'the consumer's bible'"[31] after its first publication in 1893, is not about stepping into the role of the consumer but of achieving a connection beyond the domestic sphere, one denied to her but not her husband. Such fantasies of connection, however, only mask the wife's underlying mental illness, and she takes Lil's passive suicidal ideation to the next step when she attempts to kill herself in front of her son by slicing open an artery with a razor blade. Just as Wright implies that *Unity* cannot fundamentally alter the causes of Lil's problems, Nordan suggests that while the catalog may become a temporary coping mechanism, it does little to address the physical realities that force the wife to turn to it in the first place.

If these women suffer from physical alienation, the men in *Lawd Today!* undergo an alienation of labor that highlights what workers lose in the shift from the small rural post office in the South to the large postal hub in the urban North. Though Jake prizes his relatively well-paid government job at a time when many cannot find work, his position at the Chicago post office is anything but ideal. As Fabre notes, the historical Chicago post office where Wright worked and which he later depicts in the novel "bore the unfortunate distinction of having the worst working conditions of all United States post offices."[32] Jake stands for the duration of his eight-hour shift under glaring lights, inhaling dust that dries his throat, listening to noise that "imperceptibly dulled his senses" (130), all under the panoptic gaze of the foreman whose "legion of catfooted spies and stoolpigeons . . . snoop eternally" (129). Though these hardships and physical exertions exact a toll, the most dehumanizing aspect of the job remains the mental erosion the workers suffer due to the alienating act of production. Giving complaint to this exploitative process in the second section of the novel, Wright collapses Jake and his three friends into one collective character, forming what critic Yoshinobu Hakutani describes as the singular voice of "the proletarian pluralistic novel."[33]

"I wouldn't get so damn tired if I knowed where some of this mail was going."
"Some people asking for money to get home, maybe."
"And somebody telling somebody that somebody else is dead, maybe."
"Yeah, maybe a lot of great things in these letters."
"It's hard to just move your hands all day and not see what you're doing."
"Like a squirrel turning in a cage." (150)

Not privy to the human dramas that compel such correspondences, the men become little more than mechanized sorters, fundamentally estranged from the benefits of the communication process. Unlike the singular postmistress in Welty's fiction who becomes intimately intertwined in the interplay between mail and recipient, the men in Wright's sorting room are reduced to interchangeable, unknown entities, revealing how the postal service enhances the connection of some only at the expense of others. Engaged in mindless, repetitive tasks without knowing the end benefit of their work, the men lose part of their humanity and become trapped in an unfulfilling and seemingly futile cycle of labor.

Postscript

No discussion of the Postal South would be complete without mention of William Faulkner's participation in it, both as a writer and, more infamously, as an incompetent postmaster at the University of Mississippi branch. Absent the fatalism and despair characterizing postal work in *Lawd Today!*, Faulkner's personal statements about his postmaster stint nevertheless resonate with Wright's novelization of the labor as mindless and unfulfilling, burdening the shoulders of potentially imaginative but unprosperous people. Devotees of Faulkner's writings and legacy are familiar with his reported comments upon leaving his post in October 1924: "I reckon I'll be at the beck and call of folks with money all my life, but thank God I won't ever again have to be at the beck and call of every son of a bitch who's got two cents to buy a stamp."[34] Speaking in Oxford, Mississippi, in 1987 at the dedication of the first issue of the United States Postal Service's William Faulkner stamp, Welty rejoins the caustic humor of his reported comments with a slightly softer carp, imagining herself and her audience as patrons looking to purchase a two-cent stamp only to find the stamp window unattended: "So we holler his name, and at last here he is. William Faulkner. We have interrupted him. . . . [H]e was out of sight in the back—writing lyric poems."[35]

Notably, Welty's speech rehearses the perspectives of many of her characters—women seeking correspondence and community. Elsewhere, Welty's fiction retains Faulkner's vision of reproof: much like Emily Grierson from Faulkner's "A Rose for Emily" (1930), Sabina McGinnis in Welty's "Asphodel" (1942) rejects modernized mail delivery, viewing it as an intrusion on her privileged independence. Ultimately, the Postal South collects a cacophony of voices, memories, and conflicts, all reflective of the diverse lives inhabiting the region or recalling their experiences in it. In these crucial moments, where southern writers evoke a shared, though varied, imagination and condition—be it mail order reprieve from seclusion and alienation as in Welty, Wright, and Nordan, or a Black woman's tenuous attachment with the postal service either as postmistress in Yarbrough or addressee in Walker—definitive patterns emerge relative to the impact of modern mail delivery on southern life and culture. Repeatedly, these stories of the Postal South tell readers who southerners are, what they have been to one another, what their aspirations, ambitions, and destinies communicate about the region's past and ever-changing future.

NOTES

1. W. E. B. Du Bois, *The Souls of Black Folk*, ed. Brent Hayes Edwards, rev. ed. (1903; repr., Oxford, UK: Oxford University Press, 2007), 3.

2. Devin Leonard, *Neither Snow nor Rain: A History of the United States Post Office* (New York: Grove Press, 2016), 20–21.

3. Winifred Gallagher, *How the Post Office Created America: A History* (New York: Penguin, 2017), 156. Hereafter cited in the text.

4. William B. Galewood, "Theodore Roosevelt and the Indianola Affair," *Journal of Negro History* 53, no. 1 (1968), 60.

5. Steve Yarbrough, "'Dogged by Some Sins from Their Past': An Interview with Steve Yarbrough," interview by Tom Williams, *Arkansas Review: A Journal of Delta Studies* 33, no. 2 (Aug. 2002): 117–18.

6. Steve Yarbrough, *Visible Spirits* (New York: Knopf, 2001), 94. Hereafter cited in the text.

7. Thomas E. Dasher, "Steve Yarbrough: Transplanted Mississippian," *Rough South, Rural South: Region and Class in Recent Southern Literature*, eds. Jean W. Cash and Keith Perry (Jackson: University Press of Mississippi, 2016), 197.

8. David McWhirter, "Secret Agents: Welty's African Americans," *Eudora Welty, Whiteness, and Race*, ed. Harriet Pollack (Athens: University of Georgia Press, 2013), 119.

9. For examples of this type of racial discrimination, see "Segregation—Postal," *Freedom Just Around the Corner: Black America from Civil War to Civil Rights*, Smithsonian National Postal Museum, https://postalmuseum.si.edu/exhibition/freedom-just-around-the-corner-segregation/segregation-postal.

10. For a discussion of how the RFD program improved the quality of life for those living in isolated, rural places, see Gallagher, *How the Post Office Created America*, 192.

11. Eudora Welty, interview by Alice Walker, "Eudora Welty: An Interview," *Conversations with Eudora Welty*, ed. Peggy Whitman Prenshaw (Jackson: University Press of Mississippi, 1984), 132.

12. Alice Walker, *In Love and Trouble: Stories of Black Women* (San Diego: Harvest, 1973), 89. Hereafter cited in the text.

13. Eudora Welty, *Losing Battles*, in *The Complete Novels*, ed. Richard Ford and Michael Kreyling (New York: Library of America, 1998), 784. Hereafter cited in the text.

14. Rebecca Mark, "Cross-Mark Ploughed into the Center: Civil Rights and Eudora Welty's *Losing Battles*," in *Eudora Welty and Politics: Did the Writer Crusade?*, ed. Harriet Pollack and Suzanne Marrs (Baton Rouge: Louisiana State University Press, 2001), 129.

15. Eudora Welty, interview by Charles T. Bunting, "'An Interior World': An Interview with Eudora Welty," *Conversations with Eudora Welty*, ed. Peggy Whitman Prenshaw (Jackson: University Press of Mississippi, 1984), 48.

16. Alice Walker, *The Color Purple* (Boston: Mariner Books, 1982), 22. Hereafter cited in the text.

17. Linda Seltzer, "Race and Domesticity in *The Color Purple*," in *Alice Walker's "The Color Purple*," ed. Harold Bloom (New York: Chelsea House Publishers, 2000), 139.

18. Gallagher, *How the Post Office Created America*, 192.

19. bell hooks, "Writing the Subject: Reading *The Color Purple*," in *Alice Walker's "The Color Purple*," ed. Harold Bloom (New York: Chelsea House Publishers, 2000), 64.

20. Mark, "Cross-Mark Ploughed into the Center," 142.

21. For a discussion of Julia Mortimer's failure to fully acknowledge the Black man's unjust killing, see Marrs, "Cross-Mark Ploughed into the Center," 152. In considering this case, Vaughn lacks the same insight.

22. Suzanne Marrs, introduction to *What There Is to Say We Have Said: The Correspondence of Eudora Welty and William Maxwell*, ed. Suzanne Marrs (Boston: Mariner Books, 2012), 2.

23. Richard Wright, *Black Boy (American Hunger)*, in *Richard Wright: Later Works*, ed. Arnold Rampersad (New York: Library of America, 1991), 246. Hereafter cited in the text.

24. Lewis Nordan, *Boy with Loaded Gun* (Chapel Hill, NC: Algonquin Books, 2000), 84. Hereafter cited in the text.

25. Michael Fabre, *The Unfinished Quest of Richard Wright*, trans. Isabel Barzun (New York: William Morrow, 1973), 79.

26. See Fabre, *The Unfinished Quest*, 78, for a discussion of the connections between Wright's experiences working at the post office and his treatment of it in *Lawd Today!* Fabre notes that "Wright used the details of his duties at the central post office in his novel *Lawd Today*.... Like Jake in *Lawd Today*, Wright even had a box at home to practice for his examination."

27. Richard Wright, *Lawd Today!*, in *Richard Wright: Early Works*, ed. Arnold Rampersad (New York: Library of America, 1991), 4. Hereafter cited in the text.

28. Gallagher, *How the Post Office Created America*, 210.

29. Brannon Costello, "Richard Wright's *Lawd Today!* and the Political Uses of Modernism," *African American Review* 37, no. 1 (2003): 46–47.

30. Lewis Nordan, *Sugar among the Freaks* (Chapel Hill, NC: Algonquin Books, 1996), 16. Hereafter cited in the text.

31. Gallagher, *How the Post Office Created America*, 205.

32. Faber, *The Unfinished Quest*, 78.

33. Yoshinobu Hakuntani, "Richard Wright's Experiment in Naturalism and Satire: *Lawd Today!*" *Studies in American Fiction* 14, no. 2 (Autumn 1986), 175.

34. Joseph Blotner, *Faulkner: A Biography*, rev. ed. (1974; repr., New York: Random House, 1984), 118.

35. Eudora Welty, "Speech in Celebration of the William Faulkner Stamp," in *On William Faulkner* (Jackson: University Press of Mississippi, 2003), 72.

"Burning in His Own Heart"

Contrasting Visions of Blindness and Invisibility as Social Death in Wright's *Native Son* and Faulkner's *Light in August*

BERNARD T. JOY

Both William Faulkner's *Light in August* (1932) and Richard Wright's *Native Son* (1940) are substantially shaped by the legacy of the transatlantic slave trade. As Orlando Patterson writes, "Jim Crow was neoslavery, pure and simple, a system ... enforced by a police state and collectively reinforced ... not by marginal white mobs ... but by ordinary white citizens often led by ordained ministers of religion."[1] Just as Paul Gilroy draws on Primo Levi's discussion of the "useless violence"[2] of Auschwitz and its utility to its perpetrators as a means of producing a solidarity based upon the dehumanization of those marked by racial, ethnic, or cultural difference, Patterson too draws parallels between the Jim Crow laws and Nazi atrocities. Both are considered—by Patterson and by Gilroy—to be historical circumstances whose destructive aftereffects continue into the twenty-first century as part of the "lineaments of the culture of slavery [that] still haunt African American life" (*SSD*, xix).

Writing specifically on the transition from slavery to the social worlds described and interpreted by African American writers such as Wright, Abdul R. JanMohamed has argued that "one feature that links the [ante- and postbellum] periods is the reliance of both societies on the threat of death and the systematic use of lynching to coerce subject populations."[3] In my emphasis on the specific historical period of the early to mid-twentieth century and what I view as its distinctiveness from earlier realities, I stop short in what follows of adopting JanMohamed's heuristic, in which he uses the terms "slave" and "black" interchangeably in a manner that brackets the differences between a society built upon institutionalized slavery and one suffering from its hangovers while retaining its own species of de facto slavery (*DBS*, 5).

However, in my readings of *Native Son*'s Bigger Thomas and *Light in August*'s Joe Christmas, I do draw upon JanMohamed's insights into the important commonalities between the practical lives of Black people decades after slavery and those of their enslaved forebears. I particularly share JanMohamed's emphasis, after Patterson, on the "powerlessness, social-death, and lack of honour" (*DBS*, 5) that typify conditions such as those of Joe and Bigger.

In the reading that follows, I offer an extension of JanMohamed's reading of Bigger as a subject bound on a trajectory from social death through actual death to symbolic death. I then highlight those parts of Bigger's narrative in which we may observe a commonality with Joe's own racially determined trajectory. However, I also examine the opportunity that Joe's light skin affords him throughout the novel to escape the epidermalization that the visibly Black Bigger cannot escape. In addition, I extend JanMohamed's use of Patterson's constituent elements of slavery by suggesting that in addition to powerlessness, social death, and lack of honor, another central element in the definition of the slave experience (and through inheritance, the experience of the descendants of enslaved Africans) is the invisibility of their social condition in the United States. What slavery really means, as Patterson puts it at one point, is "direct and insidious violence . . . namelessness and invisibility . . . endless personal violation, and . . . chronic inalienable dishonour" (*SSD*, 12). This second pairing, namelessness and invisibility, is of particular interest in my discussion. Patterson's association of the terms coincides with my reading of the sense of being unseen that Bigger and Joe both experience at various stages of their complex negotiations with "natal alienation," framed as "a loss of native status, [a] deracination" (*SSD*, 7). In my reading of both novels, though the implications are markedly distinct in each, to be invisible is to be deracinated. While I join JanMohamed in tracing scopic, specular registers across *Native Son*, and while I extend his Freudian observations into my reading of *Light in August*, I turn to intersections in the phenomenological work of Frantz Fanon and Maurice Merleau-Ponty in order to frame the concepts of blindness and invisibility in the two novels. As I hope to show, the clearest picture of characters like Bigger Thomas and Joe Christmas may arise out of a consideration of both the limitations on and the possibilities for redemption inherent in how Black bodies see and are seen, how Black people have sought to represent themselves and how they have been represented by the societies they inhabit, and how the conditions of that seeing prompt those subjected to its dehumanizing operations toward emancipatory (often violently emancipatory) action.

Blackness, Visibility, and the Body: Wright, Fanon, and Merleau-Ponty

In this opening discussion of *Native Son*, I will draw centrally upon Fanon's racial interventions into phenomenology, and particularly his well-known objections to—but also extensions of—aspects of the phenomenology of Merleau-Ponty. From a Fanonian perspective, the racial epidermal schema is imposed over or undergirds the socially unimposed corporeal schema, the biological universality of which, as presented by Merleau-Ponty, Fanon sought to characterize as a concept of white philosophers that failed to consider the problems of racialization. Fanon considered a transparent, unmediated access to the dialectic between body and world as foreclosed to a Black experience forever structured by the "thousand details, anecdotes [and] stories" of the white societies through which Blackness is seen and against which, for Fanon, "no ontological resistance" is possible.[4] In Fanon's own reading, Bigger Thomas's acts of violence in *Native Son* are responses "to the world's anticipation" (*BSWM*, 107), to the fear within white societies that Black subjects are always more capable of savagery than white subjects. In this sense, the acts of violence perpetrated against Bigger and those that he perpetrates can be read as predetermined, as proceeding out of his visibility as Black and his refusal to recede into the kind of social invisibility (a kind of social death) that would render him inoffensive, though it would prolong the tension of his eventual discovery as the violent, animalistic, and amoral Black man of white imagination. Living under this white gaze and having thoroughly internalized it, Bigger—unlike Joe Christmas in *Light in August*—is never free to imagine himself outside the racial or the social. As such, Bigger rigidly associates social death with physical death in that he experiences his physical, biological, corporeal self as always already imposed upon by a white construct: the Black man. It is by this same token that the sense of aliveness Bigger derives from asserting his will on the white world is continually conflated with his perception of himself as socially alive, socially aware, and socially visible. In the Fanonian sense, Bigger accepts that it is "impossible ... to get away from an inborn complex" and so he focuses his energies on his attempt "to assert [him]self as a BLACK MAN" (*BSWM*, 87).

This inescapable visibility as Black, which Bigger experiences throughout the novel and which he will ultimately embrace as a resource of emancipatory resistance against his dehumanization, like the comparable inescapable visibility of his social circle, finds continual expression in the imagery of the text that works to emphasize and juxtapose whiteness and Blackness. Even in moments alone with friends, as in his first meeting with Gus, the visual significance of their black skin within a white society forms a major part of how Bigger and other Black characters are seen: "lean[ing] their backs against the red-brick wall of a building, smoking, their cigarettes slanting white across their black chins."[5]

From early in the novel, Blackness is sharply delineated and set against a homogenous whiteness. Bigger inhabits a visual landscape in which even the cigarettes Black people smoke emphasize their racial difference via a contrast with their skin. It is a contrast that readers may experience visually by way of its verbal evocation of a painterly, photographic, or filmic chiaroscuro. Techniques of this kind, which draw upon the visually saturated cultural context within which *Native Son* exists and to which Wright explicitly refers throughout the novel, act to mark vision as a central diegetic mechanism through which the formation of both perspective and identity are achieved. One instance of Wright's direct reference to visual culture, in particular, that cues up our reading of the imagery used to represent the novel's Black characters is his repeated reference to the movies in the pages directly preceding Bigger's meeting with Gus (*NS*, 42–43).

Additionally, the racial homogeneity of Bigger's social world— against which Blackness is marginalized to the point of invisibility and set in stark contrast to the point of hypervisibility— is equally represented via a binary delineation of colors and their social imports within a ubiquitously visible supremacist taxonomy in which every symbol of authority is coded as white. In the space of only a few pages, we encounter a communally experienced Black mental space overbearingly populated by exploitative "old white landlords," "white policemen," "the white world's rule," and State's Attorney Buckley's "white face . . . fleshy but stern" emblazoned on a billboard that seems to Bigger to watch him "unblinkingly," mimicking the pervasiveness of a white gaze capable of structuring racial difference and racial subjecthood, and thereby engendering the typologies upon which the policing of racial boundaries is founded (*NS*, 43–45). "IF YOU BREAK THE LAW," reads the legend on Buckley's campaign poster, "YOU CAN'T WIN!" (*NS*, 43). However, despite these continual cues of a visually evident racial hierarchy, there remain interspersed references to a dimension of experience that seems to escape the rigidity of a racialized, socially imposed visual coding.

Consider, for instance, the specificities of Bigger's interaction with Buckley's optically disorienting billboard image. What becomes apparent is that, despite the seemingly omnipresent power of the white gaze, what regulates Bigger's interaction with the image is not Buckley's vision (in any case, his printed image has no vision) but rather Bigger's own visual attention and bodily movements through space. As he does elsewhere, with regard to the billboard, Wright represents multiple layers to Bigger's visual attention, from his vague perception of the object as a peripherality ("he brooded and watched the men at work across the street. They were pasting a huge colored poster to a signboard" [*NS*, 42]) to his active visual appraisal allied to a range of associated thoughts and affects ("He looked at the round florid face and wagged his head" [*NS*, 43]). This latter, invested layer of attention is emphasized in this passage via repetition. From the first instance of Bigger having "looked" at Buckley's image—as opposed to having "watched" it—there are three further references to looking within eighteen lines. The implication is that the optical illusion of Buckley's visual power very much relies upon the inability of subjected persons like Bigger to look away. It is Bigger's vision, in other words, which supplies the power. The end of this interaction is also instructive in that it is not ultimately Bigger's conscious decision concerning where he directs his vision that breaks the dynamic of looking and being looked at in which Bigger engages with Buckley. Rather, what breaks the interaction is Bigger's physical location in space in relation to Buckley's image itself, "so far from it you had to take your eyes away" at which point "it stopped, like a movie blackout" (*NS*, 43). Here, in a decidedly phenomenological manner, we are presented with a visual world regulated by the physical orientation of the body.

The formulation is Merleau-Pontian. It involves a visible object existing in space, though seen only within the eye's or the body's "radius of action," a vision "formed from a certain point of the world."[6] However, even if this brief interaction with the image of a white face reveals Bigger's body, his movement, and his look as the organizing factors of the world he visually experiences, it is also clear that they are by no means the only factors. Nor can we conclude they are the primary factors. For Merleau-Ponty, the visible (speaking dualistically, the sensible world) and the invisible (speaking dualistically, thought, meaning, ideas, ideality, and mind) interact in a complex interplay wherein the visible thing ("a concretion of visibility . . . not an atom") "holds with all its fibers onto the fabric of the visible, and thereby onto a fabric of invisible being" (*VAI*, 132). Though a sustained interrogation of Merleau-Ponty's phenomenology of the visible and the invisible is beyond the scope of this discussion, I allude to it here not only to draw attention to the parallels between his understanding of the structuring power of body, movement, look, and Wright's similar understanding but also to suggest the nuanced ways in which both Wright and Fanon (proceeding out of their own specific positionalities as marginalized Black men) offer new possibilities to a predominantly white philosophical and social discourse for understanding the place of the body in the world from a greatly neglected historio-racial perspective. Being in the world, both Fanon and Wright seem to reveal to us, is indeed akin to the experiences described by phenomenologists such as Merleau-Ponty. However, being *Black* in the world comes with its own perspectives, its own problematics, and its own requirements for certain kinds of emancipatory action. In this way, we might think of the contributions to our understanding of (Black) visibility and invisibility made by writers such as Wright or Fanon not as rejections but as extensions of the contributions of (white) philosophers such as Merleau-Ponty.

Robert Bernasconi has recently made just such a case. In his analysis, Fanon challenges Merleau-Ponty's neglect of the importance of racial schemata to (Black) bodily experience. However, Bernasconi also places strong emphasis on the dual analysis of the problem at work in Fanon's *Black Skin, White Masks* (1952), wherein the consciousness of a history of dehumanization (the imposition of racial epidermal schemata) is balanced by a "forward-looking"[7] approach, what Fanon called "a progressive infrastructure ... toward disalienation" (*BSWM*, 184). "The importance of this sentence," as Bernasconi notes, "cannot be exaggerated given that the original title Fanon gave the book ... was *Essay on the Disalienation of the Black*" (*FFEP*, 393). Gilroy too challenges the widely held view of Fanon's rejection of phenomenological conceptions (like those of Merleau-Ponty) in which the body interacts, structures, and is structured by the world in a manner unimposed upon by social arrangements such as race. For Gilroy, "against what Fanon identified as the intensity of epidermalization and its racial corporeal schema, something like a 'real dialectic between ... [the] body and the world' (*BSWM*, 111) can begin, unanticipated, to reassert itself," and "despite its eternal, fixed appearance, the unstable equilibrium of the racial corporeal schema can be overthrown."[8]

Bernasconi, drawing on Jean-Paul Sartre's progressive-regressive method (which he argues Fanon anticipates), traces these two complementary strands of Fanon's project (the regressive and the progressive) through various sections of *Black Skin, White Masks*. The regressive sections of the book, Bernasconi argues, amount to Fanon's diagnostic "focus on those Black people who seek an exit or escape from being locked into their racial identity by embracing the white world and seeking acceptance by it ... [by choosing] to exist [in] their racial facticity" (*FFEP*, 395). However, even in these regressive sections, and far more explicitly elsewhere via his engagements with Karl Jaspers, Merleau-Ponty, and others, Fanon embraces a progressive infrastructure, "the task of which was to explore the possibility of a healthy relation between Blacks and Whites" (*FFEP*, 395). For Bernasconi, this Fanonian method is analogous to that of the clinician who "approaches the patient already equipped with an implicit understanding that the patient is not healthy, so that the passage from diagnosis to a possible cure is already immanent within the task" (*FFEP*, 396). As Bernasconi notes, "Fanon made this point repeatedly. In the very first chapter he had paraphrased Marx's famous eleventh thesis that the point is to change the world," not just to understand it (*FFEP*, 396). Gilroy makes similar parallels when he notes that "two things about Fanon that his many American readers have largely failed to really grasp" are his status as both a doctor and a soldier. "He had a doctor's mentality," Gilroy writes; "[H]e wanted to heal. . . . In Fanon, every argument about violence, every single comment on violence is framed or qualified by an argument about healing."[9] As such, Fanon's analysis of the racial epidermal schema becomes his diagnosis of a collective malady, and his calls to emancipatory action become akin to a cure aimed at the reclamation of a certain ontological immediacy, an unmediated, real relationality between the body and the world.

If Fanon recognized racialization as a malady, then the emancipatory action he proposes as a cure involves the counter-Hegelian rejection of social death and the embracing of the possibility of actual death. Rejecting racialization is only possible under this analysis, as Bernasconi writes, in those cases when the racialized subject, "after having 'reflected,' becom[es] 'actional' in a fight for freedom in which [s/he] is willing to accept death" (*FFEP*, 396). For Merleau-Ponty, freedom from the fatality of the structuring of consciousness is available only via consciousness of the body and its specific operations. Fanon denies such a possibility for Black subjects in that the Black body is the object not of its own consciousness but of the white gaze. His insistence on the need for actionality beyond mere consciousness marks one of his clearest disagreements with Merleau-Ponty's approach. For Fanon, the escape of "an inauthentic attitude in which [the Black] body is locked into its facticity by the white gaze" (*FFEP*, 403) and the attainment of a "real dialectic between . . . [the] body and the world" (*BSWM*, 111) require the Black body's "willingness to be its own nothingness, to accept death for the creation of a better world," and thereby to engender a state of affairs in which "'cultural crystallization' is put in question" "through an alternative bodily experience" of the embracing of actual death (*FFEP*, 403).

To return to Bigger, in whose narrative I read clear parallels to a Fanonian extension of a vision of embodied phenomenology typified most closely perhaps by Merleau-Ponty, it is clear that his consciousness of himself operates through a panoptic white gaze, but it is equally clear that his entrapment within that prison implies Fanon's "real dialectic between . . . [the] body and the world" just as the diagnosis of a malady implies the possibility of a cure and the reestablishment of good health. What is also clear is that the cure Bigger adopts for himself is a Fanonian one, wherein he embraces not only a violent actionality but also a willingness to die rather than to accept the social death of racial facticity and its concomitant powerlessness, lack of honor, deracination, and invisibility. I further argue that *Native Son* registers an emancipatory dimension of Bigger's characterization via representations of his vision even as his vision (of Buckley's overbearing image, for example) registers the conditions of his subjection to racializing operations. Throughout *Native Son*, Wright represents Bigger's multiple layers of visual attention. It is in the softening of the focus of that visual attention that Wright is able to present a prereflective, socially unimposed dialectic between body and world that hovers always on the peripheries of Bigger's consciousness:

> He puffed silently, relaxed, his mind pleasantly vacant of purpose. Every slight movement in the street evoked a casual curiosity in him. Automatically, his eyes followed each car as it whirred over the smooth black asphalt. A woman came by and he watched the gentle sway of her body until she disappeared into a doorway. He sighed, scratched his chin and mumbled. (*NS*, 45)

Here, the "pleasantly vacant" state of Bigger's mind speaks to a brief cessation in the negative affects around which his interactions with his environment generally revolve. It is a cessation Bigger owes to his mind's vacancy, to the absence of thought, analysis, judgment and categorical knowledge that typifies prereflectivity. As a result, rather than obeying the dictates of a mind conditioned to interpret visual information through the lens of racial subjugation, the things Bigger sees in this passage inspire only "a casual curiosity" that borders on the sensorily soothing, conditioned as it is by the smoothness of "the smooth black asphalt" and the sexualized image of "the gentle sway" of a woman's body. Here vision is not the result of racial codes and categories. It is unmediated, innate, automatic, and it comes punctuated by Bigger's small, personal, meaningless interactions with his body: a sigh, a scratch, a mumble.

It is, of course, eminently arguable that Bigger's social and racial conditioning exist even at the prereflective, unconscious, bodily level. For instance, we may think of the imaginary game Bigger and Gus play ("'Let's play "white,"' Bigger said" [*NS*, 47]), through which, by placing himself into various "white" situations, Bigger comes anew to realize (talking like he is "just now finding . . . out" [*NS*, 49]) the stark reality of white privilege and Black subjugation in the United States of the 1930s. Abdul JanMohamed uses his own discussion of this game to make a case for the somatic or psychosomatic effects of racialization. Together with feelings of "drastic exclusion" and "incarceration," Bigger and Gus experience the feeling of being penetrated (an experience linked, for JanMohamed, to the "trope of 'rape' that will come to dominate the novel") as well as a feeling of not being able to breathe (*DBS*, 89). "I feel," Bigger says, "like somebody's poking a red-hot iron down my throat" (*NS*, 49). Such feelings, as represented by Wright, speak specifically to the use of overkill, torture, and theater utilized in white-on-Black lynching to build solidarity among members of the mob. Additionally, Wright has captured the element of sexualized violence characteristic of white supremacist lynching culture wherein objects were often inserted into the victim's anus or throat. What JanMohamed concludes specifically from Bigger's difficulty with breath "is that since breathing, controlled normally by the parasympathetic nervous system, is an entirely unconscious activity, the process of racialization controls not only the conscious mind but also the unconscious, somatic apparatus and the automatic functions of the body" (*DBS*, 89). For JanMohamed, then, if Bigger, as a principal example of the "death-bound-subject" in Wright's corpus, hopes to achieve a measure of emancipation from the lineaments of racialization, he "will have to undergo a process of profound destruction of subjectivity, down to bodily and even cellular levels."

Although JanMohamed mentions Fanon only once in his long chapter on *Native Son*, his conclusions do align with my understanding of the novel's parallels to a Fanonian emphasis on the historio-racial elements of the creation and maintenance of subject positions. Additionally, the parallels I read between Fanon's insistence upon actionality, violence, and the need to face and embrace actual death as avenues toward emancipation from the workings of racialization all apply to JanMohamed's formulation. Under both these analyses, the conscious, actional turn toward death is necessary to the "profound destruction of subjectivity" that results, in JanMohamed's reading of Bigger's racially determined trajectory, from his passage from the "thesis" of social death (whereby the slave in fear of actual death as an idea accepts slavery as the condition of his life), through the "antithesis" of actual death (whereby the slave decides to risk closer proximity to actual death in order to escape the position of slavery), and toward the "synthesis" of symbolic death (whereby the slave's acceptance of actual death unseats his/her subject position as slave with a new, reborn subject position) (*DBS*, 17). I subtly differ with JanMohamed, however, in suggesting that it may not be so clear-cut that Bigger's subject position is inflected by racialization down to the level of his cells.

Certainly, race and race-thinking follow Bigger everywhere. It is how he is seen and how he sees himself. It constitutes a great deal of his interactions with his environment, and it influences how he feels inside his own body. But as noted above, Wright depicts various layers in Bigger's attention, which oscillates between a thoroughly reflective, conscious state in which acute racial awareness is a significant component and a prereflective, unconscious state in which thinking and specifically race-thinking are represented as absent, and Bigger's interactions with his environment appear more transparent, less mediated, more innate and automatic. In this light, it is important to consider how Bigger qualifies his account of being unable to breathe: "I know I oughtn't think about it, but I can't help it. Every time I think about it, I feel like somebody's poking a red-hot iron down my throat" (*NS*, 49). It appears, then, that just as a certain kind of looking—as opposed to a prereflective "watching"—grants Buckley's white gaze its power, so too a certain level of reflection—of *thinking*—either produces or reveals the somatic effects of racialization upon Bigger. Throughout *Native Son* and particularly after his murder of Mary Dalton, there remains a distinction between Bigger's reflective and prereflective looking. Though Bigger favors the reflectivity around which the things in his visual environment cohere, including the racial structuring of his subject position—though he prefers, that is, to admit his visible Blackness into the core of his ontological being—the prereflective component of his vision never ceases to be a condition of how he sees and thus interacts with his own subjecthood and with the world. Thus, the reader is left to question what these prereflective interactions with raw visual stimuli might mean or achieve.

Bigger Thomas, Joe Christmas, and the Phenomenology of Mass Media

With reference to "individual characters' acts of seeing" in Faulkner's *Pylon* (1935), Peter Lurie has noted that in Faulkner's descriptions of his characters' visual experiences of reading newspapers, we see an "abrogating of verbal and cognitive processes to what Faulkner depicts as the specifically unreflexive, acritical experience of looking."[10] Lurie specifically cites the instance in which the reporter's "eye, the organ without thought speculation or amaze, ran off the last word."[11] Lurie further suggests that this abrogating of language and cognition to unreflexive—or, to use the term I have employed here, *prereflective*—looking is a common feature in Faulkner's work of the 1930s. I argue that features such as these place phenomenological insights of the kinds discussed in the previous section at the very center of Faulkner's literary project as well as Wright's, and nowhere is this particular phenomenology—what we might call a phenomenology of mass media, or of the experience of *looking* at mass media—made more apparent than in Joe Christmas and his interactions with both movies and pulp magazines. Lurie argues, for instance, that Joe's acts of reading a pulp crime magazine and passing a picture house on the day he murders Joanna are examples of mass culture interpellating him to violent action. As Lurie lays out, Joe's identity has always been constituted both by the embodied gazes of others—of Doc Hines and the dietitian in childhood, of McEachern in adolescence, and of fellow millworkers in adulthood—and by a "pervasive gaze" displaced into the text itself, which introduces a ghost of "looking" into even those passages that pertain to Joe's most private, isolated moments (*VI*, 75–78).

This analysis invites a return to Wright. For instance, Lurie's discussion of the "all-seeing and maleficent" (*VI*, 77) image of the kitchen light at the McEachern house—which greets Joe after his sexually violent encounter with a Black woman, seeming "to watch him, biding and threatful, like an eye"[12]—pairs with JanMohamed's ideas concerning the pervasive specularity of sexual violence in *Native Son*. For JanMohamed, rape may be considered "a 'trope' which . . . functions as the center of a specular world characterized entirely by the metonymic spread of 'rape'" (*DBS*, 111), from Bigger's symbolic rape of Gus—forcing him to lick his dangerously phallic blade, "his body tingling with elation" (*NS*, 69), and threatening to cut out his belly button (the violent penetration of an orifice)—to his assumed rape of Mary and his actual rape of Bessie. On these readings, both Joe and Bigger can be thought of as driven deterministically by the ways in which they are seen within the mass culture they inhabit (always already as rapists and murderers, imbued with a dangerous Blackness). Additionally, their final physical crimes against women are long anticipated by the shadows of a dominant (white) seeing that pervades the visual landscape they inhabit and that they themselves actively court as consumers of their material culture.

As mentioned earlier, Bigger's perspective and identity are greatly informed by the power of the movies. This is a structuring force in Bigger's life of which he is vaguely aware, and we quickly become privy to his understanding of the intricate relationship between looking at the movie screen and the creation of social imaginaries: "In a movie he could dream without effort; all he had to do was lean back in a seat and keep his eyes open" (*NS*, 43). For Bigger, the concrete visual coherence of the screen image (despite its reduction of his organic aliveness) represents the "sense of fullness" (*NS*, 179) to which he aspires, for which "his senses [have] hungered" (*NS*, 43), and that he only feels he can appropriate to himself by rendering himself as visible and as ontologically reduced as an image on screen—as an incarnation, that is, of the socially sensible image of the dangerous Black man. Joe too is, in Lurie's words, "object of a gaze that is both authoritative and cinematic" (*VI*, 78). He, too, owes aspects of his identity and of the representation of his visual presence in the novel to the screen image. It is while passing the picture house in Jefferson, for instance, that his isolated image appears lit (as though by cinematic lighting) "from street lamp to street lamp, the heavy shadows of oak and maple leaves sliding like scraps of black velvet across his white shirt" (*LIA*, 87). Notice here the inversion (like a photographic negative) of the image of Bigger and his friend, "their cigarettes slanting white across their black chins" (*NS*, 45). Much could be said about how the physical properties of light and color interact with Bigger's visibly black form and Joe's visibly white form, and about the political and phenomenological implications of those properties. For now, however, consider what the whiteness of Joe's skin in particular tells us about the visibility and invisibility of his physical form in space, as his appearance to the sensible world contrasts with the phenomenological invisibility of his interiority. In the sequence, for instance, in which he stands naked beside the road by the cabin and is lit by a passing car, "his body grow[ing] white out of the darkness like a kodak print emerging from the liquid," his physical body is again marked as visually white against the contrasting blackness or darkness of his falling garment, "the dark air," and "thightall" weeds themselves darkened by the "dust of a month of passing wagons" (*LIA*, 82). This short passage offers one of Faulkner's greatest representations of the visual. The high contrast of dark/black and light/white throughout projects a visual image. However, Joe's visibility as white is also shown here to amount to a phenomenological invisibility of his interiority. His words contradict his visual presentation and speak to a contradiction between appearance and being. Despite being visibly white, he denies ontological whiteness by attacking it ("'White bastards!' he shouted"), and his attempted outing of himself as the dangerous and sexually transgressive Black man of white nightmares during the Jim Crow period by drawing attention to his penis ("'That's not the first of your bitches that ever saw . . .'") is not met by his greater visibility as Black. Rather his protestations of an invisible self under and distinct from his visible whiteness fall on blind eyes and deaf ears: "There was no one to hear, to listen."

Joe's attempt to shout out from a Black internality through the medium of a visibly, shiningly white form betrays certain philosophical intuitions that he and Bigger do not ultimately share but with which both characters interact. It is Joe's fundamental perspective for much of *Light in August* (by no means his only perspective, but a dominant one) that visible form masks invisible essence and that invisible essence is an avenue to an undifferentiated universalism. This is a universalist perspective that Joe has felt drawn to, at least in part, due to his ability to pass as white. The racially indeterminate Joe, unlike Bigger, is able to entertain the feeling of being solipsistically removed from his surroundings, of being a universal, deracinated human being untouched by social arrangements. Additionally, he, unlike Bigger, is periodically able to evade the essentializing, dehumanizing effects of racist blindness, the kind that leads to the death of his own father at the hands of his grandfather, Doc Hines, who commits the murder blinded both by physical darkness and by the prejudice that sees the threat of Blackness everywhere, even (possibly) in the person of a Mexican (*LIA*, 282). At times seemingly free of racial categorization, Joe is represented from childhood in a state of presocial, deracinated transcendence. At the orphanage, for instance, before his violent racialization at the hands of the dietitian, Joe is described as walking the "empty corridor, during the quiet hour . . . like a shadow, small even for five years, sober and quiet" (*LIA*, 91). His smallness, his insubstantiality, and his isolation in the empty halls code him as socially invisible. It is an invisibility—a seeming absence of social identity—that Joe seeks and longs for. Sequestered behind the curtain in the bedroom where the dietitian will find him, Joe inhabits a state of corporeality prior to the imposition of social accounts of his being. Here he is alone only with the corporeal sensations of sweating, eating, digestion, and vomiting. Only as he is being discovered by the dietitian does he become aware of himself as a subject, called to, interpellated, and imposed upon by the social world, and says "to himself with complete and passive surrender: 'Well, here I am'" (*LIA*, 93). The state of presociality Joe is represented as experiencing in childhood is one he attempts and fails to recapture throughout his life. To Joe, unlike Bigger, social aliveness is not akin to physical aliveness. Rather, for Joe, to die as a social and racial subject is to "sink back" (*NS*, 304), to use the words of *Native Son*, into a transcendent and universal human condition conceived of as beyond and behind social groupings and racial categories. Joe courts this transcendence in his absurd attempt at a presocial, Edenic togetherness with Bobbie the prostitute, in his fifteen years of nomadic wandering, in his taciturn manner, and in his refusal to commit fully to either Black or white belonging, though both at various times are open to him.

Lurie has convincingly argued that even Joe's moments of solitude come associated with a sense of him as "'accompanied,' visualized, or seen": "someone, that is . . . is insistently present at [these moments] to see Joe, to note how lonely or how much like a phantom or spirit he 'looked'" (*VI*, 77-78). As Lurie writes, the five-year-old Joe's isolation is one that "Faulkner nevertheless 'fills' . . . with the narrator's presence and gaze," aligning readers "with the centralized, panoptic power of the institution" by rendering them able "to watch Joe even, or especially, when he thinks he is not being seen" (*VI*, 92-93). For this specific phenomenological analysis, it is less helpful to think of visibility and invisibility as mutually exclusive or as contradictory than as mutually imbricated. The visible thing, as Merleau-Ponty has it, "holds with all its fibers onto the fabric of the visible, and thereby onto a fabric of invisible being" (*VAI*, 132). As such, Joe's visibility admits into its very constitution the invisible components of experience, as indeed does Bigger's in those moments of prereflectivity in which "his mind [is] pleasantly vacant of purpose." Likewise, when Joe reads the pulp magazine before the murder of Joanna, an act that certainly informs how he is seen and how he sees himself reflectively, Faulkner signals that he partakes also in a prereflective, presocial, primally embodied state of foundational experience, "apparently arrested and held immobile by a single word which had perhaps not yet impacted, his whole being suspended by the single trivial combination of letters in quiet and sunny space" (*LIA*, 85–86). In this phenomenological frame, it does not make conceptual sense to ask whether Joe or Bigger are encountering the visible *or* the invisible. They encounter both, always, each superimposed upon the other. What remains of interest, however, is the often very different though sometimes related ways in which Joe (a character passing as white, invented by a white American writer) and Bigger (the visibly Black invention of an African American writer) interact with these phenomenological conditions and what those various reactions tell us about what visibility and invisibility are, and how they inform our perspectives and identities.

To return for a moment to *Pylon*, as a line of approach to my closing comments on *Native Son* and *Light in August*, that novel (*Pylon*) presents us with a clear dynamic between two seemingly incompatible dimensions of the printed text and of the manner in which it is received by the reader on the level of vision. On the one hand, a prereflective looking reacts to text as a physical phenomenon in space, as nothing more than a "symmetrical line of boxheads" (*P*, 96). On the other, a reflective, critical seeing appraises the meaning of the text, its place within a national discourse, and registers it as a concrete sedimentation of social, cultural, and political forces. Here, "the fragile web of ink and paper" has become "assertive, proclamative; profound and irrevocable . . . the dead instant's fruit of forty tons of machinery and an entire nation's antic delusion." The distinction recalls Merleau-Ponty's critique of the Cartesian "*spoken* cogito" via his positing of a "*tacit* cogito" ("the presence of self to self . . . prior to every philosophy") formed through contact with a prereflective, prelinguistic experience of the world—as when, for instance, a young boy puts on his grandmother's glasses and opens her book, "believ[ing] he will be able to find for himself the stories that she has read to him" but finding instead, since he's unable to read, "nothing but black and white."[13]

This same dynamic of a prereflective seeing that responds to text as an asemantic visual object in space and a reflective seeing that responds to text as a signifying object (which may even signify "an entire nation's antic delusion," including its delusions around race) also characterizes Bigger's interactions with printed text, and specifically with newspapers.

When, for instance, Bigger first flees the law, he conflates his murder of Mary with the internal feelings "burning in his own heart" (*NS*, 252) and further conflates both of these phenomena with the socially visible (socially legible) accounts of his deeds carried by newspapers. It is worth noting that *Native Son* itself drew liberally on press coverage of the sensational Robert Nixon murder trial in Chicago in 1939 and that in writing *The Man Who Lived Underground* a year after the publication of *Native Son*, Wright drew for inspiration on the pulp magazine *True Detective*. If popular print culture was important to Wright's creative process, it is equally important to his protagonists, a feature, as previously noted, that Wright shares with Faulkner.

Where on balance, however, Joe Christmas is more aligned with a vision of a solipsistic, idealized, universal, and invisible internality, Bigger's internality, his thoughts, his affects, his lived experience, all find expression, he feels, in acts of violence against a violent system, and those expressions are concretized in the "tall black type" (*NS*, 252) of the newspapers. Triggered by his killing of Mary, Bigger comes to think of his bodily aliveness (which he encounters experientially at times) as having no social reality and thereby no de facto reality. In a decidedly Fanonian move, Bigger rejects the possibility that a Black subject may structure his subject position according to an unimposed corporeal schema and accepts the racial epidermal schemata against which there can be "no ontological resistance" (*BSWM*, 83). Additionally, Bigger mirrors Fanon in resisting the dehumanizing effects of this accepted racial reality. He becomes, that is, actional, violent, and willing to accept the possibility of the actual death that would, in JanMohamed's words, render it "absolutely impossible to have the structure of social death imposed upon" him (*DBS*, 102). This perspectival shift relegates Bigger's bodily actuality, his invisible somatic sensations, and his affective life to the status of a phantom.

That phantom, however, can be *lent* reality by its conversion into socially visible concretizations, a human life converted, among other things, into the texts of mass culture and sensationalist journalism:

> The papers ought to be full of him now. It did not seem strange that they should be, for all his life he had felt that things had been happening to him that should have gone into them. But only after he had acted upon feelings which he had for years would the papers carry the story, *his* story. He felt that they had not

wanted to print it as long as it had remained buried and burning in his own heart. But now that he had thrown it out . . . the papers were printing it. (*NS*, 252)

The specifically visual dimension of this emergent perspective can be seen clearly in the way Bigger reads the papers. For what Bigger finds in the *Chicago Tribune* is no mere "symmetrical line of boxheads" (*P*, 96). Nor is it the visual, corporeal, prereflective "arrested" state, the sense of being "held immobile by a single word," "not yet impacted" by its meaning, though "suspended by the single trivial combination of letters" (*LIA*, 85–86), which Joe experiences in his isolation. Rather, the information Bigger gleans from his reading becomes increasingly, preternaturally "assertive, proclamative; profound and irrevocable" (*P*, 96), not only in what it reveals about "an entire nation's antic delusion" but also in what it reveals about the actual, practical effects of that national mindset.

What Bigger sees, in other words, are neither asemantic shapes or colors nor texts that signify within the limits of their content. Instead, newspapers become, for him, a kind of rudimentary radar technology by which he can sight (without physically seeing) the layout of the entire city, the movements of law enforcement through its streets and within its buildings, together with events that are yet to take place. For instance, his first look at the *Tribune* after fleeing from the Dalton house grants Bigger visions of the reporters finding Mary's remains, discovering the reality of her decapitation, and noticing his flight (*NS*, 252). There is something cinematic about how these images of moments he has lived and moments he imagines project onto Bigger's consciousness via the mediation of the newspaper. Later, Bigger collates a series of distinct data points drawn from the newspapers: a black-and-white map of the South Side with shaded sections where searches for him (the "Negro rapist") have already been carried out, his own knowledge of local geography, the date on the paper, the location where the manhunt has started the night before, and the likely pace it will maintain (*NS*, 276). Bigger uses this information to draw a moving mental picture of the actions and likely actions of the pursuing police and vigilantes of whom, from his physical place in a dark "building . . . quiet save for the continual creaking caused by the wind," he cannot possibly have sensory knowledge. Through this process, which follows not so much his crime itself as its discovery, its being made visible by the detection of Mary's bones in the Dalton furnace, Bigger unconsciously revokes his visceral being (and so his need for direct sensory data) in favor of a social being (cognitive, critical, reflective) that entirely subsumes his physical body.

Compare, for instance, the Bigger who, late in his flight, sees only through print media to the earlier Bigger who, escaping through the window of his room at the Dalton house, experiences a moment of non-egoic bodily awareness wherein his reflections, judgments, and knowledge concerning his subject position are all temporarily suspended by the visceral experience of falling through thin air into the snow. As he falls, he becomes a dizzying confusion of bodily sensation not reflected upon, not even *seen*—"he looked into the snow and tried to see the ground below; but he could not" (*NS*, 250-51)—but felt: "twisting in the icy air," "eyes . . . shut," "hands . . . clenched," "the muscles of his body contract[ing] violently, caught in a spasm of reflex action," "his groin laved with warm water . . . urine," he "sneezed" (*NS*, 251). This series of prereflective bodily responses, proprioceptional awareness, and visceral sensations represents the invisible Bigger—Bigger as only he experiences his own embodiment—that he begins from this point resolutely to eschew in order that he might better appropriate the socially visible, racial subject that he cannot in any case escape, according to his own analysis.

Given, as he sees it, his inescapable visibility as he contends with "the white world's rule" (*NS*, 44) in the form of both the police who pursue him for his crimes and the court that will indict him, it becomes Bigger's mission to appropriate the privilege he thinks of as typically reserved for white subjects: the privilege, that is, of visibility in a shape and form responsive to one's own inventions. In this sense, Bigger's desire to merge with the crowd, expressed explicitly near the novel's end, is a desire not for anonymity but for the self-determination and self-possession he associates with full citizenship. In a sense, it is primarily the need to attain the socially visible state of the citizen that compels Bigger toward his crimes and becomes concretized for him by the mass-cultural materials that surround him. Long before Bigger resolves to take that social visibility and social aliveness by force, he felt the need for the "sense of fullness he had so often but inadequately felt in magazines and movies" (*NS*, 179). Popular print culture, film, and news media are therefore avenues for Bigger toward the sovereignty via social visibility that is the goal of his rebellion both against the blindness of his society, fixated on its imagined Black man, and against a deracinating, universalizing color blindness. Both of the latter, I argue, Bigger conceives of as avenues to social death as invisibility—just as, conversely, the visibly white-skinned Joe Christmas suffers from the Jim Crow system's racist blindness despite attempting to benefit from his (mis)recognition within that system by seeking to occupy a universal, color blind space outside his society's rigid and dangerous taxonomies of race. For Joe, this universalized position remains a redemptive possibility that his own physical death can be considered to represent. Despite its physical brutality, his moment of death is akin to Bigger's short-lived turn toward "the dark face of ancient waters" (*NS*, 304) before he elects to resist all such visions of apocalyptic peace. Joe's dying moment articulates with a sense of corporeal, organic, phenomenologically embodied experience: his "eyes open and empty of everything save consciousness," his image "of itself alone serene, of itself alone triumphant" (*LIA*, 349-50). For Bigger, on the other hand, physical death remains entangled with the social and symbolic world he inhabits; far from constituting a release from racial subjugation, his impending execution at the hands of a white supremacist system is a central means by which that system maintains itself and against which Bigger must "[spring] back into action, alive, contending" (*NS*, 306), in a manner akin to Fanonian actionality.

Conclusion: The Body and Black Representation

The representation of Black subjects—Bigger, Joe—has been a central concern here. The stakes involved in such representations present themselves distinctly in the intersection between phenomenology and antiracism and reach their greatest urgency where they pertain to the ways in which the human body may retain or be deprived of self-possession, self-making, and access to the corporeality, the phenomenality of lived experience, that is the "real dialectic between . . . [the] body and the world" (*BSWM*, 111). Part of this question involves a recourse to scholarship around those bodies (for instance, Black bodies) that have been historically and are still today subjected to the structurations and interpellations of those dominant modes of seeing, looking, and reading invested with the capacity to racialize—or, as Christine Okoth put it in a recent discussion of Fanon, the capacity to provoke "a total crisis of embodiment, one that ultimately results in the substitution of the corporeal with the discursive."[14] It is this rendering of the corporeal, phenomenal embodiment of complex human beings into discourses to be seen, looked at, or read that I see taking place in the stories of Bigger and Joe. In both cases the characters' racializations involve an imposition of a certain kind of visibility (visible as Black and as a symbol of Blackness as a historical, imagined construct) and also a certain kind of invisibility (that of corporeal, phenomenal internalities not yet captured by the workings of racial schemata). Under these circumstances, visibility and invisibility become like laminates, palimpsestic, one existing atop or beneath the other and both coexisting in the same space and moment. Okoth, too, touches on this palimpsestic relationship in her account of racializing encounters (with law enforcement, for example) that construct the racial body ("the Black body") as "a double of the real body of a Black person, a 'shadow' without clear boundaries that, in the moment of racialisation, merges with the visual presence of the subject of racialisation" (*BBRR*, 230). This sense of shadowing and merging is precisely how I have described the relationship between the visible and invisible in *Native Son* and *Light in August*. The visible and racialized occupies the same space as the invisible and phenomenal self. What is of further interest, however, is how the interplay among race, epidermalization, and racial passing helps account for the pronounced variance between Bigger's and Joe's responses to their societies' racializing practices—where, unlike dark-skinned Bigger, light-skinned Joe can experience the privilege of viewing himself (at times) as a representative of a universalized human experience. As I have discussed, there are moments for Bigger of internality, corporeal aliveness, and an opacity of lived experience unresponsive to the structurations of the racial schema. However, this is an invisibility that Bigger eschews largely because, through the process of racialization, the sense of aliveness he might otherwise associate with that invisible internality has long been overcome by what Okoth calls "a progressive erosion or a slow encroachment of Blackness on Black corporeality" (*BBRR*, 229). As such, Bigger experiences his corporeality as synonymous with his Blackness, so that to erase that Blackness via invisibility is to erase his corporeal self via physical death.

The importance of phenomenological and antiracist interventions into literary works seeking to represent Black being revolves around questions of the centrality of lived experience, of the body's unimposed, idiosyncratic relationality to environment: to race, class, gender, sexuality, ability, age, and their many complex intersections. Neither Bigger nor Joe (for very different reasons) is able to achieve a real dialectic between his embodied self and the world. Labyrinthine complications of racialization in the Jim Crow South offer them paths either to an obliterating, deracinating invisibility or to visibility as an ossification into rigid racial facticity undergirded by the lineaments of social death. What future work in this area must continue to explore is how a greater understanding of the body as it exists in the world may offer generative avenues beyond this oppressive either/or binary.

NOTES

1. Orlando Patterson, *Slavery and Social Death: A Comparative Study* (Cambridge, MA: Harvard University Press, 2018), xix. Hereafter cited in text as *SSD*.
2. Paul Gilroy, *Against Race: Imagining Political Culture Beyond the Colour Line* (Cambridge, MA: Harvard University Press, 2000), 300–301.

3. Abdul R. JanMohamed, *The Death-Bound-Subject: Richard Wright's Archaeology of Death* (Durham, NC: Duke University Press, 2005), 5. Hereafter cited in text as *DBS*.

4. Frantz Fanon, *Black Skin, White Masks*, trans. Charles Lam Markmann (London: Grove Press, 1967), 84. Hereafter cited in text as *BSWM*.

5. Richard Wright, *Native Son* (1940; repr., London: Vintage, 2000), 45. Hereafter cited in text as *NS*.

6. Maurice Merleau-Ponty, *The Visible and the Invisible*, ed. Claude Lefort, trans. Alphonso Lingis (Evanston, IL: Northwestern University Press, 1968), 7. Hereafter cited in text as *VAI*.

7. Robert Bernasconi, "Frantz Fanon's Engagement with Phenomenology: Unlocking the Temporal Architecture of *Black Skin, White Masks*," *Research in Phenomenology*, 50 (2020): 393. Hereafter cited in text as *FFEP*.

8. Paul Gilroy, "Agonistic Belonging: The Banality of Good, the 'Alt Right' and the Need for Sympathy," *Open Cultural Studies* 3, no. 1 (2019): 8.

9. Paul Gilroy and Sindre Bangstad, "A Diagnosis of Contemporary Forms of Racism, Race and Nationalism: A Conversation with Professor Paul Gilroy," *Cultural Studies* 33, no. 2 (2019): 180.

10. Peter Lurie, *Vision's Immanence: Faulkner, Film, and the Popular Imagination* (Baltimore: Johns Hopkins University Press, 2004), 15. Hereafter cited in text as *VI*.

11. William Faulkner, *Pylon*, rev. ed. (1935; repr., New York: Vintage International, 2011), 96. Hereafter cited in text as *P*.

12. William Faulkner, *Light in August*, rev. ed. (1932; repr., London: Vintage, 2005), 121. Hereafter cited in text as *LIA*.

13. Maurice Merleau-Ponty, *Phenomenology of Perception* (New York: Routledge, 2012), 426, 423. Hereafter cited in text as *PP*.

14. Christine Okoth, "The Black Body and the Reading of Race," in *The Cambridge Companion to American Literature and the Body*, ed. Travis M. Foster (Cambridge, UK: Cambridge University Press, 2022), 230. Hereafter cited in text as *BBRR*.

Criminality, Sexuality, and Violence in Faulkner and Wright

Sanctuary and *The Long Dream*

JOHN WHARTON LOWE

If the book we are reading does not wake us, as with a fist hammering on our skull, why then do we read it? So that it shall make us happy? Good God, we would also be happy if we had no books, and such books as make us happy we could, if need be, write ourselves. But what we must have are those books which come upon us like ill-fortune, and distress us deeply, like the death of one we love better than ourselves, like suicide. A book must be an ice-axe to break the sea frozen inside us.
—FRANZ KAFKA[1]

William Faulkner always viewed *Sanctuary* (1931) as his most notorious novel, and few have since disagreed, in light of the novel's seamy voyeuristic look into prostitution, gangsters, addiction, and kinky sexuality, not to mention rape, murder, and other sundry crimes. Most of these horrific elements are also present in Richard Wright's last published novel, *The Long Dream* (1958), whose central character, Fishbelly (his actual first name is Rex), becomes initiated into corruption by his own father and is then forced to develop strategies within the web of transgression to ensure his survival. Many of these issues continue in the unpublished sequel to *The Long Dream*, *Island of Hallucinations*, which transfers Fish's story to his new home in France. This paper will explore the ways in which the two writers' display of the sordid underbelly of Mississippi echoes real events—especially Wright's employment of the tragic 1940 Natchez nightclub fire that killed over two hundred innocent patrons alongside gangsters, pimps, and prostitutes. Faulkner and Wright saw an indissoluble link between criminality, sexuality, and violence. I will also suggest that both Faulkner and Wright, influenced by gangster films and pulp fiction, sought to attract a larger public through sensationalism, but in a way that would lead to a new and disturbing literary aesthetic. Both writers understand the distinction that "like sentimental fiction, sensational literature is a form of melodrama that aims to move its audiences to experience intense feelings, but it emphasizes thrills, shock, and horror more than virtuous and socially redemptive feelings. . . . Sensationalism [seeks] to linger on bodies and explore intense emotions rather than regulating, refining, or transcending them."[2]

There is good reason to compare these books; according to Margaret Walker, Wright read Sanctuary and was "ecstatic" about it.[3] He had purchased all of Faulkner's works as they were published and was thrilled when Faulkner wrote him praising Native Son, and Wright framed the letter and hung it over his desk. Both writers enjoyed and appreciated crime novels, and elements of the genre appear in many of their works. Wright, of course, with the exception of his "white" novel, Savage Holiday, combined his treatments of these subjects with race, as African Americans, before and after his time and in ours as well, have too often been charged with crimes, many of which they have not committed. Further, as a former communist, Wright had always been a critic of bourgeois culture, and as Ernest Mandel has claimed, the crime story became more prominent with the rise of industrial society, one that "in and of itself breeds crime, originates in crime, and leads to crime."[4] All crimes, of course, are transgressions; as such, they represent a breaking down of social norms, laws, and moral codes. Sexuality, so often on the edge of violence, can attract because of its exhilarating sense of transgression; as Georges Bataille observed, "Eroticism always entails a breaking down of established patterns . . . of the regulated social order."[5]

Faulkner's daring challenges to this order, in all of his works, were appealing to Wright, who no doubt felt that the high regard Faulkner enjoyed with other Black writers of both the US and the circum-Caribbean came from his willingness to interrogate racial and sexual violence; Trinidad's C. L. R. James, applauding their daring, had asserted that Faulkner and Wright were the two greatest American writers of the twentieth century. Indeed, in terms of the theme of this collection, Walker herself declared, "It is in Wright, Faulkner, and Welty that we see the southern writer rising above time and place, struggling beyond the racist limitation of the society, reaching into the truly rarified world of the artist, where human values and universal truths take precedence over provincial notions and bigoted minds. Like all great writers in the world, they move from the local to the universal, from the immediate to the timeless, from the simple to the sublime."[6]

The Long Dream revisits the Mississippi of Wright's youth but changes the scene quite significantly by concentrating on the Black middle-class family of an undertaker, Tyree Tucker, who supplements his income from his funeral home with illegal profits drawn from prostitution and slumlording, activities undertaken through an unholy alliance with a corrupt and racist white police chief. The partnership succeeds partly from the fact that each man has the goods—blackmailing goods—on the other; both offer crass examples of hypocrisy, using bourgeois culture and the mask of institutional position to flaunt not only laws but standards of decency.

The Long Dream constitutes Wright's most scathing portrait of the Black upper class. In his famous essay, "Blueprint for Negro Writing" (1937), he had bemoaned the way that "the petty bourgeois sections of oppressed minorities strive to assimilate the virtues of the bourgeoisie in the assumption that by doing so they can lift themselves into a higher social sphere," and indeed, Tyree Tucker not only has these ambitions, he has realized them; he has a big house, a fancy car, and respect in the Black community.[7] As Fish and the reader eventually see, however, this proper facade masks a seedy backdrop of criminal activity and of Tyree's fleecing of his customers in the mortuary. Wright once commented in an interview, "[I]n real life, undertakers are among the richest Negroes. They are allowed to bury Negroes only. It is a kind of trust, a monopoly. It is the most lucrative Negro job because whites do not want to touch Negro dead. I take it as a symbol of the black bourgeoisie. They make a living out of the sufferings of other Negroes and the whites allow them to do what they wish in the ghetto."[8]

Sexuality and Prostitution

As in *Sanctuary*, there is more overt sexuality, often conjoined with violence, in *The Long Dream* than in Wright's earlier fictions. The initial nicknaming of Rex as Fishbelly involves a scene where his father teaches him to inflate white fish bellies; the boy associates the smell with his mother. One scene makes comic use of condoms, and another (also set in a lavatory) involves Fish and friends looking at white pornography. Fishbelly's childhood plays a variation on Freud, whose "primal scene" consists of a child inadvertently witnessing his or her parents having sex. Here, Fishbelly's "scene" takes place in his father's mortuary, where his father is having sex with a client; Fish sees "two staring red eyes, a strained humped back" on top of an embalming table and later asks his father, "what was you doing to the lady? I thought you was acting like a train."⁹ His father bribes Fish's silence with ice-cream money; Fish, happy, thinks

> he shared a dark secret with his father; he did not grasp the nature of that secret, but he was confident that time would reveal it.... [He had] a hunger to get home and play with his electric trains.
>
> From that day on, thundering trains loomed in his dreams—hurtling, sleek, black monsters whose stack pipes belched gobs of serpentine smoke, whose seething fireboxes coughed out clouds of pink steam ... panting trains that roared yammeringly ... hauled brutally forward by red-eyed locomotives. (22-23)

These early scenes provide Fish with multiple signals that sex is "nasty," obscene, forbidden, dangerous, and associated with death. The violent, industrial nature of Fish's perceptions of sexuality here aligns with the train imagery that *Sanctuary*'s Horace Benbow associates in his dream vision of Little Belle/Temple tied naked to a train's flatbed, but also with what Jay Watson has recently presented as an age of modernist speed, something he finds in abundance in *Sanctuary*.¹⁰

In a key episode that Wright drew from his earlier autobiographical sketch, "The Ethics of Living Jim Crow," we read about a Black bellboy caught in an affair with a white prostitute. In the earlier work, he is castrated and run out of town. Here, the dismemberment is coupled with death. Wright spares neither Fish nor the reader, as Dr. Bruce methodically does a post-mortem on Chris's mutilated body; vigilantes had beaten him, dragged him behind a car, and then lynched and castrated him, taking "souvenirs" like an ear. We peer with Fish into the dark bloody void between the corpse's legs. One has to think that Wright has the horrid images of the lynched body of Emmett Till in mind here: the fourteen-year-old Chicago teenager was brutally murdered and mutilated in Money, Mississippi, in 1955, after supposedly whistling at a white woman; his mother insisted his coffin be open and that photographs be made, which were widely circulated.

In a subsequent scene of instruction, Tyree tells Fish, "A black man's a dream, son, a dream that can't come true. Dream, Fish. But be careful what you dream. Dream only what can happen.... The main thing for a black man is to live and not end up like Chris.... When it happens every day, it ain't no accident no more. It's a law, a law of life.... To outwit that law's your main business in life.... I'd do anything on this earth to keep from dying like that. I'd kill myself first" (80). Unsurprisingly, thereafter, Fish has nightmares about castration, particularly after he and his friend Zeke are arrested for trespassing; cruel cops pretend they are going to castrate him repeatedly, wielding a knife near his groin and causing him to faint three times.¹¹ Fish's terror stems from his realization that he could meet Chris's fate if his photo of a leering white woman were discovered by the police; surreptitiously, he swallows it. As Earle V. Bryant has noted, "Fish has enthroned within himself the image of the white woman, has incorporated it into his being forever."¹² This action replicates two scenes in the Bible: in Revelations, an angel instructs John to eat a book ("Take it, and eat it up; and it shall make thy belly bitter, but it shall be in thy mouth sweet as honey") and then commands John to prophesy (Rev. 10: 9-11). God similarly calls on Ezekiel to eat a scroll (Ezekiel 3:1) in which is written woe, mourning, and lamentations, enabling him to warn the people in his prophecies.¹³

After viewing the horror of Chris's mutilated body, Fish comes to see that the violence of castration has a psychological version too, after viewing his usually proud father fawn, grin, and grovel before his supposed partner, Police Chief Cantley. Yet after he sees his father's "fear and weakness" coupled with his pleading and grinning with the white authorities, Fish weeps. "He knew in a confused way that no white man would ever need to threaten Tyree with castration; Tyree was already castrated" (151).¹⁴ But Tyree is *not* castrated, as his son believes; late in the novel, before his assassination (which Tyree knows is coming), he determines to bravely save his "kingdom" for his son. And it is Tyree who indicts the ultimate form of the state, its power to curdle Black dreams: while *Sanctuary* will always be read as a literary classic (albeit an often repellent one), *The Long Dream* has more relevance today than ever before in its portrait of the dangers this young Black man faces as he confronts his father's tangled relationship with the police in particular but with the myriad cultural menaces Black men faced at that time in general, many of which are still with us. As Wright stated in an interview with the French periodical *L'Express*, "[W]hen [Tyree] tells [Fish], 'Don't allow yourself to be carried away too far by your dream,' this means, 'If you really believe what is written in the Constitution, you will get killed.'"¹⁵

After the horrifying lesson taught by watching his father prepare Chris's mangled body for interment, Fishbelly has a nightmare: "[H]e was in Mama's and Papa's bedroom and there was a big white clock with a white face and two white hands flung wide as in warning and the white face was like God's face that Reverend Ragland said would burn you forever in a lake of fire if you didn't behave and he tiptoed to the door to see if anybody was watching . . . and under the little bench that Mama sat upon was a strange little thing he stooped yes it was a fish belly wet stinking crumbled with fuzzy hair and he laughed nervously and suddenly he started for the clock began a loud striking like somebody beating a drum TICK TOCK and the clock began striking thunderingly DONG

DONG and he was amazed when the clock spoke DON'T DON'T and he heard a puffing like a train HMPFF HUMPFF and he saw a locomotive with coaches like he got at Christmas and the locomotive's stack pipe touched the fish belly" (82–83; italics removed), a reprisal of the association of trains with his father's infidelity at the mortuary, and a coupling with the dominant female image of the fish.

The clock in Miss Reba's whorehouse in *Sanctuary* is similarly connected with sexuality; Michel Gresset notes the way in which this baroque presentation of a familiar object shows Faulkner "playing with psychology," but as he elaborates, "often, indeed, the sheer visual intensity of his 'psychological' scenes results in a surreal representation of reality."[16] There is, however, a very realistic element to Miss Reba's clock—or there was before it ceased to run: a sex worker provides timed companionship, working by the hour, so to speak. But in *Sanctuary*, the face of the clock is also a mirror: "Temple began to hear a clock. It sat on the mantel above a grate filled with fluted green paper. The clock was of flowered china, supported by four china nymphs. It had only one hand, scrolled and gilded, halfway between ten and eleven, lending to the otherwise blank face a quality of unequivocal assertion, as though it had nothing whatever to do with time."[17] Faulkner embroiders on this a bit later: "The china figures which supported the clock gleamed in hushed smooth flexions: knee, elbow, flank, arm and breast in attitudes of voluptuous lassitude. The glass face, become mirror-like, appeared to hold all reluctant light, holding in its tranquil depths a quiet gesture of moribund time, one-armed like a veteran from the wars" (150). Here, we are reminded of what Oscar Wilde's Dorian Gray sees in the mirror—a reflection of his aging and his growing depravity—which is not unlike what Temple sees or what Fishbelly intuits from his dream. But the clock also indicates that Temple is suspended in time, in a perpetual nightmare, or as Wright might say, "a long dream." Temple often looks into the *actual* mirror in this room as well: "[I]n the wavy mirror of a cheap varnished dresser, as in a stagnant pool, there seemed to linger spent ghosts of voluptuous gestures and dead lusts" (155). Cheating mirrors find a counterpart in the tacky floral furnishings of Miss Reba's brothel, where cheap art covers all bodily functions, not just sex: "[I]n the corner . . . sat a slop jar dressed also in fluted rose-colored paper" (155).

Prostitution runs like a tawdry red thread through both novels. Popeye relies on Miss Reba's institution as his—and later Red's—"love nest," and both he and the madame are prime examples of a time—the Prohibition era—when criminality and capitalism were closely conjoined. Wright's novel, while set in another decade, offers a similar scenario, but the unholy bond between the police and the brothel-capitalists is much tighter. The trade in women's bodies has special resonance in *Sanctuary*; as Bataille has remarked, "With prostitution, the prostitute was dedicated to a life of transgression. The sacred or forbidden aspect of sexual activity remained apparent in her, for her whole life was dedicated to violating the taboo" (133). But Faulkner complicates the matter: as many critics have noted, almost every character in *Sanctuary* has a double, and Temple's is Ruby. Her fidelity to Lee Goodwin time and again leads her to trade her body for money to help him, and he beats her for doing so. However, the text avoids making Ruby a saint, for like Temple, she too apparently reveled in the fine clothes and jewelry that once came her way. In equipping her with a sickly infant—who, by the end of the novel, when we learn of Popeye's drastic condition as a baby, registers as the gangster's double—Faulkner makes her a kind of double Mary, both the Blessed Virgin with her sacred child and the scarlet Mary Magdalen.

On the other hand, Ruby's efforts when she is impoverished situate her in what Bataille calls "low prostitution," and in her conversations with Horace—but not with Temple—she does indeed seem to show that she has fallen as low as she can go. As Bataille says of this entire class of sex workers, "[S]he cannot attain an absolute indifference; not only has she fallen but she knows she has. She knows she is a human being. Even if she is not ashamed of it, she does know that she lives like a pig" (135). Further, as Bataille also claims, Christianity profited from having "low prostitution" as an extreme "other" for feminine identity. "Degradation ... continued to signify evil" (138). Peter Lurie has suggested that Ruby is an example of a familiar figure in popular fiction, the "fallen-yet-virtuous woman," a type epitomized in Donald Henderson Clarke's 1929 gangster novel, *Louis Beretti*.[18]

Faulkner, by contrast, brings us into Miss Reba's world indirectly at first, through aspersions cast on Temple by town boys. We learn early on that the loose-living coed's name has been written on the wall of an Oxford lavatory. She is first called a whore by Popeye, when she asks him to drive her and Gowan Stevens back to town. "Make your whore lay off of me, Jack" he says to Gowan (49). But then Popeye makes her *his* whore at Miss Reba's, incarcerating and manually violating her, before turning voyeur after bringing Red in to have more conventional sex with her.

Unlike Ruby, the madame Miss Reba is a grand comic invention. Her cruelty toward her dogs and her fake motherly concern for both Popeye and Temple are opposite sides of a counterfeit coin. Her amusement over the innocence of the bumpkin Virgil Snopes and his friend Fonzo Winbush, who think they are staying at a boarding house and go out at night looking for hookers, is shared by readers. One has to think that Faulkner is at once impressed by the agency that madames have and deconstructing the "whore with a heart of gold" syndrome that would be epitomized in Margaret Mitchell's Belle Watling. Miss Reba's mawkish, melodramatic memories of her departed mate and partner in crime, Mr. Binford, make her criminally entertaining, and her drunken session with her fellow madames after Red's assassination by Popeye provides a kind of mock chorus to the murder. We would do well to consider Faulkner's method here; Andre Malraux famously wrote that *Sanctuary* represented the intrusion of Greek drama into the detective story. Certainly, one convention of Greek drama is to have murder, incest, and rape take place offstage, and we do not, in fact, see Temple's rape, Red's murder, or Lee's lynching in detail. Faulkner will leave a "blank" for the reader to fill in, or alternately, create a comic retelling of otherwise grim events. For instance, Miss Reba tells of her servant Minnie walking into Temple's room where Popeye is watching Temple and Red have sex: "Minnie said the two of them would be nekkid as two snakes, and Popeye hanging over the foot of the bed without even his hat took off, making a kind of whinnying sound" (258). Thus, we hear this twice removed, and through the filter of comedy. Temple's earlier link with Ruby is posed when the latter tells the story of her father shooting her lover and then telling her, "Get down there and sup your dirt, you whore," to which Temple replies, "I have been called that" (58).

Virgil and Fonzo similarly provide a comic lens on rituals of initiation. While Fishbelly's father takes him to the whorehouse he owns for a passage to "manhood," the Yoknapatawpha boys look around for a brothel, not realizing they are staying in one. Nevertheless, they are initiated, not by their father, but by their cousin Senator Clarence Snopes, who instructs them that the bodies of Black women are cheaper. We might remember here that Greek tragedies were paired with often priapic comedies, such as Aristophanes's *Lysistrata*, and Faulkner's use of macabre humor provides the kind of counterpoint that fascinated him, especially in earlier works like *As I Lay Dying* and later ones like the separate stories of *The Wild Palms*.

While prostitution is a major topic in both stories, its base in capitalism is, unsurprisingly, much more starkly presented by Wright, the former communist. According to Walker, one of Wright's favorite books was Stephen Crane's tale of a young girl's path into the sex industry, *Maggie: A Girl of the Streets*,[19] and his portrait of "the Grove," a nightclub that doubles as a brothel, meets a fiery end, as Wright plays on the actual horrific Rhythm Club fire that killed 209 patrons in Natchez on April 23, 1940. The fire inevitably brings attention to Tyree, the club's owner, and simultaneously threatens the exposure of his "silent" partner, Cantley, while also immolating Fishbelly's near-white mistress, Gladys.

Both male protagonists—Tyree and Fishbelly—profit from the trade in women's bodies. As an interviewer once pointed out to Wright, Fishbelly is in love with Gladys, a light-skinned woman who is, unknown to him, working as a prostitute at the Grove. As Fish gives money to Gladys, who gives it to Tyree, who gives it to his son, we see the circular motion of crime, or as Wright said, the "vicious circle in the ghetto."[20] But Wright had spelled it all out in his novel: after the Grove fire kills Gladys, Fish realizes that "he and his family had been living off the immoral earnings of Gladys! The money he had paid her for the right to sleep with her had found its way back into his own pocket! . . . He was a kind of superpimp" (246–47). The sensational presentation in both novels of prostitution provides a seamy but productive milieu for an exploration of the interbraiding of commerce, perverse sexuality, and violence.

The big difference in the novels, curiously, is that Faulkner doesn't deal extensively with interracial sexuality in *Sanctuary* (although Clarence Snopes steers Virgil and Fonzo to a Black whorehouse he frequents), while Wright makes it a central focus in his narrative. Both novels, however, reflect the authors' fascination with criminality and incarceration, subjects also central to another shared preoccupation: detective narratives. Faulkner, of course, would go on to feature a convict as his central figure in "Old Man," while Harry Wilbourne, the main protagonist in the accompanying "The Wild Palms," also winds up in prison. Then, too, we have the detective narratives Faulkner wrote, including the stories in *Knight's Gambit* (1949) and the novel *Intruder in the Dust* (1948), while Wright would leave behind an unpublished detective novel, *A Father's Law*, posthumously released in 2008.

Just as Miss Reba's whorehouse becomes a central locus for *Sanctuary*, the Grove nightclub—where many of Tyree's prostitutes go to snare johns—is that space in *The Long Dream*. Wright based the Grove on the Rhythm Club of Natchez. On that night in April 1940, the club, filled to capacity by a crowd drawn to hear the Chitlin' Circuit sensations, Walter Barnes and His Royal Creolians, erupted in flames. The owner had decorated the club with festoons of Spanish moss, which he drenched in volatile insect repellent. He knew everyone would want to hear the Creolians, so he boarded up all the windows and doors except the entrance to keep gatecrashers out. When the fire erupted, the crowd sprang toward the entrance doors, but they only opened inward, so the push kept the only exit blocked.

Wright, who spent his childhood near Natchez, knew families who had lost loved ones in the conflagration, and he was also aware that segregation dictated that only Black undertakers could bury Black bodies. The historical marker that still stands in Natchez notes that the dead included "civil and cultural leaders"; Wright, however, makes his Grove more sinister, as a place mainly for whores and pimps. He also reduces the number killed in the fire to forty, which makes Tyree's assumption of all mortuary duties central, since multiple undertakers shared the burden after the Rhythm Club burned. Cantley's involvement in the club's operations also emerges more saliently with the simplification. Dr. Bruce is the main owner, but the operations of the club are masterminded by Tyree and Cantley. As Fish and friends survey the twenty "gals" seated at the Grove's tables, three stand out: Gladys, who immediately draws Fish's attention; the yellow Beth; and the "fat, jet black" Maybelle, who represent the color hierarchy of the race (176). Rejected, Maybelle screams to Gloria, "Go to hell, you white-looking bitch! . . . I ain't blind! I know they made their goddam choice! They want *white* meat! But you sluts ain't *white*! You n-----s like me! But you the nearest thing that they can git that *looks* white!" (177). She then taunts the boys: "If you-all just dying for white meat, why don't you go 'cross town where there ain't *nothing* but white meat? . . . I'll tell *you*! You scared of being killed like a dog!" Before being thrown out by the bouncer, whom she calls a "black baboon" (179), Maybelle concludes, "You goddamn *white-struck* black fools just hungry for the meat the white man's done made in n----r town! Go on, you cheap n-----s, and lap the white man's crumbs!" This extended harangue is one of the most powerful in Wright's *oeuvre*, offering a tribute to the Black woman of words while performing a devastating critique of colorism within the race, but also underlining Fish's obsession with white women, a thread that runs throughout the novel and its sequel, *Island of Hallucinations*.

Confinement and Surveillance

Eventually, Cantley becomes tormented by the knowledge that Tyree has incriminating evidence against him and takes measures that lead to the undertaker's murder. Despite being fully aware of this, Fishbelly, terrified of the alternatives, takes up his dead father's businesses and the accompanying payments to Cantley. He, too, however, eventually falls under suspicion from Cantley and is subject to a sting whereby he is set up by a hired prostitute, then sent to prison.

The presentation of Mississippi as a virtual prison for Blacks finds expression in several of Wright's books, and indeed, the original title of *The Long Dream* was *Mississippi*. Fishbelly's growing sense of psychological confinement, as the social boundaries and opportunities around him paradoxically seem to shrink even more rapidly after he inherits his father's empire, proceeds to his actual incarceration in a section of *The Long Dream* that inevitably recalls the final chapters of *Native Son*. As Wright stated in that 1960 interview, "Mississippi is only an immense black ghetto, a vast prison where the whites are the jailers and the Negroes are the prisoners. And the new movement for integration which is taking shape in the United States has not really reached the state yet."[21] We remember that *Sanctuary*, too, ends in prison, with Popeye's demise in what is literally gallows humor. Both figures, however, are transformed by criminality—be it their own or others'—and both have to pay for crimes committed by others.

Temple is also linked symbolically with the prison system: her dorm is called the "coop," and she has been placed on probation for "slipping out at night" (57). Subsequently, after her abduction and installation in Miss Reba's brothel, she is a prisoner in her room, which becomes the scene of her obsessive couplings with Red and her transformation to immorality. She ultimately expands beyond unrestrained sexuality to the monstrous crime of falsely accusing Lee Goodwin of her rape; this in turn leads to *his* rape, torture, and incineration by a mob. In her "cell" at Miss Reba's, Temple is watched continually, and as Jay Watson has noted, Popeye, whose deformities and aberrant behavior caused his confinement in a series of social and medical institutions during his childhood, has acquired "the Foucauldian competence that will make him the novel's most expert administrator of discipline, punishment, surveillance, and other techniques of knowledge/power."[22]

The Corruption of the Self and the State

We see plainly in each text that small transgressions can lead to larger ones. Temple's corruption does not begin with Popeye or her life at Miss Reba's. It begins to build much earlier, in a quotidian detail: she has a Latin "pony" (152)—a cheat book. Her violation of college rules and teasing of the local male population leads to her name being scrawled on lavatory walls. Conversely, the moral decay of other "proper" characters remains under the surface. *Sanctuary* is a sequel to *Flags in the Dust* (1929); ten years have passed since Bayard Sartoris made his wife Narcissa a mother and a widow, and since her brother Horace married Belle Mitchell. Narcissa, a much more malignant figure in *Sanctuary* than in the earlier text, struggles constantly to thwart Horace's efforts to take care of the former prostitute Ruby and her child in town, all in the name of outraged respectability. Here and in many other concealed maneuvers by Narcissa we see evil infecting the seemingly tranquil town, whose borders with both the natural world and the underworld are continually under threat in the novel.

Similarly, Fish's moral disintegration is gradual. His first job is collecting rent from Tyree's slums and cathouses. The Tucker family's share is equal to that given to the corrupt police chief. These duties give Fish—and the reader—a panoramic view of the variety, the idiosyncrasies, and the struggles of the Black community, where desperation makes people turn on each other, even in the same family. Fish's Black high school teacher recites a rhyme to "help you to understand our folks":

> Big n-----s have little n-----s upon their back to bite 'em.
> And little n-----s have lesser n-----s, and so on ad infinitum.
> And the big n-----s themselves, in turn, have bigger n-----s to go on;
> While these again have bigger still, and bigger still, and so on. (207-8)

The principal provides a gloss: "The white folks are on top of us, and our own folks are on top of our folks, and God help the black man at the bottom" (208). Fish comes to see this as accurate: "His Black Belt teemed with crimes against the person: assaults, knifings, shootings stemming from drunken brawls. 'We n-----s fighting each other and we don't even know it,' he told himself with amazement."

The novels portray sexual corruption among men as well as women. The preoccupation of men with proof of their sexual prowess plays a key role in crime and personal corruption in both texts. Wright and Faulkner have male characters flaunt sexual trophies as a masculine accessory. An unnamed "town man" early on in *Sanctuary* pulls a female undergarment saved from a sexual encounter from his pocket, "and flip[s] it out, whipping the sheer, faintly scented web across their faces.... 'Doc got that step-in in Memphis ... off a damn whore'" (31). Similarly, Fishbelly's friend Zeke, the first among their crowd to "score," flaunts his "rubbers" and brags that he got even with a girl by cutting a hole in one he used with her. In both novels, Memphis, with its seedy bars, whorehouses, and corrupt officials, is the Dantean city of Dis—of depravity and death.

More generally, the body's corruption is suggested many times in both texts, especially through a focus on excreta. St. Augustine long ago remarked, "Inter faeces et urinam nascimur": "we are born between faeces and urine" (quoted in Bataille, *Erotism* 57-58). Twice in *Sanctuary* we are told of Temple's name being inscribed on a lavatory wall, meant to be read by a man defecating. We also see her, in fact, defecating at the Old Frenchman Place as three men scheme to rape her. The obscenity of the sexual organs and the violence of the sexual act is repeatedly referenced in both Faulkner and Wright's texts.

The corpse, perhaps the most dramatic form of excreta, plays a key role in both novels. Chris's dead body, as we have seen, becomes a shattering example and warning for Fish. Later, when he discovers a dying dog, Fish kills it to put it out of its misery, and then, mimicking Chris's autopsy, he opens its belly to stare at its organs, lifting them out. This epiphany crystalizes his sense of death: "When the whites came at him now, he would know what death was, just as he had anticipated death by fainting when the white men had threatened to castrate him" (141). Yet just after this scene, Fish encounters a white man gravely injured in a car accident, another example of modernist machine violence; but the man calls out "G-Goddammit, n----r! S-stop talking and h-help me" (143). It turns out this man had swerved to avoid the dog Fish just killed, but he had hit it anyway. Leaving the injured man, Fish thinks about flagging a passing car, but the first one turns out to be not only a police car, but one driven by the officer who pretended he was going to castrate Fish. This rather overdetermined and unlikely sequence of events nevertheless pulls together the thematics of killing speed, death, the physicality of the body, racism, and the violence and oppression of white policemen. It also parallels Popeye's childhood torture and killing of animals. As Olga Vickery observes, in terms that fit Fish and the dog as well, "[O]nly by eschewing life can Popeye prolong his existence, and only by affirming the reality of death can he, by implication, affirm that existence. . . . It is his attempt to gain a fleeting and illusory sense of life through the very act of destroying it."[23] These scenes may additionally illustrate the "connection" noted by Bataille "between death and sexual excitement. The sight or thought of murder can give rise to a desire for sexual enjoyment" (11–12). "In essence," he concludes, "the domain of eroticism is the domain of violence, of violation," and "the most violent thing of all for us is death which jerks us out of a tenacious obsession with the lastingness of our discontinuous being" (16).

The violated corpse occupies pride of place in the grim gallows humor of Red's funeral, held in a gambling casino. The proprietor tries to keep it solemn—no dancing—and when one of the friends of the deceased says that "Red wouldn't like it solemn," the proprietor replies, "Let him go somewheres else, then. . . . I just done this as an accommodation. I aint running no funeral parlor" (245). The crowd gets drunk and Red's pal Gene, the bootlegger, gets maudlin; all hell breaks loose among the mourning thugs and floozies; the bouncer is attacked by four men, upsetting the coffin as the orchestra flees; and the poorly embalmed "corpse tumbled slowly and sedately out and came to rest with its face in the center of a wreath. . . . When they raised the corpse, the wreath came too, attached to him by a hidden end of wire driven into his cheek. He had worn a cap which, tumbling off, exposed a small blue hole in the center of his forehead. It had been neatly plugged with wax and was painted, but the wax had been jarred out and lost. They couldn't find it, but by unfastening the snap in the peak, they could draw the cap down to his eyes" (248-49). Faulkner had of course perfected this graveyard humor in *As I Lay Dying* with the ghastly things done to Addie's body, and he would do it again in *Absalom, Absalom!* when Sutpen too falls out of his coffin on the way to the cemetery.

Excretion becomes linked with sexuality prominently in a key bathroom scene in *The Long Dream*, when Fish reaches for toilet paper after a bowel movement and spies an old newspaper with "a photograph of a white woman clad only in panties and a brassiere . . . looking straight at him, her hands on her hips, her lips pouting, ripe, sensual. A woman like that had caused Chris to die" (69). Magnetically attracted, he tears the photo off the page and secretes it in his wallet. We see a similar scene of bathroom excretion in *Sanctuary*, where Horace Benbow's pornographic fantasies triggered by Little Belle's photo cause him to run into the bathroom and vomit into the toilet.

Associations with excreta are paralleled with the thematic of the degradation of beauty. When Popeye is unable to consummate his attraction to Temple because he is impotent, he resorts to the corncob. This heinous act—the most remembered fact about the novel for many—is followed by his choreographing for his viewing pleasure the sex-play of Temple and Red at Miss Reba's. Again, Bataille provides a gloss on the scene: "Beauty is desired in order that it may be befouled; not for its own sake, but for the joy brought by the certainty of profaning it. . . . A woman's beauty (her humanity, that is) [makes] the animal nature of the sexual act obvious and shocking. . . . To despoil is the essence of eroticism" (144–45), and further, "In sacrifice, the victim is chosen so that its perfection shall give point to the full brutality of death" (144).

Fishbelly, like Temple, goes down a slippery slope of corruption, dropping out of school to participate in his father's illegal activities and taking advantage of the poor and sex workers. After the Grove burns, we expect Fish to be heartstruck by the death of his mistress, but when the evil police chief arrives, Fish suddenly realizes that he and his father can make money taking care of the bodies. He brilliantly suggests this to the chief, adding that the high school gym can serve as a makeshift morgue. "You know Papa and if you just tell the coroner to give us the death certificates, we'll handle 'em all" (237). Cantley pays Fish a bitter compliment—"You and your papa are go-getters. . . . You deal in hot meat, cold meat, and houses" (238)—but he also says Tyree will need this extra money, which suggests that the undertaker will take the fall for the deaths at the club.

To avoid this, Fish comes up with a plan to blame the fire on Fats, the bouncer; they agree to pay him off to "confess." This scene shows us that Fish, in scapegoating Fats, is no better than Tyree or Cantley and that his moral decline has accelerated. However, his plan collapses when he learns that Fats has died. Like Faulkner in *Sanctuary*, Wright is portraying how a victim can become a victimizer. For René Girard, the origin of violence is in mimetic rivalry. In *The Long Dream*, Tyree's corruption parallels the police chief's, but his criminal activities surely also come from patterns of white crime that he has studied and imitated. Moreover, one of the aspects of mimetic rivalry is a determination to prevent a rival from taking one's illicit gains. Even dying, Tyree seeks to prove his superiority and manhood by handing evidence that implicates Cantley over to Fish. Earlier, Tyree had decided to expose the chief by showing this evidence to the town's somewhat liberal white politician, McWilliams. As Fish and Tyree ride to McWilliams's house, Fish thinks, "Were they doing right or wrong? Then he realized that there was no right or wrong in their lives. Life was a fight to keep from being killed, to keep out of jail, to avoid situations that induced too much shame. Tyree and the doctor were doing what they had to do. It was that or they fled" (284).

Before his death, on being accused of corruption, Tyree objects: "I ain't corrupt. I'm a *n----r*. N-----s ain't corrupt. N-----s ain't got no rights but them they *buy*. . . . I want a wife. A car. A house to live in. The white man's got 'em. Then how come I can't have 'em? And when I git 'em the only way I can, you say I'm corrupt. . . . If we n-----s didn't buy justice from the white man, we'd never git any. . . . I can't vote. There ain't no black men in office in this town. . . . If I'm corrupt, who made me corrupt? Who took the bribes? The law, and the law's white. . . . When you have to do wrong to live, wrong is right" (289–90).

More troubling than personal degradation, however, is the venality of the state. The municipal authorities of *The Long Dream* have long been corrupt. Reacting to the novel, Maurice Nadeau told Wright, "You show that everything can be bought: the police, the judges, love, and even the right to live. This is a very somber picture,"[24] to which Wright replied, "Just like truth. But it is, at the same time, the novelist's truth. If Fishbelly prefers money to honesty, this is due to his having seen his father build a fortune on the whites' corruption and, though he was black, manage to corrupt them. If he deals with his unsuccessful racial brothers with contempt, this is because he has understood that despising black people leads to success. He is at the same time shy and aggressive, ignorant and kind-hearted. He wants to live but he does not know how, and this is the reason why he is dangerous to others as well as to himself."[25] In *Sanctuary*, Faulkner makes it clear that the state legislature is crooked through the comic figure of Senator Clarence Snopes. As Snopes holds forth before Horace Benbow in a smoking car, "there emerged gradually a picture of stupid chicanery and petty corruption for stupid and petty ends, conducted principally in hotel rooms into which bellboys whisked with bulging jackets upon discreet flicks of skirts in swift closet doors" (175). The state's corruption is also evident in the machinations of the attorneys during Goodwin's trial for the murder Popeye committed, which provides a telling and appropriate illustration of the truth of Benjamin's assertion that any critique of violence—which both *Sanctuary* and *The Long Dream* perform—can be summarized as that of "expounding its relation to law and justice."[26] At the trial, the ruthless, corrupt, and self-centered District Attorney Eustace Graham, who intends to run for Congress, succeeds in obtaining a unanimous conviction, although he knows Goodwin is innocent. By the end of the novel, Popeye is hanged in Alabama for a murder he similarly did not commit. Meanwhile, in Memphis, Miss Reba reports that her clientele includes "lawyers, too. I had the biggest lawyer in Memphis back there in my dining-room, treating my girls. A millionaire. He weighed two hundred and eighty pounds and he had his own special bed made and sent down here. It's upstairs right this minute" (211). In both novels, then, the principal agents of the laws of society, lawyers, judges, and legislators, are presented as thoroughly corrupt.

The Erotics of Violence

In *Sanctuary* and *The Long Dream*, Wright and Faulkner justify Bataille's declaration that "the domain of eroticism is the domain of violence, of violation" (16), and the most violent thing of all is death. Indeed, the erotic and death are linked repeatedly in both novels. One of *Sanctuary*'s finest critics, André Bleikasten, could also be speaking about *The Long Dream* when he observes, "whether repulsed by horror or anguish or aroused by desire, the body speaks the same language: the convulsions of terror resemble sexual spasms, and erotic scenes make one think of scenes of torture. An ambiguity carefully nurtured throughout the novel repeatedly links desire with horror and death. Ultimately, terror, nausea and sexuality are joined in the same poisonous sheaf."[27]

The Roman playwright Terence famously proclaimed, "Nothing human is foreign to me." Both Wright and Faulkner seem to share this position, as they systematically reveal the malignant side of every section of society; even "good characters" like Wright's Fish and Faulkner's Horace are ultimately revealed to be tainted by the same flaws they oppose in others. At the same time, both authors take great pains to provide a context for the transgressions of their female characters. Temple Drake emerges as one of Faulkner's most multifaceted figures; her corruption clearly stems from misogynistic patterns of patriarchy that limit her agency to modes of seduction, and from the outset, she is subjected to violence, predation, and kidnaping into an underworld that opens her up to uncontrollable desires. Wright, too, gives us more complex portraits of women in *The Long Dream* than we see in his other works. Gladys, especially, becomes sympathetic to readers when we see the history of her subjugation by her father, her rapist, her clients, and ultimately, by Fishbelly. Tyree's mistress Gloria does better, by seizing her opportunities and fleeing with Doc at the end of the novel. Then there is the angry, heavy, and voluble hooker Maybelle, a fiery indicter of the violence, prejudice, and misogyny that has made her who she is. Significantly, although we see much more of Temple in Faulkner's narrative, we have to wait until *Requiem for a Nun* (1951) to plunge deeply into her reactions to the negative factors that have forged her identity, from her patrician family to her underworld experiences. Her bored and blank demeanor in the Luxembourg Gardens after her flagrant deceptions at Goodwin's trial needed a sequel, and Faulkner, understanding the dramatic possibilities, wrote *Requiem,* whose three acts were adapted into an actual play mounted on Broadway for Faulkner's friend Ruth Ford and her then husband Randolph Scott in 1959. *Sanctuary*, of course, had itself been adapted—for the screen—in *The Story of Temple Drake*, released only two years after the novel's publication. While the ending was shifted to indicate "redemption," the movie makers realized the potential of the novel's violence and sexuality.[28] There was a dramatic afterlife for *The Long Dream* as well. The novel was clearly rife with theatrical possibilities, and in 1960, Ketti Frings, who had had great success dramatizing Thomas Wolfe's *Look Homeward, Angel* (which won the Pulitzer Prize for drama in 1957), presented her adaptation of Wright's novel on the New York stage. The play unfortunately closed after only a few performances; Brooks Atkinson, writing in the *New York Times*, praised the acting but found the drama never came alive.

A final note: both *The Long Dream* and *Sanctuary* end with a central character relocated to Paris. Wright had fled to the City of Light himself in 1946, unwilling to raise a family in the racist United States. Fishbelly, by contrast, is fleeing Cantley and his minions while seeking, like Wright, an opportunity to live a life in a country freer from racial prejudice. Temple has been taken to France by her ever-watchful father, most likely to keep her out of the public eye until the scandal of the Goodwin trial has subsided. She seems numb and indifferent to her surroundings, however, and is certainly not portrayed as hopeful. Fishbelly, by contrast, is full of hope in Paris, if tempered by trepidation.

Interestingly, each of these novels led to a sequel. As noted above, *Requiem for a Nun* was published twenty years after *Sanctuary* and focuses on the now married Temple's plans to elope with Red's brother, abandoning Gowan Stevens, now her husband, and their two children. Wright seems to have planned from the beginning to write not one but *two* sequels to *The Long Dream*, though he completed only one. In *Island of Hallucinations*, he has Fish, recently released from prison but in danger of death at the hands of Cantley, flying to exile in Paris, an echo of the author's own permanent relocation there in 1947. Addison Gayle provided a chilling comment on Fish's survival and flight: "Americans educate their children to become professionals; Blacks educate their children to survive the Americans."[29] While Temple and Fish escape life-threatening entanglements, then, at least for a time, they leave behind a cast of broken or ended lives, victims of violent, often lawless white cultures, whose hypocritical members give lip service to respectability, Christianity, and moral uplift. Both Wright and Faulkner succeed in mounting fiery jeremiads, which are propelled by the flight fuel of sensation, sexuality, and violence, but in the service of hastening a stern reckoning.

NOTES

1. Franz Kafka, *Letters to Friends, Family, and Editors*, trans. Richard and Clara Winston (New York: Schocken, 1977), 16.
2. Jesse Alemán and Shelley Streeby, introduction to *Empire and the Literature of Sensation: An Anthology of Nineteenth-Century Popular Fiction*, ed. Jesse Alemán and Shelley Streeby (New Brunswick, NJ: Rutgers University Press, 2007), xvii.
3. Margaret Walker, *Richard Wright, Daemonic Genius: A Portrait of the Man, A Critical Look at His Work* (New York: Amistad, 1988), 74.
4. Ernest Mandel, *Delightful Murder: A Social History of the Crime Story* (Minneapolis: University of Minnesota Press, 1984), 135.
5. Georges Bataille, *Erotism: Death and Sensuality*, trans. Mary Dalwood (San Francisco: City Lights Books, 1986), 18. Hereafter cited parenthetically.
6. Walker, *Richard Wright, Daemonic Genius*, 49.
7. Richard Wright, "Blueprint for Negro Writing," *Richard Wright Reader*, ed. Ellen Wright and Michel Fabre (New York: Harper and Row, 1978), 38.
8. Richard Wright, interview by Georges Charbonnier, "A Novel by Richard Wright, *The Long Dream*," *Conversations with Richard Wright*, ed. Keneth Kinnamon and Michel Fabre (Jackson: University Press of Mississippi, 1993), 218. Wright's presentation of Black undertaking parlors would find a powerful echo in Gloria Naylor's novel, *Linden Hills* (1985), which I find quite indebted to *The Long Dream*.
9. Richard Wright, *The Long Dream* (1958; repr., New York: Harper Perennial, 1987), 18, 22. Henceforth cited parenthetically.
10. Jay Watson, *William Faulkner and the Faces of Modernity* (New York: Oxford University Press, 2019), 102–15.
11. The policemen's amazement over Fish fainting shows that Wright is dealing with the racist canard that Black people can't faint. Laughing, the men repeat this act, over and over.
12. Earle V. Bryant, "Sexual Initiation and Survival in *The Long Dream*," *Southern Quarterly* 21, no. 3 (Spring 1983): 64.
13. John Lowe, "Wright on Patmos: The European Refiguration of Mississippi in *The Long Dream*," in *Richard Wright: Writing America at Home and from Abroad*, ed. Virginia Whatley Smith (Jackson: University Press of Mississippi, 2016), 142.

14. Wright's complex meditation on racial castration finds a variant in David Eng's book-length study, which concentrates on this concept as it has been applied to Asian American men. See David L. Eng, *Racial Castration: Managing Masculinity in Asian America* (Durham, NC: Duke University Press, 2001).

15. "Interview with Richard Wright," in *Conversations with Richard Wright*, ed. Keneth Kinnamon and Michel Fabre (Jackson: University Press of Mississippi, 1993), 205.

16. Michel Gresset, *Fascination: Faulkner's Fiction, 1919–1936*, trans. Thomas West (Durham, NC: Duke University Press, 1989), 168.

17. William Faulkner, *Sanctuary*, rev. ed. (1931; repr., New York: Vintage International, 1993), 148. Hereafter cited parenthetically.

18. Peter Lurie, *Vision's Immanence: Faulkner, Film, and the Popular Imagination* (Baltimore: Johns Hopkins University Press, 2004), 36.

19. Walker, *Richard Wright, Daemonic Genius*, 74.

20. Wright quoted in Charbonnier, "A Novel by Richard Wright, *The Long Dream*," 219.

21. "Interview with Richard Wright," 202.

22. Watson, *William Faulkner and the Faces of Modernity*, 117.

23. Olga W. Vickery, *The Novels of William Faulkner: A Critical Interpretation* (Baton Rouge: Louisiana State University Press, 1964), 110–11.

24. Richard Wright, interview by Maurice Nadeau, "Richard Wright Explains His Work and *The Long Dream*," *Conversations with Richard Wright*, ed. Keneth Kinnamon and Michel Fabre (Jackson: University of Mississippi Press, 1993), 199.

25. Nadeau, "Richard Wright Explains His Work and *The Long Dream*," 199.

26. Walter Benjamin, "Critique of Violence," *Selected Writings*, vol. 1, *1913–1926*, ed. Marcus Bullock and Michael W. Jennings (Cambridge, MA: Harvard University Press, 1996), 236.

27. Quoted in Gresset, *Fascination*, 169.

28. For a definitive analysis of *The Story of Temple Drake*, see Deborah Barker, "Moonshine and Magnolias: *The Story of Temple Drake* and *The Birth of a Nation*," *Faulkner Journal* 22, nos. 1–2 (2006–7): 140–75.

29. Addison Gayle Jr., *The Way of the New World: The Black Novel in America* (Garden City, NY: Anchor, 1975), 177.

William Faulkner, Richard Wright, and the Writing of African American Consciousness

ANITA DEROUEN AND ANNE MACMASTER

Although William Faulkner and Richard Wright were born in Mississippi within eleven years of each other, came of age there, and rose to international recognition as novelists in the 1940s, their lives—except for a single letter from Faulkner to Wright in 1945—never crossed.[1] With their works, it is otherwise: confluences of theme and technique at significant points in the authors' careers make a theory of mutual interaction hard to resist. We know that Wright read Faulkner's works beginning in the early 1930s,[2] and we can estimate with some certainty that Faulkner began to read Wright's works in or around 1940.[3] Because Wright expressed enthusiasm for Faulkner's novels while he was still preparing to write one of his own (Walker 84), we might expect the main flow of influence to be from Faulkner to Wright, yet we find the more substantial impact to be the other way around. This essay examines how Faulkner's reading of Wright coincides with a turning point in Faulkner's career, when, according to Jay Watson, "Faulkner's depiction of race relations and his portrayal of black characters became more nuanced, sensitive, and progressive."[4]

In exploring the confluence between Wright and Faulkner, we focus on the representation of African American characters and the rendering of Black consciousness into fiction. As Watson notes, it is rare that "Faulkner gives readers . . . direct access to the interiority of his black characters" (209). Although Faulkner never affords a Black character the kind of modernist, interior monologue (in which thought is rendered through sentence fragments and in the character's own words) that he gives to white characters such as Quentin Compson, Faulkner employs other modernist techniques to render into narrative what might be considered Black interiority. Here, it is worth comparing Faulkner's 1932 novel, *Light in August*, with Wright's *Native Son* (1940), especially in their rendering of consciousness into prose. In making this comparison between the two novels, we are wary of reducing Wright's work to a response to Faulkner's; instead, we examine their respective attempts to depict Black consciousness and consider the degree to which each achieves credibility.

In works immediately preceding *Light in August*, Faulkner seems to be working his way up to the theme of racial justice, treating it obliquely or from a white point of view. In the 1931 short story "Dry September," Faulkner dissects and indicts the system of white supremacy, but, in this account of the lynching of a Black man, does not enter the mind of any Black character; instead, he probes the experiences of three white characters, each of whom is responsible for the lynching to a different degree. In the novel *Sanctuary*, also published in 1931, Faulkner again broaches the theme of lynching, but this time the victim, Lee Goodwin, is white, and this novel does not deal primarily with race relations. Then, in *Light in August* in 1932, Faulkner creates Joe Christmas, a character who is lynched on account of his being categorized as a Black man and whose consciousness Faulkner develops in some depth. Thus, in *Light in August*, Faulkner comes closer to confronting racial injustice directly and to representing an African American character from the inside. Faulkner is limited, however, in his approach to issues of race by the ambiguity of Joe Christmas's racial identity. In entering the mind of Joe Christmas, the narrator does not have to assume a Black consciousness but can instead explore modernist liminality.

By "modernist liminality," we mean that Faulkner seems to be engaging here in what Eric Lott in *Love and Theft* identifies as the "textual blackface" adopted by those white modernists who wished—in the words of Aliyyah I. Abdur-Rahman—"to distort, to experiment, to transform, and to invent wholly new ways of writing [...] by importing and infusing elements of racial blackness into their artistic creations."[5] Abdur-Rahman notes that for these modernists, "blackness was itself believed to be the very condition of fracture, radical uncertainty, and resultant chaos both within oneself and in one's relation to the culture at large" (173). In a novel focused on the quest for legitimacy in a rapidly changing landscape, the story of Joe Christmas's growing up in a white world where he is never seen as legitimate underscores the inability of this fragmented consciousness to find wholeness.

Native Son, published in early 1940, is another modernist work in which a fragmented consciousness struggles to find wholeness, but here the narrative is liberated from textual blackface; in fact, Wright lays bare the limitations of Faulkner's approach when he brings the reader on Bigger's inner journey to self-knowledge and understanding. Bigger Thomas and Joe Christmas share a good deal of overlapping circumstance: each character is viewed by his community as a Black man who has murdered a white woman, a position that puts legal rights beyond his reach. Although the mixed-race status of Christmas's father is far from a certainty in *Light in August*, Christmas feels himself nevertheless to be divided between racial identities (Watson 211). And once the rumor of his mixed-race parentage reaches the sheriff and the people of Jefferson, Christmas is also viewed as Black by his pursuers, with the result that his identity, combined with the racial identity of the victim of the homicide, rules out any chance of a fair trial or even a genuine investigation of the crime, just as it does for Bigger Thomas.

In both investigations, crucial facts get obscured. No one in *Light in August* except Joe Christmas knows that Joanna Burden drew a gun on him before her throat was cut, so that Christmas may have a legitimate plea of self-defense to make. But we cannot say with certainty that Christmas killed her (and not, say, Brown the next morning) since there are no witnesses to the crime, not even the reader. Similarly, no one in *Native Son* besides Bigger puts any stock in Bigger's claim that he killed Mary Dalton accidentally and not—as the charge against him reads—"during the course of criminal rape."[6] In this case, a killing to which the reader *is* witness, Wright enlists us in the novel's sense of injustice, while Bigger's attorney, Boris Max, never fully understands his client's point of view. Max advises the Court to disregard Bigger's claim that his causing of Mary Dalton's death was inadvertent: "Let us not concern ourselves with that part of Bigger Thomas's confession that says he murdered accidentally, that he did not rape the girl. It really does not matter" (824). Instead of focusing on the facts of the case, Max attempts to defend his client by setting Bigger's life within the broad sweep of history. Although Max is trying to help, it is but a short step from his statement that "it really does not matter" whether Bigger "murdered accidentally [or] that he did not rape the girl" to the State Attorney's claims that "he killed her because he *raped* her! Mind you, Your Honor, the central crime here is *rape*! Every action points toward that!" (833). And while the State Attorney gets the facts of the case wrong, he gives clear voice to the myth of white purity, a myth which, claiming "that intercourse between white women and black men could only result from rape," operated as a pretext for violence against African Americans.[7] Both Wright and Faulkner demonstrate the legal ramifications of this myth. Had either Bigger Thomas or Joe Christmas been viewed as a white man, the crucial facts at the center of each case would have mattered to the investigators. But since both are deemed Black, the questions at the center of each case—Was this murder? And if so, what was the motive?—really do not matter at all.

Both Faulkner and Wright offset the racist myth by immersing the reader in the inner world of the accused character's consciousness. Using free indirect discourse, Faulkner and Wright create intimacy between character and reader, setting up a tension between the character's inner world and the external world that would deny depth and nuance to his reality. Alienated from much of the world outside their minds, Bigger Thomas and Joe Christmas pursue modernist inner journeys; each attempts to make sense out of an external world that may have no intrinsic meaning.[8]

Throughout *Light in August*, Joe Christmas responds to nature with the sensibility of a poet, and, when he is in flight from the sheriff's posse and its dogs, he is driven by starvation and exhaustion into an almost mystical state. Toward the end of the chase, Christmas's sensitivity to nature culminates in a transcendental experience in which the boundary between self and world breaks down: "It is just dawn, daylight: that gray and lonely suspension filled with the peaceful and tentative waking of birds. The air, inbreathed, is like spring water. He breathes deep and slow, feeling with each breath himself diffuse in the neutral grayness, becoming one with loneliness and quiet that has never known fury or despair."[9] Christmas's "feeling . . . himself diffuse in the neutral grayness, becoming one with [the] loneliness and quiet" of the place suggests the Buddhist ideal of impersonal loneliness aimed at in the poetry of haiku master Matsuo Bashō. "[T]he finest of Bashō's poems," writes Makoto Ueda, "seem to be devoid of ordinary human emotions. . . . All there is is the atmosphere of the quiet, the vast, or the swift."[10] Given the influence of the haiku on the high modernist penchant for the image and impersonality, Joe Christmas's impersonal emotion, like that of the speaker in Ezra Pound's "In a Station of the Metro," transforms Bashō's Buddhist ideal into a modernist spot of time. By giving the reader access to Christmas's mind when it reaches this spiritual state, Faulkner reveals the distance between a rich inner world and the flattening stereotype held by Joe's pursuers.

Working with the same technique of free indirect discourse, Wright also emphasizes the gap between Bigger and the stereotype to which "both white public and white law" (McMillen 15) would reduce him. Like Joe Christmas, Bigger Thomas is spurred by physical duress to reach heightened states of mind. Having been pried from the water tower with a fire hose and dragged down flights of stairs, having refused food for three days, Bigger withdraws into his mind. He finds unexpected solace in the imagery of the religion he has rejected: "[H]e turned away from his life and the long train of disastrous consequences that had flowed from it and looked wistfully upon the dark face of ancient waters upon which some spirit had breathed and created him, the dark face of the waters from which he had been first made in the image of a man with a man's obscure need and urge; feeling that he wanted to sink back into those waters and rest eternally" (701). The sheer length of the sentence is an index of Bigger's interior complexity and depth. When Bigger is alone, Wright brings us close to him, allowing the reader to understand a character who is alienated from all others. Faulkner similarly uses free indirect discourse to create intimacy between Joe Christmas and the reader.

In *Light in August*, Christmas's consciousness shapes eight consecutive chapters (more than a third of this novel of twenty-one chapters), before Faulkner abruptly breaks off the reader's access to Christmas's mind. During the chase that ensues after Joanna Burden's death, the narrative point of view shifts from Christmas's perspective to that of his pursuers and then reverts to his perspective only briefly one last time. Our final access to Christmas's mind comes when Christmas, just before entering Mottstown, feels that one side of his divided identity is overtaking the other: looking at the pair of brogans on his feet (which he's traded with a Black woman in order to elude his pursuers), Christmas interprets the shoes as emblematic, as "the gauge . . . of the black tide creeping up his legs, moving from his feet upward as death moves" (339). Like a cinematographer using a wipe to move one picture off the screen, Faulkner wipes Christmas's consciousness out of the novel as that "black tide" moves up his body. We get no further narration from Christmas's point of view—not of his time in Mottstown, nor of his time in jail in Jefferson. A character whose consciousness has been central drops out when he comes to be regarded as Black by himself and others. This fact invites comparison with Wright's treatment of Bigger Thomas.

In *Native Son*, Wright narrates the entire novel from Bigger Thomas's point of view, alternating between the objective reporting of events that register on Bigger's mind and the subjective flow of his thoughts. In the first two-thirds of the novel, there is much action and interaction with other people as Bigger moves through the streets of Chicago and various venues of the city—from pool hall and movie theater to the abandoned buildings and empty rooms where he hides during the chase. In the last third of the novel, once Bigger is incarcerated, Wright plunges the reader deeper and deeper into Bigger's mind until the movement of his thoughts becomes the main action of the novel. Between interactions with the external world (the coroner's inquest, the interview with his attorney, and several moments during the trial), Bigger returns to his solitary cell—the cell indicating the character's interior "architecture"—to reflect at length on his experiences. The narrative continues right up to the eve of Bigger's execution and ends only after Wright has traced the course of Bigger's long, inner endeavor to make sense of his experience.

Unlike Bigger's inner journey, Christmas's is cut off abruptly and (compared to Bigger's) prematurely. *Light in August* continues for another third of its length after Faulkner drops Christmas's perspective and replaces it with an array of others' speculations on his motives, and then with Gail Hightower's interiority as well as with passages from Byron Bunch's point of view. Toward the end of *Light in August*, then, Hightower supplants Christmas as the character whose interiority is rendered in depth. As long as Christmas's consciousness is central, Faulkner takes pains to represent it on several levels of thought,[11] but he reserves the sudden illuminations of self-awareness for Hightower. Christmas is granted a layered interiority, but Hightower is given the novel's epiphanies.

In *Native Son*, both Christmas's experiences of injustice and Hightower's modernist epiphanies belong to Bigger Thomas. Wright contrasts Bigger's expanding understanding of himself and his world to the stunted insight of the mob that bays for his blood. "Though he could not have put it into words," Bigger grasps on some level that the people in the crowd "were determined to make his death mean more than a mere punishment; that they regarded him as a figment of that black world which they feared and were anxious to keep under control" (703). This is one of Bigger's first insights into the system that he's caught up in, and it rouses him from a stupor into resistance. As Bigger perceives the narrative imposed by white supremacist culture, Wright's narrative rejects his white counterparts' tendency to defer to stereotypes. Wright exposes racist attitudes via the words of newspaper editors, university professors, the State's Attorney, and even—at times—Bigger's own lawyer, while the gap between these stereotypes and Bigger's insight only grows wider.

In reading *Native Son*, Faulkner would have taken note of Wright's sustained rendering of Bigger's inner journey after his arrest and incarceration, and Wright's treatment of Bigger's interiority may have played a significant part in Faulkner's endowing Black characters, after 1940, with interiority. While this shift arguably constitutes an improvement in Faulkner's representation of Black characters, we nevertheless acknowledge its limits. What Faulkner achieves, short of representing African American experience credibly, forms part of a larger literary trend described by Abdur-Rahman: "Representations of African Americans in white American-authored texts of this era have not tended overall to reflect African American people, their inner or cultural life; these representations have, instead, marked crucial moments in the development of white American culture and consciousness" (173).

We can trace such moments in the development of Faulkner's consciousness by exploring his different treatments of the character Lucas Beauchamp from magazine story to *Go Down, Moses* (1942) to *Intruder in the Dust* (1948). In early 1940, Faulkner sent his agent three stories, two of which featured Lucas: in January, Faulkner submitted "A Point of Law";

in February, "Gold Is Not Always"; and in March, "Pantaloon in Black."[12] Each of these stories represents a new point of departure for Faulkner in that each one is told, wholly or in significant part, from the point of view of a Black character. Significantly, the characters Lucas and Rider, unlike Joe Christmas and Charles Bon, are not racially ambiguous: they are not "characterized by" the "self-division . . . that makes [Joe Christmas] a paradigmatic modernist figure" (Watson 211). But this move on Faulkner's part away from characters who can "pass" for white and toward characters who are culturally Black is not necessarily a departure from "textual blackface" (Abdur-Rahman 173)—at least not at first.

Faulkner's first versions of the stories about Lucas depend upon extremely flattening cultural stereotypes. The magazine story "A Point of Law" is a tightly composed tale of intrigue in which all the Black characters are comic types. Lucas is a bootlegger who plans to knock out his competition, George Wilkins, by reporting George to the white landowner, Roth Edmonds. Lucas's plan backfires when his own daughter, Nat, teams up with George to turn the tables on her father. Nat means to overcome Lucas's opposition to her marrying George, but not without assuring herself of George's obtaining a well, a stove, and a porch before she moves in with him. When the young couple's scheme goes awry, both Lucas and George end up charged with bootlegging, and the authorities plan to make George testify against Lucas and Nat testify against George. Suddenly, a wedding license is produced to show that Nat and George are already married. Thus, everyone's plot is overturned, even law enforcement's, and the story ends with a comic denouement: Lucas and George start the bootlegging business anew, using the money for Nat's well, stove, and porch to buy a new still.

"A Point of Law" is a comic tale, unified in tone as well as in plot, but even in this first version of Lucas, certain stretches of narration from his perspective strain against the flattening of comic stereotype.[13] When Faulkner, in 1941, revised this story into the first chapter of "The Fire and the Hearth" for *Go Down, Moses*, he took the tightly woven comic tale and deepened it by plunging at greater length into Lucas's consciousness and thereby transforming the comic intrigue into a family tragedy of loss and betrayal. Now, Lucas Beauchamp and the landowners share a common progenitor in old Carothers McCaslin, who is Lucas's grandfather and the patriarch of the other branch of the family, which descends through "Cass" Edmonds to his son Zack and grandson Roth. When Lucas goes to Roth's door to report George's still, his mind travels back forty-three years to the time Roth was born. During a flood, Roth's mother (Zack Edmonds's wife) went into labor, and Lucas, in crossing a river to fetch a doctor, nearly lost his life. After Zack's wife dies giving birth to Roth,

Lucas's wife, Molly, moves into Edmonds's house to care for the newborn Roth and her own infant son, Henry, a set of events that brings Lucas's life to a crisis. After six months, when Lucas begins to suspect that something is going on between Molly and Zack Edmonds, he decides that he must kill Zack. The gun misfires, sparing Zack's life, and Lucas demands that Molly come back to live at home again; it is unclear whether Lucas's suspicions were unfounded or not. All this is narrated from Lucas's point of view as a memory, and the comedy of "A Point of Law" gets submerged underneath the serious matters of racial injustice and of the white family's disowning of their Black cousins.

Lucas's thoughts are now more complex than they were in "A Point of Law," and the free indirect discourse gives Faulkner scope for passages of lyrical prose that capture the rhythms of Lucas's thought and deepen his interiority. As Philip M. Weinstein observes, "'The Fire and the Hearth' takes nine pages to establish Lucas Beauchamp's interiority," and in those pages "we enter a subjective drama more compelling than any plot it may release."[14] Weinstein's reading of Lucas in this story concurs with Abdur-Rahman's generalization about Black characters created by white writers in this period—that they tend to reveal more about the "culture and consciousness" of their authors than about the "inner or cultural life" of African Americans (Abdur-Rahman, "White Disavowal, Black Enfranchisement," 173). In "The Fire and the Hearth," Weinstein argues, Lucas "becomes a full participant in humanity, a blood-brother to Faulkner's brood of resonant, memory-laden, white protagonists" but at a cost: "Lucas can join them, however, only as a white man" ("'He Come and Spoke for Me,'" 241). Thus "Lucas's heroic status is conditional upon his being figuratively removed from his own black heritage" (237). This Lucas, Weinstein maintains, identifies with his white grandfather at the expense of ties to his Black family (239–43). Weinstein's reading is persuasive, but it does not rule out other readings of "The Fire and the Hearth" that view this Lucas as part of a progressive turn in Faulkner's treatment of Black characters and themes after 1940.

Faulkner had multiple reasons for developing Lucas into a three-dimensional character. In order to support his unremunerative work as a novelist, he wrote short stories to sell to the wide, middle-brow audience of popular magazines; he wrote the novels, on the other hand, to be judged by the standards of high art. In building a novel out of various stories written for magazines, he would deepen the stories' content and characters. More to the point for our arguments, when Faulkner was revising the stories about Lucas he may well have been influenced by Wright's treatment of African American consciousness in *Native Son*. By 1940, it would have been impossible for Wright's work to have escaped

Faulkner's notice, given his fellow Mississippian's meteoric success as a best-selling novelist—especially as Faulkner's own novels were selling poorly—and given the fact that in *Uncle Tom's Children*, Wright had set his novellas in the rural South. The unflinching directness with which Wright confronted the brutality of this culture could not have been lost on Faulkner, nor the speed with which Wright turned the world of American literature upside down.

When Wright first "surged into the limelight of the mainstream literary scene" in March of 1938 with the publication of the collection *Uncle Tom's Children*,[15] Faulkner's financial affairs were beginning to hit bottom. In 1940, when *Native Son* was featured as one of two choices in the Book-of-the-Month Club, Faulkner's publisher itemized the poor sales of his last four novels to show that "these figures do not justify any additional advance" (Gresset 57). Meanwhile, the sales of Richard Wright's novel were breaking records: "Within a few weeks," according to biographer Hazel Rowley, "*Native Son* had sold more copies than any novel Harper had published in the previous twenty years.... After three weeks, 215,000 copies had been sold, and the novel was still selling at a rate of two thousand copies a day. *Native Son* was a literary phenomenon."[16] "It is no exaggeration," one journalist wrote in 1940, "to say that at one stroke [Wright] has become a national figure."[17]

All this publicity enabled Wright to provide a wide American audience with a new image of itself: Wright's "*Story* prize and the Book of the Month Club selections were," in the words of Laurence Cossu-Beaumont, "mediators for the emergence of a new discourse on race, of an indisputable aesthetics of violence, of a perilous vision of America, until then contained in radical or activist spheres and invisible in popular readings" (233). Since Faulkner spent the 1930s mostly between Hollywood and Oxford, Mississippi—quite apart from the "radical ... spheres" in which Wright spent the same decade—Wright's "new discourse on race" must have taken Faulkner, too, by surprise in or around the year 1940. As Irving Howe put it in 1963: "The day *Native Son* appeared, American culture was changed forever."[18]

Arguably, then, Wright's fiction played a role in the changes that Faulkner brought to his treatment of Lucas Beauchamp between "A Point of Law" and *Go Down, Moses*. And Faulkner continued to develop both Lucas's interiority and the theme of racial injustice in his reworking of the second comic story about Lucas revised for *Go Down, Moses*. In the magazine story "Gold Is Not Always," Faulkner pits Lucas against a white traveling salesman, and the intrigue involves the device of "stocking the pool"—burying coins to fool the salesman out of the metal detector. To this comic intrigue, Faulkner adds Molly Beauchamp's desire to divorce Lucas on account of religious scruples against taking things out of the earth that have been buried there. This addition in itself might have contributed to the comedy's flattening stereotypes were it not for Faulkner's cross references in *Go Down, Moses* that connect Molly's desire for a divorce with this novel's complex exploration of the relations between Black and white members of the same family. In *Go Down, Moses*, Lucas and Zack are cousins (one generation removed), sharing a common ancestor in Carothers McCaslin, so their sons, Henry and Roth, are also related, and much of the serious content that Faulkner adds to "Gold Is Not Always" in revising it for *Go Down, Moses* is made more poignant by the family themes. Roth's memory of ending his friendship with Henry at adolescence again brings up the whole story of Roth's birth and Henry's infancy, and Molly's demanding a divorce causes Roth to feel that Lucas is "breaking up [. . .] the home of the woman who had been the only mother he, Edmonds, ever knew."[19] Although the narrative perspective in chapter 2 of "The Fire and the Hearth" is not exclusively Lucas's—it shifts to Roth's at times, and at other times the narrator maintains some distance from all of the characters—nonetheless, in this chapter as in the first one, Faulkner attempts to inhabit the mind of a Black character who is not racially ambiguous, and he attempts, from this perspective, to address racial justice.

Besides Lucas, Rider in "Pantaloon in Black" is the other significant Black character from whose point of view Faulkner addresses the theme of racial justice. Sent to magazines at the same time as the stories about Lucas and also included in *Go Down, Moses*, "Pantaloon in Black" had no comic prototype. Faulkner sustains Rider's perspective all the way through the story, right up to the ironic coda, which serves as a brutal indictment of the whites' inability to grasp a Black man's humanity. Faulkner's use of Rider's point of view is arguably his most effective critique of the system of white supremacy. And although Rider appears only in this single tale, he may be Faulkner's finest achievement in writing from a Black point of view.

Just as Wright does in *Native Son*, Faulkner in "Pantaloon" limits dialect to the characters' spoken words and relays the protagonist's thoughts and sensations in rhythmical prose. When Rider rebuffs his uncle's attempts to console him and takes flight from all entreaties that he come home, Faulkner immerses the reader in the protagonist's sensitive and poetic sensibility:

"You cant keep up," he said, speaking into the silver air, breasting aside the silver solid air which began to flow past him almost as fast as it would have flowed past a moving horse. The faint frail voice was already lost in the night's infinitude, his shadow and that of the dog scudding the free miles, the deep strong panting of his chest running free as air now because he was all right. (Faulkner, *Go Down, Moses*, 144)

In passages like this one, Faulkner shapes the world of Rider's consciousness with all the nuance and depth that he gives to white characters—such as Darl Bundren—whose thoughts defy the power of speech. In rendering Rider's sensations lyrically, Faulkner creates a level of intimacy with the character equivalent to—albeit not as sustained or as self-consciously modernist as—those he achieves with the interior monologues of Benjy and Quentin Compson.

While Rider may be Faulkner's finest achievement in Black interiority, Lucas Beauchamp may be more revealing of the stages of the author's developing awareness of the limits of his ability to represent Black interiority. Weinstein sees Faulkner's 1948 return to Lucas in *Intruder in the Dust* as a regression for both character and author: "The perspective is Chick Mallison's, and Lucas as seen in his eyes has receded in a number of ways from the mobile figure of *Go Down, Moses*" ("'He Come and Spoke for Me,'" 243). It is true that Lucas recedes into the background throughout much of *Intruder*, but there is a way to read this development as an advance in Faulkner's treatment of Black characters and of racial issues between 1942 and 1948. Both Lucas as character and Faulkner's approach to his interiority arguably evolve in tandem with confluences between Faulkner and Wright. Between Faulkner's revisions of Lucas in 1941 for *Go Down, Moses* and his return to Lucas in *Intruder in the Dust* in 1948, a few events relevant to the relationship between the two authors occurred, all in 1945. In March, Wright published *Black Boy: A Record of Childhood and Youth*; in June, US Senator and former Mississippi Governor Theodore Bilbo denounced *Black Boy* from the Senate floor in a "tirade" that was "widely quoted in the newspapers" (Rowley 319); and in September, when "*Black Boy* was selling twice as well as *Native Son*" (Rowley 321), Faulkner wrote to Wright with qualified praise for both books, but expressing a clear preference for the novel over the autobiography, going so far as to exclude the genre of autobiography from the category of art:

> Dear Richard Wright:
> I have just read *Black Boy*. It needed to be said, and you said it well. Though I am afraid (I am speaking now from the point of view of one who believes that the man who wrote *Native Son* is potentially an artist) it will accomplish little of what it should accomplish, since only they will be moved and grieved by it who already know and grieve over this situation.

You said it well, as well as it could have been said in this form. Because I think you said it much better in *Native Son*. I hope you will keep on saying it, but I hope you will say it as an artist, as in *Native Son*. I think you will agree that the good lasting stuff comes out of one individual's imagination and sensitivity to and comprehension of the suffering of Everyman, Anyman, not out of the memory of his own grief. (Faulkner, *Selected Letters*, 201)

Faulkner may protest too much in denying the connection between the art of the novel and the experience of the author; so dogmatic a view aligns with the New Critical zeitgeist cresting in the midforties. But Faulkner's asserting these opinions to Wright is telling, given the differences between their positions in American society. Faulkner assumes that readers of autobiography are swayed only by what confirms their own experiences, whereas readers of novels enter into some common human experience. But Faulkner had to know on some level that his art came out of "the memory of his own grief" and that Wright's art was rooted in the experience of being a Black man in America. In stating such claims so authoritatively, Faulkner may betray defensiveness about his ability to create Black characters—or about the turn of Wright's critique of Jim Crow and white supremacy pointedly southward in his autobiography (after *Native Son* had aimed it at Chicago, or more broadly, at the nation rather than the region). Yet in the sharpness with which Faulkner draws his lines here—between autobiography and fiction, between life and art—he seems to be setting himself up to see the contradictions in his own pronouncements.

There is evidence that Faulkner came to acknowledge the limitations of his experience when it came to creating Black characters from the inside when, a few years after he wrote his letter to Wright, he returned yet again to the character Lucas Beauchamp. In *Intruder*, Lucas's legal situation now resembles those of Joe Christmas and Bigger Thomas. The official investigators of Vincent Gowrie's murder don't bother to question Lucas about the facts of the case because he's a Black man accused of killing a white one. Even before hearing Lucas's version of events, Gavin Stevens comes up with a legal strategy: "[Y]ou'll plead guilty; I'll persuade the District Attorney to let you do that. . . . Then they wont hang you; they'll send you to the penitentiary."[20] In the failure of Lucas's attorney to understand him, we are reminded of Bigger's attorney, Boris Max, whom Wright likens to a blind man groping his way out of Bigger's cell when he leaves it for the last time (Wright, *Native Son*, 849). In Faulkner's calling up the shade of Boris Max in Gavin Stevens, as in his abjuring Lucas's point of view this time to filter Lucas's story through the perspective of the white boy, perhaps we may read an acknowledgment on Faulkner's part of the limits of his understanding of the inner lives of his Black characters. With the death of Caroline Barr, Hutchinson notes, Faulkner gained a "sudden awareness of her separate life and family" ("Tracking Faulkner," 65), separate worlds to which he'd previously been blind. "Faulkner seemed suddenly aware of how much of her life was outside his ken," Hutchinson argues, and "the shock of this recognition infuses his fiction after 1940" (66). Perhaps this recognition explains Faulkner's decision to render Lucas Beauchamp from the outside in *Intruder in the Dust*, where, even without interiority, Lucas is arguably a more human character than Faulkner's two previous versions of him. Lucas's dignity, charm, and wit work together in this novel as a counterweight to Chick's strenuous efforts to confine him to his place as a "Negro."

In *Intruder*, Faulkner sets up a tension between the mindset of racism that Chick has been steeped in—already at age twelve, Chick was intent upon putting Lucas in his place—and the pull of another set of values that Chick feels whenever he comes into contact with Lucas. Chick's is the consciousness in this novel, but the resistance to racism is Lucas's. Lucas refuses to accept the attempts not only of Chick, but also of the whole white county to put him in his place. As a landowner in *Intruder*, Lucas (who was a tenant farmer in the earlier works) is a symbol of Black independence and therefore a target of white hostility throughout Yoknapatawpha. Lucas's refusal to capitulate to open threats or economic pressure is the kind of quality that contributes to the "increasing humanity" of "Faulkner's black characters in the 1940s" (Hutchinson, "Tracking Faulkner," 65).

The seeds of Lucas's resistance to racism were sown in "Gold Is Not Always," when he confronts the salesman "not only with dignity but with command" (Faulkner, *Uncollected Stories*, 226). And in *Go Down, Moses*, Lucas put up a certain resistance to the Jim Crow codes of the South, not only in attempting to kill Zack Edmonds but also in everyday life. Roth Edmonds notices "even as a child . . . how Lucas always referred to his father as Mr Edmonds, never as Mister Zack, as the other negroes did, and how with a cold and deliberate calculation he evaded having to address the white man by any name whatever when speaking to him" (101). In *Intruder*, Faulkner increases Lucas's resistance to Jim Crow customs, to the point where Lucas—like one of the protagonists of *Uncle Tom's Children* through whom Wright presents "the evolution of what might be called a black revolutionary consciousness"[21]—values his dignity over his life. The powerful indictment of the brutality of the Jim Crow South in *Uncle Tom's Children* must have been known to Faulkner by the time he was writing *Intruder*, a decade after the publication of Wright's collection of novellas. In *Intruder*, although Lucas Beauchamp appears only in the first three (of eleven) chapters and then returns at the novel's end, somehow Lucas's dignity survives the long passages of Gavin Stevens's racist rhetoric in between. The parts of the novel in which Lucas appears far excel those in which Gavin Stevens speaks at length; Lucas is the memorable character, stealing the show from the white characters, as when, in jail, he replies to Chick's whining about the difficulty of his own situation:

> He looked at Lucas: "I'll have to get out there and dig him up and get back to town before midnight or one oclock and maybe even midnight will be too late. I dont see how I can do it. I cant do it."
> "I'll try to wait," Lucas said. (71)

Lucas's wry humor cuts through Chick's self-absorption, his tendency to think the plight is his and not Lucas's. If *Intruder*'s Lucas Beauchamp rises above Gavin Stevens's racist rhetoric, perhaps he does so partly because Faulkner owes something to the characters who resist racism in the fiction of Richard Wright.

NOTES

1. In 1945, after the publication of *Black Boy*, Faulkner wrote to Wright, comparing the autobiography to *Native Son*: see *Selected Letters of William Faulkner*, ed. Joseph Blotner (repr., New York: Vintage, 1978), 201. Hereafter cited in the text.

2. According to Margaret Walker in *Richard Wright: Daemonic Genius* (New York: Warner Books, 1988), Wright in the early 1930s "deeply admired" Faulkner, was "ecstatic . . . about *Sanctuary*" (74), and had "learned language from Faulkner by reading *Sanctuary*, *Light in August*, and *Absalom, Absalom!*" (84). Hereafter cited in the text.

3. For a comprehensive analysis of how reading the fiction of Richard Wright and of other African American authors contributed to a shift in Faulkner's fiction beginning around 1940, see George Hutchinson, "Tracking Faulkner in the Paths of Black Modernism," in *Faulkner and the Black Literatures of the Americas: Faulkner and Yoknapatawpha, 2013*, ed. Jay Watson and James G. Thomas, Jr. (Jackson: University Press of Mississippi, 2016), 59–73. Hereafter cited in the text.

4. Jay Watson, *William Faulkner and the Faces of Modernity* (Oxford, UK: Oxford University Press, 2019), 284.

5. Eric Lott, *Love and Theft: Blackface Minstrelsy and the American Working Class* (New York: Oxford University Press, 1993); Aliyyah I. Abdur-Rahman, "White Disavowal, Black Enfranchisement, and the Homoerotic in William Faulkner's *Light in August*," *Faulkner and Whiteness*, ed. Jay Watson (Jackson: University Press of Mississippi, 2011), 173. Abdur-Rahman hereafter cited in the text.

6. Richard Wright, *Native Son*, in *Early Works*, ed. Arnold Rampersad (New York: Library of America, 1991), 756. Hereafter cited in the text.

7. Neil McMillen, *Dark Journey: Black Mississippians in the Age of Jim Crow* (Ubana: University of Illinois Press, 1990), 15. Hereafter cited in the text. "Whites remained 'absolutely

pure,'" McMillen explains, quoting Mississippi Governor Theodore Bilbo, "because 'white women have preserved the integrity of their race'" (McMillen 15). Black Mississippians knew better and saw "the mystique of white feminine 'purity'" for what it was: "an excuse for lynching [and] not a description of social reality." In *Native Son*, Wright demonstrates that the legal consequences of this myth were not confined to the Deep South.

8. For the inner journey as a modernist motif, see Craig Hansen Werner, *Playing the Changes: From Afro-Modernism to the Jazz Impulse* (Urbana: University of Illinois Press, 1994), 190–97. Werner connects Bigger as "questing hero" with other "'metaphysical picaros' from Leopold Bloom to Ellison's invisible man" and likens Bigger's "metaphysical journey" to similar journeys in the works of Joyce, Eliot, Pound, Beckett, Faulkner, and Ellison (194). In his "attempt to wrest meaning from his isolation" (195), Bigger—like Joe Christmas—travels through the territory that Michael Levenson describes as "the inward universe of consciousness, which becomes its own vast and subtle region." See Levenson, *Modernism* (New Haven: Yale University Press, 2011), 91.

9. William Faulkner, *Light in August*, rev. ed. (1932; repr., New York: Vintage International, 1990), 331. Hereafter cited in the text.

10. Makoto Ueda, "Bashō on the Art of the Haiku," *Japanese Aesthetics and Culture: A Reader*, ed. Nancy G. Hume (Albany: State University of New York Press, 1995), 157. An example that Ueda gives of such a haiku in which the poet's self dissolves into the impersonal loneliness of nature is this one: "Quietness— / The cicada's cry / Penetrates the rocks" (Ueda 157).

11. On the "stratification of Christmas's consciousness," see Dorrit Cohn, *Transparent Minds: Narrative Modes for Presenting Consciousness in Fiction* (Princeton, NJ: Princeton University Press, 1978), 65.

12. Michel Gresset, *A Faulkner Chronology* (Jackson: University Press of Mississippi, 1985), 53. Hereafter cited in the text.

13. See, for example, paragraphs three through five of this story, in which the narration progresses along with the flow of Lucas's thoughts: William Faulkner, *Uncollected Stories of William Faulkner*, ed. Joseph Blotner (New York: Random House, 1979), 213–14. Hereafter cited in the text.

14. Philip M. Weinstein, "'He Come and Spoke for Me': Scripting Lucas Beauchamp's Three Lives," in *Faulkner and the Short Story: Faulkner and Yoknapatawpha, 1990*, ed. Evans Harrington and Ann J. Abadie (Jackson: University Press of Mississippi, 1992), 238. Hereafter cited in the text.

15. Laurence Cossu-Beaumont, "The Literary Mainstream: *Story* and the Book-of-the-Month Club," in *Richard Wright in Context*, ed. Michael Nowlin (Cambridge, UK: Cambridge University Press, 2021), 225. Hereafter cited in the text.

16. Hazel Rowley, *Richard Wright: The Life and Times* (New York: Henry Holt, 2001), 191–92. Hereafter cited in the text.

17. Mike Gold, in the *Sunday Worker*, quoted in Rowley, *Richard Wright*, 192.

18. Irving Howe, "Black Boys and Native Sons," quoted in Cossu-Beaumont, "The Literary Mainstream," 233.

19. William Faulkner, *Go Down, Moses*, rev. ed. (1942; repr., New York: Vintage International, 1990), 113. Hereafter cited in the text.

20. William Faulkner, *Intruder in the Dust*, rev. ed. (1948; repr., New York: Vintage, 2011), 63. Hereafter cited in the text.

21. Richard Yarborough, introduction to *Uncle Tom's Children: Novellas* by Richard Wright, rev. ed. (1940; repr., New York: Harper Perennial, 1993), xxviii.

The Transit of Memory

William Faulkner, Jesmyn Ward, and Eudora Welty

SARAH GILBREATH FORD

When asked in an interview about the prevalence of ghosts in contemporary fiction, Jesmyn Ward responds, "[W]riters are resisting. We're pushing back against this trend that seems to be happening right now, where people in politics are attempting to rewrite history and attempting to undermine our understanding of what came before."[1] Although contemporary debates may have shifted from which monuments should be removed to how schools teach about racial oppression, the decision about what history we tell still provokes heated controversy. Ward employs two ghosts in *Sing, Unburied, Sing* to resist the erasure of Black history: Given, a Black man whose murder at the hands of a white man is covered up by the justice system, and Richie, a twelve-year-old boy who became an inmate at the notorious Parchman prison.[2] These ghosts confront efforts to bury stories like theirs by claiming the right to reenter the timeline and tell their stories to the present world. While Eric Foner's question of "who owns history" undergirds those battles over Civil War monuments, critical race theory, and the appropriate year to identify the founding of the United States, Ward's fictional text asks a related question: who owns narrative?[3]

In exploring the stakes of narrative, Ward explicitly references two earlier Mississippi writers: Eudora Welty and William Faulkner. A quote from Welty's memoir *One Writer's Beginnings* serves as epigraph to Ward's novel: "The memory is a living thing—it too is in transit. But during its moment, all that is remembered joins, and lives—the old and the young, the past and the present, the living and the dead."[4] Ward explains that the quote is "applicable to the story I'm telling" because "memory being a living thing is another way to say that the past is not the past, and that time isn't linear,"[5] echoing Faulkner's famous line from *Requiem for a Nun*,

"The past is never dead. It's not even past."[6] She further reveals that when she was crafting *Sing, Unburied, Sing* as a "novel about a journey," she was "thinking about *As I Lay Dying*."[7] Although Ward uses the word "love" to describe both Welty's words and Faulkner's novel, positing simple influence does not provide sufficient context for her connection to these writers.[8] Greg Chase argues that Ward is not "a mere legatee of Faulkner" and that she "actively invites us to understand her novels as conversing with Faulkner's,"[9] while Sinéad Moynihan proposes the term "recycling" to indicate a "more politically engaged model of rewriting."[10] The framing I propose in this essay draws from what Ward inherits from Faulkner and Welty: a gothic sense of the fluidity of time. Haunting signals a rupture, a thwarting of the arrow of time to put two temporalities together. Instead of positing an earlier narrative with precedence or a contemporary narrative with hindsight, a framing that imagines mutual hauntings leaves the ownership of narrative in flux. By allowing her novel to be haunted by Faulkner and Welty, Ward puts her work in conversation with the past. By haunting that tradition in turn, Ward claims ownership of a narrative of racial injustice, the song being the "unburied" in her title "sing."

Haunting and claiming are bound together in the gothic tradition, as gothic texts often play out anxieties about the ownership and transfer of property. Ruth Bienstock Anolik explains that the "English Gothic is taken up by the issue of possession and is preoccupied with the legal and seemingly literal questions of ownership: the questions of who actually owns the *property* (the frequently contested castle), who owns the *self*, including the body and mind, who owns the *narrative* and the *text*."[11] American gothic texts likewise explore issues of property, although the concern shifts from inheritance to the means of acquisition, specifically whether the property was obtained ethically. The haunting of Nathaniel Hawthorne's 1851 novel *The House of Seven Gables*, for example, begins with Colonel Pynchon accusing Matthew Maule of witchcraft so he can acquire his property and build the magnificent dream house with seven gables. Hawthorne then describes the house as having "spacious apartments" and "ceilings gorgeously painted" but also "some low and obscure nook" containing a "corpse, half-decayed and still decaying."[12] A ghost lingering in a building's halls signals a problem with the title.

The texts of Welty, Faulkner, and Ward, however, portray a twist on this connection of haunting and claiming. Through their attention to movement—the transit of memory, the movement of a body, the journey by car—haunting in these texts is not bound to a place or centered on the ownership of a physical property. Instead, Ward borrows from Faulkner and Welty a haunting that claims the property of narrative. Instead of the legal possession of a place, the various ghosts rend the fabric of time to claim spectral possession of a story. Anolik argues that the gothic "posits a ludic, supernational world in which the principles of legal ownership grounded in rationality and an existing social order, must give way to the irrational, to ghostly possession."[13] Ghosts can, in other words, travel through time to resist the death of their story, claiming ownership of their narrative.

In exploring how Welty's conception of memory in transit haunts *Sing, Unburied, Sing*, I will discuss two of Welty's texts: the memoir *One Writer's Beginnings* that contains the words of the epigraph and the closely related novel *The Optimist's Daughter*. While Ward borrows from both Welty and Faulkner the sense that the past survives into the present, what is key to that survival is the portal, the passage that allows the past to enter the present. Transit becomes both form and content in Welty's memoir. As she details aspects of her youth and family life in the first section, "Listening," she connects her stories with travel. She remembers riding in the family's first automobile, always sitting in the back seat between her mother and one of her mother's friends. The young Eudora would tell them, "Now *talk*," and then she would delight in their stories. Welty structures her second section, "Learning to See," by using the family's summer car trips to visit both sets of grandparents. In the last section, Welty "[finds] a voice" through train trips with her father that taught her about differing perspectives. Journeys shape her memoir and her understanding of narrative in general: "The trips were whole unto themselves. They were stories. Not only in form, but in their taking on direction, movement, development, change."[14]

Given the built-in temporal arc of a journey, Welty strangely does not present her life story chronologically. She begins the book by explaining, "[I]n our house on North Congress Street in Jackson, Mississippi, where I was born, the oldest of three children, in 1909, we grew up to the striking of clocks" and then claims that the entire family "have been time-minded all our lives."[15] However, as Gary M. Ciuba argues, Welty's "fragmented and wayward memories ultimately reject the external organization of clocks and calendars."[16] Transit becomes not just the scaffolding of her text but the very portrait of the artist, as Welty allows memory to move back and forth in time, layering the present onto the past. Welty recalls, for example, the magic of children's books with the "enchanted-looking initials" at the beginning of each story.[17] She then links the books to a later memory: "When the day came, years later, for me to see the Book of Kells, all the wizardry of letter, initial, and word swept over me a thousand times over, and the illumination, the gold, seemed a part of the word's beauty and holiness that had been there from the start."[18] Instead of chronology's marks on a timeline, creating a before and after or a cause and effect, Welty values an atemporal coming together that she labels "confluence," with the "greatest confluence of all" being "the individual human memory."[19] Welty thus locates a transit through time in her memoir, eschewing clock time to posit memory with the power to join the past and the present.

Ward allows this description of memory's transit to haunt her narrative by using it as epigraph. Epigraphs occupy a liminal position in a text; while they are not included in the fictional narrative, they still bear meaning into that narrative. Gérard Genette labels contextual material, such as epigraphs, titles, and dedications, "paratexts" and describes them as a "threshold" into the text, an apt image for how Welty's description of the layering of time carries over into Ward's depiction of her protagonist Jojo.[20] Jojo experiences memory as an entity that can travel with seeming volition. At the beginning of the novel, he recalls a tense scene between his parents. He then tries to "leave the memory of Leonie and Michael fighting outside, floating like fog in the damp, chilly day. But it follows."[21] Richie, the boy killed at Parchman, also experiences agentic memory when he describes what happens after his death. As he starts to remember the horrors of Parchman, he tries to dive "into the dirt, and it parted like a wave. I burrowed in tight."[22] Richie tries "to be blind to the men above. To memory. It came anyway."[23] Alive or dead, characters find that despite their attempts to flee or hide, memory as somehow existing outside of their minds can follow them.

Abstract memory then becomes figured by ghosts in Ward's text, which also follow people unbidden. The ghosts of Given and Richie initially present as classic haunts, tied to the places of their murders. Leonie first sees the ghost of her brother Given when she gets high at a party at the aptly named Kill, where Given had died. Given had gone to a party at the Kill with his white football teammates against the advice of his father. His belief that these teammates "were like brothers to him" becomes cruelly ironic when one of those teammates shoots Given after Given wins the hunting contest by killing a buck first.[24] Despite Given's death, Leonie dates and then marries the cousin of the shooter, and she continues to visit the Kill. By haunting this particular place and appearing to a sister who did not pay heed to the lesson of not trusting white people, Given follows the standard gothic logic of a ghost tied to the place of his violent death and haunting those who ignore the past.

Richie also at first appears to act as the specter of a place where terrible things happened. Richie tells of waking into the afterlife to converse first with a snake and then with a vulture.[25] The vulture gives Richie a scale that allows him to fly, but those unbidden memories come and pull him back to the earth, specifically back to the dirt of Parchman: "This is where I was worked. This is where I was whipped. This is where

River protected me. The bird dropped to the ground, dug its beak into the black earth, and I remembered my name: Richie. I remembered the place: Parchman prison."[26] He haunts the prison for years until Jojo shows up with Leonie to pick up his father, who has finished serving a sentence for drug possession.

As specters of place, Given and Richie become the images of memory, ghostly reminders of their murders. Memory in *Sing, Unburied, Sing*, however, does not stay in place, and the ghosts become weirdly "in transit" as they move with the living via automobiles. Just as Welty connects stories with travel, the memories represented by Given and Richie journey by car. Ward's choice of traveling by car has resonance for the racial oppression her book details. As Nicole Dib argues, the "road [is] a political space."[27] The open road touted in much of American literature as the method and symbol of freedom becomes fraught for Black characters whose movements have historically been monitored and controlled by white society. A terrifying encounter with a police officer in *Sing, Unburied, Sing* brings this to the surface, as Leonie swallows a bag full of drugs to hide it and the police officer points a gun at Jojo. Movement thus promises both possible freedom and potential danger.

Ghosts riding in cars with the living further indicates that the living are not saved by avoiding the particular places made metaphysically thin by past violence. When Leonie first sees Given at that party, she runs to her car because Given looks "murderous": "I was shaking so hard, I could hardly put my key in the ignition. Given climbed in next to me, sat in the passenger seat, and turned and looked at me with a face of stone."[28] Richie also climbs into the car with Jojo, recognizing him by his smell as "River's child" and deciding to ride along to see if he can find Jojo's grandfather, whom he calls River: "I fold myself and sit on the floor of the car."[29] Since Richie and Given are supernatural beings who can fly and walk through doors, both surely do not need a car to get from one place to another. Riding in cars, though, puts them in close, confined proximity to the living people they wish to haunt, so that the movement of enghosted memory through time becomes doubled by their movement in automobiles with the living. As in Welty's memoir, memory becomes in transit, joining the living and the dead.

Despite Ward's use of Welty's words as epigraph, no one has linked Ward and Welty, but several critics have followed Ward's hints about Faulkner's influence to investigate those connections.[30] Jojo's journey with his family through the Mississippi landscape clearly echoes the journey of the Bundrens in *As I Lay Dying*. Greg Chase explores how "Ward claims a county of her own, carving out space for her oeuvre alongside the long shadow Faulkner casts over the state's literary landscape" (202), while

Sodam Choi specifically addresses how *Sing, Unburied, Sing*'s reworking of Faulkner's road trip fills in gaps about the "unspeakable, the invisible, the excluded to deconstruct white narratives" (435). My reading of how Faulkner haunts Ward focuses on how the ghosts of Addie, Given, and Richie allow for a conversation between past and present because of their disruptions of chronological time. *Sing, Unburied, Sing* becomes haunted by the way in which Faulkner uses physical movement through space to signal the disruption of a transit through time, confirming that the haunting becomes about movement instead of about place.

Late in *As I Lay Dying*, as Addie's dead body is in transit to her ultimate burial, she narrates a chapter of the text. This placement puzzles and fascinates critics; as Diane York Blaine explains, "[Addie] speaks after she's already decomposed, she remains a literal presence for almost the entire length of the novel, she goes away without leaving; in short, her character resists the now seemingly secondary concern over whether 'to be or not to be' by foregrounding the issue of what it means 'to be' in the first place."[31] What Addie might "be" troubles a simple gothic reading of the novel. Brian Norman, for example, claims that Addie is "no ghost" and that "she is simply and strikingly a dead woman, lying in a box, talking."[32] Even as the text insists on the physicality of her dead body with characters referring to its smell and buzzards following the decaying corpse, her still-embodied voice lives on, and Gabriele Schwab formulates the problem as "the grotesque life of a dead body"[33] (209). Although the issue may be simply that the chapters are out of chronological order, the way the reader experiences the narrative has Addie seemingly speaking from the dead. John Limon points out the effect on the reader: "When you read the Addie section, three-fifths of the way through *As I Lay Dying*, you had better start over. You had been reading things that had to have seemed inexplicable."[34]

Things become inexplicable because of the blurring of death and life with a transit between what should be past and what should be present. Addie may not appear as an ethereal specter, but she still functions as a ghost in the way her temporal movement ruptures the narrative. Had her narrative appeared earlier in the text, her voice would not shock the reader. Although her confessions about motherhood and adultery would be radical wherever they were located, they seem distinctly out of place when she has already been mourned by her family.[35] The first scene of *As I Lay Dying* hints that the path through this text will be circuitous instead of straight. Darl walks "fifteen feet ahead of Jewel" on a path that "runs straight as a plumb-line."[36] When Darl reaches a cottonhouse, though, he follows a path around it while Jewel walks straight through, using the windows as doorways. Jewel then ends up ahead of Darl on the path. Darl's diversion from the straight trajectory that Jewel follows affects the timing of their journeys, as the past in the form of Jewel walking behind becomes the future. While events may have occurred on a timeline, the telling of them in the novel follows Darl's swerve.

By waiting until late in the text to allow Addie to tell her story, Faulkner turns her into a ghost, layering the past and the present. This play with chronological order affects other sections of *As I Lay Dying* as well. Tull, for example, narrates the story of Cash finishing Addie's coffin and driving in "the last nail" but claims even after going home, he can "still see Cash going up and down with that saw."[37] He describes how the family finds the finished coffin the next morning "bored clean full of holes," as Vardaman apparently wanted his dead mother to be able to breathe.[38] The next section narrated by Darl, however, rewinds the action back to Cash building the coffin again, as the text moves back and forth in time so that the coffin-building seems an ongoing activity. Cora's section, right before Addie's, acts as a flashback to a conversation they had earlier about sin and love. The section after Addie's from the perspective of Whitfield describes his reaction upon finding out Addie, his former lover, was dying and then his discovery that she had already died. Addie does not then just seemingly come back to life in her own chapter; she lives and dies repeatedly through the text's play with chronology, much as Philip Weinstein describes the cycle of Charles Bon's life and death in *Absalom, Absalom!*: "Charles Bon enters the novel dead, is brought back to life, is shot, is resurrected, is shot again, is resurrected again, is shot again."[39] Tamara Slankard points to the present progressive verb tense in the title, "dying," to argue that "dying is a continual process in Faulkner's work."[40] The confusion of the line between living and dying provides that transit.

Sing, Unburied, Sing likewise confuses this boundary. Although the first lines in the novel are Jojo claiming, "I like to think I know what death is. I like to think that it's something I could look at straight,"[41] when he meets the ghost of Richie that straightness, as in *As I Lay Dying*, falters: "I can't look at him straight. Not with him sitting on the floor of the car, squeezed between Kayla's car seat and the front, facing me."[42] Jojo's grandmother later explains to him that "we don't walk no straight lines. It's all happening at once. All of it. We all here at once. My mama and daddy and they mamas and daddies."[43] Although Richie, like Addie, clearly dies in the text, the muddled description of his death suggests an indefinite line between life and death. To Richie, he simply "woke in a stand of young pine trees on a cloudy, half-lit day."[44] Given's exact status also appears vague. At times, Leonie calls him "Given-not-Given" to distinguish the spirit she sees from the brother who died. She then calls him "Phantom Given" when the police officer threatens Jojo's life, perhaps indicating the possibility that Jojo, too, could die and become a being who exists as more phantom than person.[45]

Even supposedly living characters in Ward's novel cross the barrier between living and dead. Jojo explains that Stag, his grandfather's brother, walks around Bois Sauvage singing to himself. Jojo's grandmother explains that Stag is "sick in the head," and Pop tells the story of how he and Stag ended up in prison because Stag "felt dead inside" so he got in fights to "feel more alive."[46] After Parchman, Stag does not even speak sense when he interacts with the other living characters. Leonie, too, exists in a liminal space between living and dying when she gets high, perhaps explaining why she can see Given when she is on drugs. Her friend Misty claims that when Leonie lies about what she sees when high, she gets "dead still."[47] The book's supernatural elements, from Leonie hearing voices and Jojo seeing Richie to the tree of ghosts at the end, suggest that the living, the dead, and the undead are not distinct categories.

If Ward's gothic portrayals follow the lines of Welty and Faulkner in attesting to the transit of memory and the lack of barriers between life and death, we could, in one sense, say that all three authors simply employ the gothic's amplification of fiction's license to mess with time. In her essay, "Some Notes on Time in Fiction," Welty explains how fiction can play with temporality. While "clock time has an arbitrary, bullying power over daily affairs that of course can't be got around," Welty argues that "it has not the same power in fiction as it has in life."[48] Instead, fiction, as the product of the imagination, has the force to alter time: "Fiction does not hesitate to accelerate time, slow it down, project it forward or run it backward, cause it to skip over itself or repeat itself."[49] Most significantly, fiction "can set a fragment of the past within a frame of the present and cause them to exist simultaneously."[50] The gothic turns up fiction's power to manipulate time, and Ward, Faulkner, and Welty certainly employ the tools of fiction to do so. However, in unbinding memories and ghosts from particular places, they use the joining of past and present for a specific purpose: to allow the dead to wrest ownership of their identity from the living. Through time travel, narrative becomes a kind of property that can be claimed.

Laurel in Welty's *The Optimist's Daughter* discovers this as she confronts the specter of her mother, Becky. Sally Woolf explains the novel's close relationship to *One Writer's Beginnings*: "Passages echo and reflect one another from book to book, suggesting the imaginative interplay between fact and fiction."[51] The transit of memory Welty announces at the end of her memoir threads through the quasi-autobiographical experiences of Laurel as she tries to assess the meaning of her parents' lives. Laurel's return to her Mississippi home occurs because of her father's eye surgery and subsequent death. In the years after her mother's death, her father had married a pretty, young, brash woman named Fay, who takes the occasion of her husband's death to claim the property of his house and its contents.[52] When Laurel and Fay arrive at the house after his death to find members of the community gathering, Fay exclaims, "What are all these people doing in my house?"[53] When she sees Laurel's friends come to pay their respects, she asks, "Who's making themselves at home in my parlor?"[54] Her late husband's friend tries to reassure her that she was provided for: "I reckon you know you get the house and everything in it you want," but Fay has no need of reassurance: "I sure do know whose house this is."[55] Laurel witnesses Fay's assumption of ownership in the drops of nail polish carelessly left on her father's desk and the damage done to a breadboard that Laurel's late husband had made for her mother. When Laurel confronts Fay over her vandalism, Fay responds, "I'll have you remember, it's my house now, and I can do what I want to with it . . . With everything in it. And that goes for that breadboard too."[56] If Laurel wants to retain a connection to her parents, legal possession of their belongings will not work.

And it would not suffice, as Laurel discovers the night she confronts the specter of her mother. Welty sets this scene with gothic markers: during a storm late at night Laurel gets trapped in her mother's old sewing room because a bird flying around the house terrifies her. À la Poe, the bird "touched, tapped, brushed itself against the walls and closed doors, never resting."[57] In her fear, Laurel returns to her childhood, as the sewing room was also her nursery. Although earlier Laurel had found no papers in her father's desk, her mother's desk, "exiled" to a room used for storage, still contains letters, garden diaries, school notes, recipes, a snapshot book containing pictures of her parents before they were married, and a reader with her mother's favorite poetry. As Laurel examines the objects, she remembers her mother's stories. As she remembers, she hears (in direct quotes) Becky's voice. When Laurel looks at a picture of her mother in a blouse her mother made, she hears, "I'll never have anything to wear that to me is as satisfactory as that blouse."[58] When the house shakes with the thunder of the storm, Laurel's mother seems to buck up Laurel's courage: "Up home, we loved a good storm coming, we'd fly outdoors and run up and down to meet it."[59] Laurel hears her mother's request during her last days as she was bedfast: "Don't let them tie me down."[60] When Laurel remembers her mother reciting a poem, Laurel hears it clearly in her mother's voice.

What is striking about this scene is how strong Becky's voice still is. Although her image does not appear in ghostly form, her words seemingly spoken in that dark room provide a spectral effect. Through memory,

Laurel has made the transit and summoned her mother into the present. On her deathbed, Becky had accused Laurel of not helping her enough in her last days: "You could have saved your mother's life. But you stood by and wouldn't intervene. I despair for you."[61] Laurel, though, saves her mother after her death by remembering her stories and bringing her back to life. Rebecca Mark explains that Laurel tells Becky's story "in a way that shows not only empathy and compassion but deep understanding of the incredible complexity and depth of passion, anger, love that was her mother's life."[62] Drawing out the last piece of paper from the desk, Laurel summons her grandmother as well, as she "met her own name on a page" when reading "I will try to send Laurel a cup of sugar for her birthday."[63] A flood of emotions overcomes Laurel as she then hears the specter of her late husband crying, "I wanted [life]" with his voice rising "with the wind and [going] around the house and around the house."[64] When Laurel leaves her family home, she does not fight for possession of her parents' belongings or even take the breadboard that her husband made. Through her memories, the specters from her past tell their stories to claim their lives. Witnessing their stories come to life again, Laurel has no need for mere material reminders.

Spectral possession of a narrative provides further justification for Addie's out-of-place narrative in *As I Lay Dying*. She returns from the dead as a spectral voice to counter every other character's claim over not just her physical body but also her constructed identity in language. As the narrative repeats Cash's crafting of the coffin, Vardaman at one point realizes, "When they get [the coffin] finished they are going to put her in it" and then exclaims, "Are you going to nail it shut, Cash? Nail it? *Nail* it?"[65] His later boring of holes indicates his horror of the coffin's confinement, and Louis Palmer identifies the coffin as "[preserving] the function of the Gothic house."[66] If we attend to Vardaman's panic, Addie, much like Laurel cowering in the dark sewing room and Becky begging not to be tied to the bed, will be trapped within that box like a gothic damsel imprisoned in a dungeon, an apt metaphor for the container the characters create through language to define her.

Vardaman's repeated line, "My mother is a fish," demonstrates these linguistic binds.[67] He does not think of a simile (my mother is *like* a fish) that would connect the fish he brings home and his mother in that scary box as both lifeless. Instead, the equation of the metaphor turns his mother into a fish, with the "is" acting as an equal sign.[68] Addie is not a person but an object now subject to her son's construction of her being. Darl's observation that "Jewel's mother is a horse," though seemingly a comment on how Addie's death reveals what Jewel values, amplifies the reduction of Addie's life to someone else's linguistic trap.

Addie's complaint, then, that she "had been tricked by words" and that "love" was a word "like the other: just a shape to fill a lack" demonstrates her awareness of how language, specifically the discourse of "love" and "motherhood" that others use to define her, leaves her without agency. Brian Norman explains, "Words swap experience for lies; convert doers into the done-to; introduce dishonesty between body, experience, and utterance. Addie's semiotic theory is as homespun as it is complex and devastating. The result is not a silent nihilism, but rather a full-throated meditation on the violence of language, whose hypocrisy and patriarchy can only destroy a woman like Addie."[69] Just as the coffin confines her corpse, words confine her person, both in life and death.

That confinement proves significant, as it provides the occasion for the other characters to craft stories. In examining the connections between the dead female body and art, Elisabeth Bronfen argues that art comes to fruition "over her dead body" because "culture can repress and articulate its unconscious knowledge of death which it fails to foreclose even as it cannot express it directly."[70] The characters need Addie's dead body as the blank space for storytelling to the point that they imagine her body as dead before she expires.[71] The doctor, the supposed representation of logic, first observes that Addie "turns her head and looks at us," but then says, "[S]he has been dead these ten days" and he only sees "a bundle of rotten sticks."[72] At the moment Addie actually dies, Darl describes Dewey Dell shaking her mother's body, which is just "a handful of rotten bones," as if Addie's flesh had already disappeared while she was living, making her immediately a skeleton. The other characters use Addie's death (much like Caddy's absence in *The Sound and the Fury*) to provide a space for narrative; her death is productive.

By evading the boundary between life and death, though, Faulkner's texts work against how the dead can become, in Solveig Dunkel's words, "a metaphor for the silenced subjects in general."[73] Addie may look like a corpse on her deathbed and may present as a dead body in the coffin, but her voice is "harsh and strong."[74] What Addie constructs in her own chapter is a self apart from others' claims on her. She tosses "motherhood" aside as a word "invented by someone who had to have a word for it," and she dismisses "love" as something her husband Anse uses: "Let Anse have it, if he wants to. So that it was Anse or love; love or Anse: it didn't matter."[75] Instead, Addie seeks "aloneness" and, as Karen S. Sass argues, "insists on her subjecthood."[76] The subject her narrative reveals is shocking in her hatred of her pupils and in the scandalous affair that produced Jewel, but it is hers. In speaking late in the narrative against the constructions other people create of her as mother, wife, fish, horse, or skeleton, Addie claims the property of her story and thus her self.

This spectral claim made by whatever Addie might be—specter, ghost, dead body, or character—works against the legal possession of property and happens because of the movement through space and time. The journey of Addie's body to Jefferson for burial structures the text, a movement that is by Addie's volition. Her neighbor Cora objects to the plan that Addie be buried in the town of her birth rather than where her husband and children reside, pronouncing: "A woman's place is with her husband and children, alive or dead."[77] Placing her "in the same earth" as her husband's family would contain her.[78] The place, the earth, and the question of ownership keep her within the legal narrative of property. Addie recalls how her first conversation with Anse, the one in which she decided to marry him ("And so I took Anse"), concerns his ownership of a house, as if his property entitled him to marry her.[79] Her "revenge" on Anse for the feeling that she was "tricked" by his words, is insisting that her body be taken to Jefferson to be buried.[80] Anse acknowledges that his ties to property counter her desire to seek other ground when he complains that their problem has been living "on a road" because, he argues, his wife was "well and hale as ere a woman ever were, except for that road."[81] Against Anse's insistence on house and property, Addie values the movements of her body to Jefferson and of her dead voice to the present.[82] Against his legal possession, she posits the spectral possession of her story.

Haunted by Welty's conception of memory and Faulkner's spectral journey, *Sing, Unburied, Sing* likewise speaks to how movement through time and space can result in spectral claims over the property of narrative. Just as Addie presents her story to counter how others construct her identity, the true story of Given's murder has to counter the coverup. And just as Becky uses the portal of Laurel's memory to speak her identity back into present existence, Richie needs Jojo and River to tell the parts of his story he does not remember, particularly his violent death. In Ward's hands, the ability to time travel allows ghosts to reveal and claim narratives of racial injustice.

As the first specter appearing in the novel, Given's initial haunting of Leonie may appear less than effective because he cannot speak. Until he battles Richie in one of the novel's final scenes, Given appears only as image and has to mouth words or use facial expressions to communicate with Leonie. Even before his voice can be heard, however, Given's presence protects his family, particularly against the dangers of white people. Leonie reveals that Given appears to her when she does drugs with her white friend Misty, and while Leonie may think of Misty as "my best friend," when Given shows up and Misty questions Leonie about what she seems to be staring at, Leonie has to admit, "I'm Black and she's White, and if someone heard us tussling and decide to call the cops, I'd be the one going to jail. Not her. Best friend and all."[83] When Leonie finally admits to seeing Given, Misty denies Leonie's experience, saying, "[Y]ou ain't supposed to be seeing nothing on this shit," prompting Given to mouth, "What the fuck does she know?"[84] As flippant as Given's response sounds, who knows what becomes a key reason for his haunting? When he initially appears to Leonie at the party at the Kill, his presence causes her to remember the true story of his death, murdered by Michael's cousin and covered up with the help of Michael's father, Big Joseph. Given reminds Leonie that the white family she is entangled with is vicious and violent, and Leonie's two interactions with Big Joseph evidence Given's warnings: Big Joseph comes after her on a tractor and later announces that she and her children are not welcome in his house. When Leonie reunites with the newly released Michael, Given sits in the hallway outside of Jojo and Kayla's room, guarding the children against a father who later also shows his violent streak, hitting the three-year-old.

Given's role as protector appears again in the terrifying encounter with the white police officer. When Leonie swallows the bag of drugs to hide them, she sees Given when they take effect. At this point, the officer has already pointed his gun at Jojo's head and handcuffed him. As the officer searches the trunk of the car, Leonie sees that "Phantom Given is sitting next to Jojo on the ground, reaching out as if he could touch him."[85] Given appears to be trying to shield or comfort Jojo. Then Leonie sees Given reach out to Kayla, "as if he can actually touch her."[86] Whatever Given does causes Kayla to vomit all over the officer's uniform, forcing him to retreat and the incident to end. Leonie understands now that Given's movement through time makes him "the heart of a clock" so that he can pause time.[87]

The true story of Given's death reveals the need for wariness while his spectral presence speaks a message of protection. When Given finally speaks out loud, he claims the right to sound this message by claiming his family. During the deathbed scene of Given's mother, Richie appears to be trying to claim her as a way of entering the other world. Leonie hears Given twice say, "Not . . . Your . . . Mother" as Given tries to thwart Richie.[88] Given then takes his mother, saying, "I come for you Mama" and "I come with the boat, Mama."[89] Because Given appears and speaks his story of protection, she chooses the way she dies. Given's initial appearance to Leonie sparks her to tell the story of his death while his ending words claim the story of his family.

While Given's spectral claim to narrative protects Jojo's family, Richie's spectral claim threatens them all. Jojo can retell the first part of Richie's story, but he has not heard the whole narrative: "Pop's told me some parts of Richie's story over and over again. I've heard the beginning at least too many times to count. There are parts in the middle, about the outlaw hero Kinnie Wagner and the evil Hogjaw, that I've only heard twice. I ain't never heard the end."[90] He hears the parts that Pop has told him while riding in the car to Parchman, so that the journey through space and the journey through time align. Even though his grandfather does not go on the trip with them, when Jojo remembers the sections he has heard, he speaks of the storytelling in present tense: "I hear Pop."[91] He remembers/hears how Richie at only twelve was too young to endure the labor at Parchman, so River tried to protect him. Assigned to care for the dogs, River could not always be in the fields, so when Richie breaks a hoe, River cannot prevent his punishment by brutal beating. When Richie, however, climbs in the car and jokes, "I guess I didn't make it . . . But I don't know how. I need to know how," Jojo understands the stakes:

> I don't want to hear no more of the story. I shake my head. I don't want him talking to Pop, asking him about that time. Pop has never told me the story of what happened to Richie when he ran. Every time I ask about it, he changes the subject or asks me to help him with something in the yard. And I understand the sentiment when he looks away or walks off, expecting me to follow. I know what Pop's saying: *I don't want to talk about this. It wounds me.*[92]

Richie, however, wants to possess the story, thinking, "It's how I get home."[93] He forces his way into the car so that he can confront River and find out the end of the story.

At Bois Sauvage, Jojo understands Richie's threat to Kayla, his dying grandmother, and the rest of the family, so he thinks that if he can get Pop to tell the ending, Richie will disappear. When Pop starts telling of how a prisoner named Blue first raped one of the prostitutes that visited the jail and then decided to run, forcing Richie to go with him, the telling seems to open Richie's memory. He and Pop alternate telling the story, although only Jojo can hear them both. When Pop finally tells of having to kill Richie so that Richie would not be brutally lynched as Blue was, Richie's voice turns into a scream. Earlier, when Richie had first encountered Jojo, he used the metaphor of a shirt for his story: "The story of me and Parchman, as River told it, is a moth-eaten shirt, nibbled to threads: the shape is right, but the details have been erased. I could patch those holes. Make that shirt hang new, except for the tails. The end."[94] The end, however, does not give Richie the comfort he seeks or send him home. The story cannot give him that newness that he desires. Richie tries to gain control by knowing and owning his story, but unlike Becky,

Addie, and Given, he does not succeed, and Jojo sees his spirit at the end, trapped in the present world: "The boy floats and wanders, still stuck."[95]

Like Faulkner and Welty, Ward depicts a haunting based on movement instead of place to explore the spectral possession of narrative, but her text also haunts backward to Faulkner's and Welty's texts by amplifying the larger racial dimensions of memory and narrative. The epigraph Ward pulls from Welty's memoir in its original context celebrates the transit of memory as a positive force. Just before the quote, Welty includes a passage from *The Optimist's Daughter* that elucidates her conception of confluence. Laurel dreams of crossing a bridge with her late husband Phil and seeing the place where the Ohio and Mississippi Rivers converge, a "confluence of the waters."[96] Welty then declares, "Of course the greatest confluence of all is that which makes up the human memory—the individual human memory. My own is the treasure most dearly regarded by me, in my life and in my work as a writer."[97] The ability of the memory to elide chronology and to join the past and the present allows Welty to link events and concepts across time. This "treasure" undergirds not just Welty's autobiographical writing but enhances her ability to make intriguing links in her fiction between, for example, a German piano teacher living in small-town Mississippi and the myth of Perseus and Medusa.[98] The "confluence" of ideas, events, or people coming together aptly describes Welty's writing and her attempt to "enter the mind, heart, and skin of a human being who is not myself. Whether this happens to be a man or a woman, old or young, with skin black or white, the primary challenge lies in making the jump itself."[99]

While Laurel in *The Optimist's Daughter* might discover the power of memory's transit in being able to hear her mother once more, when Leonie sees Given and when Jojo encounters Richie, they understandably fear what these specters from the past may bring into the present. And while Welty's focus is on the "individual human memory," Ward's target is the larger memory of a family and a race of people. Leonie may be the only one to see Given, but his death still affects her family, his family, and the Black and white communities of southern Mississippi. Richie's story is likewise intended to be representative, demonstrated by his accounts of traveling to different periods of Parchman's existence. Richie tries to understand how "Parchman was past, present, and future all at once."[100] Given and Richie are figures of pain and racial injustice, so that when Ward uses Welty's quote about the past and the present joining to introduce a narrative of ghosts who haunt because they died brutally, she shifts the tone of Welty's words from celebratory to threatening.

This shift becomes sharper considering the two other epigraphs Ward uses, appearing before and after Welty's quote, literally framing Welty's words. The first is a Kwa chant about the disappearance of an African boy, which begins: "Who are we looking for, who are we looking for? It's Equiano we're looking for." The verses reference Olaudah Equiano, whose slave narrative details a childhood in Africa, followed by kidnapping, then enslavement on a series of ships.[101] In the narrative, Equiano never returns home, so the chant haunts in its reference to a family and village who never see this boy again. Richie, as the boy in *Sing, Unburied, Sing*, also never returns to his family home, and while he sees River and finally hears the circumstances of his own death, his ghost remains without a home. Memory is a recounting of loss.

The other epigraph is from Derek Walcott's 1969 poem "The Gulf" and again details the experience of having "no home."[102] As the speaker makes a voyage by airplane from Dallas to the Gulf Coast, his detachment from the land "at this height" mirrors his detachment from the country below. In the air, "our old earth" "again looks new," yet the speaker still senses that the "divine union" seen below is actually in "detached divided states" where the "air, heavy with gas/sickens the state, from Newark to New Orleans."[103] As he approaches the Gulf, he continues to feel the separation: "The Gulf, your gulf, is daily widening."[104] Although he says, "the South felt like home," by the end, the speaker proclaims, "I have no home" because of those "whose gospel is the whip and flame."[105]

When encircled by and conversing with these narratives of isolation and loss, Ward significantly alters Welty's works by reframing them in different social, economic, and racial contexts. By referencing both the Kwa chant and Walcott's poem, Ward connects the dispossession of Jojo's family to the history of the African slave trade. Richie explains that he had to learn that "time is a vast ocean, and that everything is happening at once."[106] The ocean imagery appears again when Jojo's grandmother dies.[107] Given offers a boat because, as Leonie witnesses, "[t]ime floods the room in a storm surge."[108] The epigraphs framing Welty's quote point to the Atlantic scene of the slave trade, the passage to Africa, and the waters that in the present come into the Gulf and into Jojo's home in Bois Sauvage. Ward haunts Welty's conception of individual human memory as depicted by Laurel's imagination of the two rivers coming together by depicting an ocean of horrific memories coming to bear on her characters.

Sing, Unburied, Sing's haunting of *As I Lay Dying* likewise troubles the limits of Faulkner's aperture, as Ward expands Faulkner's timeline to bring the haunting of the past into the future. Brian Norman points out that "what remains curiously unnarrated" in *As I Lay Dying* is "Addie's actual burial, the ostensible point of the whole plot."[109] Once Addie has narrated her chapter, she falls silent. The family reaches Jefferson with each member seeming to have an agenda unconnected to Addie's burial. Anse quickly replaces Addie, introducing his new wife to his children.

Addie's defiance of the boundaries of life and death might then be limited, much like the speaker in Emily Dickinson's "I died for Beauty—but was scarce," who can chat with the entity who died "for Truth" in the adjoining burial chamber but only "[u]ntil the Moss had reached our lips—/ And covered up—Our names—"[110] When Addie's family buries her and moves on, she perhaps ceases to exist as a speaking subject.

Ward, on the other hand, imagines an afterlife for her characters. While the text depicts this state as a kind of place when Given offers a boat to take his mother on to the next world, the characters also speak of it as a song. When Richie tells Jojo that he needs the rest of his story so that he can "get home," Jojo at first hears "home" as literal and responds, "[Y]ou ain't even from Bois."[111] Richie tries to explain that what he is seeking is a "song. The place is the song and I'm going to be part of the song."[112] At the end of the narrative, when Jojo sees Richie still trapped in this world and time, Richie admits that he hopes to "cross the waters. Be home . . . Become. The song."[113] This collective song is the narrative of suffering writ large. Jojo sees a tree with branches "full of ghosts" all telling stories of violence and murder. Kayla, in her innocence, can sing a song to them that temporarily gives them "relief," but they do not disappear.[114] Eden Wales Freeman notes the location of the tree behind Jojo's house: "The placement of the tree suggests that Americans cannot escape racial trauma. It is growing in our backyards,"[115] and Joanna Davis-McElligatt argues that the ghosts "emerge as metaphysical representations of the afterlife of slavery."[116] Figuring a tree of ancestry, generations of "Black and brown" people continue to haunt the present. In Ward's rewriting of Faulkner's journey, the end remains out of reach for those who haunt because of atrocities of the past. The movement, the transit, is ongoing, and the title in its imperative form asks the unburied to keep singing.

When Jojo's grandmother sees Richie, she describes him as "pulling all the weight of history behind him."[117] *Sing, Unburied, Sing* explores how to carry that weight and tell that history. By borrowing the gothic power revealed in Welty's and Faulkner's texts to elide time, Ward can put the ghosts of Given and Richie into the present to tell their stories in a world that might want to "undermine our understanding of what came before."[118] Ward does not dismiss or ignore the white Mississippi writers who came before her, but that "love" she shows is also not blind. She instead borrows the tools they have used to build her own narratives, especially the powerful tool of time travel allowed by the gothic. If haunting is a bid for spectral possession, a way to claim rightful ownership, *Sing, Unburied, Sing* claims and exposes a narrative of continued racial oppression. In his analysis of the gothic, David Punter argues that while "the law is the imposition of certainty," ghosts have their "armies" too.[119] With Given and Richie as tools of battle, Ward mounts a resistance.

NOTES

1. Jesmyn Ward, interview by Louise McCune, "Ghosts of Our Past: An Interview with Jesmyn Ward," *Los Angeles Review of Books*, October 11, 2017, blog.lareviewofbooks.org/interviews/ghosts-past-interview-jesmyn-ward.

2. For more on Ward's depiction of Parchman, see Catherine Calloway, "Parchman, Imprisonment, and Liminality in Jesmyn Ward's *Sing, Unburied, Sing*," *Philological Review* 45, no. 2 (2019), 55-82; Greg Chase, "Of Trips Taken and Time Served: How Ward's *Sing, Unburied, Sing* Grapples with Faulkner's Ghosts," *African American Review* 53, no. 3 (2020): 201-16; Sodam Choi, "The Haunted Black South and the Alternative Oceanic Space: Jesmyn Ward's *Sing, Unburied, Sing*," *English Language and Literature* 64, no. 3 (2018): 433-51.

3. Eric Foner, *Who Owns History: Rethinking the Past in a Changing World* (New York: Hill and Wang, 2003).

4. The epigraph appears before the page numbers in *Sing, Unburied, Sing* and is taken from *One Writer's Beginnings*.

5. Ward, "Ghosts of Our Past."

6. William Faulkner, *Requiem for a Nun* (1951; repr., New York: Vintage International, 2011), 73.

7. Jesmyn Ward, interview by Isabella Biedenharn, "Jesmyn Ward on the Evolution of Her Haunting Novel *Sing, Unburied, Sing*," *Entertainment Weekly* (September 11, 2017), ew.com/books/2017/09/11/jesmyn-ward-sing-unburied-sing.

8. Ward comments that she loves the Welty quote in her interview with McCune ("Ghosts") and that she loves *As I Lay Dying* in the interview with Biedenharn ("Jesmyn").

9. Chase, "Of Trips Taken and Time Served," 201.

10. Sinéad Moynihan, "From Disposability to Recycling: William Faulkner and the New Politics of Rewriting in Jesmyn Ward's *Salvage the Bones*," *Studies in the Novel* 47, no. 4 (2015): 551.

11. Ruth Bienstock Anolik, *Property and Power in English Gothic Literature* (Jefferson, NC: McFarland, 2016), 2.

12. Nathaniel Hawthorne, *The House of Seven Gables*, ed. Milton R. Stern (1851; repr., New York: Penguin, 1965), 229, 300.

13. Ruth Bienstock Anolik, "Horrors of Possession: The Gothic Struggle with the Law," *The Legal Studies Forum* 24, nos. 3-4 (2000): 677.

14. Eudora Welty, *One Writer's Beginnings*, in *Eudora Welty: Stories, Essays, & Memoir*, ed. Richard Ford and Michael Kreyling (1983; repr., New York: Library of America, 1998), 914.

15. Welty, *One Writer's Beginnings*, 839.

16. Gary M. Ciuba, "Time as Confluence: Self and Structure in Welty's *One Writer's Beginnings*," *Southern Literary Journal* 26, no. 1 (1993): 79.

17. Welty, *One Writer's Beginnings*, 847.

18. Welty, *One Writer's Beginnings*, 847.

19. Welty, *One Writer's Beginnings*, 948.

20. Gérard Genette and Marie Maclean, "Introduction to the Paratext," *New Literary History* 22, no. 2 (1991): 261.

21. Jesmyn Ward, *Sing, Unburied, Sing* (New York: Scribner 2017), 11.

22. Ward, *Sing, Unburied, Sing*, 136.

23. Ward, *Sing, Unburied, Sing*, 136.

24. Ward, *Sing, Unburied, Sing*, 47. Given's death because he won a contest, preceded by his attesting to his bond with his white football teammates, reflects aspects of Ernest Gaines's *A Gathering of Old Men* (New York: Knopf, 1983), suggesting that Ward may be rewriting Gaines's text in this novel as well. In *A Gathering of Old Men*, the men remember Silas who was killed by white men after he won a plowing contest. Gil Boutan tries to

convince his father not to seek revenge for his son's death by telling him about the importance of Black teammates.

25. Dolores Flores-Silva and Keith Cartwright explain how this imagery comes from Ward's Afro-Creole heritage in south Mississippi. See "The Scaly Bird Sings 'Remember Me': Gulf Fiestas of the Dead and Tribalography in Jesmyn Ward's *Sing, Unburied, Sing*," *Xavier Review* 38, no. 2 (2018): 140-54.

26. Ward, *Sing, Unburied, Sing*, 136.

27. Nicole Dib, "Haunted Roadscapes in Jesmyn Ward's *Sing, Unburied, Sing*," *MELUS* 34, no. 2, (2020): 135.

28. Ward, *Sing, Unburied, Sing*, 52.

29. Ward, *Sing, Unburied, Sing*, 133.

30. In addition to Chase and Choi, for critics who examine *Sing, Unburied, Sing* and *As I Lay Dying*, see Dib, Flores-Silva, and Cartwright. See also Megan Ashley Swartzfager, "'Ain't No More Stories for You Here': Vengeful Hauntings and Traumatized Community in Jesmyn Ward's *Sing, Unburied, Sing*," *Mississippi Quarterly* 73, no. 3 (2020): 313-34. Moynihan examines the connections between *Salvage the Bones* and *As I Lay Dying*. Sherita L. Johnson's "Emancipating Faulkner: Reading *Go Down, Moses* and Jesmyn Ward's *Sing, Unburied, Sing*," in *Faulkner and Slavery*, ed. Jay Watson and James G. Thomas, Jr. (Jackson: University Press of Mississippi, 2021), 194-210, examines the connections between *Sing, Unburied, Sing* and *Go Down, Moses*. Marie Liénard-Yeterian examines Ward's connection to *Light in August* in "Review of Jesmyn Ward's *Sing, Unburied, Sin*g," *Xavier Review* 38, no. 2 (2018): 164-66.

31. Diana York Blaine, "The Abjection of Addie and Other Myths of the Maternal in *As I Lay Dying*," *Mississippi Quarterly* 47, no. 3 (1994): 422. For readings of Addie's section, see also Solveig Dunkel, "Toni Morrison and William Faulkner's Verbose Ghosts," *Faulkner Journal* 32, no. 1 (2018): 51-66; Doreen Fowler, "Matricide and the Mother's Revenge: *As I Lay Dying*," *Faulkner Journal* 4, nos. 1-2 (1988-89): 113-25; Marc Hewson, "'My Children Were of Me Alone': Maternal Influence in Faulkner's *As I Lay Dying*," *Mississippi Quarterly* 53, no. 4 (2000): 551-67; Harriet Hustis, "The Tangled Webs We Weave: Faulkner Scholarship and the Significance of Addie Bundren's Monologue," *Faulkner Journal* 12, no. 1 (1996): 3-21; Paul S. Nielsen, "What Does Addie Bundren Mean, and How Does She Mean It?" *Southern Literary Journal* 25, no. 1 (Fall 1992): 33-39; Brian Norman, *Dead Women Talking: Figures of Injustice in American Literature* (Baltimore: Johns Hopkins University Press, 2012); Patrick Samway, "Addie's Continued Presence in Faulkner's *As I Lay Dying*," in *Southern Literature and Literary Theory*, ed. Jefferson Humphries (Athens: University of Georgia Press, 1990), 284-99; Karen R. Sass, "At a Loss for Words: Addie and Language in *As I Lay Dying*," *Faulkner Journal* 6, no. 2 (1991): 9-21; Gabriele Schwab, "The Multiple Lives of Addie Bundren's Dead Body: On William Faulkner's *As I Lay Dying*," in *The Other Perspective in Gender and Culture: Rewriting Women and the Symbolic*, ed. Juliet Flower MacCannell (New York: Columbia University Press, 1990), 209-41; Amy Louise Wood, "Feminine Rebellion and Mimicry in Faulkner's *As I Lay Dying*," *Faulkner Journal* 9, no. 1 (1993): 99-112.

32. Norman, *Dead Women Talking*, 51.

33. Schwab, "The Multiple Lives of Addie Bundren's Dead Body," 209.

34. John Limon, "Addie in No-Mans-Land," in *Faulkner and War*, ed. Noel Polk and Ann J. Abadie (Jackson: University Press of Mississippi, 2004), 38.

35. The shuffling of narrative pieces is a trick that Faulkner plays in other gothic works. A classroom exercise I have tried is rearranging the events of "A Rose for Emily" in chronological order. Once the buying of arsenic, the disappearance of Homer Barron, and the bad smell emanating from Emily's house are lined up chronologically, the confusion disappears, and students agree that the disordered narration enables the suspension of understanding. *Absalom, Absalom!* famously allows the reader to learn of events as Quentin does instead of in their

chronological order, leading to a succession of multiple possibilities for why Henry Sutpen has to kill Charles Bon to prevent him from marrying his sister: bigamy, incest, miscegenation.

36. William Faulkner, *As I Lay Dying*, rev. ed. (1930; repr., New York: Vintage International, 1990), 3.

37. Faulkner, *As I Lay Dying*, 72.

38. Faulkner, *As I Lay Dying*, 73.

39. Philip Weinstein, "'Thinking I Was I Was Not Who Was Not Was Not Who': The Vertigo of Faulknerian Identity," in *Faulkner and the Craft of Fiction: Faulkner and Yoknapatawpha, 1987*, ed. Doreen Fowler and Ann J. Abadie (Jackson: University Press of Mississippi, 1989), 184.

40. Tamara Slankard, "'No Such Thing as Was'": The Fetishized Corpse, Modernism, and *As I Lay Dying*," *Faulkner Journal* 24, no. 2 (2009): 11.

41. Ward, *Sing, Unburied, Sing*, 1.

42. Ward, *Sing, Unburied, Sing*, 169.

43. Ward, *Sing, Unburied, Sing*, 236.

44. Ward, *Sing, Unburied, Sing*, 134.

45. Ward, *Sing, Unburied, Sing*, 165.

46. Ward, *Sing, Unburied, Sing*, 18.

47. Ward, *Sing, Unburied, Sing*, 35.

48. Eudora Welty, "Some Notes on Time in Fiction," in *On Writing* (1973; repr., New York: Modern Library, 2002), 97.

49. Welty, "Some Notes on Time in Fiction," 97.

50. Welty, "Some Notes on Time in Fiction," 97.

51. Sally Wolff, "Eudora Welty's Autobiographical Duet: *The Optimist's Daughter* and *One Writer's Beginnings*," in *Located Lives: Place and Idea in Southern Autobiography*, ed. J. Bill Berry (Athens: University of Georgia Press, 1990), 84. For connections between Welty's memoir and novel, see also Peggy Whitman Prenshaw, *Composing Selves: Southern Women and Autobiography* (Baton Rouge: LSU Press, 2011).

52. In examining consumer culture in the novel, Travis Rozier argues that Fay "represents the new consumer culture that puts less emphasis on lineage and social standing than on what one can buy and own" (139). See "The Whole Solid Past: Memorial Objects and Consumer Culture in Eudora Welty's *The Optimist's Daughter*," *Southern Quarterly* 53, no. 1 (2015): 137–51.

53. Eudora Welty, *The Optimist's Daughter,* in *Eudora Welty: Complete Novels*, ed. Richard Ford and Michael Kreyling (1972; repr., New York: Library of America, 1998), 913.

54. Welty, *The Optimist's Daughter*, 914.

55. Welty, *The Optimist's Daughter*, 940.

56. Welty, *The Optimist's Daughter*, 988.

57. Welty, *The Optimist's Daughter*, 962.

58. Welty, *The Optimist's Daughter*, 966.

59. Welty, *The Optimist's Daughter*, 971.

60. Welty, *The Optimist's Daughter*, 970.

61. Welty, *The Optimist's Daughter*, 975.

62. Rebecca Mark, "Wild Strawberries, Cataracts, and Climbing Roses: Clitoral and Seminal Imagery in *The Optimist's Daughter*," *Mississippi Quarterly* 56, no. 2 (2003): 347.

63. Welty, *The Optimist's Daughter*, 977.

64. Welty, *The Optimist's Daughter*, 978.

65. Faulkner, *As I Lay Dying*, 65.

66. Louis Palmer III, "Bourgeois Blues: Class, Whiteness, and Southern Gothic in Early Faulkner and Caldwell," *Faulkner Journal* 22, nos. 1–2 (Fall 2006–Spring 2007): 129.

67. Faulkner, *As I Lay Dying*, 84.

68. My thinking about simile and metaphor in this novel is informed by Judy Butterfield's examination. See "'An *Is* Different from My *Is*': The Lost Mother and the Subjectivity of the Motherless in Faulkner's *As I Lay Dying* and Welty's *Delta Wedding*," *Eudora Welty Review* 14 (2022): 25–42.

69. Norman, *Dead Women Talking*, 53.

70. Elisabeth Bronfen, *Over Her Dead Body: Death, Femininity, and the Aesthetic*. (New York: Routledge, 1992), xi.

71. Similar descriptions occur in other Faulkner texts. Emily in "A Rose for Emily" is described as "bloated, like a body long submerged in motionless water, and of that pallid hue" while Rosa in *Absalom, Absalom!* is described as "one of the ghosts which had refused to lie still even longer than most had, telling [Quentin] about old ghost-times." See William Faulkner, "A Rose for Emily," in *Collected Stories of William Faulkner* (New York: Random House, 1950), 92; and William Faulkner, *Absalom, Absalom!*, rev. ed. (1936; repr., New York: Vintage International, 1990), 5.

72. Faulkner, *As I Lay Dying*, 43.

73. Dunkel, "Toni Morrison and William Faulkner's Verbose Ghosts," 57.

74. Faulkner, *As I Lay Dying*, 46. Addie's protest against words through the medium of words is admittedly problematic, as many critics acknowledge.

75. Faulkner, *As I Lay Dying*, 171, 172.

76. Sass, "At a Loss for Words," 9.

77. Faulkner, *As I Lay Dying*, 23.

78. Faulkner, *As I Lay Dying*, 23.

79. Faulkner, *As I Lay Dying*, 170.

80. Faulkner, *As I Lay Dying*, 173.

81. Faulkner, *As I Lay Dying*, 37.

82. Anse continues to show his connection to property as he steals from his children to purchase his new set of teeth.

83. Ward, *Sing, Unburied, Sing* 36. Dib points out the connection between the journey by car and the "trip" on drugs (143). Choi explains that both the drugs and Given's appearance demonstrate Leonie's trauma (441).

84. Ward, *Sing, Unburied, Sing*, 36, 37.

85. Ward, *Sing, Unburied, Sing*, 165.

86. Ward, *Sing, Unburied, Sing*, 166.

87. Ward, *Sing, Unburied, Sing*, 167.

88. Ward, *Sing, Unburied, Sing*, 165–66.

89. Ward, *Sing, Unburied, Sing*, 269.

90. Ward, *Sing, Unburied, Sing*, 72.

91. Ward, *Sing, Unburied, Sing*, 75.

92. Ward, *Sing, Unburied, Sing*, 181.

93. Ward, *Sing, Unburied, Sing*, 182.

94. Ward, *Sing, Unburied, Sing*, 137.

95. Ward, *Sing, Unburied, Sing*, 280.

96. Welty, *The Optimist's Daughter*, 947.

97. Welty, *The Optimist's Daughter*, 948.

98. This allusion occurs in *The Golden Apples* as Virgie thinks about how her piano teacher, Miss Eckhart, has a painting on the wall of her studio of Perseus cutting off the head of Medusa.

99. Eudora Welty, preface to *Collected Stories*, in *Eudora Welty: Stories, Essays, & Memoir* (1980, repr., New York: Library of America, 1998), 829.

100. Ward, *Sing, Unburied, Sing*, 186.

101. Jennifer Farley, "A Forced Migration," *Anchor: A North Carolina History Online Resource*, Spring 2006, ncpedia.org/anchor/forced-migration.

102. Derek Walcott, "The Gulf," in *Collected Poems: 1948–1984* (New York: Farrar, Straus, & Giroux, 1986), 107.

103. Walcott, "The Gulf," 106, 107.

104. Walcott, "The Gulf," 107.

105. Walcott, "The Gulf," 107, 108.

106. Ward, *Sing, Unburied, Sing*, 186.

107. Choi argues that Ward creates a "'home' for blacks in an atemporal oceanic space where the past and the present are able to meet simultaneously" (435).

108. Ward, *Sing, Unburied, Sing*, 269.

109. Norman, *Dead Women Talking*, 52.

110. Emily Dickinson, "I died for Beauty—but was scarce," in *The Poems of Emily Dickinson*, ed. R. W. Franklin (Cambridge, MA: Harvard University Press, 1999), 207.

111. Ward, *Sing, Unburied, Sing*, 182.

112. Ward, *Sing, Unburied, Sing*, 183.

113. Ward, *Sing, Unburied, Sing*, 281.

114. Ward, *Sing, Unburied, Sing*, 284.

115. Eden Wales Freeman, *Reading Testimony, Witnessing Trauma: Confronting Race, Gender, and Violence in American Literature* (Jackson: University Press of Mississippi, 2020), 177.

116. Joanna Davis-McElligatt, "And Now She Sings It: Conjure as Abolitionist Alternative in Jesmyn Ward's *Sing, Unburied, Sing*," *Mississippi Quarterly* 74, no. 1 (2021): 120.

117. Ward, *Sing, Unburied, Sing*, 265.

118. Ward, "Ghosts of Our Past."

119. David Punter, *Gothic Pathologies: The Text, the Body, and the Law* (New York: St. Martin's Press, 1998), 2, 3.

"We Listen for What the Waves Intone"

Writing Black Women's Liberatory Voices as Dialectical Ghosting in Eudora Welty's "The Burning," Margaret Walker's *Jubilee*, and Natasha Trethewey's *Native Guard*

REBECCA MARK

Eudora Welty, Margaret Walker, and Natasha Trethewey would never be considered traditional Civil War writers, nor would they want to be. Their fiction does not conform to either the nostalgic Lost Cause/*Gone with the Wind* romance genre or the brutally realistic Civil War battle prose of texts in the style of Michael Shaara's *Killer Angels* (1974). However, all three Mississippi women writers have penned works that have, at their core, the self-emancipation of enslaved African peoples in the United States during and after the Civil War. By reclaiming Black women's agency and voices, the three writers explore previously unchartered territory in southern literature and effectively throw death blows at both the tenacious romanticization of southern slavery and the enthrallment with battle lore. Raped and abused for reproductive eugenics economies, forced to grow, harvest, and cook the food that kept the master, mistress, and their families alive, made to wet nurse and raise white women's children, Black women sustained the early plantation care economy of unpaid labor. Welty, Walker, and Trethewey give voice to all women, but it is Black women, whom Zora Neale Hurston calls "the mules of the world," that these three writers free from previously stifling, degrading, and repressive Mammy/Jezebel narratives.

Growing up and living in a Mississippi torn into shreds by violent segregationists and white supremacists, Welty, Walker, and Trethewey embodied the visceral experience of racism in their fiction and understood the deadly serious nature of their work. Over three generations and more than a century, these writers created an interconnected Mississippi web of what we would now call feminist and racial-justice storytelling.

Eudora Welty knew Margaret Walker, and in their later years, they became the "Sister Act," speaking together at colleges and universities. Margaret Walker had read "The Burning" and Eudora Welty had read *Jubilee*; Natasha Trethewey read both Margaret Walker and Eudora Welty's works. All three had read Faulkner.

Eudora Welty's photographs had such a profound effect on Trethewey that she agreed to write the introduction for the 2019 edition of *Photographs*.[1] In this introduction, Trethewey focuses on the image of Windsor Plantation: "I return to the haunting image of the ruins of the antebellum mansion at Windsor Plantation. The ornate columns that remain stand as monument to the past, the history of slavery, the wealth amassed by cotton planters in Mississippi. Welty captured that, but she captures something else as well."[2] What is most compelling to Trethewey is Welty's shadow "on the ground in front of the ruins, the Rolleiflex camera in her hands. You might imagine her a ghost of history, hands clasped before her as if to pray. You might see how the shape of her dress, the position of her arms gives the appearance of an angel, an intermediary showing us her guardianship and reverence not for the nostalgia of the past, but the truth of it."[3] Not the nostalgia, but the truth. To pull back the gauzy curtain of nostalgia, the delusion that emboldened both the fictional and tourist industries of Mississippi, to discover "the truth" had tortured southern white and Black writers for decades. For Trethewey, Welty's photographs are a rich touchpoint for her imaginative journey and shadowing of history, a doorway into the world that her maternal grandmother, a Black woman born in Gulfport, Mississippi, in 1916 had experienced.

As Annette Trefzer reminds us in *Exposing Mississippi: Eudora Welty's Photographic Reflections*: "Offering nuanced insight into such landscape just beyond the younger artist's vantage point, Welty's photography, 'a record of what she had seen,' was Trethewey's visual bridge into her culture of that past."[4] Trefzer asserts that "[a]s we have seen in the pages of *One Time, One Place*, Welty reshapes Mississippi geography to correct racial erasures from southern space, visualizing the formerly invisible with emotional intelligence. . . . Welty, in her photography, and Trethewey, in her poetry, reclaim Mississippi as southern cultural space, a home for African Americans."[5] To fill in the faint lines and amplify the stories hovering behind these erasures is the work of Natasha Trethewey. It is done not for some abstract reason, but quite literally to bring her Black mother, grandmother, and friends back to life, to create a living visual history of place.

• • •

Certainly, Faulkner's maxim in *Requiem for a Nun*, "The past is never dead. It's not even past" has become a too-often unexamined mantra.[6] For Faulkner, there is no such thing as history or facts that we can sear to in the past. Instead, everything that has ever happened becomes a mirage that constantly appears and disappears on the horizon, what Trethewey has referred to from the artist's point of view as the perspective of a "nearsighted watchman."[7] Walter Benjamin, writing in his description of the Angelus Novus, helps us unknot Faulkner's statement. The angel "would like to stay, awaken the dead, and make whole what has been smashed. But a storm is blowing from Paradise; it has got caught in his wings with such violence that the angel can no longer close them. The storm irresistibly propels him into the future to which his back is turned, while the pile of debris before him grows skyward. The storm is what we call progress."[8] Benjamin's angel, although longing to fix broken things in the past, is paralyzed by the force of the forward-moving wind, thus unable to return to the past and change it—*he* can only let the debris grow skyward. What distinguishes the view of the past, particularly the history of enslavement in the American South that Welty, Walker, and Trethewey imagine from Faulkner's *decree* and Benjamin's *angel*, is that all three writers find multiple ways to return to the past and engage in repair, a form of literary reparation. Their imaginative engagement with history creates a space of temporal dissonance, a neither "then" nor "now," that is not stuck and thus allows constant reconciliation, call and response, recognition, and regeneration of the unacceptable and violent destructive force of trafficking and enslavement of human beings.

In Sarah Ford's *Haunted Property: Slavery and the Gothic*, Ford introduces and explicates the concept of "haunting backwards," exploring the literary characters who do return and try to make whole what has been smashed. These angels move from past to future—back and forth, a call and response, sometimes violently, sometimes lyrically: "Octavia Butler and Natasha Trethewey mold the gothic into a useful tool for their narratives, taking its supernatural disruption of chronological time and reversing it. This disruption opens up the possibility of traveling through time to witness nineteenth-century slavery, a Civil War encampment, and a 1907 parade celebrating King Cotton. Butler uses the conduit of a troublesome house to propel her character into the past, while Trethewey uses point of view, tense shifts, and photography to erase the passage of time. In both texts, however, the writers are reversing haunting to teach their readers that there is no safe barrier between past and present."[9] In this moment of devastating white supremacist violence in the United States, we are reminded daily that there is indeed no safe barrier between past and present.

The nuance and subtlety with which each of these authors effectively discovers, invents, and prophesizes the southern narrative of Black women's autonomy depends on their identity and life experience, the historical moment at which they are writing, the ways in which they embrace the intersectionality of their characters' life experience, and, most significantly, their willingness to explore daring, at times weirdly figurative, modes of experimental writing. Imagining an unspeakable, unfathomable moment of freedom, in which the former enslaved and oppressed Black woman can speak her own liberation, her own self and sense of embodiment into being, is not easy and certainly not formulaic. Liberation fiction can appear tricky, thickly metaphoric, symbolic, even unwritable. Here, I think of Beloved's ghostlike first words, "I come out of blue water after the bottoms of my feet swim away from me I come up I need to find a place to be the air is heavy I am not dead"[10] or the science fiction time travel world of Dana in Octavia Butler's *Kindred*. What these writers are inscribing into prose and poetry does not have a literary scaffolding or established written tradition, not like the many-volumed piling on of the Lost Cause myth. The most historically reliable renderings of the moment of liberation have come from WPA narratives of enslaved people themselves who were children during emancipation. These oral narratives provide accurate truths but do not replace the literary texts. The voice and body of the enslaved woman coming into form by the pen of her literary sisters needs, as Beloved voices, "to find a place to be the air is heavy I am not dead."[11]

• • •

The Lost Cause lie did irreparable damage to generations of Black people by legitimizing domestic terror, Ku Klux Klan violence, and national amnesia. Originally perpetrated by Edward A. Pollard, *The Lost Cause: A New Southern History of the War of the Confederates* (1866), articles by Jubal A. Early (1870s), Thomas Dixon Jr.'s turn-of-the-century trilogy, *The Leopard's Spots* (1902), *The Clansmen* (1905), and *The Traitor* (1907), and of course, Margaret Mitchell's *Gone with the Wind* (1936), the Lost Cause narrative attempted, and often succeeded, in erasing southern memory of and culpability for slavery. Pollard, Dixon, Mitchell, and a host of others' distorted lies ask that we believe that slavery was never the cause for which the states went to battle. Instead, in their gauzy magnolia-laced mint julep façade of a world, the South fought to preserve a chivalric way of life, the virtue of white women, the honor of their great soldiers, but most importantly, the supremacy of the white race. Entangled with honoring war hero masculinity and the reality of ungrieved, unfathomable numbers of southern dead, the myth took hold and never let go.

Literature has always had the opportunity to put flesh and blood on the sketchy skeleton of American history, but novelists and poets can be blinded by their own biases and miss the mark as spectacularly as historians. Welty, Walker, and Trethewey take the job of mourning and the task of renewal seriously. Each in their own unique way recover the drumbeats, heartbeats, footsteps, of Black female self-determination, the deep ravine of grief, fury, and self-emancipation. They understand on a visceral level that healing from the disease called the Lost Cause falls firmly on the shoulders of creative writers and artists. While southern literature can never be the same after Faulkner, after the Lost Cause myth dies a thousand deaths at the hand of his spectacular genius, when it comes to unghosting Black women during the Civil War—any women for that matter, as many of Faulkner's feminist critics have shown us— he does not tell us the truth of it, nor does he find a place from which Beloved can speak.

"A Rag Bundle" / Faulkner

Faulkner's *The Unvanquished* is decidedly not a Lost Cause novel in the *Gone with the Wind* tradition. In this tale, Faulkner writes a characteristically experimental and bold narrative of the last years of the Civil War from the home front, as he does in *Absalom, Absalom!* As the story progresses, particularly in the last chapters, Faulkner is critical of and scathing toward the male characters—including the war hero, Colonel John Sartoris—who use their weapons as if they are still in battle to kill indiscriminately. In fact, Colonel Sartoris kills the carpetbaggers, the Burdens, to keep Blacks from voting, revealing that he is not that different from Grumby and Snopes. What differentiates Bayard Sartoris from his father is his unwillingness to use his gun unless it is to avenge his grandmother's murder; he will only kill Grumby, who, in this southern social order, is scum of the earth, and go after Ab Snopes, coded in the story as the white league.

Sutpen is no chivalric planter; Miss Rosa and Ellen no magnolia-scented southern belles; Colonel Sartoris no honorable, fallen, grey-coated hero. Ringo is too savvy to be an Uncle Tom; Clytie and Louvinia no mammies, and both Rosas no smelling-salt old ladies of the South. Faulkner leaves the southern myth in questionable shape in *The Unvanquished* and seemingly in embers in *Absalom, Absalom!* However, as Michael Gorra argues in *The Saddest Words: William Faulkner's Civil War*, while Faulkner in *The Unvanquished* grapples with recognizing the full humanity of his Black neighbors—James Baldwin's call to action—he never does it "adequately as we will see; not in ways that would satisfy us today, or that could satisfy Baldwin then."[12] As Gorra states, Faulkner "never depicts a slave auction, or a family broken by sale. Nor does he describe a whipping, still less the salt and pepper that were often rubbed into the skin the leather had broken: none of his people have a tree of scars upon their back.... Slavery there is made to look almost innocent, and not just because it's seen from a white child's point of view."[13]

Many astute feminist Faulkner critics over the years have thoroughly documented Faulkner's failure of imagination when it comes to his portrayal of women of all ages, all races, and particularly those in their sexual, childbearing years. But when it comes to Faulkner and his Civil War heroines, something truly reactionary occurs. Faulkner simply cannot imagine Black or white women living fulfilled, powerful lives outside of the constraints of the Lost Cause myth. Ellen will marry Sutpen, who she knows to be a monster, to secure herself the respectability of a southern wedding and fulfill her dream of southern womanhood. Aunt Rosa will die an angry, jilted woman because she does not get a chance to participate in the wedding ritual. Faulkner's women maintain the southern-lady hysteria of Aunt Louisa in *The Unvanquished*, who compels Drusilla to marry Sartoris, leave the military, and wear a dress. Like Rosa in *Absalom, Absalom!* they uphold the Confederacy by writing poetic odes to the Confederate dead.

Two of Faulkner's most powerful women, Judith and Drusilla, gender-bend into men, only to let love slay them. Although Faulkner lets them run the household, tend the gardens, find and forage for food, take care of the finances, join the army, ride horses better than any man, write poetry, run a successful horse-stealing enterprise, feed the community, and on and on, he traps them in romantic longing for fallen heroes. Butch Judith and butch Drusilla turn into femme southern belles yearning for their men. Drusilla bathes herself in verbena to attract Bayard and throws herself at him the first chance she gets. Judith pines away for Charles Bon and the loss of the possibility of marriage to her fiancé. There were many upper-class white women who held onto their status, their racism, and their entitlement by glorifying the Confederacy. But the fact that no liberated Black woman makes her voice and story heard in *Absalom, Absalom!* or *The Unvanquished* is simply inexcusable. Not Clytie. Not Philadelphy. Certainly not Louvinia, who goes as far as to tell Granny to whip her son Loosh for resisting, for siding with the Yankees and telling them where the silver was buried.

As powerful as he makes her, Faulkner never allows Clytie her own autonomy. She uses all her strength to protect the legacy of Sutpen's offspring, Black and white, even if she must burn down the plantation house and herself so that Henry will never be taken by the law. Patricia Yaeger clearly analyzes Faulkner's failure in creating Clytie: "The lightness of her being glosses over what should be most heavy—not only the long line of neglected, disowned, never-acknowledged children but the marginalized acts of neglected, disowned, never-acknowledged laborers—the naked Black men who 'tear' Sutpen's Hundred out of the earth, the never-mentioned being of Clytie's never-mentioned mother, the way the white architect clings to his mildewing vestments to separate himself from Black men who are never quite acknowledged as men. Clytie may be a Haitian rebel who burns down the House of Sutpen, but she is reduced by the end of *Absalom, Absalom!*, to 'a rag bundle,' to fuel for the fire, grist for the mill."[14] Building an antiracist post-Civil War South would mean letting Clytie burn down the master's house without killing herself.

Throughout *The Unvanquished* and *Absalom, Absalom!* Faulkner burns and destroys but he does not build or seed. Regenerating the world of the Old South plantation would mean allowing Jim Bond to be more than a howling presence, a fear lurking in the ashes, a specter, whom Shreve can hold up to Quentin as the threat of the future, that Jim Bonds's tainted Blackness will conquer the Western hemisphere. A New South story would celebrate Jim Bond, not leave him unable to speak. In *The Unvanquished*, Faulkner introduces the enslaved people who are freeing themselves by walking behind the Yankee troops as "a cloud of dust," one with the earth and not human. Ringo, who is smart enough to know to run toward freedom, tells Granny to turn in the other direction, away from the self-liberating enslaved Black people—his people. "'Cant you see um coming?' Ringo hollered, 'Get on away from here.'"[15] As the group of Black people escaping slavery moves past them, Faulkner has Bayard describe them as animals: "They were coming up the road. It sounded like about fifty of them; we could hear the feet hurrying, and a kind of panting murmur. It was not singing exactly, it was not that loud; it was just a sound, a breathing, a kind of gasping murmuring chant and the feet whispering fast in the deep dust. I could hear women too and then all of a sudden, I began to smell them. 'N[----]s,' I whispered."[16] Bayard, who we are expected to think of as honorable and manly at the end of the text for not killing his enemy, is portrayed here as profoundly racist, unable to see the escaping enslaved as people. Instead, he refers to body parts—their feet and their smell—and uses a racial slur.

Faulkner forfeits telling the most poignant and powerful story of the Civil War, the autonomy of enslaved peoples walking toward freedom and forcing Lincoln and the northern generals to write and sign the Emancipation Proclamation, for the right to tell an old worn-out farce.

In *The Unvanquished*, the enslaved people who are taking their lives and the lives of their children into their hands to walk toward freedom exist not as individuals but as water, a sea of faces, a flood of bodies. The Black woman whom Granny, Bayard, and Ringo find crouching in the road holding her child, sick, tired, and desperately needing food, never has an opportunity to tell her story, to even speak her name. She will not, as Granny commands her to, go back "home" to the plantation where she was enslaved. She takes food handed to her, catches a ride in the wagon, and then she steps down to meet the group moving toward the river. Ringo and Granny do not think she will be able to keep up with the group for long. Faulkner never tries to imagine her plight, her excitement, her desire for freedom. There is no understanding. Instead, he portrays them all as headed toward an imaginary Jordan, ill-informed and in a religious trance. The horses drown, and Faulkner chooses the tale of Granny and Ringo setting up a horse-stealing business rather than the story of the liberation of the enslaved. Faulkner enters the foggy river and returns his protagonists to a racist social order.

We are stuck in a modernist abyss, mourning the inadequacy of Colonel Sartoris, the fallen hero, rather than celebrating the hundreds of thousands of heroines and heroes who rewrote American history by walking away from slavery through self-emancipation. If one chooses to see history as one long moment of futility, then one will never see transformation or regeneration or anything remotely resembling freedom. Writing to Robert K. Haas in a letter dated July 8, 1938, Faulkner states, "*The Unvanquished*, the title of the story, [is the story] of Granny's struggle between her morality and her children's needs."[17] The idea that Granny must break from her morals to steal two horses from the Yankees and eventually start a lucrative horse- and mule-stealing business is ironic and absurd given the fact that Rosa Millard grew up and benefited from the free labor of enslaved Black people, including Marengo (Ringo), Joby and Louvinia, Loosh and Philadelphy, and Simon her entire life, seemingly without a troubled conscience. The enslavement of fellow human beings does not bother Granny, but rough language and horse stealing worries her something terrible.

By being unable to imagine the Black or, in this case, white women as liberated and liberator, Faulkner minimizes the potentiality of their selfhood. The embers of the Lost Cause myth are still burning. The fact that Zora Neale Hurston wrote *Their Eyes Are Watching God* in 1937 and Faulkner *The Unvanquished* in 1938 and *Absalom, Absalom!* in 1936 indicates that Faulkner's failure to understand the interiority of Black women had little to do with "the times" and everything to do with his inability to take off the blinders and privileges of white supremacy.

"Stretching Her Throat Like a Sunflower Stalk above the River's Opaque Skin" / Welty

Eudora Welty's only Civil War story, "The Burning," is wildly problematic and yet it more definitively calls out the death of the Lost Cause narrative and resurrects the power of the Black woman than any of Faulkner's Civil War fiction. In Welty's now-famous rebuttal to interviewer Patricia Wheatley when she asked Welty if there was something about the Civil War that captures the imagination, Welty made it abundantly clear that the Civil War did not capture her imagination: "I abominate the Civil War and everything about it, and I don't feel anything but horror and infinite regret, even just despair sometimes that it happened. I mean, despair over the tremendous loss of life, which is the way people felt about the First World War in England."[18] For Welty, her answer came from a deep hatred of war but was also fueled by the fact that, as a white southern woman writer living in Jackson, Mississippi, it was imperative that she disavow all connection to Margaret Mitchell and the scores of white-privileged United Daughters of the Confederacy who were writing romance novels about the Civil War. However, "The Burning" haunted Welty: "As for 'The Burning,' I think that is a bad story. I don't know why I tried to write anything historical. . . . I think the story is too involved and curlicued around with things."[19] Albert Devlin, one of the first critics to give this story serious consideration, disagreed, calling "The Burning" "a daring kind of experiment."[20]

Welty rewrote "The Burning" eight times and published a version in *Harper's Bazaar* in March of 1951 and another much-altered version in *Bride of the Innisfallen* in 1955. In the second version, Welty transforms Florabel from a downtrodden enslaved woman to an empowered liberated woman named Delilah. In the *Harper's Bazaar* version, Welty describes Florabel, foreshadowing this transformation: "[H]erself was an unknown, like a queen, somebody, she had heard called, even cried for."[21] In *The Bride of the Innisfallen* version, when Delilah is dragged behind the white mare by the Yankees and raped, "She screamed, young and strong, for them all—for everybody that wanted her to scream for them, for everybody that didn't; and sometimes it seemed to her that she was screaming her loudest for Delilah, who was lost now—carried out of the house, not knowing how to get back."[22] Delilah screams for herself and her whole community. She is not a strange Jim Bond character howling in the wilderness. She is not symbolic of the end of white civilization. She is powerful, "young and strong." In both versions, Welty makes the selfhood and identity of her Black woman character central to the narrative; she is an autonomous subject, not an object.

"The Burning" does not describe a Margaret Mitchell Yankee invasion. In fact, as Susan Donaldson argues, Welty directly repudiates *Gone with the Wind* and the Lost Cause narrative in this text.[23] Miss Theo and Miss Myra horrifically wait too late to escape the Yankees, get raped, offer Delilah up as a substitute victim, allow Phinny to be burned to death, take "[t]he Dickson's perfectly good hammock,"[24] and calmly hang themselves. Delilah finds her way back to the burned house, spots the Venetian mirror, and in it, sees a vision of herself as powerful. With several rapes, the murder of a child, and two suicides in just a few pages, we almost wish Miss Theo would rise from the grass, grasp a handful of dirt, and swear, "I'll never be hungry again." But instead, Delilah imagines Miss Theo writhing like a snake in the grass.

"The Burning" is indeed "curlicued around" with so many textual allusions that they cannot be fully explicated in this essay. Alluding to *Snow White and the Seven Dwarfs*, Samson and Delilah, the myths of Astarte and Epona, Jonah and the whale, the story of King Solomon and the Queen of Sheba, the myth of Phineas and the harpies, and the story of the Phoenix bird, Welty transforms what could be a formulaic southern Civil War story into a story of regeneration and redemption. As Carey Wall warns us, we cannot think about the story from a realistic point of view: "While everyday thought considers suicide an impossible means of fomenting new energy and life, ritual transformation can make death an effective means of creating an opening to new life.... The three women of 'The Burning' are working in sacred rather than profane territory."[25] Welty, like Faulkner, tears down, burns, and sacrifices the white ladies of the Lost Cause myth, but unlike Faulkner, she provides a sustaining narrative of regeneration.

Theo and Myra's brother's name is Benton. His name comes from the English name for a town and means "bent grass." Following Wall's admonition to pay attention to the ritualistic elements of the story, we can see Benton as the fertility god or the grain god who has been killed in the autumn and burned, to be reborn in the spring. After the burning, Miss Theo and Miss Myra find and take hold of Delilah "face down in a ditch with her eyes scorched open, who did at least go beyond the tramped down gate and away through the grand worthless field they themselves had had burned before."[26] In the *Harper's Bazaar* version of "The Burning," Welty makes the fertility connection abundantly clear: "For soon this poor set-up black girl's screams began outside, low in the yard and around that house, springing up everywhere she ran, *like all the green in the world after a hard rain*."[27] We can see the full Moirai, the triple goddess in Theo, Myra, and Delilah, and the renewal of the fertility god in the emancipation of the enslaved.

Between Benton as the grass god and Delilah as a fertility goddess raining down on the earth with her screams, the ritualistic reading is highly suggestive.

There are numerous intertextual traces that link Phineas to the Phoenix. In the story of the ancient bird, he builds a nest of myrrh, honey, and cinnamon every five hundred years, and when he is finished, he makes an egg out of the myrrh, lifts his nest into the air, flies to the god of the sun, and bursts into flames. Out of the ashes of his body a new Phoenix bird is born. When Delilah is standing in the hall while the soldiers are trying to rape Miss Myra and Miss Theo, she looks up the stairs to where Phinny should be, and she sees that "the bare yawn of the hall was at her back, and the front stair's shadow, big as a tree and empty."[28] She says later, "Could be he got out" (489), and when the three women come to the hammock, a type of nest in the open sun, they find a familiar cup with a sweetness in it—like Phinny's cup that he throws down the stairs when he is hungry or thirsty (490). After helping to hang Miss Theo and Miss Myra, Delilah takes the cup back to the house, and in the feathery ashes, finds Phinny's bones. It took the Phoenix bird three days to build a nest and make the journey. In this reading, by waiting two days after the general tells her that their house will be burned, Miss Theo gives the Phoenix/Phinny Bird three days to build a nest and rise from the ashes. Delilah, Phinny, and all the enslaved become the Phoenix bird rising from the ashes. And yet Delilah carries Phinny's actual burned bones, a sacrificial offering bundled on her head as she walks toward the river and freedom.

When Delilah is looking in the mirror at the end of the story, Welty writes, "Behind her the one standing wall of the house held notched and listening like the big ear of King Solomon into which poured the repeated asking of birds" (492). King Solomon controlled the birds and could make them do his bidding. When Solomon finds out that Queen Sheba is the ruler of a land that does not know him as their king, he demands that she come and bow down to him. He threatens her with all the beasts and demons of the world, and she acquiesces to his wishes. When Delilah returns to the house, she envisions an army of bats and insects and butterflies coming to attack her. But unlike Queen Sheba, Delilah does not acquiesce. Instead, she imagines "the motherly image—head wagging in the flayed forehead of a horse with ears and crest up stiff, the shield and the drum of big swamp birdskins, the horns of deer sharpened to cut and kill with. She showed her teeth. Then she looked in the feathery ashes and found Phinny's bones. She ripped a square from the manifold fullness of skirts and tied up the bones in it" (493). Delilah sees in the mirror a warrior woman with sharp teeth, anger, power, mother right, and horns with which to go into battle. Eudora Welty has her two southern belle white women who tell racist jokes about the death of a child commit suicide for the good of the community, and, like Virginia Woolf killing off the angel in the house, for the good of her writing. She murders them and all that they stand for. True to their entitlement to the end, they demand that Delilah help them hang themselves, but Delilah emerges from this insane past, not in rags like Clytie but with a manifold fullness of skirts, and most importantly, with Phinny's bones:

> Light on Delilah's head the Jubilee Cup was set. She paused now and then to lick the rim and taste again the ghost of sweet that could still make her tongue start clinging—some sweet lapped up greedily long ago, only a mystery now when or who by. She carried her own black locust stick to drive the snakes.
>
> Following the smell of horses and fire, to men, she kept in the wheel tracks till they broke down at the river. In the shade underneath the burned and fallen bridge she sat on the stump and chewed for a while, without dreams, the comb of a dirtdauber. Then once more kneeling, she took a drink from the Big Black, and pulled the shoes off her feet and waded in.
>
> Submerged to the waist, to the breast, stretching her throat like a sunflower stalk above the river's opaque skin, she kept on, her treasure stacked on the roof of her head, hands laced upon it. She had forgotten how or when she knew, and she did not know what day this was, but she knew—it would not rain, the river would not rise, until Saturday. (494)

In direct contrast and direct response to Faulkner, Welty lifts the unknown enslaved woman walking next to Granny's wagon and gives her a life, a voice, a purpose, and power. Welty allows Delilah to luxuriate in her freedom, her Jubilee. She tastes sweetness, the lingering honey of the rising Phoenix. Phinny's Jubilee Cup? Delilah easily follows the Yankee troops' wheel tracks. She sits by the river and chews on a blade of grass, rests, drinks from the river, and submerges herself. Welty imagines her feeling the water on her free body, her waist, her breast, and the description "stretching her throat like a sunflower stalk above the river's opaque skin" lifts Delilah from a slave to a free woman. Phinny's bones are her treasure, and she "laces" her fingers around them. Unlike Faulkner, Welty creates a Black female queen who, in this moment of her self-liberation, her white mistresses dead, the plantation house burned to the ground, carries the Phoenix bones of her Phinny, her son, the future of her people, on her head. Admittedly, Welty's image of the African warrior can be read as stereotypical and thus limited, but it at least gives the character power and a potential future of revenge.

"Chick, Chick, Chick, Chick" / Margaret Walker's *Jubilee*

"My grandmothers were strong. / Why am I not as they?"[29] When Margaret Walker asks this question at the end of her poem "Lineage," she is not saying that she and her generation of women are not strong. The words "not as they" indicate to this reader that she is saying that she has a different kind of strength. She is strong but not "bent to toil" strong. She is not willing to say only "clean" words. Throughout her life as a writer, Margaret Walker never shied away from the whole truth, all the sad, horrific, damning, and jubilant veracity of it. In her bestseller, *Jubilee*, Walker rejects romantic, nostalgic amnesia.[30] Phyllis R. Klotman in her essay "Oh, Freedom: Women and History in Margaret Walker's *Jubilee*" quotes Walker as reminding her readers that "I am not a romanticist in *Jubilee*. It is a realistic book."[31] *Jubilee* is a fiction based on the oral history told by her great-grandmother Elvira Ware Brown, in which Walker tracks the experience of enslaved peoples for the duration of the war to liberation and Reconstruction. She writes nothing about battles, strategies, and Lost Cause narratives, does not create an intertextual maze in the style of Welty; instead, she creates an experimental epic that traces Black women's lives through a genealogical, human, and historical perspective. Klotman emphasizes that "*Jubilee* is definitely Vyry's story; she is at the center of the novel, which begins with the imminent death of her mother, Sis Hetta, in 1839. It ends in 1870 with the news of an impending birth—Vyry's fourth child—some thirty years later."[32]

Not only is this Vyry's story, but this is Walker's story by a Black woman, for Black women, and to educate all others. Although she does not have her white women kill themselves like Welty does in "The Burning," they are presented realistically, committing some of the greatest atrocities, brutality, and outright torture of Vyry and others. Walker, in the very first pages of *Jubilee*, demands that we face reality: once she has described regal Hetta—only twenty-nine years old, as "bloated and swollen beyond recognition" (6), having "terrible fits and hemorrhaging" (6), and dying in childbirth after having given birth to fifteen children forced on her by master John Morris Dutton's raping her most of her life—she has cured any readers who needed curing of layering nostalgic myths on the enslavement of human beings. If the loss of Hetta to her whole Black community is not enough, the white plantation doctor, who arrives two days late and blames Granny Ticey for not "getting all the rotten pieces" (6) after a dead baby, reveals that Walker in 1966 in Mississippi at the height of the civil rights movement is decidedly not interested in nostalgia. Unlike "The Burning" which *ends* with Delilah seeing herself in the Venetian mirror as an African queen/warrior, *Jubilee starts* with the queen Hetty, whom her master John imagines as "some African Queen from the Congo" with "gold rings around her neck" (8), broken and dying from bearing the master's children.

Walker is not authoring a book that is "curlicued around" like Welty's "The Burning" but is instead rich in cultural allusion, folklore, African storytelling, and the Black blues and spiritual traditions. She is deeply committed to telling the Black woman's story of enslavement, not just of her protagonist Vyry, but of Black women Sis Mammy Sukey, Granny Ticey, Hetta, Caline, May Liza, Lucy, Aunt Sally, and her daughter Minna—and many of the men. Unlike in sentimentalized Civil War romances of the 1930s and 1940s, Vyry does not end up in a romantic relationship with the man of her dreams. She will not even consider Randall Ware until he promises that he will secure her freedom. Instead, because of the historical and economic realities of slavery, war, and Reconstruction, Vyry creates a life with Innis Brown.

As Eleanor Traylor reminds us in her essay "Music as Theme: The Blues Mode in the Works of Margaret Walker":

> Music is the leitmotif of Margaret Walker's *Jubilee*. . . . Through her songs, the personal history of Vyry, Elvira Ware Brown, central dramatic figure, actual maternal great-grandmother of the author, merges with the history of a community, a time, a place, a space—a mythical zone—within the history of world story. Vyry, "adrift" as in a "wide world alone," is a unique wayfarer whose journey, as charted in the bluesman's song, is a series of new beginnings. Her rhythmic movement through experience is not the movement of the ritual tragic hero: she does not topple from the heights of a social order and die in affirmation of a value. Nor does she muddle through the comic hero's bumbling acquiescence to the social norm . . . her movement through time is a continual process of dissolution, absorption, conversion, and realignment. She locates within her personal experience the public experience of the tribe. . . . [L]ike the strategy of the bluesman's song whose tale of woe controlled by form invites the world to dance, is the rhythmic motion, the consummation of the model heroine of the blues.[33]

Traylor brilliantly refers to a passage in the novel in which John Morris Sutton rides home to his plantation: "From the live oak trees hung the weird gray veils of Spanish moss waving wildly in the wind and trailing like gray tresses of an old woman's hair, lost from the head of some ghost in the wilderness. Often during daylight hours, the sky was completely obscured by an archway of these trees" (35). Walker then writes: "Here in the stillness of the forest one was cut off from reality and lost in a fantastic world of the jungle. In this world of half-darkness and half-light he had often felt as though eyes were watching him" (35). Eyes are indeed watching this white master of the plantation South. Margaret Walker's eyes, and because of her, Eleanor Traylor's eyes, and all the eyes of her students and readers, and finally from 1966 to the present, the eyes of the millions of readers who have read *Jubilee* throughout the world. John Morris Dutton does not know this, but he is riding home to find out that disease has claimed Granny Ticey and Mammy Sukey. All the old women, all the "gray tresses," "the heads of ghosts in the wilderness," are watching him.

John Morris Dutton returns to find that his wife Saline—who has seen her husband sleep with Hetty for years, has watched Hetty bear fifteen light-skinned children, the last one being Vyry who looks like a twin to her daughter—has strung Vyry up by her thumbs in a closet. Eyes are watching him indeed. Vyry is watching. Saline is watching. His daughter Lillian is watching. The novel begins with the death and dying and torture of women but moves forward in Traylor's words "as a constant dissolution, absorption, conversion, and realignment."[34] By creating a blues character like Vyry, Walker's rhythmic narrative force never loses power. She is not strong like her grandmothers. She is strong like herself because the ghosts of her grandmothers have infused her with the knowledge of the trees. Her own great-grandmother Elvira Ware Brown is the ghost force haunting backward and transforming forward through a cross-generational dialectic exchange creating a song motif that allows Walker to control the text within overlapping artistic formal structures.

Haunting backward and allowing Vyry to walk slowly onward to liberation, Margaret Walker reminds us that getting out on paper all the rotten pieces of enslavement is almost impossible, but she will not hold back. *Jubilee* moves forward to presenting Hetta's child Vyry as an independent woman, the proud owner of a farm of her own, pregnant with her man Innis's child, a child who will be born free, and watching her son Jim headed off to college with his father, Randall Ware. Even at this moment of closure, Walker reminds us that while Jim and his father are about to board the train to college, "[t]he colored people shared half their car with the baggage and the freight including squawking chickens, pigs, and a goat" (496). Realistic. Political. Radical. Forward and back and forth simultaneously. No caught angel wings. Call and response.

Walker follows Vyry from the torturous hands of Miss Saline—in the big house stringing her up in the closet by her thumbs for breaking a dish—to standing over her own farm: "Now, with a peace in her heart she could not express, she watched her huge flock of white leghorn laying-hens come running when she called. This time, she was feeding her own chickens and calling them home to roost. It was this call Minna heard her mother crooning: 'Come biddy, biddy, biddy, biddy, Come chick, chick,

chick, chick!'" (497). But this is not just a sweet ending to an epic tale of injustice and resilience. The folk saying "chickens have come home to roost" is used to indicate that when a person has hurt someone in the past, their actions will come back to haunt them. Call and response. The violence that Miss Saline visited on her as a child is not dead. It will always linger in her memory. Chick, chick, chick. These are white chickens, and they have come home to roost. She has called them home to roost.

But unlike for Faulkner, the violence and horror of her life of enslavement, if not dead, is indeed in the past. Walker allows her characters to transform, to thrive, to rebel, to savor a moment of justice and retribution. Vyry is pregnant with another child, and although we could read this as a romanticized ending to a life of struggle, violence, and oppression, activists know that one moment of liberation will always unveil what has not been liberated yet. At this very moment, Minnie has been crying in bed by herself because Randall Ware has taken her brother Jim away on a train to college. He asks her to come. Jim asks her to come but she knows she must stay with her mother. A liberation story is never complete. There is never closure. The reader is asked to haunt forward to the day Minnie will be able to free herself and attend college like Jim. The chicks symbolize affluence, comfort, well-being but they also symbolize the future—unknown and radical. The chickens are coming home to roost. In *Jubilee*, as in *For My People*, Walker creates cohesive and coherent life stories where there could simply be despair and dissolution. In *For My People*, Margaret Walker writes the poem "The Struggle Staggers Us" in 1938, around the time she began work on *Jubilee*. In this poem she is speaking, haunting backward to her great-grandmother Elvira and haunting forward to her own children and great-grandchildren: "There is a journey from the me to you / There is a journey from the Me to You. / There is a journey from You to Me. / A union of the two strange worlds must be."[35]

"We Listen for What the Waves Intone": Natasha Trethewey

Natasha Trethewey does not actually enter the territory of Civil War literature. Instead, she enters the South: the place of her birth, the Civil War, enslavement, and the Native Guard are all part of this journey. Her mother is Black, her father white, and her relationship with her home state of Mississippi is complex. Trethewey, from a nuanced position, brings together family stories, stories of the South, stories of the Civil War, stories of her parents all dedicated "to my mother in memory" punctuated with the epigram by Charles Wright: "Memory is a cemetery / I've visited once or twice, white / ubiquitous and the set-aside /

Everywhere under foot."[36] These words combined with the words of the spiritual she uses as the epigraph for the first section—"I am going there to meet my mother / she said she'd meet me when I come" (1)—reminds us that Trethewey's journey is maternal, womanist, and genealogical.

Taking a deep dive into archival materials—letters, journals, photographs, and oral narratives from the Native Guard—she asks poignant questions that upend traditional Civil War narrative structures in a poetic exploration that seeks to follow shadows, ghosts, fragments, and what cannot and has not been known. She walks the fine line between what is dead, what is alive, and how and whom we choose to remember. Trethewey is as interested in the silences, the land itself, the metaphoric ellipses, and the vibrations and songs that still resonate as she is in telling a fully formed story directly confronting and interrogating the white, ubiquitous "everywhere under foot" myths.

In the first poem of *Native Guard*, "The Southern Crescent," she tells a story of her mother as a young girl seeking to meet up with her own father, Trethewey's grandfather, by taking the train across the country to California, only to face deep disappointment when there is no one like him on the platform to greet her. She juxtaposes the story of her mother's failed journey with a trip she and her mother take together the last day the Southern Crescent makes its run: "She is sure that we can leave home, bound only / for whatever awaits us, the sun now / setting behind us, the rails humming / like anticipation, the train pulling us" (5-6). In *Native Guard*, Natasha Trethewey is bound only by what awaits her, haunting backward and forward, and even sideways, weaving memories of her mother's murder at the hands of her ex-husband with the historical account of the Native Guard Union soldiers, an all-Black regiment, with the tourist Civil War South of Vicksburg, with the literary South of Robert Penn Warren, and with the Gulf South of her childhood.

It is as important for her to memorialize her mother, left out of history, as it is to create a literary monument to the Native Guard, enslaved Black men of the 1st, 2nd, and 3rd regiments stationed in Ship Island guarding Confederate prisoners of war, also erased from history. This radical juxtaposition makes the undeniable statement: the embattled body of her abused mother must be memorialized, remembered, just as the bloated, neglected bodies of the dead Native Guard who fought for the Union. Trethewey owns the land of the Gulf South. She tells us: this is my South. Complex. Layered. Literary, full of unburied ghosts. On this train ride with no destination, Trethewey asks us to bear witness to a new kind of historical evidence. In the poem "What Is Evidence," she will ask us to see that her mother's beaten body, the "fleeting bruises," "quiver of her voice," and " teeth she wore in place of her own" are not evidence: "Only the landscape of her body—splintered / clavicle, pierced temporal / —her thin bones settling a bit each day, the way all things do" constitute evidence (11).

For Trethewey the line between life and death, between past and present is so gossamer that hearing a neighbor call her cat in the poem "At Dusk" "left me to wonder that I too might lift / my voice, sure of someone out there" (15). Each morning, in the poem "The Myth," she realizes, as mourners do, that her mother has slipped away while she was sleeping. But in dreams you live. "So, I try taking / you back into morning. Sleep-heavy, turning, / my eyes open, I find you do not follow" (14). In the poem "Monument" when she visits her mother's grave and sees the ants climbing all around, there is a sense that she has not done her job of properly attending to the grave. But the ants are doing this job for her (43).

The commitment to remember her mother and to tell the history of the Native Guard in the same collection reveals a writer who understands that the history of enslavement and her mother's death are inextricably tied together. She journeys back and forth in time between the Gulfport of her youth and the Gulfport / Ship Island of the Native Guards, and in doing so, she weaves a web of acknowledgment. In the poem "June 1863," she writes, "Yesterday, word came of colored troops, dead / General Banks was heard to say *I have / no dead there*, and left them, unclaimed" (28).

One poem, "Incident," tells all: Trethewey writes of the family story they tell every year, looking out the window with drawn shades: "At the cross trussed like a Christmas tree, / a few men gathered, white as angels in their gowns." Trethewey's historical angels become the Ku Klux Klan, the ones who smash, burn, and terrorize. Trethewey, bearing witness, writes: "Nothing really happened. / By morning all the flames had dimmed" (41). What Trethewey reminds us in her collection *Native Guard*, and I do mean "us" quite literally, the scholars, the storytellers, and keepers of the past, the ones who haunt the archives, is that we must stand eyes wide open at the scene of the crime and bear witness. We must find the festering wounds in the texts that we read and expose and heal them. If we do not, then "nothing really happened." Quite simply, these three women writers, a different kind of triad, refuse to believe that nothing happened or that we are stuck in a violent paralysis in which the past is never past. "The Burning," *Jubilee*, and *Native Guard* start with the dead, buried, forgotten, and silenced bodies of their ancestors and give them voice, life, and a future. They begin with the death of Black and white women and end with the resurrection of Black women's voices.

Trethewey's pointing out Welty's angel-shaped shadow reminds us in a Brechtian metacontextual way that there is, in this present moment, a woman artist standing taking a picture of these ruins. The ruins do not catch in her wings. They do not overwhelm her. While they may haunt her, Welty and Trethewey capture and haunt them right back. They are haunting backward, imagining forward, demanding that their world, their subjectivity and autonomous voice and vision, prevail. If we take Faulkner literally and believe that the past is not dead, then we are even more responsible for listening backward and writing forward. While the volume *Undead Souths: The Gothic and Beyond in Southern Literature and Culture* takes us far beyond earlier notions of these words, there is plenty more to explore concerning this topic. "To see dead people is to face the past and its many cultural eruptions in the present. In analyzing diverse images of southern necrologies, we unveil how these eerie figures record, critique, and/or invent convulsive, disruptive constructions of the South. In so doing, they force us to reimagine an already imaginary South."[37] Indeed, the past has haunted the southern present and the national imagination so treacherously that we are left with ghosts following ghosts to the steps of the Capitol with Confederate flags not able to distinguish the difference between then and now and not having a nuanced grip on an embodied historical language that allows our better angels to sift through the debris. They are trying to make us believe that "nothing really happened"—here and now or there then.

To expel the poison of enslavement and violence of civil war from our national imaginative body is impossible, but to starve it of its romanticized allure, to live more fully in the present, camera in hand, like Adrienne Rich, searching for "the thing I came for: / the wreck and not the story of the wreck / the thing itself and not the myth," is another thing entirely.[38] At this moment in our national history, when Walter Benjamin's pile of debris has grown skyward and caught in the wings of the angel of history, it is our responsibility to highlight the voices of those who do not look longingly back to a plantation past for inspiration but instead insist on a solid, hard, personal narrative that cannot be ignored, walked past or through and that must be grappled with. The unique experiential narrative structures that these three writers employ and deploy demand our attention. It is no mistake that for Walker and Trethewey, the lives of the characters they unbury are directly connected to the lives of the living for whom they write—in Trethewey's case, for her mother, and in Walker's, her grandmother. For Black writers for whom slavery presented not nostalgia but nightmare, their writing lives are not complete until they have gone back and opened this wound and made whole what has been smashed. The wound does not throb and bleed and manifest until they demand that it do so and only then, only in particular, familial, real ways does the story pour forth, a story written in blood, blues, and bones.

Eudora Welty, Margaret Walker, and Natasha Trethewey bring the buried voices of a different kind of civil war back to life. As Trethewey remarks, there are no names carved for the Native Guard. She asks: "What is their monument?" Margaret Walker left her preferred genre, poetry, to write the epic novel *Jubilee* that she published in the middle of the confluence of the civil rights movement and the Black Power movement. These characters return not as debris, not as ghosts, but as loam. Their lives are not caught in an endless cycle. They are imagined into freedom.

The artists of Mississippi lived neck-high in dead bodies, bleeding angels, and debris. For three Mississippi writers to tell the story of the lost lives of the Civil War is to discover radical new ways of writing. The writing that pours forth from this intimate engagement with time and space is strange, often wild, expressing voicings that find in the figurative spaces of symbol, metaphor, and upended structure a regenerative place of text/ile that is not frayed or torn or easily silenced—a secret voice often extratextual, masked, and expansive. This triumvirate of geniuses built an alternative narrative for Mississippi writers that answers the storm of progress with quiet, persistent, listening, witnessing, and experiential voicing. What has been left out will emerge as each of these writers uses her imagination to follow Trethewey's words in "Elegy for the Native Guards" and "listen for what the waves intone" (44).

NOTES

1. Eudora Welty, *Photographs*, rev. ed. (1989; repr. Jackson: University Press of Mississippi, 2019).

2. Natasha Trethewey, "That's Just the Way it Was," in *Photographs*, by Eudora Welty, xi.

3. Trethewey, "That's Just the Way it Was," xi.

4. Annette Trefzer, *Exposing Mississippi: Eudora Welty's Photographic Reflections* (Jackson: University Press of Mississippi, 2022), 109.

5. Trefzer, *Exposing Mississippi*, 109.

6. William Faulkner, *Requiem for a Nun* (1951; repr., New York: Vintage International, 2011), 85.

7. Trethewey, "That's Just the Way it Was," ix.

8. Walter Benjamin, "Theses on the Philosophy of History," *Illuminations*; ed. Hannah Arendt (New York: Houghton Mifflin, 2019), 249.

9. Sarah Ford, *Haunted Property: Slavery and the Gothic* (Jackson: University Press of Mississippi, 2020), 181.

10. Toni Morrison, *Beloved* (1987; repr., New York: Vintage International, 2004), 270.

11. Morrison, *Beloved*, 270.

12. Michael Gorra, *The Saddest Words: William Faulkner's Civil War* (New York: Norton, 2020), 10.

13. Gorra, *The Saddest Words*, 177.

14. Patricia Yaeger, *Dirt and Desire: Reconstructing Southern Women's Writing, 1930–1990* (Chicago: University of Chicago Press, 2000), 90.

15. William Faulkner, *The Unvanquished*, rev. ed. (1938; repr., New York: Vintage International, 1991), 82.

16. Faulkner, *The Unvanquished*, 83.

17. Faulkner to Robert K. Haas, July 8, 1938, *Selected Letters of William Faulkner*, ed. Joseph Blotner (New York: Random House, 1977), 106.

18. Patricia Wheatley, "Eudora Welty: A Writer's Beginnings," in *More Conversations with Eudora Welty*, ed. Peggy Whitman Prenshaw (Jackson: University Press of Mississippi, 1996), 120–21.

19. Jan Norby Gretlund, "An Interview with Eudora Welty," in *Conversations with Eudora Welty*, ed. Peggy Whitman Prenshaw (Jackson: University Press of Mississippi, 1984), 221.

20. Albert Devlin and Peggy Whitman Prenshaw, "A Conversation with Eudora Welty, Jackson, 1986," *Mississippi Quarterly* 39, no. 4. (Fall 1986): 447.

21. Eudora Welty, "The Burning," *Harper's Bazaar* (March 1951), 247.

22. Eudora Welty, "The Burning," in *The Collected Stories of Eudora Welty* (New York: Harcourt, Brace, Jovanovich, 1980), 485.

23. Susan Donaldson, "Faltering Narrative: Eudora Welty's 'The Burning,' Slavery's Ghosts, and the Politics of Grief," in *New Essays on Eudora Welty, Class, and Race*, ed. Harriet Pollack (Jackson: University Press of Mississippi, 2020), 133–49.

24. Welty, "The Burning," 489.

25. Carey Wall, "Extreme Reversal to Meet Life's Obligations," *Mississippi Quarterly* (April 2009): 130.

26. Welty, *Collected Stories*, 487.

27. Welty, "The Burning," *Harper's Bazaar*, 247. Italics mine.

28. Welty, *Collected Stories*, 483. Hereafter cited parenthetically.

29. Margaret Walker, "Lineage," in *This is My Century: New and Collected Poems* (Athens: University of Georgia Press, 1998), 21.

30. Margaret Walker, *Jubilee* (Boston: Houghton Mifflin, 1966).

31. Phyllis R. Klotman, "Oh, Freedom: Women and History in Margaret Walker's *Jubilee*," quoted in *Fields Watered with Blood: Critical Essays on Margaret Walker*, ed. Maryemma Graham (Athens: University of Georgia Press, 2001), 211.

32. Klotman, "Oh, Freedom," 184.

33. Eleanor Traylor, "Music as Theme: The Blues Mode in the Works of Margaret Walker" quoted in *Fields Watered with Blood: Critical Essays on Margaret Walker*, ed. Maryemma Graham (Athens: University of Georgia Press, 2001), 197.

34. Traylor, "Music as Theme," 197.

35. Margaret Walker, "The Struggle Staggers Us," in *For My People* (New Haven: Yale University Press, 1989), 58

36. Natasha Trethewey, *Native Guard* (New York: Houghton Mifflin, 2007), 8–9. Hereafter cited parenthetically.

37. Eric Anderson, Taylor Haygood, and Daniel Cross Turner, introduction to *Undead Souths: The Gothic and Beyond in Southern Literature and Culture*, (Baton Rouge: LSU Press, 2015), 10.

38. Adrienne Rich, *Diving into the Wreck* (New York: W. W. Norton & Co. 1973), 22, 23.

About the Contributors

Anita DeRouen teaches English at Murrah High School in Jackson, Mississippi. DeRouen has published on race and media representation, digital literacy, and most recently, Richard Wright. DeRouen serves as community liaison for the Millsaps College Truth, Racial Healing, and Transformation Center and is an independent racial dialogue consultant.

Susan V. Donaldson is National Endowment for the Humanities Professor of English and American Studies, Emerita, at the College of William and Mary, where she taught from 1985 to 2020. Donaldson is the author of *Competing Voices: The American Novel, 1865–1914*, which won a *Choice* "Outstanding Academic Book" award, and some sixty essays and book chapters as well as coeditor of *Haunted Bodies: Gender and Southern Texts* and editor and coeditor of several special issues of *The Faulkner Journal* and *Mississippi Quarterly*. During her retirement, she is working on three book projects: "The Politics of Storytelling, Race, and Visual Culture in the US South," "Mississippi Writers and the Fall of Jim Crow," and "Utopias in the Americas."

Julia Eichelberger is Marybelle Higgins Howe Professor of Southern Literature at the College of Charleston and directs the undergraduate minor in Southern Studies. A former president of the Eudora Welty Society, she has published essays and two edited volumes on Welty (*Tell About Night Flowers: Eudora Welty's Gardening Letters, 1940–1949* [2013]; *Teaching the Works of Eudora Welty* [2018]) and is completing a monograph on Welty's forty-five-year correspondence with her friend Frank Lyell. She has also published scholarship and public history on Charleston for the Committee on Commemoration and Landscapes, a committee charged with telling a fuller story of the College of Charleston and the city.

W. Ralph Eubanks is faculty fellow and writer-in-residence at the Center for the Study of Southern Culture at the University of Mississippi. He is the author of *A Place Like Mississippi: A Journey through a Real and Imagined Literary Landscape*, as well as two other works of nonfiction, *Ever Is a Long*

Time and *The House at the End of the Road*. A writer and essayist whose work focuses on race, identity, and the American South, his writing has appeared in *Vanity Fair*, the *American Scholar*, the *Georgia Review*, and the *New Yorker*.

Sarah Gilbreath Ford is professor of American literature at Baylor University where she serves as the director of the Beall Poetry Festival. She is the author of *Tracing Southern Storytelling in Black and White* (2014) and *Haunted Property: Slavery and the Gothic* (2020). She serves as coeditor of the *Eudora Welty Review*. In 2018, she won the Eudora Welty Society's Phoenix Award for scholarship and service. In 2019, she was named a Baylor Centennial Professor.

Bernard T. Joy is an educator, writer, and researcher living in Scotland. He has taught in the secondary sector since 2012 and has also held teaching positions at several institutions of further education, including the University of Glasgow, where he earned his PhD in 2021 with a thesis on William Faulkner. He is a frequent speaker at the annual Faulkner and Yoknapatawpha Conference, at the Faulkner Studies in the UK Conference, and at the Faulkner network at Amiens, France. His publications include two books of poetry and one solo collection of prose fiction, and his essays and book chapters have been included in the *Faulkner Journal*, the *Journal of American Studies*, the Faulkner and Yoknapatawpha book series, and elsewhere. In addition to Faulkner, he has written or is currently writing about Richard Wright, Cormac McCarthy, Charles Baudelaire, Paul Cézanne, Maurice Merleau-Ponty, and others. Joy was the 2022 recipient of the John W. Hunt Memorial Scholarship.

John Wharton Lowe (1945–2023) was Barbara Methvin Distinguished Professor of English and Latin American Studies at the University of Georgia. His books include *Calypso Magnolia: The Crosscurrents of Caribbean and Southern Literature*, which won the C. Hugh Holman Award and the Sharon L. Dean Award. He served as president of the Society for the Study of Southern Literature, the Southern American Studies Association, and the Louisiana Folklore Society.

Anne MacMaster is professor of English and director of the women's and gender studies program at Millsaps College. Her recent publications include (with Anita DeRouen) "Realism and Modernism, Solipsism and Solidarity" in *Richard Wright in Context* and (with Michael Gleason) "The Pull of the Land: Indigenous Spirituality and Authorial Guilt in 'Roger Malvin's Burial' and Faulkner's 'The Bear'" in the *Nathaniel Hawthorne Review*.

Rebecca Mark is director of the Institute for Women's Leadership and professor in the department of Women's, Gender, and Sexuality Studies at Rutgers University. Her books include *The Dragon's Blood: Feminist Intertextuality in Eudora Welty's Fiction* and *Ersatz America: Hidden Traces, Graphic Texts, and Mending of Democracy*.

Suzanne Marrs is professor emerita of English at Millsaps College. She received the 1998 Phoenix Award for Outstanding Welty Scholarship from the Eudora Welty Society and was Mississippi's Humanities Scholar of the Year in 2009. Marrs is the author of *Eudora Welty: A Biography*, *One Writer's Imagination: The Fiction of Eudora Welty*, and *The Welty Collection*. She is also the editor or coeditor of three works—*What There Is to Say We Have Said: The Correspondence of Eudora Welty and William Maxwell*, *Eudora Welty and Politics: Did the Writer Crusade?* (with Harriet Pollack), and *Meanwhile There Are Letters: The Correspondence of Eudora Welty and Ross Macdonald* (with Tom Nolan). Along with Michael Pickard and Lee Anne Bryan, Marrs is currently writing a book to be titled *Eudora Welty and the House of Fiction*.

Donnie McMahand is associate professor of African American literature at Towson University. His publications include essays on works by Toni Morrison, Langston Hughes, Eudora Welty, Bebe Moore Campbell, Lewis Nordan, Harper Lee, Truman Capote, and Randall Kenan. His essay "Strange Bedfellows: Randall Kenan 'Talks Back' to the Southern Renaissance" was shortlisted for the Louis D. Rubin Prize in Southern Literary Criticism. With coauthor Kevin Murphy, McMahand won the Ruth Vande Kieft Prize for a 2013 essay about Welty's novel *The Optimist's Daughter*. He dedicates the essay to his mother, Gloria D. McMahand.

Kevin Murphy is a faculty member at Towson University. Murphy writes about modern and contemporary southern fiction and has published essays and reviews in the *Eudora Welty Review*, the *Southern Quarterly*, the *Mississippi Quarterly*, and the *Southern Literary Journal*. Most recently, he and coauthor Donnie McMahand published their essay "The Lynched Earth: Trees, Trespass, and Political Intelligence in Welty's 'A Worn Path' and Morrison's *Home*" in the 2020 volume *New Essays on Eudora Welty, Class, and Race*, edited by Harriet Pollack. Murphy and McMahand are the 2022–24 copresidents of the Eudora Welty Society.

Harriet Pollack, College of Charleston, is the author of *Eudora Welty's Fiction and Photography: The Body of the Other Woman* (2016). In 2019, she inaugurated and now edits the University Press of Mississippi series

Critical Perspectives on Eudora Welty. Her eight edited and coedited volumes include *Eudora Welty and Mystery: Hidden in Plain Sight* (with Jacob Agner, 2023); *New Essays on Eudora Welty, Class, and Race* (2020); *Emmett Till in Literary Memory and Imagination* (with Christopher Metress, 2008); and *Eudora Welty, Whiteness, and Race* (2013). She is currently at work on Eudora Welty's Modernist Multimedia Interactions.

James G. Thomas, Jr. is associate director for publications at the University of Mississippi's Center for the Study of Southern Culture. He is an editor of the twenty-four-volume *New Encyclopedia of Southern Culture* and *The Mississippi Encyclopedia*; coeditor (with Jay Watson) of the Faulkner & Yoknapatawpha Series; and editor of *Conversations with Barry Hannah*. His work has appeared in *Ethnic Heritage in Mississippi: The Twentieth Century, Southern Cultures, Southern Quarterly,* and *Living Blues*.

Annette Trefzer is professor of English at the University of Mississippi. She is the author of *Exposing Mississippi: Eudora Welty's Photographic Reflections* and *Disturbing Indians: The Archaeology of Southern Fiction* and coeditor of *Global Faulkner*; *Faulkner's Sexualities*; *Faulkner and Mystery*; *Faulkner and Formalism: Returns of the Text*; and *Faulkner and the Native South,* all published by University Press of Mississippi, and her work has appeared in many journals.

Jay Watson is Howry Professor of Faulkner Studies and Distinguished Professor of English at the University of Mississippi. He is the author of many publications, including *William Faulkner and the Faces of Modernity*, *Forensic Fictions: The Lawyer Figure in Faulkner*, and *Fossil-Fuel Faulkner: Energy, Modernity, and the US South*. He is also coeditor of multiple volumes in the Faulkner and Yoknapatawpha Series.

Ryoichi Yamane is associate professor of English at Tokyo Institute of Technology. His essays have appeared in journals and edited collections both in English and Japanese, including the *Journal of the American Literature Society of Japan, Studies in English Literature,* and *William Faulkner no Nihon houmon: reisen to bungaku no politikusu* (*William Faulkner's Visit to Japan: Politics of Cold War and Literature*).

Index

Page numbers followed by "f" indicate figures
Page numbers followed by "t" indicate tables

Abdur-Rahman, Aliyyah I., 203, 207, 209
Absalom, Absalom! (Faulkner), 20, 50t, 90, 94, 103; death in, 196, 223, 237n71; ending, 245; narrative, 235-36n35, 244-46; southern myth in, 243
Agee, James, 130, 132
All Things Considered, 110n24
American Association of State Colleges and Universities, 31-32
American Dilemma, An (Myrdal), 127
American Exodus, An (Lange and Taylor), 132
American Mercury, 48t, 49
Anderson, Sherwood, 5
Anolik, Ruth Bienstock, 218, 219
Aristophanes, 190
"Asphodel" (Welty), 149, 160
As I Lay Dying (Faulkner), 47, 94-97, 109, 190, 218, 221, 232; death/ghosts in, 196, 222-23, 226-28, 233; narration, 227-28; temporality of, 222-23
Aswell, Edward, 34, 51
Aswell, Mary Lou, 34, 38, 51
Atkinson, Brooks, 199
atomic/nuclear power and weapons, 39; America's nuclear unconsciousness, 122; America's radioactive nation-building project, 122; arms race, 112-23; bombing of Bikini Atoll, 112; bombing of Hanoi, 39; bombing of Hiroshima, 112, 114; bombing of Nagasaki, 112, 114-15; military-industrial complex, 123n10; and nuclear southern studies, 121-23
"Atoms for Peace" speech, 112
"At the Landing" (Welty), 25, 27, 149

Bagdanov, Kristin George, 122
Baldwin, James, 7, 8, 244

Bambara, Toni Cade, 21, 92
Bandung Conference, 114, 119
Barnhisel, Greg, 113
Barthes, Roland, 127
Bashō, Matsuo, 205
Bataille, Georges, 184, 189, 195-96, 198
"Bear, The" (Faulkner), 5, 75
Belikasten, André, 198
Bell, Derrick, 65, 82
Bellocq's Ophelia (Trethewey), 107
Beloved (Morrison), 242-43
Benjamin, Walter, 241
Bent, Tim, 37
Bernasconi, Robert, 168-69
"Between the World and Me" (Wright), 49, 50t
"Big Boy Leaves Home" (Wright), 50t
Bilbo, Theodore, 31, 52t, 212, 216n7
Black, Patti Carr, 29, 36, 38
Black Boy (Wright), 6, 21, 35, 51, 52t, 65, 90-92, 154-55, 212
Black dual consciousness, 127
Black Lives Matter, 63
Blackness, 165-72; bodily experience of, 168; the body and Black representation, 180-81; understanding of, 168
Black Power (Wright), 126, 128, 133-34, 136f, 142
Black Power movement, 134, 258
Black Sharecropper, The (Delano), 142f
Black Skin, White Masks (Fanon), 168
Black Yeomanry (Woofter), 127
Blaine, Diane York, 222
"Blueprint for Negro Writing" (Wright), 8, 185
Bourke-White, Margaret, 132
Bowen, Elizabeth, 31, 33
Boyer, Paul, 113, 114
Boy with a Loaded Gun (Nordan), 154-55
"Bride of the Innisfallen, The" (Welty), 28, 247

INDEX

Bronfen, Elisabeth, 227
Brookhart, Mary Hughes, 25
Brown, Elvira Ware, 251, 253–54
Brown v. Board of Education, 66, 116
Bryant, Earle V., 187
Burnett, Whit, 35
"Burning, The" (Welty), 239–40, 247–50, 252, 256; Lost Cause narrative in, 247–48; mythology in, 248–50
Burroughs, Floyd, 136
Butler, Eliza Rhees, 30
Butler, Judith, 78
Butler, Nicholas Murray, 30
Butler, Octavia, 241
By the Bomb's Early Light (Boyer), 113

Caldwell, Erskine, 132
Calloway, Thomas, 139
Camera Lucida (Barthes), 127
Capers, Charlotte, 25, 29–30, 38
Carlson, Tucker, 64
Cave Canem, 106
Chase, Greg, 94, 218, 221
Chaucer, Geoffrey, 33
Chekhov, Anton, 5, 33
Chicago Defender, 47
Choi, Sodam, 222
Ciuba, Gary M., 219
civil rights movement, 63–64, 77–78, 106, 113, 115, 258; backlash to, 66
Civil War, 64, 116, 145, 247, 255–56, 258
Clansman, The (Dixon), 242
Clarion-Ledger, 40n8
Clark, Kenneth B., 75–76
Clarke, Donald Henderson, 189
Club Float, Black State Fair Parade, Jackson, Mississippi (Welty), 137f
Coen brothers, 99
Cold War, 13, 112–23
Cold War Modernists (Barnhisel), 113
Color Purple, The (Walker), 146, 151–54
Columbia University, 30, 31, 48t, 49; Johnson Hall, 30
Communist Party, 49, 50t, 119–20
comparative analysis, purpose of, 9
Confederacy, 116; monuments to, 45, 217
Congo (Lindsay), 36
Congress for Cultural Freedom, 114
Cox, Minnie, 145–47, 149
Crane, Stephen, 5, 190

Creating Faulkner's Reputation (Schwartz), 113
Creekmore, Hubert, 6
Crenshaw, Kimberlé Williams, 65, 67–68
Crisis, 47
critical race theory, 63–85, 217; critique of white supremacy in, 65–67; definition of, 67–68; in education, 64–65; opponents of, 64
Critical Race Theory (Delgado and Stefancic), 66–67
cultural appropriation, 146–47
"Curtain of Green, A" (Welty), 28
Curtain of Green and Other Stories, A (Welty), 4, 8, 52t

Daly, Elizabeth, 33
Darda, Joseph, 123n10
Dasher, Thomas E., 148–49
Daugherty, Beth Rigel, 37
Davis, Jefferson, 116
Davis-McElligatt, Joanna, 233
Day's End, Jackson (Welty), 142f
de Beauvoir, Simone, 6
Delano, Jack, 130, 131f, 142f
Delgado, Richard, 66–67
"Delta Autumn" (Faulkner), 75
Delta Wedding (Welty), 32, 35, 52t, 58
"Demonstrators, The" (Welty), 66, 77–80; narrator, 80–81; whiteness in, 80–81
Devlin, Albert, 247
Dib, Nicole, 221
Dickinson, Emily, 233
Dickson, Thomas, Jr., 242
Domestic Work (Trethewey), 106–7
"Domestic Work, 1937" (Trethewey), 107
Dominy, Jordan J., 113, 122
Donaldson, Susan, 62n29, 248
Dostoevsky, Fyodor, 5
Douglas, Ellen, 29
Dreiser, Theodore, 5
"Dry September" (Faulkner), 203
Du Bois, W. E. B., 113, 127, 139, 144, 148; submerged tenth, 127, 139; "Talented Tenth," 127, 139
Duck, Leigh Ann, 87
Dyer, Geoff, 129

Early, Jubal A., 242
Eddington, Arthur Stanley, 43–44
Eight Men (Wright), 69

Einstein, Albert, 43, 112–13
Eisenhower, Dwight D., 112
"Elegy for the Native Guards" (Trethewey), 258
Ellison, Ralph, 34–35, 128, 216n8
Encounter, 114
Engel, Lehman, 62n21
Equiano, Olaudah, 232
Essay on the Disalienation of the Black (Fanon), 168
"Ethics of Living Jim Crow, The" (Wright), 50t, 52t, 54–55, 68, 186
Eubanks, W. Ralph, 27, 86
Eudora Welty: A Biography (Marrs), 37
Eudora Welty Day, 38
Evans, John, 26
Evans, Walker, 135–36
Evers, Medgar, 31, 77
"Everybody's Protest Novel" (Baldwin), 7
Excitable Speech (Butler), 78
Exposing Mississippi (Trefzer), 240
Eye of the Story, The (Welty), 5, 122

Fabre, Michel, 155
Fanon, Frantz, 164–65, 168–71, 180
Farm Security Administration (FSA), 126–27, 129–30, 141
Father's Law, A (Wright), 191
Faulkner, Estelle, 34, 47, 49, 61n19, 62n20
Faulkner, Sally Murray, 45
Faulkner, William, 35, 43, 184, 240–41, 243, 254; birth, 3, 46t, 202; caricature of, 4; and the Civil War, 243–47; correspondences with Welty, 4, 34, 52t; correspondences with Richard Wright, 6, 51, 52t, 62n23, 184, 202, 212–13, 215n1; distortion of time in work, 5, 222–23; education, 46; employment at post office, 46t, 47, 48t, 61n16, 160; in Europe, 47, 48t; finances, 49, 51, 210; Gold Medal for Diction, 34; and haunting in writing, 196, 218, 222–23, 226–28, 231, 233; literary modernism of, 66, 113; marriage, 48t; meeting Welty, 33–34, 52t; and Mississippi moment, 87, 89–98, 101–5, 108; Nagano Seminar lecture, 112, 114; Nobel Prize Banquet Speech, 116; and nuclear arms race, 112–15, 120–21, 123; postage stamp, 4, 160; and privilege, 44–47, 61n15; race as social death as a theme, 104, 164, 173–75, 179–81; realism of, 6; reception in France, 7; repurposing of writing, 94–96, 105, 109, 217, 221–22, 232–33; Rowan Oak home, 34; screenwriting, 49, 50t; statue of, 3, 7; treatment of Black employees, 51, 53; treatment of women characters, 244–45, 250; writing of African American consciousness, 202–15; writing about race relations, 8, 63, 66, 67, 116–17, 202, 211, 215
Federal Writers Project, 5, 49, 50t
Fellowship of Southern Writers, 31
Felski, Rita, 9
feminist storytelling, 239
field of affordances, 43, 59
"Fire and Cloud" (Wright), 55
"Fire and the Hearth, The" (Faulkner), 72–74, 208–9, 211
"First Love" (Welty), 25
First World Conference against Atomic and Hydrogen Bombs, 113
Flags in the Dust (Faulkner), 193
Flaubert, Gustav, 4
"Flowers for Marjorie" (Welty), 27
Floyd, George, 63, 71
Floyd Burroughs, Hole County Alabama (Evans), 135f
Foner, Eric, 103–4, 217
Foote, Shelby, 32
Ford, Ford Madox, 39
Ford, Ruth, 199
Ford, Sarah, 241
"For My People" (Walker), 87
For My People (Walker), 254
"For Rent" (Wright), 129
Forster, E. M., 33
Foucault, Michel, 193
Frankenberg, Ruth, 76
Freeman, Eden Wales, 233
Freeman, Lindsey A., 121–22
Friedman, Susan Stanford, 9
Frings, Ketti, 199

Gaines, Ernest, 234n24
Gallagher, Winifred, 144, 152, 158
Gathering of Old Men, A (Gaines), 234n24
Gayle, Addison, 200
Genette, Gérard, 220

Gerald, Tom, 26
Ghostly Matters (Gordon), 77
Gibson, James, 43
Gilroy, Paul, 118, 163, 168–69
Ginsberg, Allen, 122
Girard, René, 197
"Go Down, Moses" (Faulkner), 8, 75
Go Down, Moses (Faulkner), 52t, 58, 66, 71–74, 77, 207–8; narration, 208–9, 212; systemic racism in, 71–75, 208–10; white abandonment in, 76
"Going to Naples" (Welty), 28
Golden Apples, The (Welty), 4, 52t, 59, 237n98
"Gold Is Not Always" (Faulkner), 208, 210–11, 214
Gone with the Wind (Mitchell), 239, 242–43, 248
Gordon, Avery, 77
Gorra, Michael, 243–44
gothic literature, 218, 233, 241; American, 218; English, 218; property and, 218–19, 226
Granger, Gideon, 144-45
"Graveyard Blues" (Trethewey), 111n36
Great Depression, 47, 48t, 128, 138, 156–57
Great Falls Tribune, 40n8
Great Migration, 68, 71
Greenway, George, 30
Gresset, Michel, 188
Grisham, John, 87
"Gulf, The" (Walcott), 232

Haas, Robert K., 246
Hakutani, Yoshinobu, 159
Hale, Grace Elizabeth, 140
Hamilton, Edith, 95
Hamilton, William, 35
Haney, David, 101-2
Harding, Sandra, 44
Harm in Hate Speech, The (Waldron), 78
Harper's Bazaar, 34, 51, 247–48
hate speech, 78, 82
Haunted Property (Ford), 241
Hawthorne, Nathaniel, 218
Heavy: An American Memoir (Laymon), 20–22, 88, 90–92, 108
Helmerich Award, 31
Hemingway, Ernest, 5
Hicks, Granville, 117
Higashiyama, Masayoshi, 112, 114, 123n1
Hillerman, Tony, 33

History of the Literature of the U. S. South, A (Stecopoulos), 121
House of Seven Gables (Hawthorne), 218
Howard University Dental School (Calloway), 139f
Howe, Irving, 210
"How I Write" (Welty), 102
How the Post Office Created America (Gallagher), 145
How to Kill Yourself and Others in America (Laymon), 87, 89–90, 92
Hudson Review, 4
Hughes, Langston, 113
Hughes, Mary, 25
Hurston, Zora Neale, 34, 239, 246

imperialist nostalgia, 76
"In a Station of the Metro" (Pound), 205
"Incident" (Trethewey), 256
"Indonesian Notebook" (Wright), 114
"Inheritors of Slavery" (Delano), 130
Intondi, Vincent J., 113–14
Intruder in the Dust (Faulkner), 8, 52t, 191, 207–8; film adaptation, 4, 51, 52t; narration, 212, 214–15; reviews of, 34; systemic racism in, 213–14
Island of Hallucinations (Wright), 183, 192, 200

Jackson Junior League, 49, 50t
James, C. L. R., 184
James, Henry, 4, 5
JanMohamed, Abdul R., 163–64, 170–71, 173
Jaspers, Karl, 168
Jim Crow, 7–8, 54, 58, 68, 102, 105–7, 116, 145, 163, 181; color line, 82, 140, 144; hardening of laws, 149; miscegenation law, 104; white gaze of, 62n29
John Reed Club, 49, 50t
Journal of Mississippi History, 35
Joyce, James, 4, 5
Jubilee (Walker), 87, 239–40, 251–54, 256, 258; inspiration for, 251, 253–54; narrative, 253; women characters in, 251–54
Judith Basin Farmer, 40n8
"June Recital" (Welty), 89

Kafka, Franz, 183
"Keela, the Outcast Indian Maiden" (Welty), 8, 35

Kenan, Randall, 34
Khrushchev, Nikita, 117
Killer Angels (Shaara), 239
Kinchy, Abby J., 113
Kindred (Butler), 241-42
King, Martin Luther, Jr., 102, 113
King's College, 33
Klotman, Phyllis R., 251
Knight's Gambit (Faulkner), 191
Kreyling, Michael, 32-33
Ku Klux Klan, 242
Kwa people, 232

"Ladies in Spring" (Welty), 149
landscape of affordances, 43, 59
Lange, Dorothea, 126, 132
Lawd Today! (Wright), 146, 156-60
Lawrence, D. H., 5
Laymon, Kiese, 20, 87-89, 106; education, 87, 89-90; and Mississippi moment, 86-89, 108
Lee, Hermione, 27
Leonard, Devin, 144
Leopard's Sports, The (Dixon), 242
Let Us Now Praise Famous Men (Agee), 130, 132
Levenson, Michael, 216n8
Levi, Primo, 163
Lewis, Elva, 25
Lewistown Democrat-News, 40n8
L'Express, 187
liberation fiction, 242
Life magazine, 114-15, 120-21; "A Bold Boycott Goes On," 115-16; "The Golden Youth of Communism," 115-17; "A Letter to the North," 115-16; "The New Communist Line," 117; "The Trials of Uncle Daniel," 115
Light in August (Faulkner), 50t, 202; ending, 207; narration, 206-7, 213; popular media in, 172-80; race as social death as a theme, 104, 164, 173-75, 179-81, 203-6
Limon, John, 222
Lindsay, Vachel, 36
"Lineage" (Walker), 251
"Livvie" (Welty), 27, 51, 56-58
"Livvie is Back" (Welty), 52t
Locke, Alain, 6
"Long Black Song" (Wright), 50t, 55-57
Long Division (Laymon), 89, 92

Long Dream, The (Wright), 185; corruption in, 194, 197-99; criminality in, 183, 188, 190-92, 196-97; death in, 186-88, 190-91, 194-96; ending, 199; excreta in, 196; original title, 192; sexuality and prostitution in, 185-87, 190-92, 194, 198
Longing for the Bomb (Freeman), 121
Look Homeward, Angel (Wolfe), 199
"Looking at Short Stories" (Welty), 5
Los Angeles Evening Express, 45
Losing Battles (Welty), 25, 98-101, 109, 146, 149, 151, 153; Black suffering in, 150-51; inspiration for, 26
Lost Cause, 239, 242-43, 246, 248, 251
Lost Cause, The (Pollard), 242
Lott, Eric, 203
Louis Beretti (Clarke), 189
Love and Theft (Lott), 203
Lucky Dragon No. 5, 112
Lumumba, Ebony, 60n4
Lurie, Peter, 172-73, 175, 189
Lyell, Frank, 4, 33, 38
lynchings, 45, 171
Lysistrata (Aristophanes), 190

Macdonald, Ross, 33, 38
Maggie: A Girl of the Streets (Crane), 190
Malraux, Andre, 5, 50t, 190
Mandel, Ernest, 184
Mansfield, Katherine, 5
Mansion, The (Faulkner), 100
"Man Who Lived Underground, The" (Wright), 52t, 58, 66, 69
Man Who Lived Underground, The (Wright), 69-71, 177; inspiration for, 69, 177; Library of America edition, 69
Maran, René, 6
Mark, Rebecca, 151, 153, 226
Marrs, Suzanne, 5, 125n35, 154; first meeting Welty, 25-26; friendship with Welty, 24-41; sabbatical, 25; training as a generalist, 24-25; as Welty Scholar in Residence at MDAH, 26, 29, 36
Marrs, Wanda, 26
Marx, Karl, 169
Masco, Joseph, 122
Matthews, John T., 94
Maxwell, Emmy, 38
Maxwell, William, 24, 38
McHaney, Pearl, 103-4

270 INDEX

McMillen, Neil R., 71–72
McWhirter, David, 149
Memorial Drive (Trethewey), 103
"Memories of My Grandmother" (Wright), 69
"Memory, A" (Welty), 89
Memphis Commercial Appeal, 49
Mencken, H. L., 5, 21, 35, 47, 49, 92
Men We Reaped (Ward), 99
Meriwether, James B., 123n1
Merleau-Ponty, Maurice, 164–65, 167–69, 176
Metro-Goldwyn-Mayer, 4, 50t
Meyer, George, 152
Midway, Mississippi State Fair (Welty), 138f
Millar, Ken, 38–39
Millar, Margaret, 38
Millsaps College, 20–21, 29, 31, 34
"Miscegenation" (Trethewey), 102–4
Mississippi Department of Archives and History (MDAH), 25; Archives Welty Collection, 26, 29, 36
Mitchell, Margaret, 190, 239, 242, 247–48
Mizener, Arthur, 33, 39
modernist liminality, 203
Montgomery Bus Boycott, 115–16
"Monument" (Trethewey), 256
Monument: Poems New and Selected (Trethewey), 103, 107, 111n36
"Moon Lake" (Welty), 51, 52t, 56, 58–59, 62n24, 89; inspiration for, 28
Moorhead, Rod, 3, 7, 19
Morris, Willie, 29
Morrison, Ann, 29
Morrison, Toni, 78, 137, 242; 1993 Nobel Prize address, 78
Mosquitos (Faulkner), 48t
Moynihan, Sinead, 94, 95, 218
"Music as Theme: The Blues Mode in the Works of Margaret Walker" (Traylor), 252
"Music from Spain" (Welty), 51
Myrdal, Gunnar, 127
"Myth, The" (Trethewey), 256
Mythology (Hamilton), 95

NAACP, 116
Nadeau, Maurice, 197
Nagano Seminar, 112–14
National Book Award, 20, 93
National Institute of Arts and Letters Gold Medal for Fiction, 34

Native Guard, 255–56, 258
Native Guard (Trethewey), 111n36, 239; Civil War narrative, 255; Faulkner poems in, 102–3; poems about mother in, 255–56; poems about Native Guard in, 255–56
Native Son (Wright), 6, 7, 50t, 51, 52t, 58, 62n23, 126, 128, 159, 184, 202; ending, 192; film adaptation of, 34, 51, 52t; narration, 206–7, 211; popular media in, 177–79; race as social death/invisibility as a theme, 164–66, 170–71, 175–76, 179–81, 204–7, 209–10; reviews of, 6; sexual violence in, 170–71, 173, 177–78, 204; success of, 6, 210
Nature of the Physical World, The (Eddington), 43–44, 50t
Neither Snow nor Rain (Leonard), 144–45
Newspapers.com, 40n8
New Stage Theatre, 29
New Yorker, 4, 31, 34, 36–37, 44, 52t, 64, 77, 79
New York Public Library, 35–36
New York Times, 199; "Eudora Welty in Type and Person," 122
New York Times Book Review, 35, 52t
New York Times Magazine 1619 Project, 64
Night Blooming Cereus Club, 49
Nisetich, Rebecca, 60n4
Nixon, Ralph, 177
Nixon, Richard, 39
Nkrumah, Kwame, 120
Nolan, Tom, 38–39
Nordan, Lewis, 144, 146, 154; birth, 155; mail delivery as a literary device, 155–56
Norman, Brian, 222, 227, 232
Norton Book of Friendship (Welty), 29

Oak Ridge National Atomic Laboratory, 121
Obama, Barack, 113–14
O'Connor, Flannery, 7
"Oh, Freedom: Women and History in Margaret Walker's *Jubilee*" (Klotman), 251
Oh, Lady, 47
Okoth, Christine, 180
"Old Man" (Faulkner), 191
One Time, One Place (Welty), 107, 138, 240
One Writer's Beginnings (Welty), 9, 61n13, 98, 101, 217, 219, 224, 231; "Learning to See," 219; "Listening," 219; temporality/transit of memory in, 219–20, 224; Trethewey introduction, 105

INDEX

One Writer's Imagination (Marrs), 40n7
Ongoing Moment, The (Dyer), 129
On Photography (Sontag), 130, 141
Opportunity, 6
Optimist's Daughter, The (Welty), 9, 27, 98, 219, 231; inspiration for, 39; temporality/transit of memory in, 224-26, 231
Oshinsky, David M., 99, 110n24
Outside, The (Wright), 52t, 117-21

Padmore, George, 120
Palmer, Louis, 226
"Pantaloon in Black" (Faulkner), 8, 208, 211-12
Parchman Farm, 98-101, 109, 110n24, 220-21, 224, 230-31
Paris Exposition (1900), 127, 139
Paris Review, 95
Passage to India, A (Forster), 33
"Pastoral" (Trethewey), 102-4
Patterson, Orlando, 163-64
Patton, Lawson "Nelse," 45
Pepperdene, Jane, 32
Percy, Walker, 33
Perelman, S. J., 37
Perry, Imani, 87
Petry, Ann, 35
Petty, Jane, 29
phenomenology, 165, 167-68, 181
Photographs (Welty), 107; Trethewey introduction, 26-27, 106, 108, 240
"Piece of News, A" (Welty), 28
Place Like Mississippi, A (Eubanks), 86
"Place of Fiction" (Welty), 4
"Plutonian Ode" (Ginsberg), 122
"Point of Law, A" (Faulkner), 207-10
Polk, Noel, 3, 43
Pollack, Harriet, 35
Pollard, Edward A., 242
Ponder Heart, The (Welty), 115, 117
Portable Faulkner, The (Faulkner), 52t
Porter, Katherine Anne, 33
Pound, Ezra, 205
"Powerhouse" (Welty), 8, 31, 34-35
Prejudices (Mencken), 5
prereflectivity, 170, 172, 176-77, 179
Presence Africaine, 52t
Price, Reynolds, 29, 36-38, 122
Pritchett, V. S., 33
Punter, David, 233
Pylon (Faulkner), 172, 176

Quintana, Ricardo, 30

racial epiderma schema, 165, 168-69, 177
racializing encounters, 180-81
racial justice storytelling, 239
racism: self-destructive behaviors caused by, 60, 90, 92-93; systemic racism, 63, 74
Rainey, Ma, 152
Rankin, John, 31
Reconstruction, 64, 144-45, 149
Regarding the Pain of Others (Sontag), 132
Requiem for a Nun (Faulkner), 8, 199, 217-18, 241
Rhythm Club, 183, 190-92; historical marker for, 191
Rickover, Hyman, 115
Ring Dove, 4
Robber Bridegroom, The (Welty), 4, 52t
Robertson, Pat, 64
Robeson, Paul, 113
Robinson, John, 4, 29, 34, 125n35
Rocky Flats nuclear weapons plant, 122
Rony, Fatimah Toby, 62n29
Roosevelt, Eleanor, 33
Roosevelt, Theodore, 145-46
Roots (Haley), 88
Rosaldo, Renato, 76
"Rose for Emily, A" (Faulkner), 43, 49, 51, 53-55, 160, 237n71; Black characters in, 53-56; narrator, 56, 235n35; unpublished version, 55
Rosskam, Edwin, 127, 159
Rosskam, Louise, 127
Rowley, Hazel, 210
Rubin, Louis, 25
Rufo, Christopher, 64
Russell, Bertrand, 112
Russell, Diarmuid, 57, 58, 116-17
Russell & Volkening, 51
Russell-Einstein manifesto, 112

Saddest Words, The (Gorra), 243-44
Salvage the Bones (Ward), 93-94; allusions in, 109; doubled doubling in, 96-98, 109; Faulkner references in, 94-98, 109
Sancton, Tom, 62n33
Sanctuary (Faulkner), 47, 184, 187; clock in, 188; corruption in, 193-95, 197-99; criminality in, 183, 190, 193, 197-98; death in, 195-96; doubles in, 189; ending, 193,

199; excreta in, 195–96; racial injustice in, 203; sexuality and prostitution in, 185–86, 188–91, 194, 198
Santa Barbara Writers Conference, 38
Sartoris (Faulkner), 48t
Sartre, Jean-Paul, 6, 168
Savage Holiday (Wright), 184
Schlesinger, Arthur M., Jr., 122
Schwab, Gabriele, 222
Schwartz, Lawrence H., 113, 122
Scott, Rudolph, 199
"Sears and Roebuck Catalog Game, The" (Nordan), 156, 158–59
Segregated entrance of movie house on a Saturday afternoon, Belzoni, Mississippi, 1939 (Wolcott), 141f
Segregated Theater Entrance, Jackson, Mississippi (Welty), 137f
Seldes, Tim, 37, 51
Selzer, Linda, 151
700 Club, 64
Sewanee Review, 62n24
Shaara, Michael, 239
"Shadow Club, The" (Welty), 35
Shahn, Ben, 130, 132f
Sharecropper and Wife, Georgia (Delano), 131f
Ship Island, 255
"Shower of Gold, A" (Welty), 27
Silver, James W., 116, 124n20
Simmons, Dorothy, 28
Sing, Unburied, Sing (Ward), 60, 93–94, 98, 102; Faulkner allusions in, 222, 232–33; ghosts and haunting in, 217–18, 220–24, 228–31, 233; temporality in, 220–22, 228, 232–33; Welty allusions in, 94, 99–101, 109, 219, 231–32; Welty epigraph, 101, 217, 219, 221, 231–32
Sipper, Ralph, 38
Slankard, Tamara, 223
slavery, 64, 256; culpability for, 242; de facto, 163; definition of, 164; institutionalized, 163; Jim Crow and, 163; lasting legacy of, 64, 232–33, 257; transatlantic slave trade, 163
Smith, Bessie, 152
Smith, William Jay, 38
"Social Factors in *Native Son*" (Creekmore), 6
Soldiers' Pay (Faulkner), 48t
"Some Notes on Time in Fiction" (Welty), 5, 224

Sontag, Susan, 130, 132, 141
Souls of Black Folk, The (Du Bois), 148
Sound and the Fury, The (Faulkner), 47, 48t; distortion of time in, 5; southern burden in, 103
"Southern Crescent, The" (Trethewey), 255
Southern Literary Festival, 31
Southern Literature, Cold War Culture, and the Making of Modern America (Dominy), 113
Southern Register, 47
Southern Renaissance, 86, 94, 121
Spaatz, Carl "Tooey," 114
Spencer, Elizabeth, 29
"Spotted Horses" (Faulkner), 4–5
Stecopoulos, Harilaos, 121
Stefancic, Jean, 66–67
Stein, Gertrude, 6
"Still Moment, A" (Welty), 25
Story of Temple Drake, The, 199
Stout, Maxine, 40n8
Stout, Tom, 40n8
Stowe, Harriet Beecher, 7
"Strong Horse Tea" (Walker), 150
"Struggle Staggers Us, The" (Walker), 254
Sullivan, W. V., 45

Tate, Allen, 103
Taylor, Paul, 132
Taylor, Peter, 32
Tennant, Stephen, 31
Terence (playwright), 198
Teresi, Christian, 102
textual blackface, 203, 208
"That Evening Sun" (Faulkner), 48t, 49, 54; Black characters in, 53–56; racial injustice in, 54–55; women in, 53, 55–56, 59
Their Eyes Were Watching God (Hurston), 246
These 13 (Faulkner), 49
Thompson, Liz, 37
Thrall (Trethewey), 107
Till, Emmett, 116, 155, 186
Time magazine, 50t
Tougaloo College, 31
Tour d'Argent, 31
Traitor, The (Dixon), 242
Traylor, Eleanore, 252–53
Trefzer, Annette, 240
Trethewey, Natasha, 239–41, 243, 254–58; on being a southern writer, 104–6, 109, 111n34, 254; introduction to Welty's *One*

Writer's Beginnings, 105; introduction to Welty's *Photographs*, 26–27, 106, 108; grandfather, 255; grandmothers, 106–8, 240; and Mississippi moment, 86–87, 101–8; mother, 103, 111n36, 240, 255–57; stepmother, 107
True Detective, 69, 177
Truman, Margaret, 33
Trump, Donald, 63–64
Tucker, Neely, 87
Turnbough, Gwendolyn Ann, 103, 111n36
Turner, Daniel Cross, 104
12 Million Black Voices: A Folk History of the Negro in the United States (Wright), 52t, 68, 126–30, 132–35, 137, 141
Twentieth Century-Fox, 50t

Uhry, Alfred, 32
Uncle Tom's Cabin (Stowe), 7
Uncle Tom's Children (Wright), 7, 50t, 52t, 55, 68, 210, 214
Undead Souths (Anderson, Haygood, and Turner), 257
United Daughters of the Confederacy, 247
United Nations General Assembly, 112
United States Postal Service, 144, 146, 153–54, 160; impact on Black American's lives, 144–45, 156–57; mail delivery as a literary device, 144–61; rules and restrictions against Black employees, 145, 149; Rural Free Delivery Program, 149, 152; rural isolation and, 146, 156–57
Universal Studios, 50t
University of Chicago, 127
University of Mississippi, 4, 160
University of North Carolina, 25
University of Sussex, 37
University of Wisconsin-Madison, 30, 40n8, 48t
University Press of Mississippi, 106
University Review, 6
Unvanquished, The (Faulkner), 50t, 243–44; enslaved people in, 245–46
USSR, 13, 14, 115, 116, 117

Vanderbilt University, 121
Vardaman, James K., 147
Vickery, Olga, 195
Visible Spirits (Yarbrough), 146–49
Vital Center, The (Schlesinger), 122

Walcott, Derek, 232
Waldron, Ann, 35–36
Waldron, Jeremy, 78
Walker, Alice, 144, 146, 150–51; mail delivery as a literary device, 151–52, 161
Walker, Margaret, 19, 55–56, 87, 90, 190, 239–40, 243, 257–58
Walker, Peter, 25
Wall, Carey, 248
Waller, Fats, 31
Wandalene, Evounda, 26
"Wanderers, The" (Welty), 27, 59
Ward, Jesmyn, 20, 60, 102, 110n24; allusion in writing, 95, 217–18; brother, 99; and ghosts in literature, 217; and Mississippi moment, 86–87, 93–101, 108; and narrative, 217; recycling of mythology, 95–96
Warren, Robert Penn, 103, 255
"Was" (Faulkner), 72
Wasson, Ben, 51
Watson, Jay, 186, 193, 202
"Waves, The" (Woolf), 37–38
Weinstein, Philip M., 104, 209, 212, 223
Welty, C. W., 40n8, 46t, 47–49
Welty, Eudora, 7, 43, 51, 87–89, 184, 239–40, 243; application to work at the *New Yorker*, 36–37; biography, 36–39; birth, 3, 46t; camera collection, 26; caricatures, 4, 47; childhood, 47, 62n32; on the Civil War, 247–48, 250, 258; correspondences with Virginia Woolf, 37–38; death, 24, 36–37; education, 5, 30, 34, 46t, 47, 48t; education at Columbia University, 30–31, 47–49, 48t; education at University of Wisconsin-Madison, 30, 40n8, 48t; father's death, 28; focus on women in writing, 149–54, 160, 247–50; friendship with Suzanne Marrs, 24–41; and haunting in writing, 218, 228, 231; Helmerich Award, 31; humor in writing, 89, 100, 108; literary memory, 87, 98, 232; mail delivery as a literary device, 144, 146, 149, 153–54, 160; meeting Faulkner, 33–34, 52t; and Mississippi moment, 87–89, 98–101, 105–8; in Montana, 28; in New York, 49, 50t; and nuclear arms race, 113–15, 120–23, 125n35; in Paris, 31, 34; photography, 8, 26–27, 31, 49, 55, 62nn28–29, 106–8, 126, 128, 133, 136–42, 240, 256–57; and privilege, 44, 47, 58,

150–51; and racial justice/injustice, 31, 35, 55, 63, 66–67, 77, 82, 137–39, 150–51; and racist characters, 77–79, 88–89; readings of Faulkner's work, 3–6; regionalism, 87–89, 98–101, 105–8, 117; relationship with Ken Millar, 38–39; repurposing of, 96, 98–101, 109, 217, 231–33; review of *Intruder in the Dust*, 4, 34; speech at University of Mississippi, 4; statue of, 3, 7; temporality/transit of memory in writing, 219–20, 224, 238n107; use of allusion, 87; visual idea of the American South, 126, 128, 137–42

Welty Collection, The (Marrs), 40n7
"What I Pledge Allegiance To" (Laymon), 89–90
"What Is Evidence" (Trethewey), 255–56
Wheatley, Patchy, 29
Wheatley, Patricia, 247
"Where Is the Voice Coming From?" (Welty), 31, 66; narrator, 77–79
"Whistle, The" (Welty), 28, 55
White, Mary Alice, 37
white blindness, 11, 66–68, 82
white gaze, 62n29, 68–70, 75, 129, 165–66, 169
White Man, Listen! (Wright), 119–21
whiteness, 80–82, 165; childhood socializations to race and, 87; constructions of, 76; insecurities of, 108; under siege, 78
Who Owns History? (Foner), 103–4
"Why I Live at the P.O." (Welty), 20–21, 88–89, 149
"Why I Write" (Trethewey), 102
Wide Net, The (Welty), 52t
Wiegman, Robyn, 76
Wilde, Oscar, 188
Wild Palms, The (Faulkner), 50t, 100, 190–91
Wilson, Edmund, 4, 34
Window-Shopping, Grenada, Mississippi (Welty), 140f
"Winds, The" (Welty), 89
Windsor Plantation, 240
Wirth, Louis, 127
WJDX, 50t
Wolcott, Marion Post, 141
Wolfe, Thomas, 199
"Woman of the Thirties, A" (Welty), 27, 136
Woodburn, John, 34
Woofter, Thomas Jackson, 127
Woolf, Virginia, 33, 37–38, 250

Woolfe, Sally, 224
Works Progress Administration (WPA), 50t, 242
World War I, 46, 247
World War II, 66, 71, 113, 119
"Worn Path, A" (Welty), 8, 27, 126, 128
Worse than Slavery (Oshinsky), 99, 110n24
Wright, Charles, 254
Wright, Richard, 5–6, 21, 34–35, 43, 106, 146, 184, 215n2; absence in school curriculum, 87; in Africa, 133–35, 142; approach to African psychology, 120–21; artistic perspective, 8, 53; birth, 3, 46t, 155, 202; in Chicago, 7, 22, 47–49, 68, 120, 155, 213; childhood, 7, 34, 44–47, 154–55, 185, 191; education, 5, 34, 46t, 47, 48t; employment at post office, 47–49, 155; fear of white people, 154–55; finances, 49, 51; grandmother, 69; and haunting in writing, 218; in London, 52t, 120; mail delivery as a literary device, 144, 154, 157–59; in Memphis, 47, 68; in Mississippi, 7, 34, 44–47, 88, 120, 185, 191, 193; and Mississippi moment, 87, 89–93, 108, 210; in New York, 7, 120; and nuclear arms race, 113–14, 117–21, 123; in Paris, 5–7, 34, 51, 52t, 93, 120; photography, 126–27, 129, 133–35, 136f, 139, 141–42; poverty and, 44–45; race as social death as a theme, 164–66, 170–71, 175–76, 179–81; and racial justice/rejection of racial injustice, 6–7, 35, 44–46, 49–51, 54–55, 58, 63, 65–68, 90–91, 97, 118, 184, 193, 210, 213, 215; reasons for leaving Mississippi and the US, 21–22, 193; statue of, 3, 7; and terror in freedom, 119, 121; uncle, 46; visual idea of the American South, 126–30, 132–35, 139, 141–42; white paternalism and, 158; writing of African American consciousness, 202–15

Yaeger, Patricia, 99, 245
Yarbrough, Steve, 144, 146–49, 161
York, Jake Adam, 102
You Have Seen Their Faces (Caldwell and Bourke-White), 132
Young, Al, 34
Youngkin, Glen, 64–65